Judith Thompson

Late 20ᵗʰ Century Plays 1980-2000

heCrackwalker WhiteBitingDog PinkIAmYours LionInTheStreets Sled PerfectPie

Judith Thompson
Late 20th Century Plays
1980-2000

Playwrights Canada Press
Toronto • Canada

Late 20th Century Plays © Copyright 2002 Judith Thompson
The Crackwalker © 1980 • *White Biting Dog* © 1984 • *I Am Yours* © 1987
Lion in the Streets © 1990 • *Sled* © 1997 • *Perfect Pie* © 2000
The moral rights of the author are asserted.

Playwrights Canada Press
215 Spadina Avenue, Suite 230 Toronto, Ontario CANADA M5T 2C7
416-703-0013
orders@playwrightscanada.com • www.playwrightscanada.com

CAUTION: These plays are fully protected under the copyright laws of Canada and all other countries of The Copyright Union, and are subject to royalty. Changes to any script are expressly forbidden without the prior written permission of the author. Rights to produce, film, or record, in whole or in part, in any medium or any language, by any group, amateur or professional, are retained by the author. For professional production rights, please contact Shain Jaffe, Great North Artists, 350 Dupont Street, Toronto, Ontario M5R 1V9 416-925-2051 greatnorth@canadafilm.com. For amateur production rights, please contact Playwrights Guild of Canada, 416-703-0201 info@playwrightsguild.ca.

No part of this book, covered by the copyright hereon, may be reproduced or used in any form or by any means—graphic, electronic or mechanical—without the prior written permission of the publisher except for excerpts in a review. Any request for photocopying, recording, taping or information storage and retrieval systems of any part of this book shall be directed in writing to The Canadian Copyright Licensing Agency, 1 Yonge St., Suite 1900, Toronto, Ontario CANADA M5E 1E5 416-868-1620.

Playwrights Canada Press acknowledges the support of
the taxpayers of Canada and the province of Ontario through
The Canada Council for the Arts and the Ontario Arts Council.

Cover photo by Steve McKinley.
Production Editor: Jodi Armstrong

National Library of Canada Cataloguing in Publication

Thompson, Judith, 1954-
  Late 20th century plays, 1980-2000

ISBN 0-88754-620-X

  1. Title.

PS8589.H4883A19 2002   C812'.54   C2001-903394-X
PR9199.3.T469A19 2002

First edition: September 2003.
Printed and bound by Hignell Printing at Winnipeg, Canada.

TABLE OF CONTENTS

Introduction
by Ric Knowles   iii

The Crackwalker   1

White Biting Dog   83

Pink   169

I Am Yours   175

Lion in the Streets   253

Sled   331

Perfect Pie   409

Afterword
by Helen Gilbert   493

READING JUDITH THOMPSON

"I wonder if we could have something for the – underneathness?"
—Pony, *White Biting Dog*

How does a reader approach the plays of Judith Thompson? Thompson is among Canada's best known, most highly respected, most frequently produced, most frequently anthologized, and most frequently taught playwrights nationally and internationally. Admired by directors, celebrated by academics, and loved by actors and audiences, her plays can nevertheless be challenging for contemporary readers accustomed to the narrative pleasures of prose fiction, the scopophilic delights of film and television, or the informational rewards of non-fiction books, magazines, and newspapers.

The plots of the plays are notoriously disjunctive and unsettling. The action of *White Biting Dog* is precipitated by the voice of a small white dog on Toronto's Bloor Street viaduct who speaks to prevent the suicide of Cape Race. Part way through *Lion in the Streets* Isobel suddenly realizes that she is a ghost, Father Hayes hears the confession of a now grown man whose drowning as a boy he had witnessed decades earlier, and the severely handicapped Scarlett impossibly rises from her wheelchair to dance with her "midnight man." *I Am Yours* includes the stage direction, "*this could be a dream.*" *Perfect Pie* hinges on the visit of the adult Francesca, who both is and is not the Marie who was killed by a train as a teenager. The resolution of *Sled* is actively orchestrated by the ghost of Annie Delaney, whose murder the audience has witnessed in the middle of the first act. And so on. As Jennifer Harvie has written, arguing that they might best be read as fantasies, "Judith Thompson's plays do not precisely defy description, but they do, enigmatically, confound it" (Harvie 240).

The plays, moreover, are dramaturgically unconventional, and they employ a wide variety of structural (un)conventions. Flying in the face of dramaturgical wisdom, most of them begin with or hinge upon long, rich, and poetic monologues, many of them issue in improbable epiphanies that seem to rely upon the active evocation of the engaged imaginations and activated will power of their audiences rather than on narrative probability, and many of them have at their centre characters who are without apparent agency. *Lion in the Streets* is a twisted relay play, its so-called main plot subordinated to a series of scenes loosely held together by a single carry-over character from one scene to the next. *Perfect Pie* is perhaps best read as a revisionist memory play. *Sled* is an almost expressionist multicultural epic collage that draws on everything from realistic vignettes through historical reminiscence to mythological frames and musical numbers. *Habitat*, her most recent play as I write this, is on one level at least an issue play, *White Biting Dog* a magic-naturalist fantasia, and *Crackwalker* a mix of gritty realism and street poetry underscored by evocatively iconic religious imagery. And I never know quite how to position *I Am Yours*.

But there are some things that hold these plays together, that characterize and make fully recognizable the *œuvre* of Judith Thompson. Few who have read or seen a Judith Thompson play would fail to recognize and respond viscerally to her extraordinarily evocative ear for dialogue, coloured by both the unique circumstances of her characters and her own varied colloquial speech rhythms based on the accents of regional Ontario ranging from Kingston to Kapuskasing, Rosedale to Gravenhurst. Similarly, few would fail to recognize and respond to the range of tension-filled, contradictory, and totally recognizable characterizations that allow her to write convincing figures such as Dee in *I Am Yours* who, far from exhibiting traditional actorly throughlines, vacillates with complete conviction between professions of love and loathing for the same understandably confused partner. A Judith Thompson play is identifiably and uniquely a Judith Thompson play.

It is possible to become inhabited by the rich and twisted turns of phrase and dialogue, imagery and rhythmic musicality of Thompson's language. Anyone who has directed, acted in, or otherwise worked on one of these plays finds her own language invaded by the phrases and rhythms of the scripts. My own vocabulary has been as enriched by unforgettable phrases and speech rhythms from these plays as it has by intertexts from Shakespeare. And that's one way to read Judith Thompson.

Another, related way, is to read for character, with attention to unforgettable and often quirky portrayals of people, often women, often from the working class, and often under various kinds of stress and usually rising gloriously above it. These include: the indomitable if mentally challenged Theresa in *The Crackwalker*; the stalwart Pony and exotic Lomia in *White Biting Dog*; Pegs, in defiant maternal and class pride in *I Am Yours*; the beleaguered but heroic Rose, Thompson's first portrayal of a person with seizure disorder, in *Tornado* (both the radio play published in *The Other Side of the Dark* and the stage version published in *Canadian Theatre Review* 89); the class warrior Rhonda ("Rho-HONDA!") in *Lion in the Streets*; and the resolute Patsy Willet from Marmora, young and old, in *Perfect Pie*.

But language and character are really only clues and inroads to the best way to read Judith Thompson's work, which I suggest is through attention to what Pony in *White Biting Dog* calls "the – underneathness." In various ways and for various reasons Judith Thompson has always had an eye and ear for the not-said, not-seen reality that lurks beneath the mundane details of quotidian life that she evokes with such haunting hyper-clarity. On one level this focus derives from her ongoing interest in Freudian psychoanalysis, which leads to a recurring evocation of psychological underneathness. Her plays invoke the unconscious, the repressed, dreams, and the uncanny, in ways that tend to operate on both the level of character and of overt and often overstated symbolism, as when Lomia and Cape, mother and son, touch tongues at the end of the first act of *White Biting Dog*, provoking Cape's urge to "bash and bash and bash and bash and bash [her] head against the wall." Robert Nunn, one of the best commentators on Thompson's work, has on more than one occasion discussed her plays as "slices from the banquet of Freud," evoking on both the social and psychological levels "[t]he return of the repressed that haunts her plays" ("Strangers" 32; see also "Spatial Metaphor").

On another level, this interest in the underneathness surely resonates with Thompson's Roman Catholic background, which has come increasingly to the surface in her writing as itself, perhaps, a return of the repressed, ever since Pony, also in *White Biting Dog*, consumed and regurgitated, as a kind of unholy trinity, a communion feast of dog/God – three dead dachshunds in the basement freezer of the Race home. This religious background marks Thompson's work not only with a fundamentally Catholic sense of ritual and icon, but more importantly with the unspoken awareness of "original sin," a consciousness of sins of omission, of sins committed in thought though never acted on, and of a never quite articulated or articulatable sense of underlying, beneath-the-surface guilt together with the accompanying need for confession.

On yet another level, anyone who knows Judith Thompson might imagine another level of underneathness to her plays, at least those since *White Biting Dog*, one that has to do with pregnancy and childbirth. In *I Am Yours* and *Tornado*, which deal directly with the carrying and bearing of children, I suspect that some of Thompson's sense of "underneathness," of life beneath the skin understood both positively as fecundity and negatively as a kind of alien invasion, also derive from the material realities of her own pregnancies and birthings at the time of writing, the mid-point of her maternal experience as the mother of five. These and her later plays—most remarkably the startling monologue in *Habitat* that deals with the gap between the givens of maternal love and the quotidian grounds for human affection—are all informed by a sense of the non-integrity of the maternal subject, but also of the fierce, protective responsibility for lives that are and are not our own.

Finally, the invocation of what in *I Am Yours* is "behind the wall" and in *Tornado* is "the other side of the dark" (explicitly understood as *beneath* quotidian life) derives from Thompson's own, personal experience of seizure disorder, which she evokes so powerfully in *Tornado*, *Perfect Pie*, and, in a non-dramatic autobiographical context, in her talk, "Epilepsy and the Snake: Fear in the Creative Process," delivered as part of the Stratford Festival's "Celebrated Writers" series in 1996 and published in *Canadian Theatre Review* the same year. Thompson consistently describes the experience of having a seizure as a descent, a falling "faster and faster and faster... through space down down" a "dark tunnel" to "the middle of the earth" (Thompson 6). And she attributes much of her writerly instinct, knowledge, and creativity to her epilepsy, her contact with "the other side of the dark," and her awareness of social as well as psychological repression. "I have no doubt," she says, "that my experience with epilepsy has contributed to my creative work, partly because it helped me to understand what it is to be marginalized, to be isolated, to be fearful, and to be out of control, and even to be mortal" (qtd in Vowles).

But what "the underneathness" means for actors and audiences, whatever its complex sources, is what in the theatre is known as subtext, the unspoken impulses that motivate lines and actions and that are the bread and butter of naturalistic actor training in North America. And Judith Thompson is first and foremost an actor, as anyone who has heard her perform passages from her plays can attest. She first trained as an actor at the National Theatre School of Canada, her first writing for the stage was a monologue that she wrote for a mask class there, and that monologue eventually developed into her celebrated first play, *The Crackwalker*. According to actor Nancy Palk, for whom Thompson has written several roles, Thompson continues to write as an actor: "when Judith's working on a text, I know that she enacts it: she enters those characters just as an actor would. She allows the characters to speak and then she works" (Palk, "Redefining" 19). And all of Thompson's writing is rich in subtext, which accounts for her reputation among actors, for whom her language is a gift.

How, then, *does* a reader approach the plays of Judith Thompson? Perhaps the best advice is to approach them as an actor would, to listen to and read the subtext, the underneathness that inhabits the characters, to try to inhabit the moment-by-moment energies of the text, and ideally, to read the plays out loud and let the energies of the language and its rhythms carry us through. Palk has spoken of the need not to overindulge in analysis when approaching Thompson's plays ("Redefining" 20), of the need to "simply get out of the way" and "ride the wave" ("Working" 9):

> Her texts are so rich, and have such a powerful emotional underbelly, they're like going down a hill, like going down on a sled; I always feel like I'm on the crest of a wave and, lord love us, we're going to get to the bottom, whether I fall over or not. ("Redefining" 21)

With this collection, Playwrights Canada invites readers along for the ride.

***

Works Cited

Harvie, Jennifer. "(Im)Possibility: Fantasy and Judith Thompson's Drama." *On-Stage and Off-Stage: English-Canadian Drama in Discourse.* Ed. Albert-Reiner Glaap with Rolf Althof. St. John's: Breakwater, 1996.

Nunn, Robert. "Spatial Metaphor in the Plays of Judith Thompson." *Theatre History in Canada/Histoire du théâtre au Canada* 10.1 (Spring 1989): 3-29.

—-. "Strangers to Ourselves: Judith Thompson's *Sled*." *Canadian Theatre Review* 89 (Winter 1996): 20-32.

Palk, Nancy. "Redefining the Comfort Zone: Nancy Palk, on Acting Judith Thompson." Interview with Harry Lane. *Canadian Theatre Review* 89 (Winter 1996): 19-21.

—-. "Working on *Sled*." Introduction to Judith Thompson, *Sled*. Toronto: Playwrights Canada, 1997. 9.

Thompson, Judith. "Epilepsy and the Snake: Fear in the Creative Process." *Canadian Theatre Review* 89 (Winter 1996): 4-7.

Vowles, Andrew. "Inside Playwright Judith Thompson: Behind the Mask." *Guelph Alumnus: The University of Guelph Magazine* (Winter 1999): 20-25.

***

Ric Knowles is Professor of Drama at the University of Guelph, Past President of Playwrights Canada Press, editor of *Canadian Theatre Review* and *Modern Drama*, and author of *The Theatre of Form and the Production of Meaning: Contemporary Canadian Dramaturgies*.

The Crackwalker

The Crackwalker was first produced by Theatre Passe Muraille, Toronto, in November, 1980, with the following company:

THERESA   JoAnn McIntyre
SANDY   Jane Foster
ALAN   Hardee T. Lineham
JOE   Geza Kovacs
THE MAN   Graham Greene

Directed by Clarke Rogers
Set and costumes designed by Patsy Lang

CHARACTERS

THERESA
SANDY
ALAN
JOE
THE MAN

The Crackwalker

ACT ONE

Scene One

THERESA
Shut up, mouth, I not goin back there no more noway, I'm goin back to Sandy's! *(to audience)* You know what she done to me? She make me go livin with her up on Division near Chung Wah's, cause she say I come from God, eh, then she go lookin in my room every night see if I got guys in there cause Bonnie Cain told her I was suckin off queers down the Lido for five bucks; I wasn't doin it anyways Bonnie Cain was doin it I was just watchin. So last night, eh, I'm up there with a friend of mine, Danny, he a taxi driver – we're just talkin, eh, we weren't doin nothin, and so she come up and knock on the door and she say, "Trese I know you got someone in there" and I go "No Mrs. Beddison ain't nobody in here," and she start goin on about God and that, and how she knowed cause she got a six feelin in her, so I get scared, eh, so I tell Danny to get in the closet. We don't got no clothes on, eh, so I put his jeans and that under the bed and I get under the covers like I'm sleepin and I go "S'kay Mrs. Beddison you could come in now." So she come in lookin at me like a stupid bitch and she say she knowed there was somebody in there cause she heard talkin and I says "You feelin okay Mrs. Beddison, ain't nobody here cept me and I sleepin," then she start goin near the closet, eh, and Danny start laughin. Well she runup the closet and she pullin on the door and I'm pullin on her arm and I'm saying "Trust me Mrs. Beddison, ya gotta trus me," cause the sosha workers are always goin on about trus and that, eh, but she don't listen, she open the door and there's Danny standin stripped naked. Well that whoredog Beddison start screamin God words at him, eh, so he takes off outa the house and she takes off after him and I got his pants, eh, so I throw em out the window case he catch em and then I bawlin. I bawlin on the bed and ya know what she make me do? She make me take a bath! A bubble bath like for the baby! All bubbles and that! Then she make me put on her stupid dressin robe itch my skin and smell like chocolate bars and that and she take me to where she livin and you know what she make me do? She make me read the Bible! I don't like readin no stupid Bible! Ya get a stomach ache doin that, ya do! Stupid hose bag. I'm not goin back there no more no way, I'm goin back to Sandy's.

Scene Two

SANDY and JOE's apartment. SANDY is scrubbing the floor furiously. THERESA appears, joyous, carrying a plastic bag containing all of her belongings. As she has not seen SANDY in several weeks, she is very excited.

THERESA
Hi Sandy, how ya doin!!

SANDY does not look at THERESA.

SANDY
 What are you doin here?

THERESA
 I come callin on ya!

 In the following sequence, SANDY's anger builds. At first, however, it contains an element of teasing.

SANDY
 I don't want no houndogs callin on me. *(continues scrubbing)*

THERESA
 I not a houndog!

SANDY
 Yes, y'are.

THERESA
 No I not.

SANDY
 Whoredog houndog that's what you are.

THERESA
 (laughs, delighted) Sanny!

SANDY
 (pointing backwards) And get your whorepaws offa my sofa.

THERESA
 (jumps, removes hand, gasps) Sanny, like I don't mean to bug ya or nothin *(eating donut from bag)* but like I don't get off on livin where I'm livin no more so I come back here sleepin on the couch, okay?

SANDY
 I not keepin no cowpies here.

THERESA
 I not a cowpie!

SANDY
 (faces her) Would you get out of my house?

THERESA
 Why, what I done?

SANDY
...Ya smell like cookin fat – turns my gut.

THERESA
That only cause I eatin chip from the chipwagon!

SANDY
I don't care what it's cause of, get your whoreface out of here.

THERESA
Why, why you bein ugly for?

SANDY
You tell me and then we'll both know.

THERESA
What.

SANDY
Don't think nobody seen ya neither cause Bonnie Cain seen ya right through the picture window!

THERESA claps a hand to her mouth in "uh-oh."

On my couch that I paid for with my money.

THERESA
Wha–

SANDY
With my husband!

THERESA
No way, Sanny.

SANDY
(unable to contain her anger any longer) You touch my fuckin husband again and I break every bone in your body!

THERESA
Bonnie Cain lyin she lyin to ya she think I took twenty buck off her she tryin to get me back.

SANDY
(starts speaking after "she lying to ya") That's bullshit Therese cause Bonnie Cain don't lie and you know she don't.

THERESA
You don't trus me.

SANDY
  Fuckin right.

THERESA
  I never done it.

SANDY
  Pretty bad combination, Trese, a retarded whore.

THERESA
  That's a load of bullshit Sanny, I *not retarded*.

SANDY
  Just get out of my house and don't come back. *(pushes her)*

THERESA
  No I never I never done it! *(In angry indignation she pushes back.)*

SANDY
  Trese Joe told me, he told me what the two of youse done!

THERESA
  Oh.

SANDY
  Lyin whore, look at ya make me sick. Wearin that ugly dress thinkin it's sexy cause it shows off your fat tits and those shoes are fuckin stupid ya can't even walk in them.

THERESA
  I know.

  SANDY stares at THERESA. THERESA does not move.

SANDY
  (with an air of resignation, tiredness) Just get out, okay?

THERESA
  I never wanted it, Sanny, I never wanted it he come in he made me.

SANDY
  Bull Trese.

THERESA
  He did I sleepin I sleepin there havin dreams I seen this puppy and he come in and tie me up and push it in me down my hole.

SANDY
  What?

THERESA
He tie me all up with strings and that and he singin Ol Macdonel Farm and he say he gonna kill me if I don't shut up so I be quiet and he done it he screw me.

SANDY
Are you shittin me?

THERESA
And – and – and he singin and he take his jean down and it all hard and smellin like pee pee and he go and he put it in my mouth.

SANDY
He could do twenty for that.

THERESA
Don't send him up the river Sanny he didn't mean nothin.

SANDY
Horny bastard he's not gettin into me again.

THERESA
Me neither Sanny he tries anything I just run up to Tim Horton's get a fancy donut.

SANDY
Oh he won't be cheatin on me again.

THERESA
How come Sanny, you tell him off?

SANDY
Fuckin right I did. After Bonnie tole me, I start givin him shit, eh, and he takes the hand to me callin me a hag and sayin how he liked pokin you bettern that and look *(reveals bruise)*

THERESA
Bassard.

SANDY
He's done it before, but he won't do it again.

THERESA
Why, Sanny, you call the cops on him?

SANDY
Right.

THERESA
Did ya–

SANDY
Ya know my high heels? The shiny black ones I got up in Toronto?

THERESA
Yeah, they're sharp.

SANDY
(*obviously enjoying telling the story*) And he knows it, too. After he beat up on me he takes off drinkin, comes back about three just shitfaced, eh, and passes out cold? Well I'm there lookin at him snorin like a pig and I says to myself "I'm gonna get this bastard," I'm thinkin of how when I seen my heels sittin over in the corner and then I know what I'm gonna do. So I take one of the heels and go over real quiet to where he's lyin, and ya know what I do? I take the heel and I rip the holy shit out of his back with it.

THERESA
JEEZ DID HE WAKE UP?

SANDY
Fuckin right he did. You shoulda seen him, first I guess he thought he was dreamin, eh, so he just lies there makin these ugly noises burpin and that? And then he opens his eyes, and puts his hands up like a baby eh, and then I seen him see the heel. Well I take off right out the back door and he's comin after me fit to kill his eyes is all red he's hissin I am scared shitless; well he gets ahold of me and I says to myself "Sandy this is it. This is how you're gonna die. You got the bastard back and now you're gonna die for it." Well he is just about to send me to the fuckin angels when he stops; just like that and turns around and goes on to bed.

THERESA
How come he done that, Sanny?

SANDY
I didn't know at first either, then I figured it out. Cuttin him with the heel was the smartest thing I done. Ya see, he wasn't gonna kill me cause he don't want to do time, eh, and he knew if he just beat up on me he'd never get no more sleep cause I'd do it again. He knows it. He don't dare take a hand to me again, no way. Either he takes off, or he stays and he treats me nice.

THERESA
Did you talk to him later?

SANDY
I ain't seen him for three days. But we ate together before he took off, I fixed him up some tuna casserole and we ate it; we didn't say nothin, though. It don't matter, we sometimes go a whole week without talkin, don't mean we're pissed off at each other.

THERESA
Al and I talkin all the time when we go out.

SANDY
We did too when we first started goin together. After a while ya don't have to talk cause you always know what they're gonna say anyways. Makes ya sick sometimes. What are you bawlin for?

THERESA
I'm sorry Joe done that to me, Sanny.

SANDY
He's like that, he's a prick.

THERESA
S'okay if I come livin here then?

SANDY
…Sure, I don't care.

THERESA
Thank you Sanny.

SANDY
I like the company.

THERESA
Don't say nothin to Al, eh?

SANDY
What if I tell him what Bonnie Cain tole me about you blowin off queers down the Lido?

THERESA
Oh no, Sanny, don't say bout that.

SANDY
I guess old fags in Kingston are pretty hard up.

THERESA
You want a donut, Sanny?

SANDY
No. What kind ya got.

THERESA
Apple fritters.

SANDY
　　Jeez, Therese, ya ever see how they make them things?

THERESA
　　No, I never worked up there.

SANDY
　　It'd make ya sick.

THERESA
　　I love em.

SANDY
　　I know ya do, you're a pig.

THERESA
　　Fuck off…. Only kiddin.

SANDY
　　You watch your mouth.

THERESA
　　You love Joe still?

SANDY
　　I don't know. I used to feel like we was in the fuckin movies. Member that show "Funny Girl" where Barbra Streisand and Omar Sharif are goin together?

THERESA
　　She hardly sing pretty.

SANDY
　　Well remember that part where they start singin right on the boat, singin to each other?

THERESA
　　Yeah.

SANDY
　　We done that once. We'd been up at the Manor, eh, Chesty Morgan was up there so we'd just been havin a hoot, eh, and Joe wants to go over to the General Wolfe to see the Mayor, so we get on the Wolfe Island ferry and we're laughin and carryin on and that and then we start singin, right on the bow of the Wolfe Island ferry.

THERESA
　　Jeez.

SANDY
We didn't care when we were doin it though, we didn't give a shit what anyone was thinkin, fuck em we were havin fun.

THERESA
I love singin.

SANDY
Joe really done that to you?

THERESA
What?

SANDY
Raped ya.

THERESA
Don't like talkin about it Sanny.

SANDY
Trese.

THERESA
He done it when I never wanted it it's true.

SANDY
It is, eh?

THERESA
S'true, Sanny. Don't tell Joe, eh?

SANDY
I mighta known it.

THERESA
Still okay if I sleepin here though?

SANDY
You're gonna have to do the housework while I'm workin for Nikos.

THERESA
How come you workin down there I thought you didn't like Nikos?

SANDY
I get off on corned beef on rye, arsewipe, what d'ya think I need the fuckin money.

THERESA
Ain't Joe drivin for Amey's no more?

SANDY
No.

THERESA
What's he doin?

SANDY
Fuckin the dog, I don't know.

THERESA
Bassard.

SANDY
I know. Gimme a bite of that.

THERESA
I not really retarded am I Sanny?

SANDY
Just a little slow.

THERESA
Not like that guy walkin down street lookin at the sidewalk?

SANDY
Jeez he give me the creeps.

THERESA
He hardly got the long beard, eh?

SANDY
I know.

THERESA
Not like him, eh Sanny?

SANDY
No. No, I tole ya Therese, you're just a little slow.

THERESA
Oh.

> *JOE and ALAN barge in with a hot motorbike. They start quickly, efficiently taking it apart and packing the parts. SANDY and THERESA stand there stupefied.*

JOE
Ya hoo! We got ourselves a shit-hot mother!

ALAN
: Did we *ever*!

JOE
: Okay nice and easy we don't want to mark this babe.

ALAN
: Like this?

JOE
: That's right buddy – fuckin back door wide open shit that dog just sittin there waggin its tail at us.

ALAN
: He wanted to be buddies with us.

JOE
: I just about shit it was fuckin helpin us.

THERESA
: What kinda dog was it Al, one of them golden?

JOE
: A shepherd.

ALAN
: A German shepherd a police dog.

JOE
: A fuckin screw dog.

SANDY
: You're not bringin Martin over here.

JOE
: How's my pussycake doin? Eh? *(kisses SANDY)* Eh pussycake?

SANDY
: I says you're not bringin Martin over here.

JOE
: Don't worry babe we're meetin him over to the Shamrock he ain't comin here.

ALAN
: Down the Beachcomber Room.

THERESA
: That's hardly nice down there all them trees and that?

ALAN
You like it there?

THERESA
I love it.

ALAN
I'll take ya there sometime.

SANDY
Where you been the last three nights?

JOE
Paintin the town brown honeysuck whata you been doin?

SANDY
I said where were ya for three nights in a row?

JOE
Out with the Mayor, poochie, spookin out the Royal.

THERESA
You not out with him he dead.

ALAN
Theresa.

THERESA
He is dead.

ALAN
Joe's only kiddin, Trese.

SANDY
You tell me where ya been or you're out on your ear. I said where were ya the last three nights?

JOE
Just hold on to your pants sugar crack first things first. *(madly working on the bike)*

ALAN
This is big bucks ya know.

SANDY
You don't have to tell me cause I know. I know where ya were you were down the Embassy pissin our money away.

THERESA
Them ugly old Greeks down there anyways.

ALAN
You were takin Papa's *shirt*, eh Joe?

SANDY
I'll tell ya somethin about gamblers youse do it just so's you could lose it's true that's why.

JOE
Well fuck me blind I never knew that. Did you know that Al?

ALAN
Nope, I never heard of that.

JOE
Thars pretty good commander, where'd ya get that offa?

SANDY
It happened to be in the *Reader's Digest*, arsewipe, and it was written by a doctor, Doctor John Grant, and I guess he knows what he's talkin about.

JOE
Oooooh *Reader's Digest*, shit-for-brains is going smart on us.

THERESA
She not a shit-for-brains you stupid.

JOE
You simmer down there burger.

SANDY
Is that where ya were, pissin away my money?

JOE
(completes a physical action) Gotcha.

SANDY
Eh?

JOE
Hand me the pliers, would ya?

SANDY
(screeching) I said where were ya Joe!

> *JOE spits his mouthful of beer in her face. ALAN laughs and laughs.*

That's cute.

THERESA
Stupid dummy-face.

JOE spits on ALAN. ALAN laughs, spits back.

SANDY
You are cut off and I mean it.

JOE
From what, bitch, your ugly box?

SANDY exits to clean up.

Don't know what she's so pissed off at nice brew in the face cool ya right down.

THERESA
I'm movin back here Joe Sanny said I could.

ALAN
She did?

JOE
Is that right.

THERESA
Sleepin on the couch that okay Joe?

JOE
Sure, fuck, I don't care, long as the two of youse don't gang up on me.

ALAN
Two women together always do.

THERESA
What do two women do?

ALAN
You know, gang up on the guy.

SANDY
(entering) Only if he got it comin to him.

JOE
Do I get it comin to me commander?

SANDY
You're fuckin right you do.

JOE
Little diesel dyke this one see what she done to me?

ALAN
Holy Jeez!

JOE
She's a live one all right Pearl Lasalle the second.

THERESA
She not like Pearl Lasalle Pearl Lasalle ugly lookin.

JOE
She fights like her though don't ya honey suck? What's for supper I'm starvin.

SANDY
Nothin.

JOE
What?

SANDY
You don't bring in money we don't get no supper.

JOE
Well fuck – don't we got stuff for samiches?

SANDY
Nope.

JOE
Well fuck I'm goin over to Shirley's.

SANDY
When.

JOE
Right now fuck.

SANDY
Take your stuff with ya.

JOE
Would ya sit on this first I want fish for supper.

SANDY
Pig. I says take your stuff with ya and get out.

JOE
　You for real?

SANDY
　Fuckin right.

JOE
　All right I been wantin out of this hole. Thanks babe.

SANDY
　Is that right?

JOE
　Take care. *(starts to go)*

SANDY
　You could get in a lot of trouble rapin a retard Joe.

JOE
　Pardon.

SANDY
　I said you could get in a lot of trouble rapin a retard.

　　THERESA is motioning No! No! No! to SANDY.

JOE
　Yeah that's right you would. So?

SANDY
　You'll be up the river for twenty years when I tell the cops what you done, Joe.

ALAN
　Over fifty don't get you twenty years no way no way!

SANDY
　I'm not talkin bout the bike.

JOE
　What? What are ya talkin about eh?

SANDY
　About rapin a retard.

JOE
　What?

SANDY
　About rapin Theresa.

JOE
What.

SANDY
About rapin Theresa with me in the next room.

JOE
Rape? Rape? Who told you that did Theresa tell you that.

SANDY
Yeahhh.

THERESA
No no Sanny not rape I only said he done it when I never wanted it.

JOE
Did you tell my wife that I raped you Theresa? *(THERESA doesn't answer.)* Did you say that? Eh? *(grabs her)* Eh?

THERESA
I never – leave me alone you big ugly cock–

JOE
I'll tell you somethin about your little girlfriend buddy. I'll tell you something about this little–

ALAN
It don't matter, Joe, it – it – it just don't matter nobody don't believe her anyways.

JOE
This little girl who's callin rape was sittin on that couch beggin for it.

ALAN
She never.

SANDY
Theresa?

JOE
It's true. I come in piss drunk I'm passed out on the floor and there she is down on all fours shovin her big white ass in my face.

THERESA
No I never.

JOE
Big white bootie right in the face.

THERESA
Go away.

JOE
Tell em like it was Trese, and no crossin fingers.

THERESA
I never say that Sanny, I never mean he rape me!

SANDY
Theresa is he tellin the truth?

ALAN
Theresa you never done that, did ya? Shown him your bum?

JOE
This is your last chance, burger, now tell the fuckin truth or I get serious.

SANDY
Don't lie to me Theresa. I can forgive a lot of things but not a lie.

ALAN
You can tell the truth, Theresa, I'll take care of ya.

SANDY
Eh, Trese?

Pause.

THERESA
(laughing) Who farted?

ALAN
I never did.

JOE
Eh Theresa?

ALAN
It's – it's okay, Joe it's – she – she can't handle her booze yet she was probably drunk or sniffin and you was drunk and it don't matter, it just don't matter I'll be stayin with her all the nights from now I'm gonna take care of her it won't happen again she won't never say nothin bout ya again I promise.

THERESA
You stayin with me all nights from now Al?

ALAN
    I'm takin care of ya. I'm—

SANDY
    Could youse leave us alone, please.

ALAN
    Who, me and Theresa?

SANDY
    If you don't mind.

ALAN
    Sure, sure. We—

THERESA
    Wait for me Al I wanna get some chocolate bars and that I starvin… well I am I didn't have no dinner.

JOE
    You. You watch your mouth, eh?

SANDY
    Would youse just take off?

    ALAN pulls THERESA out.

THERESA
    See youse later don't do nothin I wouldn't do.

Scene Three

ALAN and THERESA exit. JOE is furious and trying to cool down. His back is to SANDY. She is aware of his anger. She picks something up off the kitchen floor and starts to take it in to the kitchen. JOE grabs her as she tries to pass him and throws her to the floor.

JOE
    You CUNT.

SANDY
    Keep away from me—

JOE
    I'm a fuckin rapist cause a fuckin retard SAYS so?

SANDY
    Touch me again and you go to your goddamn grave!

JOE
FUCK maybe I'm the maniac been carvin all the TELLERS out in SASKATOON! *(makes monster face and noise)*

SANDY
Go jump in a hole.

JOE
(grabs her, hard) What is fuckin with your BRAIN, woman?

SANDY
I didn't mean it.

JOE
It was a *joke*?

SANDY
I was just – you said you liked her better.

JOE
What?

SANDY
You said you liked – pokin her better.

JOE
(laughs, almost hysterically) So I go to the joint.

SANDY
I wasn't gonna tell nobody–

JOE
You're a fuckin CROW, you know that?

SANDY
I was just – seein–

JOE
(thrusting her away) Get away from me.

> SANDY *starts to run toward him, trying to scream but the sound is muffled and distorted by a stomach seizure which stops her about three feet away from* JOE.

You got your upset stomach again?

SANDY
Bastard.

JOE
(looks her up and down) You just give me a hard on.

SANDY spits on him.

Hewww you like it when I'm rough with ya, don't ya? Eh? *(moves her roughly, whispers)* Makes your nips stand up when I'm rough with ya.

SANDY's hands are still raised. SANDY and JOE are a foot apart throughout the interchange. SANDY looks at him with hatred.

What, you don't want it? Okay, see ya later!

He starts to leave.

SANDY
(head down) Joe.

JOE
What can I do for ya?

SANDY smiles.

Oh, ya do want it. Okay, why – why – don't ya take that blouse there off?

She removes her blouse.

Hm. And the skirt.

She removes her skirt. She is left in a bra and pantyhose with a low crotch. He nods, looking her up and down.

How come ya like it like this? Eh? *(shakes his head)* I gotta be somewhere.

JOE exits. SANDY remains onstage, not moving. Lights out quickly.

Scene Four

THERESA and ALAN are in a restaurant.

THERESA
Where d'ya think Joe took off to?

ALAN
I don't know probably drinkin, maybe the Shamrock.

THERESA
You think they're splitting up?

ALAN
    I hope not.

THERESA
    Me too. I love Sandy, she my best girlfriend.

ALAN
    I – Joe – he and me are good buddies, too. They go good together anyways.

THERESA
    Could I have a donut?

ALAN
    What kind, chocolate? I know you like chocolate.

THERESA
    I love it.

ALAN
    Sandy's nuts, you're not fat.

THERESA
    Don't say nothin about it.

ALAN
    You're not.

THERESA
    I don't like talkin about it.

ALAN
    Here. Two chocolate donuts.

THERESA
    Thank you Alan.

ALAN
    Jesus you're a good lookin girl. You're the prettiest lookin girl I seen.

THERESA
    Don't talk like that.

ALAN
    I love screwin with ya. Do you like it with me?

THERESA
    I don't know – don't ask me that stuff dummy-face.

ALAN
I like eatin ya out ya know.

THERESA
Shut your mouth people are lookin don't talk like that stupid-face.

ALAN
Nobody's lookin. Jeez you're pretty. Just like a little angel. Huh. Like a – I know. I know. I'm gonna call you my little angel from now on. People gonna see ya and they're gonna go "There's Trese, she's Al's angel!"

THERESA
Who gonna say them things?

ALAN
Anybody.

THERESA
They are?

ALAN
Yup.

THERESA
You're a dummy-face.

ALAN
So beautiful.

THERESA
Stop it Al you make me embarrass.

ALAN
You're – I was always hopin for someone like you – always happy always laughin and that.

THERESA
I cryin sometimes ya know.

ALAN
Yeah but ya cry the same way ya laugh. There's somethin – I don't know – as soon as I seen ya I knew I wanted ya. I wanted to marry ya when I seen ya.

THERESA
When, when did you say that?

ALAN
I never said nothin, I just thought it, all the time.

THERESA
We only been goin together for a little while, you know.

ALAN
Let's get married.

THERESA
Al stop lookin at me like that you embarrassin me.

ALAN
Sorry. Did you hear me?

THERESA
Yeah. Okay.

ALAN
When.

THERESA
Tuesday. I ask my sosha worker to come.

ALAN
No. Just Joe and me and you and Sandy. Just the four of us. I want Joe to be my best man.

THERESA
Sandy could be the flower girl. Uh. Oh.

ALAN
What?

THERESA
Hope you don't want no babies.

ALAN
Why. I do! I do want babies! I get on with babies good!

THERESA
Not sposda have none.

ALAN
How come? Who told you that?

THERESA
The sosha worker, she say I gotta get my tubes tied.

ALAN
What's that?

THERESA
Operation up the hospital. They tie it up down there so ya won't go havin babies.

ALAN
They can't do that to you no way!

THERESA
I know they can't but they're doin it.

ALAN
They don't have no right.

THERESA
Yah they do Al I slow.

ALAN
Slow? I don't think you're slow who told YOU that?

THERESA
I ain't a good mum Al I cant help it.

ALAN
Who said you ain't a good mum?

THERESA
All of them just cause when I took off on Dawn.

ALAN
Who's Dawn?

THERESA
The baby, the other baby.

ALAN
You never had a baby before did ya? Did ya?

THERESA
Las–

ALAN
You didn't have no other man's baby did ya? With another guy?

Pause.

THERESA
No, it's Bernice's.

ALAN
Who's Bernice?

THERESA
My cousin my mum's sister.

ALAN
Well how come you were lookin after her baby?

THERESA
Cause she was sick up in hospital. Jeez Al.

ALAN
Well – what happened whatdja do wrong?

THERESA
Nothin it wasn't my fault just one Friday night I was sniffin, eh, so I took off down to the plaza and I leave the baby up the room, eh, I thought I was comin right back, and I met this guy and he buyin me drinks and that then I never knew what happened and I woke up and I asked somebody where I was and I was in Ottawa!

ALAN
He took you all the way up to Ottawa? That bastard.

THERESA
I never seen him again I thumbed back to Kingston. *(crying)* I come back to the house and the baby's gone she ain't there so I bawlin I goin everywhere yellin after her and never found nothin then I see Bonnie Cain and she told me they took her up the Children's Aid she dead. So I go on up the Aid and they say she ain't dead she live but they not givin her back cause I unfit.

ALAN
Jeez.

THERESA
I ain't no more Al I don't sniff or nothin.

ALAN
Them bastards.

THERESA
Honest.

ALAN
I know. I know ya don't and we're gonna have a baby and nobody ain't gonna stop us. We're gonna have our own little baby between you and me and nobody can't say nothin bout it. You're not goin to no hospital, understand?

THERESA
But Al she say she gonna cut off my pension cheque if I don't get my tubes tied.

ALAN
Fuck the pension check you're not goin to no hospital.

THERESA
Okay Al.

ALAN
Come here. You're not goin to no hospital.

THERESA
You won't let em do nothin to me, will ya Al?

ALAN
Nope. You're my angel and they ain't gonna touch you…. Hey! I know what ya look like now!

THERESA
What, an angel?

ALAN
That – that madonna lady; you know them pictures they got up in classrooms when you're a kid? Them pictures of the madonna?

THERESA
The Virgin Mary?

ALAN
Yeah. Her.

THERESA
I love her I askin her for stuff.

ALAN
Yuh look just like her. Just like the madonna. Cept the madonna picture got a baby in it.

THERESA
It do?

ALAN
She's holdin it right in her arms. You too, maybe, eh? Eh? Hey! Let's go up to the Good Thief.

THERESA
Al I don't know you goin to church! You goin every Sunday?

ALAN
: No I never went since I was five I just want to go now. We'll go and we'll – we'll like have a party lightin candles and that a party for gettin married!

THERESA
: I love lightin candles.

ALAN
: Maybe the Father's gonna be there. They're always happy when someone's gettin married we could tell him!

THERESA
: Al I gettin sleepy.

ALAN
: Well after we party I'm gonna put ya right down to sleep over at Joe's. I won't try nothin or nothin.

THERESA
: What if Sandy be piss off.

ALAN
: No Trese, they said we could stay there together. The two of us. And we're gonna.

THERESA
: Okay… really I lookin like that madonna?

ALAN
: Just like her. Just like her.

He is rocking her in his arms. Lights fade.

Scene Five

JOE
: Me and the Mayor we'd pick up a couple steak hoagies, and a case of twenty-four, head up to Merton on the hogs – catch some shit group – you know, Mad Dog Fagin, Grapes of Wrath, somethin, get shitfaced then go back to Kingston, pick us up some juicy pie down at Lino's or Horny Tim's, drive it out to middle road, fuck it blind, and have em home by one o'clock. Then we'd go down and catch the last ferry to the island and fuckin ride from one end to the other all fuckin night. Seven o'clock we'd go into Lou's have us some home fries and a couple eggs easy over then head on back to work in Kingston. That was when I was drivin a Cat makin a shitload of money just a shitload. Huh – the Mayor was fuckin crazy wasn't nothin he wouldn't do nothin he was smart too he went to university in the States even, he just didn't give a shit about it, you know? He had about a hundred books I seen em all filled with words that long *(measures*

two feet) he knew what they meant, too, every one of them but he never let on, ya know? He never let on he knew so much… we never *talked* about shit, it was the shit we done together made us good buddies. Just doin stuff with a guy you know you're thinkin the same. Anybody touched him I woulda killed them and same goes for him… he was a damn good driver too but he wasn't drivin, Martin was. Fuckin Martin fuckin stoned on STP. Martin – Martin wasn't an asshole, but he stupid you know? Jeez he was stupid. So this Friday night we'd all gotten pissed up the Manor, eh, then we all went over to the island just to fuck around and to see the Mayor's sister, Linda, who was workin at the General Wolfe waitin on tables. So Bart, that was his real name, Bart and me and Martin had all got these new boots over at the A1 men's store really nice you know, all leather, real solid a hundred bucks a pair so we wanted to show em off to Linda, you know, bug her. So Bart gets in there and he's jumpin on tables, eatin all the limes and cherries and that for the drinks singin some gross song about his love boots, he called them. Fuck it was funny – we were killin ourselves but Linda she wasn't laughin her boss was gettin pissed off so she told Bart, she goes "Bart, get the fuck out of here I think your goddamn boots are shit." That's what she said. So he give her a big kiss right in front of her boss and we take off in Martin's car. Me and the Mayor in the backseat, Martin and his girlfriend in the front. Well we're headin down the road goin south it's dark but it ain't wet and the last thing I remember Bart looks at me and he says "I wonder what it's like to fuck an angel" and bang everything goes fuckin black. When I come to I'm in the fucking ambulance goin across to Kingston and Bart's lyin there beside me dead only I didn't know it and there's his sister Linda right there in the ambulance. I don't know how she got there – she's all red all black under her eyes and that and she's bawlin just bawlin up a storm and she's huggin his legs and she's sayin something only I can't make out what she's sayin I can't make it out I was so out of it I'm thinkin I'm gonna die I'm thinkin I'm gonna die if I don't make out what she's sayin so I kept tryin to make it out and she kept sayin it and then I knew what she was sayin and you know what it was? …She was sayin she did like his boots. "I do like your boots Bart I do like your boots Bart I do like your boots I do like your fuckin boots I do like your boots I do like your boots I do like your buots…." She wouldn't fuckin stop it.

Scene Six

ALAN and THERESA are sound asleep. The room is sometimes lit by passing cars. Noise of people on the street. THERESA's steady breathing. Suddenly we hear JOE, very drunk, half singing. As soon as ALAN hears him he springs into his jeans, legs shaking, and awkwardly tries to light a cigarette. His heart is racing. JOE enters.

ALAN
Hey Joe.

JOE
Jeeeeeeezus you gimme a scare what are you doin here?

ALAN
    Stayin with Trese member? Member ya said I could? The – the mum's got company – in from Windsor.

JOE
    Windsor – What a fuckin hole.

ALAN
    Yeah it's hot down there – in the summer–

JOE
    Look what I found in the fuckin hallway. Cheese samich with a bloody Kleenex stuck to it.

    This makes ALAN very sick.

ALAN
    Jeezus who put it there.

JOE
    I was thinkin maybe the wife left out a little snack for me. Ya want some? Blood'n Cheez Whiz samich? Hey hey hey it's hardly good.

ALAN
    Hey no – no – no thank you. No way.

JOE
    What, you don't like eatin blood or somethin?

ALAN
    I never tried it.

JOE
    Were you screwin that?

ALAN
    No! No I mean no I was just I–

JOE
    Why the hell not?

ALAN
    Oh no I mean I was eh, like I was a couple hours ago, but not right before ya came in I wasn't.

JOE
    Jeez you're strange. How come ya got dressed you goin out?

ALAN
No – no I'm not goin out – I – I couldn't fuckin sleep, you know? Ya know what that's like? Ya just keep turnin and can't lie right? So I thought I'd wait up and just shoot the shit with you when ya came in.

JOE
Strange-o.

ALAN
I guess so. Did-dju play tonight?

JOE
Papadapa dies!

ALAN
He – he was cheatin again?

JOE
Fuckin right he was.

ALAN
He dies.

JOE
Greasy fuck. Fuck once I seen Edwards get him in a half Nelson an he was so greasy he slipped out!

ALAN
Ewwww.

JOE
Slipped right out. Slimy bastard right in the middle of the game I turn to him and I says "Papa" I says, "Don't fuck with me, just don't fuck with me."

ALAN
That's hardly good. Huh. What did he say?

JOE
Nothin. He just made one of them noises.

ALAN
What, what the ones with their mouth like this? Like a chicken does?

JOE
Hah. Yeah it is kinda like a chicken. Gives me the creeps.

ALAN
Yeah. Yeah, they do that all the time and the one I worked for, Andy? He *stunk* too, he smelled like matches, you know? After ya light a match?

JOE
　He's gettin it.

ALAN
　Yeah?? Yeah? Who's gonna give it to him, are you? Are you gonna give it to him Joe? I'll help ya I hate the bastard. I hate him.

JOE
　Buddy I am pleadin the Fifth. Fuuuck. *(singing)* "I gotta get outtaaa this place if it's the lassst…"

ALAN
　I know what ya mean, Joe. Too – too – too bad there weren't no late movie on or something – hah – Mr. Ed or somethin.

JOE
　Who's he when he's at home?

ALAN
　Mr. Ed? The talkin horse, don't ya remember? "A horse is a horse of course of course and no one…"

JOE
　Hey *(indicating bedroom)* w'she bawlin or did she go out?

ALAN
　Sleepin when we come in I think.

JOE
　She's a good woman buddy.

ALAN
　I know she is Joe. So's Trese.

JOE
　Are you sure, buddy?

ALAN
　Oh – that was – she – she didn't mean nothin honest Joe she she just don't think sometimes, ya know?

JOE
　That mouth of hers is gonna send her up shit creek one day ain't it burger?

ALAN
　You – you want a smoke?

JOE
　Whaddya got – menthol, fuck, I can't smoke that shit.

ALAN
I know – I didn't buy em a guy a guy give em to me.

JOE
Hey hamburger sorry for wakin ya.

THERESA
I not a hamburger.

JOE
Ooooh I thought ya was!

THERESA
You shut up I sleepin.

JOE
Okay burger queen. Yeah. Yeah buddy she's okay too.

ALAN
Thank you, Joe. So's Sandy.

JOE
She never fucked around on me, you know.

ALAN
No?

JOE
Not once. *(goes to window and leans out)* What a fuckin hole this is eh? …K fuckin O. *(yells out window)* Fuuuuuuck.

SANDY enters.

SANDY
Would you shut it?

JOE
(singing) "I gotta get out of this place."

SANDY
Why don't ya then ya big pig.

JOE
I told ya woman don't go callin me pig in public. Jeez she got an ugly mouth, eh?

SANDY
You're shitfaced, Joe, go on and pass out.

JOE
You make me wanta piss my pants.

SANDY
Just go on makin a fool of yourself.

JOE
Down woman, me and my pal Al is gonna head up to Horny Tim's and we're gonna pick us up some tailerooonie! Then we're gonna go on over to the quarry and we're gonna get ourselves sucked and fucked–

SANDY
You're not proud, are ya.

JOE bumps into something, falls. SANDY starts to pick him up.

JOE
You never fooled around on me, did ya?

SANDY
Nope. I never… did.

JOE
(sings) "She's a hooo-o-o-o-nky tonk womannnn gimme *(goes to bedroom)* gimme gimme the *(fading)* honky tonk wom…

ALAN goes to the window and silently mouths "Fuuuuck," in imitation of JOE. He turns on TV, crouches on sofa, and sings softly, but can't remember the whole song.

ALAN
Nobody – nobody here – but us chickens, nobody here but us guys don't – don't bother me we got work – to do we got stuff to do and eggs to lay – we're busy – chickens– *(He pretends to be a car, makes sounds, mimes a steering wheel.)* Neeowwwwwwwwwww. Whaaaaaa. Fhrhuuummmm. Atta girl.

Scene Seven

Later, SANDY brings in bedding to sleep on sofa, turns on lamp, turns off TV, lights cigarette, sits on sofa.

SANDY
He pukes all over the fuckin bed.

ALAN
Oooh shit.

SANDY
  Funny.

ALAN
  I'm – I'm sorry Sandy I didn't mean to laugh at ya.

SANDY
  Can I ask you a personal question?

ALAN
  Yeah, yeah sure – what?

SANDY
  Am I gettin ugly lookin?

ALAN
  What?

SANDY
  You know, mean lookin, uglier lookin.

ALAN
  Shit no, jeez – you – you look nice I think ya do! Who, who said that?

SANDY
  No one. Are ya sure?

ALAN
  Sure, sure I am you're a good looker I even heard people say ya was.

SANDY
  Who, who said that?

ALAN
  Alf. Alf said ya was.

SANDY
  His folks are loaded.

ALAN
  I know!

SANDY
  Did – did Joe ever say anything?

ALAN
  Joe? What about?

SANDY
 About me gettin ugly, *arsewipe*.

ALAN
 No, no Joe never said nothin.

SANDY
 Are ya sure?

ALAN
 Yeah. Yeah he never – he never said nothin! No! Why?

SANDY
 None of your business.

ALAN
 What's buggin you, you got your pains?

SANDY
 No, I don't got my pains but I'm gonna get em if youse – if youse – well – no offence or nothin but when are youse gettin outa here anyways?

ALAN
 Soon as I get up the money I – wh – why is – is it buggin you me and Trese sleepin over?

SANDY
 Yeah. Yeah, it is it's – it's me and Joe gotta have – have some privacy, ya know? Ya know?

ALAN
 Yeah. Yeah I do I – I'll be out soon what can I say, we'll be out as soon as I got the cash.

SANDY
 I never heard of screwin your girlfriend on your buddy's floor.

ALAN
 I'll be out as soon as I got the cash, okay?

SANDY
 It's just strange you goin with Trese on our floor.

ALAN
 I know it's strange I know I'm strange I'm strange okay?

SANDY
 I know you're fuckin strange all right.

ALAN
You're smokin too much. You're smokin too much.

SANDY
Look who's talkin.

ALAN
Well at least I know I'm doin it you don't even know. *(takes drag off cigarette)*

SANDY
You're fuckin nuts, you know that, nuts.

ALAN
I may be nuts but I fuckin know what I'm doin. I know I'm killin myself smokin these I know it so I'm throwin them away okay? I'm throwin them away!

ALAN rips up his cigarettes and takes SANDY's cigarette out of her mouth.

Fuckin killsticks!

SANDY
(tries to stop him) Stop it you – fuckin don't you touch me – you fucker you give me back the cash for those right now right now hear?

ALAN
No! No Sandy I can't I don't have the money I gotta save it so I can fuck off outa this hole I don't have money okay??

SANDY
(starts to back out the door shaking head) You're nuts Al–

ALAN
(grabs her back into the room) I am not nuts. I am not nuts you understand? I just decided now I'm gonna quit smoking that's all. I got a flash in my head of my old man tryin to take his breath tryin to find the fuckin air and not gettin it fuckin all hunched over so's he wouldn't drown to death his his feet all puffed all that shit all that shit comin out of his mouth and they wouldn't even clean it cause they said he couldn't get nothin cause he was gonna die so he had all this shit comin out of his mouth and and I know he didn't like it cause he was clean – all the time he was washin – and then when he's dyin they don't give a shit about his goddamn mouth with all the fuck comin out of it and they got a goddamn vacuum cleaner goin – we can't hear nothin and he keeps sort of movin forward movin ahead in his chair like when you're tryin not to crash out at the show so ya keep movin forward? He didn't want to go he didn't want to go at all and he went cause of these. Cause of these goddamn ugly white killsticks these! *(shows her cigarette, lets her go)* See? See why ya can't smoke? See?

SANDY
(very moved by ALAN's speech; speaks quietly) I don't know who the fuck you think you are tearin up the place just cause you seen your old man fuckin croak.

ALAN
You don't know what it's like, man, you don't know what it's like till you been there don't you talk.

SANDY
Don't tell me what I know, arsewipe, don't you tell me nothin. I seen my mum go, I sat by her bed for three fuckin months and I don't go carryin on like a three-year-old.

ALAN
It wasn't the same I'm tellin ya it couldna been the same.

SANDY
And I'm a woman and I don't go cryin about it I never cried about it once.

ALAN
I'm not cryin about it I never cried about it I'm just tellin ya why not to smoke.

SANDY
You're just tellin me shit. Jeez if Joe seen you just now he'd think you were some kind of fag.

ALAN
I'm not a fag that's one thing I'm not I'm not a fag.

SANDY
Then start acting like a fuckin man.

ALAN
I'm not a fag you take that back.

SANDY
I'm not takin nothin back for no baby.

ALAN
I said take that back you ugly bitch.

ALAN grabs her. SANDY throws him to the floor.

SANDY
You're sad, you know that? You don't scare nobody.

ALAN
I'm no fag.

SANDY
(*goes back to lie on couch*) I seen ten-year-olds fight better than you.

ALAN
Why?

SANDY
Why what?

ALAN
Why don't I scare nobody?

SANDY
Cause you're a wimp that's why. Like one of them dogs that starts shakin when ya go to pat it.

ALAN
How come.

SANDY
How am I supposed to know?

ALAN
Don't say nothin to Joe, eh?

SANDY
What, about takin a fit?

ALAN
About you thinkin I'm like one of them dogs.

SANDY
I won't.

ALAN
Or Trese.

SANDY
Don't worry about it.

ALAN
You watched your mum go?

SANDY
Big deal.

ALAN
Couldna been the same.

SANDY
It's all the same.

ALAN
Don't you feel nothin?

SANDY
Well I'm not a baby like you.

ALAN
No.

SANDY
Anyways, bein dead ain't no different from livin anyway.

ALAN
How do you know?

SANDY
I just know. It's just like movin to Brockville or Oshawa or somethin. It ain't that different.

ALAN
Oh no. Oh no you're wrong I think you're wrong there.

SANDY
No I'm not.

ALAN
Yes you are.

SANDY
You don't know shit Al.

ALAN
I do I do know some things and I know that. I know it's different.

SANDY
Get out of my house.

ALAN
I'm goin I didn't want to stay anyways it smells funny in here.

SANDY
Garbage stinks up a place.

ALAN
And Sandy.

SANDY
What.

ALAN
No offence or nothin, but you – you – are – you are gettin ugly lookin.

SANDY looks at him.

See ya.

Scene Eight

JOE, SANDY, ALAN, THERESA sitting in bar. Otis Redding's "I've Been Loving You Too Long" is playing.

JOE
That's a shit-hot tune. Too bad he died.

ALAN
Did he die?

JOE
That's right. In a fuckin motel.

ALAN
That's too bad.

JOE
Too bad Jimi Hendrix died too.

ALAN
Yeah. Oh *yeah. (sings, drums)* "Scuse me while I kiss the sky!"

JOE
Did youse know if Hendrix hadda lived he was gonna join up with ELP?

SANDY
I seen them, Emerson, Lake and Palmer, down in Montreal.

JOE
Ya know what they woulda, been called if Hendrix hadda joined up with them?

ALAN
Hendrix, and…

JOE
(wits it out) HELP. Help. And you fuckin would need help hearin those two play together.

ALAN
Fuck would ya ever.

JOE
Fuckin straight.

ALAN
Would ya ever. Fuck, your brain'd die.

JOE
HELP. *Help.*

THERESA
I wouldn't need no help.

SANDY
You don't got no ear for music.

THERESA
I do so.

ALAN
She sings and that all the time.

THERESA
I seen Jerry uptown he got a job workin for Wilmot's.

SANDY
That right eh.

JOE
Splinter what a cocksuck.

>   *Restless, JOE goes to the jukebox, presses button. JOE walks to the urinal. After a moment, ALAN follows.*

THERESA
He be workin with all that ice cream all the time.

>   *Pause.*

SANDY
He could hardly munch out.

THERESA
I love ice cream.

SANDY
Just munch right out.

Scene Nine

JOE and ALAN. In urinal of bar.

ALAN
  Those two guys together. Geez! *(shaking head in disbelief)*

JOE
  I'm goin buddy I'm takin off.

ALAN
  Where ya goin?

JOE
  That's for me to know.

ALAN
  Oh. Sorry. How – how come gettin sick of Kingston?

JOE
  Got me a job drivin a Cat.

ALAN
  Jeez. You make a lot of cash doin that.

JOE
  Nice work if you can get it.

ALAN
  Nice work if you can get it.

JOE
  Make a shitload of money.

ALAN
  That's hard to do, drivin one of them things, ain't it?

JOE
  They're mother fuckers.

ALAN
  Jeez fuck where'd ya learn how to do that anyways?

JOE
  Hymie Beach.

ALAN
  WOW, I never knew that. You live down there?

JOE
Sure, shared a motel room with this creep who later turned out to be a queer boy. Started sayin stuff about my dink and that when I got out of the shower. "Is it always that long?"

ALAN
Fuckin queers.

JOE
I know.

ALAN
They just make me – feel like pukin–

JOE
I sent that one through the fuckin wall.

ALAN
Did ya?

JOE
Fuckin right.

ALAN
I hate em.

Pause.

JOE
Don't say nothin to Sandy.

ALAN
Don't she know?

JOE shakes his head.

What if something happens – she gets cancer or somethin?

JOE
What?

ALAN
Them things happen, I've heard of them.

JOE
…I'll let ya know where I am.

ALAN
Hey – I'd like to do that kind of shit.

JOE
 You should come out. You could get on a site dry-wallin or somethin.

ALAN
 They just take anybody?

JOE
 Sure.

ALAN
 No, no way.

JOE
 Suit yourself.

ALAN
 Hey – I forgot to tell ya, Cathy Yachuk jumped offa the Brock Towers!

JOE
 What?

ALAN
 Jumped right onto her feet Martin was sayin, fucked em up so bad they hadda take a piece of her bum and glue it on to her f-f-feet – so's she could walk on them.

JOE
 How come she done that?

ALAN
 She seen a white light in front of her, tellin her!

JOE
 Fuckin whore… yuh, I'm gettin right out of this hole.

ALAN
 You comin back ever?

JOE
 How'm I sposda know?

Scene Ten

ALAN on way to work, stumbles out door. There is an Indian MAN on the street, his wrists bleeding heavily. He is ambling past ALAN. He is very drunk.

ALAN
 Hey buddy – hey can I do something for ya?

MAN
(drunk, mumbling) Please…

ALAN
Hey, want a smoke?

MAN
Yeah. Give me a smoke.

ALAN
What are ya lookin for man?

MAN
Fuckers took it fuckers.

ALAN
Who? Did somebody jump ya? Eh? Did somebody jump ya?

MAN
Yaah. Some guys. Buncha Indians – fuckin Indians.

ALAN
Hey man you're an Indian aren't ya?

MAN
(giggling) Don't burn the fish bones! Don't burn the fishbones!

ALAN
That's okay man my fiancee she's Indian. Therese. I like Indians it's okay.

MAN
(weeping like a girl) Stupid fuckin Indians.

ALAN
Hey. Hey don't cry. Is it hurtin bad? Please – just stay here – I'll call an ambulance. Stay. *(starts to walk to phone, holds up hand)* Stay.

MAN
(sits up, screams a death scream) Aaaahh!

> ALAN comes back, takes off his own shirt, ties it around the MAN's wrist to stop the bleeding. The MAN sees a vision.

Devil-baby-eyes-devil-baby-eyes. Please. Please. Mercy. Mercy. Hand. Gimme your hand. Hand. Please.

ALAN
What? You want me to hold your hand? Okay.

MAN takes ALAN's hand, starts rubbing it in a sexual way. ALAN doesn't know what to do.

MAN
(urgently) Hey. Hey. Hey.

ALAN
What, what is it, buddy?

MAN
Hey. *(makes intercourse motion with fingers)* Let's tear off a piece. Come on let's tear off a piece. Rip off a piece. Come on.

ALAN
Stupid cocksucker!

ALAN flings MAN away, but MAN clings to his leg.

Get off me you fucker! Get offffffff me! *(He runs.)*

MAN
(lies on street, giggling) Pleeeease. (giggles)

ALAN jumps back to SANDY's living room where THERESA is asleep at his feet.

ALAN
(yells) Dieeeeeeeeeee!

Scene Eleven

It is the middle of the night.

ALAN
Therese?

THERESA
Yeah?

ALAN
Do you ever start thinkin ugly thoughts before ya go to sleep?

THERESA
No, do you?

ALAN
Yeah.

THERESA
  Like what?

ALAN
  Like fallin down and your teeth hittin the sidewalk.

THERESA
  Ewwwww.

ALAN
  Sometimes I even think of someone takin out my spine, like they do with a shrimp.

THERESA
  You crazy stupid-face, go sleepin and think of nice stuff.

ALAN
  Like what.

THERESA
  Donuts and the Wolfe Island ferry and that. Stuff like that.

ALAN
  Huh. I love ya Trese.

THERESA
  Madonna.

ACT TWO

Scene One

ALAN
Did you ever start thinkin somethin, and it's like ugly…? And ya can't beat it out of your head? I wouldn't be scared of it if it was sittin in front of me, I'd beat it to shit – nothin wouldn't stop me – but I can't beat it cause it's in my head fuck. It's not like bein crazy, it's just like thinkin one thing over and over and it kinda makes ya sick. Like when I was a kid and I used to have these earaches all the time, you know? And I would keep thinkin it was like a couple of garter snakes with big ugly teeth all yellow, like an old guy's teeth and there they were the two of them suckin and bitin on my eardrum with these yellow teeth. Makin noises like a cat eatin cat food. I could even hear the fuckin noises. *(makes the noise)* Like that. Just made me wanta puke thinkin that – made the pain worse I'd think of their eyes, too, that made me sick, black eyes lookin sideways all the time while they keep suckin and chewin on my eardrum. Fuck. Do youse know what I mean? No offense or nothin I don't mean no offense I wish youse all good luck in your lives. I was just – like I just wanted to know if any of youse like knew of a medicine or somethin ya might take for this – they gotta have somethin cause the one I'm thinkin of now is even worse it's fuckin bad it's it's somethin Bonnie Cain told me about this nurse she knows goin out to Enterprise out to one of the farms out there these folks were on the dole so she goes up to see if the kids got colds and that, and the wife, all small with her teeth all black takes her into the warsh room and tells her she got somethin wrong down in her woman's part. And Bonnie said this nurse lifted up this woman's skirt and you know what she seen? Like a cauliflower growin out of her thing! A cauliflower! Fuck! And ya know the worst part of it? When ya cut it it bleeds! It grows blood and that! It just happened last summer too, last fuckin summer in July! …How'd she go – like how'd she pee? Fuck I'll be doin the dishes where I'm workin down the Tropicana there and it's like pictures burning holes in my brain I try all the time to like put other pictures over top of that, nice things that I really get off on, eh, that I really like like – like lambs in a field, you know, with the black on their faces? Like baby sheep? I always liked them whenever I seen one in a field or someplace I always laughed at them so stupid lookin and cute fuck – I never told the other guys they were there case they burn them or something. Anyways I try puttin pictures of these baby sheep over top of the cauliflower and I'll do it and it's okay for a second then the lamb its eyes'll go all funny like slits lookin sideways just like them snakes and then it'll open its mouth and there'll be them long sharp teeth and a bunch of worms inside and the nice little sheep goes all ugly on me and the cauliflower comes back worse than ever like it ate the sheep or somethin…. Maybe if I could just have a car or get back to workin on cars, you know? Or get into Dragmasters, then maybe I'd stop thinkin of these things. I don't know. I'm lookin for somebody who knows, that's why I'm askin youse I don't know. I wish I did. *(pause)* If it was in front of me I'd beat it to shit, you know?

Scene Two

ALAN and THERESA at home. ALAN comes in after work. THERESA is watching television, laughing.

ALAN
Did ya do it did ya get it done?

THERESA
You got somethin on your mouth Al.

ALAN
(wipes) What was it?

THERESA
Look like cream from one of them Joe Louis.

ALAN
What I got on my face don't matter, Trese, I asked ya a question.

THERESA
What?

ALAN
Did ya get what I told ya done?

THERESA
Readin writin?

ALAN
Yes.

THERESA
Shhhh baby sleepin Al.

ALAN
Did – let's see. Awwwww hey Danny! He's not sleepin! Hey ya little bugger how ya doin – this is your dad –this is your dad speakin, ya know me? Hey? He does, he knows me. Don't ya Danny. Hey Danny did your angel mummy do what daddy asked her to? Eh? Yes? She did? Oh thank you Danny you are the most neatest cutest little baby boy – what's that on his chin?

THERESA
From eatin milk.

ALAN
Theresa you don't eat milk you drink it.

THERESA
　I know.

ALAN
　There. Wipe that ugly milk offa ya. Eh Danny? You are my little bugger and I'm your daddy! Hey! Your mummy gonna show me what she done! Okay mummy, now show me what ya done.

THERESA
　I lost it.

ALAN
　How could you lose it?

THERESA
　I done it, Al, but I lost it.

ALAN
　Theresa. Theresa I'm gonna try not to get mad at ya but ya can't keep doin this to me! Every day you're tellin me ya lost your homework!

THERESA
　Maybe someone take it.

ALAN
　Theresa don't you understand I am tryin to improve my family.

THERESA
　(coyly) Al.

ALAN
　What.

THERESA
　(delighted) You shoulda seen the pooh I done today it was hardly long!

ALAN
　Theresa, married ladies with babies ain't supposed to say things like that!

THERESA
　Sorry.

ALAN
　Danny could hear ya ya know.

THERESA
　I don't think he hear Al I think he deaf.

ALAN
  What?

THERESA
  I shoutin in his ear he don't do nothin.

ALAN
  Trese ya don't go shoutin in babies' ears!

  THERESA kisses ALAN. He melts.

THERESA
  I love ya Al.

ALAN
  You know I love you don't ya you know it – more than anything in this whole world you and Danny boy.

THERESA
  I know Al. How many dishes you done today?

ALAN
  Two hundred and twenty-three.

THERESA
  Jeez.

ALAN
  Yup. That's ten more than yesterday.

THERESA
  Jeez.

Scene Three

  THERESA has been sleeping over at SANDY's because SANDY is scared. Cat scream.

SANDY
  What's that noise. Trese wake up. Hear that?

THERESA
  What?

SANDY
  Listen – oh Jesus what is it?

THERESA
　Maybe it Charlie Manson.

SANDY
　Oh shut up you watch too much TV.

THERESA
　Maybe it a pussy cat.

SANDY
　Hello? Hello? Anybody there? Trese hand me somethin. The lamp.

THERESA
　Why?

SANDY
　Shut your mouth and don't ask questions.

THERESA
　Okay okay here.

SANDY
　Okay. You get the knife from the top drawer just in case he comes in here.

THERESA
　Who Charlie Manson.

SANDY
　Don't say that name Trese. Scream if anybody comes…

THERESA
　I will Sanny.

　　　SANDY goes to other room. She screams a primal scream.

SANDY
　(returns) It was nothin.

THERESA
　How come.

SANDY
　Cause.

THERESA
　How come my baby never smilin?

SANDY
　Are ya doin what the workers tell ya?

THERESA
　Al do it he don't let me do nothin.

SANDY
　Why?

THERESA
　He smarter.

SANDY
　I guess so.

THERESA
　He love Danny. He wash him with soap and he feed him and he huggin him.

SANDY
　What's he feedin him.

THERESA
　Bologna.

SANDY
　At four months?

THERESA
　He love it.

SANDY
　Oh Christ. Don't ya have baby food.

THERESA
　I don't know.

SANDY
　What am I gonna do with you?

THERESA
　I'm glad I stayin here. Al cryin nights.

SANDY
　How come?

THERESA
　I don't know. I tell him nothin's wrong everything fine but he keep cryin.

SANDY
　Trese do ya think Joe'll come back?

THERESA
> He proly comin back next Friday.

SANDY
> If he do, he can go to hell.

THERESA
> Bonnie Cain say he never comin back.

SANDY
> She did?

THERESA
> She don't know nothin. He comin back.

SANDY
> I got a letter.

THERESA
> Ya did?

SANDY
> I burnt it though, didn't read it.

THERESA
> Sandy you depress?

SANDY
> No. I just don't like stayin alone nights it ain't good for ya.

THERESA
> You could come stayin with us.

SANDY
> Uh uh. No way. I don't want to see no baby eatin bologna.

THERESA
> Oh.

SANDY
> You get in some baby food, Trese, or I'm reporting ya to the social worker.

THERESA
> Okay.

SANDY
> Okay?

THERESA
> I'm gonna.

SANDY
> You go on to sleep. Now.

THERESA
> Night Sandy. Don't go havin no bad dreams.

SANDY
> Night.

> *THERESA falls asleep instantly. SANDY stays awake, staring out.*

Scene Four

> *ALAN has just been fired from his dishwashing job. He is thrown out of a door, real or imaginary, onto a busy street. He has stolen an egg, which he carries in his hand.*

ALAN
> *(holding up egg as pointer)* I was quittin anyways, ya bastards, there's white worms in the hamburg, I seen em, there's white worms in the hamburg! *(more quietly, to himself)* I seen em wiggle– *(turning to audience, in threatening tones)* There wasn't no egg on that pan, sir, there wasn't no egg on that frypan.

> *ALAN stares at the audience for a moment, gets the idea to throw the egg at the door and turns very slowly towards door. Then in a flash, starts to throw the egg but instead, cracks it over his head. He puts the shell in his pocket, sees somebody in the distance, sticks down his hair, leans onto the sewer and discovers the Indian MAN with a bottle. ALAN grabs it and takes a sip.*

MAN
> Man, who is standing between two girly-girls in the whirly-burl.

ALAN
> Oh why don't ya just shut up…

MAN
> *(pointing at constellation in the sky)* Double devil – stuck together – cha cha cha!

> *JOE appears, wearing a new coat and a hat that says "SUCCESS." ALAN rushes to greet him. By the end of the scene, they reach the entrance to SANDY's apartment.*

ALAN
> Jesus Joe! Joe! Hey Joe, how're ya doin?

JOE
 Hey buddy how are you?

ALAN
 Okay, you know, hangin on. You – when did ya get back?

JOE
 Just now, buddy, but not for long. I'm moving Sandy out there with me.

ALAN
 No kidding? It's pretty good out there?

JOE
 It's a great place, man, lots of work, nice people. Hell of a lot better than this hole, I'm tellin you.

ALAN
 Yeah? Does Sandy know you're back?

JOE
 Nope. I'm gonna surprise her. She'll be happy as hell to see me. Then the two of us are gonna take right off.

ALAN
 That right? …Hey me and Theresa got a kid – a little boy, Danny.

JOE
 Is that right? Danny, huh? So how do you like bein a father?

ALAN
 It's all right, man. I like it. I make a good father I guess.

JOE
 Yeah? …Well, I better head off.

ALAN
 Hey – Joe – I got somethin to tell ya.

JOE
 Is this a long story or a short one?

ALAN
 Not too long – d'ju hear about Boyd's GTO?

JOE
 What the one that used to be parked on Johnson below Division?

ALAN
 Yeah, you know, green with chrome mags and chrome cut-outs.

JOE
    Yeah. What a fuckin beast. What about it?

ALAN
    He totalled it.

JOE
    Hah. Well it was a shitty lookin car anyways.

ALAN
    Yeah but fuck it had – it had them high lift cam solid lifters, and, and high compression kit and–

JOE
    You name it.

ALAN
    He had it. Yup. Hey – did you know it had four fuckin carbs?

JOE
    Eat shit.

ALAN
    No kiddin, four! But you know how come he kept it lookin so shitty?

JOE
    Beats me.

ALAN
    So the cops wouldn't notice. They all knew, though eh, they knew what he had. Fuck that thing was fast he used to shoot the main drag doin one-fifty.

JOE
    Yeah? That's fast.

ALAN
    Fuckin fast. You know how he totalled it?

JOE
    No.

ALAN
    Fuck it was funny. We were gettin polluted up at the Manor, eh, and Alfie decides he's gonna go up to Gan. He was about half pissed I guess. So parently he tries to pass three or four cars same time except one of em happens to be a truck goin left. So I guess he almost makes it but the truck catches him by his back right fender and spins him. Huh. Flipped the car six fuckin times.

JOE
>Jeez. How is he?

ALAN
>Alfie? He's okay now but he got stabbed in the heart with the rearview mirror. Had an operation.

JOE
>That right?

ALAN
>Chuck was with him and–

JOE
>The Scotty?

ALAN
>Yeah and he just jumped out and never even had a scratch on him. What's that a present for the wife?

JOE
>Yeah. That Charlie perfume shit.

ALAN
>Hardly nice. Yeah, that's nice stuff. Women – they like that kinda stuff.

JOE
>I know. Smells shitty to me.

ALAN
>Yeah.

JOE
>Well I gotta move buddy catch you later.

ALAN
>Hey! Hey!

>>*From his pocket, ALAN takes an ornamental iron monk with a hard on. It is wrapped in newspaper.*

>Here.

JOE
>What's this?

ALAN
>Just somethin.

JOE
Oh yeah. I seen one of these. Well I'm gone.

ALAN
See ya…. Bye Joe!

Scene Five

SANDY and JOE seated at a table.

SANDY
I got a fucking hole in my gut cause of you.

JOE
Who told ya that.

SANDY
Doctor Scott.

JOE
He don't know what he's talking about.

SANDY
Hurtin me all the time I had pain.

JOE
Not no more. Not no more ya won't.

SANDY
I was takin pills even – prescription!

JOE
I told ya babe I feel bad.

SANDY
I never done nothin to you why??

JOE
Ewwww Christ I missed your body there was times I wanted ya so bad I could taste ya. I'd lie in bed there and think about you and what ya looked like stripped naked, think about your nice titties.

SANDY
Two old bags.

JOE
Nothin them are peaches.

SANDY
Bullshit. I'm not goin back with ya.

JOE
Yes you are.

SANDY
Can't push me around no more.

JOE
Come on just try it a couple weeks if ya don't like it you can fuck off.

SANDY
Won't be nothin different.

JOE
It's gotta be different.

SANDY
It'll be the same as before, beatin up on me.

JOE
No way.

SANDY
How the fuck do I know?

JOE
Cause it's fuckin true that's how.

SANDY
I hate you. I hated you all the time you was gone.

JOE
I know.

SANDY
I woulda laughed if you hadda died.

JOE
I never did.

SANDY
I know.

JOE
So.

Pause.

SANDY
　　How come ya want me back.

JOE
　　Don't know. It's dog shit when you're gone.

SANDY
　　Then why'd ya stay so long.

JOE
　　Shit Sandy.

SANDY
　　I was up nights shakin.

JOE
　　Scared of the crackwalker were ya?

SANDY
　　He never hurt nobody.

JOE
　　I missed makin it with ya. Did ya miss it with me?

SANDY
　　I didn't have no one.

JOE
　　That's cause you're mine.

SANDY
　　Is that right.

JOE
　　(opens her gift) Here. Smell that.

SANDY
　　Hmmn.

JOE
　　You told me you like that shit.

SANDY
　　It's okay.

JOE
　　Soooo. You been workin for Nikos?

SANDY
    Some.

JOE
    What else you been doin?

SANDY
    Learned how to make a new drink.

JOE
    What, rum and Coke?

SANDY
    That's not new.

JOE
    What, dough brain.

SANDY
    A Dirty Mother, asshole.

JOE
    A dirty mother asshole, what's that?

SANDY
    A Dirty Mother! It's tequila, crème de cacao, and milk. It's hardly good.

JOE
    Sounds like a chocky milkshake from Mexico.

SANDY
    Arsewipe. I got a batch made up in the fridge, you want one?

JOE
    Yeah, okay. I'll try one. Gimme a beer with it though.

SANDY
    (goes to the kitchen; from kitchen) You should give Al a call he's in a bad way.

JOE
    Yeah I seen him he looked like shit.

SANDY
    They got a kid, Danny.

JOE
    He was tellin me.

SANDY
It's a medical retard.

JOE
Fuuuuck.

SANDY
It don't ever move its face – like a doll.

JOE
See this thing he give me?

SANDY
What is it?

JOE
I don't know. An iron monk with a hard on?

SANDY
Jeez where'd he get that, up at Van's?

JOE
I guess so. *(SANDY brings in tray.)* Well fuckin jumpqueen, eh, where'd ya get them glasses?

SANDY
My girlfriend Gail she scoffed em offa the 401 Inn.

JOE
Fuckin eh.

SANDY
They'd cost ya, ya know.

JOE
Hmmm. That's, ahhh that's a shit hot drink.

SANDY
Me and Gail drink it all the time when we go out.

JOE
It's not bad.

SANDY
We always order it only none of em knows how to make it so we have to tell them.

JOE
Yeah?

SANDY
  I can make any kind of drink now she taught me.

JOE
  What're you doin two women goin drinkin alone together.

SANDY
  Who said we were alone?

JOE
  Come here.

SANDY
  Joe it ain't like that no more.

JOE
  Who said it ain't.

SANDY
  I did. Keep your paws offa me.

JOE
  Jeez you're lookin good.

SANDY
  I'm doin my eyeliner different.

JOE
  Yeah?

SANDY
  Makes my eyes look bigger.

JOE
  Nice.

SANDY
  I know.

Scene Six

ALAN and THERESA's place. THERESA is playing with the baby. There are tea things set out. The baby does not respond to anything.

THERESA
  Beebeebeebee…. How come you not drinkin your tea, beebee? You got a bad cold? Poor beebee. *(singing)* My little baby is my baby my little Danny is my angel baby I take care of him, and he don't cry or nothin and he ain't never

gonna have the crib death neither– *(speaking)* No way Danny, cause I love ya. Al loves ya too but he a bastard sometime I know he don't talk nice in front of you sometime – don't you go goin into one of them deep sleeps beebee – no – hey! Hey baby Danny! Wake up cause that's how them other babies got the crib death! From sleepin too deep! S'true! You darlin little baby! You mine! That sosha worker's hardly nice, eh? Look! *(dangles Joe Louis wrapper in front of Danny)* Look at that baby, you like that? Eh? It's hardly pretty! You come on, come on, gimme a smile beebee; you thinkin too much just like Al that why you so serious all the time. 0hhhhh baby *(She rocks him.)* so soff. Skin hardly soff. Hey! I, look like that madonna lady and she holdin baby Jesus just like I holdin you so you mus look like Jesus! Baby Jesus! Oooohhh Danny you my beebee Jesus and I the Madonna lady and Al maybe he Joseph, he make stuff outa wood. You like a little horsey made outa wood carry you down Princess Street when we go to the S & R? I love ya beebee. That a little smile? Oh! Oh baby baby Jesus I love Ya!

ALAN
(comes blasting through the door, starts tearing up the place – medicines, creams, clothes, everything) No fuckin social worker's gonna fuckin tell me how to run my fuckin life! I don't take this fuckin shit from nobody! Nobody don't tell me what to do and nobody don't tell me how to take care of my baby never! That means you too you fuckin woman – I'm not takin any shit from you neither! There. We're not using any of their cocksucking medicine – they'll try to kill you with it!

THERESA
Al! Al stop it!

ALAN
They did they killed my dad with all their fuckin medicine! He didn't have no hair and he didn't have no flesh just bones all over and ugly and yellow. No way Therese no way you could stop me I'm throwin it all fuckin out! Out the window, watch! There! It's out the window! Danny! Hey Danny my boy my own son see? You don't have to be takin any of that ugly tastin shit no more!

THERESA
But he gonna get numona if he don't take his medicine doctor say so! Nurse say he hafta take it three time a day or he gettin worse! Doctor sees you done that he won't give us no more medicine for Danny! You bassard! You bassard! *(She hits him.)*

ALAN
Arsewipe! Don't you know nothin? Don't you know them doctors make money offa sick babies? That's why they like to keep em sick with all them medicines! So they make more fuckin money!

THERESA
I don't believe ya. Doctors are nice they wouldn't go makin babies sick!

ALAN
Jeez you're a dumbrain sometimes, Therese, they don't give a fuck about our fuckin baby so long as they get their TV's and golf clubs and that. They care dick! That's why they give em this poison so the baby stay sick!

THERESA
It not poison, it good for ya, the nurse say so! She don't even have no TV, she tole me. So you're crazy I know that stuff good for Danny he gettin better already!

ALAN
That baby ain't gettin no better you stupid woman you know it ain't. It looks strange. It don't look right and that's cause they're givin it all them fuckin medicines! Fuck them! So no more!

THERESA
Really would them doctors do that? Really?

ALAN
Fuckin right they would. Bastards.

THERESA
Bastards. How come? How come they hurtin my little baby?

ALAN
Money. Money and bucks. Cocksuckers.

THERESA
Well what we gonna do about all his snifflin and that?

ALAN
Well I know what to do the social worker even said I did. He said I was a great father and you even heard him. I was a great father.

THERESA
S'true Alan.

ALAN
Well, it got a cold, right? So if ya got a cold, ya gotta get warm, what else? It's fuckin simple and them doctors always do everything to make it harder! Fuck! So all we do, is ahh – turn on the oven! It's easy! Here. Put it to about five hundred – there – and open the door like that – and – now bring him over–

THERESA
Why? What you gonna do?

ALAN
Just bring the baby over, Trese. Do what I tell ya!

THERESA

Al you not cooking the baby, are ya? *(weeping with confusion)*

ALAN

(laughs) Huh. Wait'll I tell Joe that he'll laugh. Cookin the baby. Right. Jesus arsehole it's just like at the farm back in Picton when mum used to sit by the stove with Ronny to warm him up that's all! It's easy! If a guy's got a cold, warm him up!

THERESA

Oh. Don't make it too hot though.

ALAN

Keep out of it, woman. *(places crib as close to stove as he can get it)* There. There ya go Danny! How you doin anyway you little bugger – that's right it's your daddy he come to make you better! Getcha away from all them fuckin doctors! That's right.

THERESA

Al he's coughin! Cant we get back some of that cough syrup?

ALAN

Listen stupid we're not usin any of that stuff I told ya! Didn't ya hear me or what? Listen. If he's coughin we'll just get that Vicks vapour rub that my old man used to use.

THERESA

That stuff smell too much!

ALAN

If it's good enough for my old man it's good enough for my baby Therese. He used to put it all over his chest and his cough be gone the next day. Here.

He puts a whole jar of Vicks over the baby's body.

THERESA

Al you puttin too much!

ALAN

Don't tell me what to do! Shut up! I know what I'm doin I told ya the social worker said I was a great father! So shut up!

He holds the baby up. It is glistening with the stuff.

There. You're gonna be just fine now baby.

THERESA

Al you sure it ain't too much?

ALAN
Shhhhh. He's goin to sleep. Come here. I got somethin for ya.

THERESA
You did? What'dja get donuts?

ALAN
(opens perfume – orange, cheap, and it has broken in the package) Shit. It broke on me. It's okay though here I'll put it in a glass. *(He does so.)* There. *(hands it to her)*

THERESA
Smell that. That's hardly beautiful Al. Thank you I love perfume.

ALAN
I know ya do. Ya like it?

THERESA
I love it. It hardly smells nice.

ALAN
(caresses her) Guess why I brung it?

THERESA
Why?

ALAN
I love you and you're my angel madonna.

THERESA
A-l-l-l-l-l.

ALAN
It's true. Come here angel. Hey. Eh hey. You know I love makin love to ya. I love fuckin you and chewin ya out. *(whispers)* I do.

THERESA
I know.

> ALAN *starts to undress her. They start necking on the floor next to the baby.* THERESA *stops suddenly.*

Oh oh.

ALAN
What?

THERESA
We can't do it Al.

ALAN
Don't matter if you're bleedin.

THERESA
No I can't do it till I get my new IUD in. Or I get pregnant again doctor say so!

ALAN
Fuck the goddamn doctors! Goddamn doctors trying to run my life saying I can't make love to my own woman to my own wife fuck em fuck em. I don't care if you get pregnant we're gonna do it when we want and no doctor's gonna tell us nothin.

THERESA
No! No Alan, please! Get off me you bastard we're not doin it today no way! No! Get offa me or I callin the cops.

ALAN
(He hits her, sends her across the room.) You stupid dumb cunt Indian bitch face fat fat retarded whore. I don't want ya anyways! *(He collapses on floor, now meeker, almost whiny.)* Alls I wanted was a little lovin anyways there's nothin wrong with that? A man is sposda get lovin from his woman ain't he? That is how come ya get married, ain't it? All I wanted was a little lovin that's all… that's alllll.

The baby is crying.

Look what you done woman you makin the baby cry! You stupid bitch!

THERESA gets up to go to the baby.

No! No you stay down I'm the only one who can make him stop cryin. Watch. Hey baby. Hey baby here's your daddy. He's a great daddy, huh? Eh?

The baby is screaming.

THERESA
Take it away from the stove Alan! Take it away from the stove!

ALAN
(to THERESA) Shhhhh. *(to baby)* Come on baby stop that cryin daddy don't like it when you cryin! Shhhh. Now shhhhhh. Gonna buy you a car when you get older – what kind you want, a Monte Carlo? Okay. I'm gonna get you a Monte Carlo. You wait, I'm gonna get work in a station and I'm gonna buy my own and I'm gonna get you anything you want. Okay? Now shhhhhhhh. Stop cryin I'm gonna get you a Monte Carlo didn't ya hear me? Didn't ya? Shhhhhh. Be quiet your mum is tryin to sleep, okay? Shhhhhh! Come on, come on. My little Danny boy baby. Come onnnn. Shhhhhhhh!

On the last "shhh" he squeezes the baby's neck till it dies.

Shhhhhh.

From now on he is very wooden, like a sleepwalker. Looks at THERESA, who is watching in wonder.

It's okay. It's okay it's not cryin any more. See. It's quiet now. It's not cryin. I – I – I done it, see? See? I'm a good father he – you know how come he stopped? Cause I told him he was gonna get a Monte Carlo.

THERESA
What's that?

ALAN
It's a kind of car. It's a place too. One of them south sea islands. Maybe we'll go there, eh? Anyways I gotta go I gotta meet somebody… see ya.

ALAN goes. THERESA looks after him.

Scene Seven

JOE and SANDY's. ALAN, JOE and SANDY are watching a Leafs hockey game on television. ALAN is sitting away from JOE and SANDY, and he is smoking and loudly eating barbecue chips. JOE and SANDY are very much involved with each other and the game, and they virtually ignore ALAN.

JOE
Go go go you fucker – Bunnyfuck what are you fuckin doin – *get him off Nykoluk get him off the ice fuck.*

ALAN
Imlach dies.

JOE does not respond.

IMLACH DIES!!

JOE
Oh LAROUQUE –come on Sittler put that mother in come on come on FUCK OFF PERRAULT, do it Daryl hey Martin Martin put it in put it ALL RIGHT! *(jumps up)* ALL FUCKING RIGHT!

ALAN jumps up with JOE, leans into the TV, his face only one inch away from the screen, screams, wagging his head.

ALAN
ALLLLL FUCKIN RIGHT!

Looks back at JOE with a little laugh.

SANDY
(jocularly) Take a bird why don't ya?

ALAN continues yelling into TV.

JOE
Hey Al don't scare the TV away he–

THERESA appears in the doorway with a bag in her hand. She is reminiscent of Cassandra in The Trojan Women.

THERESA
YOU TOLE HIM YOU GIVE HIM A MONTE CARLO AND YA DON'T EVEN DRIVE ONE. YA DON'T EVEN DRIVE ONE.

Her presence is so strong that she immediately captures their attention.

I not goin screwin with ya no more Al, no way. No way! You stoppem breathin. I tell him "Breathin baby, breathin" and he not cause *you stoppenim.*

ALAN
(looking away from THERESA) She's lyin you guys, stop your lyin.

THERESA
You goin up the river to Penetang Al, you goin there tomorrow and you never comin out for what you done you not goin back with me I goin with Ron Harton he better than you he not stoppem breathin, he still livin up on Division up at Shuter's? I callin him up and I goin steady with him he better lookin you funny lookin I screwin him.

ALAN
YOU lyin fat COW you don't know what you're fuckin talkin about crazy fucking whore-bag – LIAR!

ALAN knocks THERESA to the floor, hesitates, grabs two glasses half-full of Dirty Mother, and runs off. JOE follows.

THERESA
You got a donut, Sanny, gimme a donut.

SANDY
What have ya got in the bag Trese.

THERESA
Ivy, Ivy gimme the bag, I not givin it.

SANDY
What's in it, though.

THERESA
 I takin him up the graveyard.

SANDY
 What for.

THERESA
 I puttin him with Grandma down St. Mary's Sanny, see ya later.

SANDY
 (stepping in front of THERESA's exit) Wait a minute what–

THERESA
 Fuck off Sanny.

SANDY
 What's inside it.

 THERESA giggles. SANDY touches the bag, flinches.

 I'm callin the cops.

THERESA
 Agghhhhh. You fuckin call anyone I takin one of my fits.

SANDY
 I'm shakin in my shoes, Trese. *(begins to dial)*

THERESA
 (grabs SANDY, rips phone from wall) You not callin–

SANDY
 (gets up, begins to exit, turns around, points at THERESA) You're not here when I get back and I'm tellin Ron Harton what ya done down the Lido, ya hear me?

 THERESA stares at SANDY in horror.

 I will, too.

THERESA
 Okay.

SANDY
 I mean it. *(exits)*

THERESA
 (to baby in bag) It okay, Danny, don't you be cryin now, you with baby Jesus sittin on the cloud and the Virgin lookin like me she with ya she sittin there wearin that long blue dress goin down to her feet hardly pretty, eh? ...Danny?

You still live? You breathin if I breathin into ya? S'okay I'm your mum! *(tries to breathe into baby)* Danny? You dead, eh? You not live. You never comin back, eh. *(puts bag to side, picks up severed phone, does not dial)* Hi Janus won't be doin readin writin today. Somethin happen. Just somethin. The baby die. The baby die. Up at Sanny's. Okay okay I waitin… Ron Harton still livin up at Shuter's? *(hangs up the phone, and picks it up immediately)* C'I speak to Ron please? Hi Ron, its Trese. S'okay if we start goin together I love ya. Okay, see ya Tuesday.

SANDY enters, breathless, leans against the door. She cannot look at THERESA.

SANDY
Don't want you tellin no stories to the cops, you hear me? Want you to tell em the truth exactly like it happened, okay?

THERESA
Don't like ya no more, Sanny.

SANDY
S'too bad.

THERESA
You a dirty faggot.

SANDY
Right.

THERESA
Not my friend no more!

SANDY
Okay…

THERESA
I not talkin to YOU.

She turns her back to SANDY. She is crying. SANDY notices.

SANDY
You should come out to Calgary sometime – visit.

THERESA
No Sanny, I workin!

SANDY
What?

THERESA
(tells story joyously with no trace of grief) Down at Kresge's up with Ivy. Hah! She hardly funny she hardly get pissed off when I eatin icin she yellin "Trese, if you eat one more chocolate icin I tellin Charlie" so I go "You tellin Charlie I tellin on you, Ivy, snitchin butter tarts!" They're hardly good, though, them tarts. Ivy English…. Sorry I can't comin with ya out west, Sanny… Ivy be piss off.

Scene Eight

ALAN and Indian MAN on warm air vent. ALAN is leaning against wall. He is clanging two glasses together. This produces a spooky sound.

ALAN
(pointing to MAN) You fuckin touch me and I'll break your head.

MAN
Hee hee hee Church'n Mondee all dee Mondee hee hee hee!

ALAN
I will break your fuckin head in!

MAN
(starts happily, becomes angry as he remembers incident with a paramedic who denied him phenobarbital) Breakin my fa fa pheno phenobarbidoll – barbidoll – NIGGER, YOU NIGGER!

ALAN
Shut it you fuck, just shut it.

MAN in panic, rushes toward the audience.

MAN
SHUT THE WINDOW, SHUT THE WINDOW, SHUT THE WINDOW… *(laughs)*

ALAN
Nothing's funny, okay, so – just – STOP LAUGHIN. Just pass out will ya, can't ya just pass out? *(MAN vomits on ALAN's sock.)* Ahhhh fuck you goddam shit. SHIT! Ecchh you keep your puke to yourself you old fuck! *(crouches, rocking)* I could drive a Monte Carlo I know I could. *(rubbing glasses together)*

JOE enters, looking for ALAN, spots him, then crosses to him.

JOE
Al?

ALAN
: Joe!

JOE
: Look – ah–

ALAN
: She's lyin Joe, I could drive a Monte Carlo.

JOE
: Al?

ALAN
: I could drive one easy.

JOE
: You could drive any car on the road. Now why don't you come on–

ALAN
: I – I – I can't.

JOE
: Why not?

ALAN
: I – I – I'm too cold, you know? I'm freezin.

JOE
: You're okay, ya probably got a flu, ya got a bug, okay?

ALAN
: No, no, I don't got a bug I'm just cold, he puked on me.

JOE
: So he puked on ya Martin used to puke on ya all the time. Come on – come on out of that shit pit and I'll get ya a coffee.

ALAN
: NO. No, I don't want to, I just don't want to, okay?

JOE
: Suit yourself. *(turns his back on ALAN, starts to leave)*

ALAN
: I done what I done and I done it and I fucked it up so I'm payin for it, get it? I'm payin for it.

JOE
: I don't know what ya done.

ALAN
Sorry, Joe.

JOE looks at him, can't think of what to say.

Joe.

JOE
Yeah.

ALAN
Could ya do one thing?

JOE
What.

ALAN
Tell her I could drive a Monte Carlo. Easy.

JOE
I will.

ALAN
Bye Joe. *(crouches in previous position, zipping and unzipping his jacket)* "Nobody here – but us chickens – nobody here but us guys – don't bother me we got work to do and eggs to lay – and guys to see–"

MAN
SHHHHHHHHHHHHhhhhhhhhh. *(with no motion, just the sound)*

Scene Nine

SANDY
I think it's better off dead. I'm not kiddin ya I'm serious. It don't hurt babies to be dead they go straight on up to heaven no hell no purgatory no nothin no problems. Cause their souls are still white as snow – they ain't had the time to get them black and ugly. Not like the rest of us – oh no if a baby dies he's just fine he don't even know he's dead. Youse shoulda seen him lyin there in that casket he looked fine. They had them little pajamas on him Trese got up at the S and R, the ones with all them dogs chasin cats all over, all yellow? They hardly looked sweet. And they had a big wreath of flowers around his neck so's to hide the strangle – you know the kind you put on your door at Christmas? Like that. It was kinda nice. We all lined up to take a look at him too – first time he got so much attention in his life – nobody broke up or nothin not even Trese. In fact I was scared she was gonna break up laughin. I'm not kiddin ya it don't bug her at all the kid's gone. Jeez y'know I don't know what goes on inside that girl but it ain't what's goin on inside the rest of us. She only got one thing on her mind now that's goin after Ron Harton. Don't ask me why, he looks like the fucking

wrath of God. He's a pig too. I don't blame Trese though, I still feel for her even –fuck – this old bag sittin behind me was goin on about how come Trese never went to the hairdressers, you know what her hair is like, eh, right in the middle of the service, so I turn around and I says, "You're gonna hardly think of goin to the hairdressers when your own baby's just been killed by your own husband, ya fuckin old hag." I called her that too, right to her face. Oh yeah I'll stand up for a friend, anytime. I'll tell ya who else I stood up for at that service… Al, and he done it. Oh yeah, I still consider him a friend. No matter what he done, nobody can say what happened in that room; so I walk into the funeral parlour, and I take one of them cookies they got lyin out, you know, just tea biscuits, and I turn around and who's standin behind me lookin me right in the eye but that goddamn Bonnie Cain. She comes up close her breath just reekin and she says to me how she seen the whole thing from the window and how he done it with a plastic bag one of them Glad bags and how Trese was lookin on and laughin. That goddamn holy bitch. "You lie" I says to her and I grab her by the tit and I says "You fuckin hound dog one more word outa you and I send you to your goddamn grave…." He never done it with a plastic bag he done it with his hands. I woulda I woulda broke every bone in her fuckin body and she knowed it too. She didn't say nothin more. Jeez I'll be glad to get outa this hole I'm tellin ya. I won't miss it neither I won't even dream about it. I won't. I worry about Trese but she'll be okay, you know? She'll – she'll go back down the Lido, start blowin off old queers again for five bucks. It's still open it won't never close…. They had them flowers round Danny's neck so's to hide the strangle but I seen it. The flowers never hid it they just made ya look harder, ya know? They just made ya look harder.

Scene Ten

Small struggle off stage. THERESA runs on stage.

THERESA
Stupid old bassard don't go foolin with me you don't even know who I look like even. You don't even know who I lookin like.

The end.

White Biting Dog

White Biting Dog was first produced at Tarragon Theatre, Toronto, in January, 1984, with the following company:

CAPE	Hardee T. Lineham
GLIDDEN	Larry Reynolds
PONY	Clare Coulter
LOMIA	Jackie Burroughs
PASCAL	Stephen Ouimette

Directed by Bill Glassco
Set designed by Sue LePage
Costumes designed by John Pennoyer
Lighting designed by Harry Frehner

White Biting Dog was winner of the 1984 Governor General's Award for Drama.

N.B. Because of the extreme and deliberate musicality of this play, any attempts to go against the textual rhythms, such as the breaking up of an unbroken sentence, or the taking of a pause where none is written in are DISASTROUS. The effect is like being in a small plane and suddenly turning off the ignition. It all falls down. This play must SPIN, not just turn around.

AUTHOR'S NOTES

CAPE: A very handsome silky young man who could seduce almost anybody in twenty minutes. He is *compulsively* seductive, extremely charming and manipulative. He thinks and speaks very quickly, changing mental gears constantly and with great alacrity. He seems to be flirting with everyone he talks to. He even flirts with the audience while telling them the most terrible things about himself. Mid to late twenties.

GLIDDEN: The kind of man others refer to as "lightweight." He is kind, loves to play pranks and wants desperately for his life to be like a Norman Rockwell painting. He is dying of a disease contracted from the constant handling of sphagnum moss –gardening was one of his chief pleasures. In the last few years he has realized that people constantly patronize him and he fights this. Without his wife he has no reason to live. Late fifties or early sixties.

PONY: Her clothing should express her directness: natural fabrics, simple walking shoes, subdued colours, no prints, nice lines. Clothes are for comfort, but are always neat. Her hair should be out of her face, but should not bring attention to itself. She is deeply ethical. Anywhere from twenty to thirty-five or so.

LOMIA: She is not knowingly campy and is not a performer. She is obsessed with her physical being. She is often very shy and girlish as well as nasty and powerful. She is buffeted by sensation. Her words are out before the thought is clear in her head. Her clothes should not conform to the stereotype of a flamboyant woman. Forty-five to fifty-five.

PASCAL: He was brilliant at physics and at chess. He strives to approach the world and every thought freshly. He spends all his time thinking about experience. His costume and hair should reflect this. He can be of any colour or ethnicity. Twenty to thirty.

AUTHOR'S NOTES

The wall to GLIDDEN's room must be transparent. Three hard baseballs are on the set. At the end of Act One, GLIDDEN had intended to play a prank to amuse his wife. However, because of his illness, he snaps and goes into his Australian fantasy for a moment. On page 3, GLIDDEN makes a sound like a cockaburro as follows: (do) oo oo oo oo   (re) ah ah ah ah   (me) ee ee ee ee
He repeats these sounds two and a half times, at an accelerating noise level.

PONY's song on page 10 is sung to the following tune:
fa	fa	sooooo	fa	me/re	fa		
You're	my	<u>dog</u>	my	dog/gie	dog		
fa	me	re	fa	me	re/do	re	
I	love	ya	<u>sooo</u>	I	al/ways	will	
				me	re/do	re	
				I	al/ways	will	

(The underlined words in the song are three times as long as the other words.)

White Biting Dog

ACT ONE

It is dark on stage. CAPE is drumming on his bongo drums. He reaches a peak, stops, doubting the reason for drumming, starts again, then stops. Unsure, as if he had heard a peculiar noise, he steps a few steps towards the audience, hands and body shy, but with a lot of energy. His voice is soft and polite, hesitant, but with a confidence underneath the gentlemanly softness.

CAPE
Did it even happen? Sure it happened. It happened, I'm not crazy, I know! I arrived at the Bloor Street bridge, and I climbed up on the wall, right? And I was gonna do it, I was just about to jump when I heard this drum sound, as if the whole city knew, boom boom boom boom BOOM BOOM BOOM BOOM BOOM BOOM *(speaks in small strange voice)* "I'm not gonna hurt you." *(turns quickly)* Who's that? A cop? There's nobody! Just! A white dog! Beside me! How did it...

"YOU'RE JUMPING TO HELL" the dog, the *dog spoke.*

So I... answered–

"BUT I'M LIVING IN HELL... ANYWAY."

"YOU'RE LIVING IN HELL, 'CAUSE YOU AIN'T DONE YOUR MISSION."

"WHAT'S THAT?"

"TO SAVE YOUR FATHER FROM DEATH. TO SAVE YOUR FATHER FROM DEATH."

The dog... spoke! I'm not kidding! This dog actually spoke she saved me from the plunge; it was the weirdest–

GLIDDEN rushes out of bed, and out of his room onto the landing.

GLIDDEN
OUT OF THE TUNNEL, OUT OF THE TUNNEL, OUT OF THE... *(makes a sound like a cockaburro; sits down, instructing)* We *don't* pull pussy by the *tail,* Gliddy, we don't pull pussy by the...

CAPE
Dad? What are you doing?

GLIDDEN
To turn my stomach.

CAPE
What?

GLIDDEN
To turny my stomach, to… *(half awakens)* Ahhh. What – what… what time is it?

CAPE
It's late, you were sleepwalking.

GLIDDEN
Isn't it way past your bedtime? You have – hockey practice tomorrow at six, don't you? You – *hop* it to *bed* right–

CAPE
DAD WAKE UP. I'm twenty-six years old and the only time I play hockey is Sunday nights with a bunch of dentists.

GLIDDEN
Oh. Yes, of course, *I* knew *that*, I was just – having you on! *Pulling your leg.*

CAPE fakes a laugh.

Never too old or too sick for a bit of a joke!! …Hey, how about a piece of toast?

CAPE
Toast? No thank you, but I could get you one, if–

GLIDDEN
Me? Oh not for me thanks. I'm for a bit of… booze. *(gets drink)*

CAPE
Were you having the nightmare? About the… boat in the ice?

GLIDDEN
What? Oh yes, no. I – don't know – one dream I had, very nice, was your mother, your mother in a taf-taffeta dress, green, at a… party…. My Gawd what a hostess, never let anyone feel – left out, you know? Even the ugliest person in the corner, why she'd talk to fellas with boils so bad you'd want to throw up just looking at them.

CAPE
Why don't I take you to bed?

GLIDDEN
Don't patronize me.

CAPE
I'm sorry. I'm sorry.

GLIDDEN is gripped by pain.

CAPE
Should I get your medication?

CAPE starts to get a drink. GLIDDEN walks across the room.

GLIDDEN
Nope, no, you know – I think I'm going to die tonight.

CAPE turns suddenly.

CAPE
But you can't. You can't you have to fight it Dad you have to kick and punch and

CAPE is holding GLIDDEN, shaking him. Peat moss falls out of GLIDDEN's pajama top.

Dad I just don't think that's very funny any more.

GLIDDEN
Sorry… It's – cool… on the… stomach…. It's…

CAPE
(cleaning up) … I just don't think you should do it any more.

GLIDDEN
I'm not… any more, I'm not any more that man who designed ships' engines… made ya wear your hockey helmet, I'm… I'mmm… a rotting tree turning into a swamp, a…

GLIDDEN sways, almost falls. CAPE catches him.

CAPE
Dad!

CAPE pulls his father onto the couch. GLIDDEN lies on CAPE's lap; CAPE strokes his father's forehead.

There. Just lie for a minute.

Sound of skateboard is heard.

GLIDDEN
What – What the heck is that sound do you know I've heard it every day now for…

CAPE
That's a skateboard. Down the steep hill.

GLIDDEN
Ohh. You know I think I should have accepted that offer. You remember from Australia? Back in – I think a hot country might have understood me. Hey, did you know that in Sydney, there are nine beaches within the city limits? WITHIN THE CITY LIMITS! Nine beaches!

CAPE
Nine!

GLIDDEN
Within the city limits! Yes…. Yes I even – have this sort of daydream… that… well… I think they might have made me Prime Minister of that country. Cornball eh?

CAPE
No! No – I've often thought of running for Alderman.

GLIDDEN
Sometimes I can even imagine being carried on the backs of the miners. I'd be Labour, of course, the miners from, say… Wogga Wogga – BUT anyway, it's too late *now*…

CAPE
Not yet.

GLIDDEN
(getting up) Maybe not – tonight. Maybe not tomorrow. But soon. When it's you, you know, you know –You know… *(pausing at stairs)* Are you sure you won't have that piece of toast?

CAPE
Yes.

GLIDDEN
Have it your way… ah – don't forget to turn out the lights and lock the door before you go to bed, eh?

CAPE
(shaking) Dad? Should I… uh… sit sit with you? What should I…?

GLIDDEN
Listen. Auntie Grace, remember? When Gracey was dying and I wouldn't eat wouldn't sleep wouldn't move from under her bed, just lay there breathing dust she said to me "Glid," she said, "Look at the kettle, and think of me. I'm WATER now, I will be STEAM." That helped. *(says it faster, like a kid's rhyme)* Look at the kettle and think of me, I'm water now, I will be steam. *I'm water now*, I will be *steam*. That's all it is. *(goes into room, returns for a moment)*

CAPE
…If I save HIM, I save my*self*, get it? I don't know why I have been given this… chance. Me, a lousy young… lawyer with a *wife* a wife who – in the whole of four years of marriage I did not smile at her once. Not once! I had never smiled at anyone, *really*, except a baby once, on the street. I couldn't. I – didn't have the… stuff to make a smile… rise up. It wasn't THERE. NOTHING WAS. Nothing *was* ever there – for other people, do you KNOW what that… I could fake it, of course, it was simple to make the faces, smiles, laughter, lust – I laughed so much, in fact, that I was… noted for my laugh. *(laughs a very infectious laugh)* But it's tiring, I couldn't keep it up, so at night in my home, I would sit in the dark, just sit in the dark on the living room brown shag carpet and Janis, would sit in the kitchen, under the light… brushing her hair. Just brushing and brushing and brushing…. Every day I felt… sicker… to hear another client – swallow his coffee – to smell the personal, unique smell of someone's bare head as they stood next to me on the subway – was excruciating pain. That's… the only way I can express it. I could not be happy. So, on a Sunday in January, I went into the kitchen – she hid her brush, I said "I think I'll get some popcorn, hon." She said "That would be neat" and made a *(purses lips as if to say "mmm")* face with her lips that she always made and I went. I went to the Don Valley Parkway bridge and was stopped by a dog. Who gave me a mission: to save myself by saving my father from death. So I staged a breakdown, crying in court, urinating in the waste paper basket. The firm gave me leave, Janis has filed for divorce, so here I am now, and…. It's failing. He is… dying… fast so I'm drumming, I'm drumming and drumming in the hopes that the dog – a dog would hear drums, don't you think? I KNOW she exists, I–

GLIDDEN drags a large bag of peat moss onto the landing, and starts holding his hands far above his head and dropping the moss on himself.

D-duh-Father? Da-Daddy what are you– *(to audience)* No, no it's nothing, eh? He he just… it's – a… mineral in the dirt, or…

GLIDDEN is breathing strangely.

Ohhhhhhh! Oh no, oh no, *(grabs GLIDDEN)* Father, Father look at me, listen I, please! Please don't give in, please–

GLIDDEN
(stands up violently) POP POP POP POP ROCK ME TO GRAVENHURST ROCK ME TO GRAVENHURST ROCK ME TO GRAVENHURST ROCK ME TO GRAVENHURST *(opens eyes wide)* I'M NOT A ROCK CONCERT NOT A

ROCKABYE ROCK, NOT A ROCKABYE, ROCKABYE CONCERT, ROCK ME TO GRAVENHURST, ROCK ME TO...

GLIDDEN passes out. CAPE catches him and puts him over his shoulder.

CAPE
Gravenhurst is where the family's all buried this is it! It's all over there is no way out.

CAPE dumps GLIDDEN on his bed, comes out, returns to throw bag of peat moss into his father's room, comes out again.

Hear that? Hear that? That's the grinding of teeth again – I – I bet it's the devils that my great aunt told us about, under the Don Valley Parkway, that's THEIR way of laughing, GRINDING their teeth – they're laughing because they think that they have me but they don't – they don't, do they? 'Cause the white dog is coming, she's coming now oh somebody tell her tell her I'm in trouble, tell her to HEEEEEEEEEEELLLLLLLLLLLP!! – the drums. Maybe she'll hear the drums *(starts drumming)* white dog, dog from the bridge oh QUEEN of dogs oh please oh help oh help oh. *(stops drumming)* It's not working. What'll I do what'll I – A SONG! A song, yes, they sing in CHURCH *(sings, to the melody of "Agnus Dei")* A – ahhhhhhhhh laaaaaaa whiiiiitee dog pleeeeeeeeease...

PONY is heard singing, off. She enters, continuing to sing until she notices CAPE when he says "Hello." CAPE speaks after he has heard the word "dog" for the second time.

PONY
Your *eyes* do shine so *bright* and clear my *dear* my Queenie dear 'cause you're my *dog* my doggie dog I love ya *sooo* I always will 'cause your *eyes* do shine so *bright* and clear my *dear* my Queenie dear and I *hope* you never *shed* a single *tear* my Queenie *dear* 'cause you're my *dog* my doggie–

CAPE
Oh my God! Oh my God that's it this is IT she's HERE – *(runs out of house)* It's – it's – a GIRL!! I guess an *angel*, kind of a.... Hello!

PONY
Oh!

CAPE
I... heard you sing!

PONY
Oh...

CAPE
Don't be... embarrassed it was... what – what–

Intending to ask PONY what the answer is, CAPE suddenly realizes that maybe she is only a girl.

What – are – you – doing out after – curfew?

PONY
Curfew? There's no curfew here!

CAPE
Yeah but that guy that guy that strangled the cheerleader, he's still loose!

PONY
I'm not afraid of some weasel. Who are you?

CAPE
I'm… you *know*?!

PONY
No.

CAPE
I'm *the guy*. That lives… here. Who are you?

PONY
Just a girl.

CAPE
Just a girl?

PONY
I think so.

CAPE
I – don't – think so, I think – I mean – if you're just a girl what are you doing wandering the streets singing songs to a dog?

PONY
Well, to tell you the truth, I'll be honest with ya, I was lying on my fold-out in my furnished bachelor on Albany and I got this UNRESISTIBLE urge to get up and go out for a walk. And when urges like that come along, I listen to them so I did. I just walked where my feet took me.

CAPE
–and they took you HERE?

PONY
Well. I don't feel like walking any further.

CAPE
: So you don't KNOW where you're going? *(realizes she is an unknowing agent of the dog)*

PONY
: Not particularly.

CAPE
: You're so brave!

PONY
: Ha. You obviously don't know me very well.

CAPE
: What, what do you mean?

PONY
: I mean that when you've done one–fifty down Thunder Bay Road and ya've jumped out and picked up an SID and watched him die right in front of your nose, going out for a midnight stroll is tiddlywinks. Seen?

CAPE
: SID–

PONY
: It stands for sudden infant death, and it is a very tragic thing.

CAPE
: Oh. You – you were an ambulance person?

PONY
: Only for four years.

CAPE
: Only.

PONY
: You want to watch me. I'm sarcastic.

CAPE
: You saved lives then, you – you saw the m-m- *(uses face and body to indicate the word "movement")*

PONY
: You better believe it. Heck my first day on we get a call from this Chinese family downtown, eh, so we walk into the house and this kid takes us to the bathroom and ya know what we see? This old Chinese guy sittin on the toity bleedin from every hole in his body; nose ears dink mouth, everything, just pourin out blood, so my supervisor looks at me and she goes "That's cute."

CAPE
Didn't all the blood make you queasy?

PONY
Who me? You kidding, dissection was my favourite subject!

CAPE
Yes? Why's that?

PONY
I don't know. It always made me feel – I don't know, like I was a top model or something.

CAPE
You– *(tries to keep her there)* –name! Name, what is your name?

PONY
Daid, Pony. *(hits herself)* I mean, Pony Daid.

CAPE
I'm Cape, Cape Race. Does – does that sound – familiar to you?

PONY
Sure. I even been there. Are you from there?

CAPE
Where? Oh! Cape Race? No. No!

PONY
Well how come you're named for it?

CAPE
'Cause 'cause you know why? 'Cause I am the way the word sounds, I think. Do you – think?

PONY
I can see that.

CAPE
You're the first person who could! Hey! Why did you leave the ambulance business?

PONY
I'm not at liberty to say.

CAPE
Oh please?

PONY
Swear you won't reveal it?

CAPE
Swear.

PONY
Speeding.

CAPE
They fired you for speeding an ambulance?

PONY
They fired me 'cause they knew I was gonna quit and their pride was hurt.

CAPE
Why, why were you gonna quit?

PONY
'Cause it was a bum operation. Like I'm an order-oriented person, eh, a neat bar my Dad even called me, and this was the slackest outfit I ever saw! Something you'd think would be the tightest, and it was the slackest! Nobody gave a fig! So I said to myself "Pony, if you want order you're gonna have to be your own boss and that's all there is to it."

CAPE
So NOW, you save lives on your *own*?

PONY
Kinda. I got my own fix-it stand, for things though eh, not people, up at the mall, out in Mississauga.

CAPE
Ah… would you – would you like to come in?

PONY
What, for a – tea?

CAPE
Tea? Sure, sure I can make tea.

Pause.

PONY
Um – just in case you're a bad guy, although I don't think you are, I think I should tell you that I have been trained by this Vietnam vet – Herb.

CAPE
Hey! Hey you think I'd hurt *you*? My life is in your hands!

PONY
Pardon?

CAPE
Just a – manner of speech – ah – well! Here it is!!

PONY
Well. This is quite the – bare room.

CAPE
Yeah? Oh yeah we – Pap and me keep breaking things – a couple of oxes.

PONY
Oh I like a clean room – although I do like the occasional knick-knack. Nice clock. Hey, ya dropped your mitten.

CAPE
P-please put that back.

PONY
Why?

CAPE
He ah – Pap wants it there he – it's been there for over a year, do you believe it? Ever since the – ah – the old duck dropped it when she left – left. He – he thinks it'll bring her back or something.

PONY
Poor guy. Is he a little–

CAPE
He – he's dying. In fact, he is going to die tonight, if nothing stops him But you – you know that, don't you?

PONY
Well – there is a kind of a creepy feeling…. Also if I do say so you're acting a little – shook up.

CAPE
Yes, yes I'm very shook up.

PONY
I don't blame you, eh, I'd flip out if anything happened to my old man.

CAPE
You understand?

PONY

Oh yeah, like I'm wild about my dad, just wild. He's very interesting you know. He collected mice!

CAPE

Mice! He was a mouser?

PONY

Kinda. He'd spend all Sundays with them, building run-wheels and such. Huh. He had two hundred and twenty-six at one time. Freaked the mum right out.

CAPE

How many now?

PONY

None any more. My dad had to gas them. Not meanly, though. He's the projectionist for Kirkland Lake, where I'm from. Us kids really lucked out, eh, got to watch every film fifteen, sixteen times.

CAPE

Look, I can't beat around any more I – listen – if you think I'm nuts just leave, but – I have to ask – are – are you here – to help us?

PONY

What, you and your dad?

CAPE

Yes.

PONY

Well, not that I was personally aware of. I guess I could be.

CAPE

Okay, I'm gonna spill the whole boodle – as I said, if you think I'm insane – just walk away. But every word is pure truth.

PONY

I'll believe you.

CAPE

Okay. See, I was a lawyer, married, making money, everything was – in place; only trouble was, I have a disease, where I hated – I hated living so much my teeth were ground down to baby teeth. One day it got so bad that I had no choice; I went to the Danforth Bridge, climbed up on the wall, and I was just about to kill myself when I saw a dog, a white dog, just sitting there. And then a real miracle happened – the dog – the dog spoke. She told me that I was JUMPING TO HELL.

PONY
 A white dog?

CAPE
 Yeah, a small white dog with bu-blue eyes.

PONY
 I don't believe it.

CAPE
 You've got to!

PONY
 No, I mean I believe what you say, but I'm freaking out because I had a white dog, like that, she was probably the being to which I was very closest of all, Queenie, and I know she had ESP in her, things happened all the time, and then just last month she died then I get this overpowering urge to come here?

CAPE
 The – the dog told me that to *save* my father was *my* only hope; if he lives, I'm cured, now you've come along, and *you* you've *saved lives*!

PONY
 Boy. Boy I knew something important would happen to me sooner or later. 'Cause – well – I feel shy to say it, but – well, I – yeah. I admit it, I, I'm a psychic.

CAPE
 Yes?

PONY
 Yeah!! Like this isn't a very good example, but up in Kirkland, whenever I wanted the traffic light to change, I'd just squeeze my bumcheeks together, eh, hard as I could, till I almost passed out but it worked, it worked every time.

CAPE
 Well!

PONY
 Oh, I did bigger things too – I – well I never used it to save a human life, but I – a couple times I found out HOW to save them.

CAPE
 You did?

PONY
 Yeah. All I would do is, I would concentrate on the question "How do I save them?" like a trance and then an answer comes out. It's worked three times. One was Queenie. That's my dog. I hooked right into her mind and she told

me what was wrong! Another was a private matter to do with my brother Wade's wife, Linda, and one was when Chrissy Pilon was missing and I took them right to the house where he – the guy – had her. Now they COULD have all been like a coincidence, but–

CAPE

No, they weren't. They weren't at all. You – are – here… to save our lives!! You have…

PONY

I knew it!! I knew I'd do something special more than work in a mall!

CAPE

…Could you go into your trance now, he's *very* bad.

PONY

Um *sure*, I don't mind but – this feels so – kinda – normal, you know? I – like I wonder if we could have something for the – underneathness?

CAPE

Oh yes! Sure. *(turns out lights; moves to drums)* How's that?

PONY

That is excellent. You keep on doing that, and I'll just *concentrate* real–

They make contact.

Oh yeah, keep up that drumming, that's–

CAPE

His name is Glidden, Glidden Race.

PONY

Glidden – Race… okayyy – mm-mm…

PONY holds her breath, sways. They both almost go into trance. The drumming is spectacular. PONY shudders and says in LOMIA's voice, or LOMIA says through a screen.

Oooooooooooh that's lovely darling could you just do the inside of my arm, oh God that is delicious I just made a lovely thick fanny burp!

CAPE jumps up, turns on the lights.

CAPE

Ahhhhh. What – what what was that?

PONY
> I don't know, I didn't even hear me, but whatever you heard, that's what it is. It's what the answer is, I know, I feel it.

CAPE
> But but but that – that was my – my mother my oh. That was her voice. That was my mother's voice. *(almost vomiting)*

PONY
> Jeeps. You obviously don't get on with your mum.

CAPE
> But her words came out of YOUR mouth, didn't they? What does that mean?

PONY
> It means her coming back is the only thing gonna save your dad.

CAPE
> What?

PONY
> I know it, I can feel it in my feet. Oh yeah, when I get it that way it's always right, right as anything.

CAPE
> That means I – I have to convince her somehow to come back for good?

PONY
> Yes. Yes it does.

CAPE
> But – but I can't. I can't bring her here.

PONY
> Why not?

CAPE
> Because she's corrupt. You know what she did to my father? She fucked around on him for years, then dumped him. He turned to mush, shaking, sweating all the time, the snakes at his office were thrilled, saying at their cocktail parties he was impotent that's why she left. He was turned to mush and it's her fucking fault it's FUCK HER. You know what I'd do if my dream came true? I'd like to get on National TV and tell them how she made me drink my own nose bleeds from fruity jam jars. She did! And she *farts* like no person should, she – oh *dear*, I-I am sorry pardon me. I guess the trance – Look, basically, I'd rather she not come back here 'cause I'm afraid we'd argue, and that I might harm her…

PONY
> I thought you said if you saved your Dad you wouldn't be strange any more.

CAPE
This is different.

PONY
Just – don't harm her. Get a grip.

The doorbell rings.

CAPE
Who – who the hell could that be?

PONY
Oh pizza fraud likely. I heard you get that all the time down here.

CAPE opens the door. LOMIA and PASCAL are standing outside. PASCAL half whispers throughout the scene and keeps his hands about his face.

CAPE
(whispers, shocked) Mu-um.

LOMIA
(in a hoarse voice) Be-before I explain this intrusion could could somebody get me a glass of water? I've got tortures in my throat worse than– *(coughs)* Please?

PONY
I'll get it!

CAPE
Mum. *(voice and hands shaking)* What-what-what-what…

LOMIA
Not – yet, darling, give me a moment, I – oh God I feel dizzy this room is so empty – and strange… I – oh uh Pascal could you hold me up OH I feel as if I'm gonna fall through the floor it's awful… is is your father in Sonny?

CAPE
My father?! I – What – Mother! It's it's four in the morning it's…

LOMIA
Is it? Well yes, I suppose that is unorthodox, but the time is not the…

PONY
Clean water's best thing for a strep for sure.

LOMIA
Thank you… is not the point. *(drinks)* Oh. You have no idea what it feels like to have a condemned house in one's throat – ah – Sonny, you've met Pascal, haven't you? Yes, yes, that time at the liquor store, with the glasses person – uh–

CAPE
Mum I-I-I told you then my-my name is Cape now–

LOMIA
(not hearing) Oh! Is that so–

PASCAL
How's it keeping, Cape?

CAPE
Yeah, yeah, Pascal, is that – ah permanent or is it there all the time? Ha ha just kidding! We – ummmmm – we were just – ah – going for a stroll.

PASCAL
It's – it's – keen out there, sharp and–

PONY
I can see the two of you have the same virus.

LOMIA
No, no Pascal's chosen to whisper, because the English language is the language of death, right foof?

PASCAL
Like box cars – shuts *out*, and kinda locks *in*. It's corrupt to the – colon– *(mimes colon)*

CAPE
Ha! That's a joke, yes? That's funny, that – what is a colon again? Oh yeah col – it – is – I–

LOMIA almost faints.

Mum? Are you – are you all right? Wh-why are you in your nightgown?

LOMIA
We've just been – in a fire!

CAPE
What?

LOMIA
My ankles are still shaking… look. Look!

CAPE
MUM what HAPPENED your your place burned down?!

LOMIA
It was blocking our path to the – ohh. It made everything so BRIGHT and…

PASCAL
It was white. White fire. Like being tied to a stake. I know how the – witches felt–

CAPE
Here Mum, put this under your head, you–

LOMIA
My heart was just – pounding it was SO terrifying, nothing could describe it nothing – the cat, Blacky *died*, he choked right in front of us and oh GOD I mean we think that the girl in Theology down the hall with that light red hair she – she had to take pills to sleep so she might have – Oh I hope NOT I mean we just ran we – Oh sorry darling I guess I'm talking your head off I-I guess I'm in shock, is this shock? Yes, I guess we're both in – shock. I mean shock. Oh.

PASCAL
The cat clawed her throat – look! Maybe trying to get – in! Her.

LOMIA
Ohhhhh. The worst thing is that it was all my fault!!

PONY
(to herself) I'll get some blankets.

CAPE gestures to his old upstairs room.

CAPE
(puts his arms around LOMIA) No, no, don't say that. I'm sure it WASN'T.

LOMIA
But I ASKED HIM TO LEAVE!! Geoffrey, this – speed freak acquaintance of Pascal's.

PASCAL
He was… depressed.

LOMIA
And we felt sorry for him but – well we finally HAD to ask him to leave after three weeks, nicely of course, and he did, but then, about seven hours later, I smelled something, and no, we hadn't left the burner on, so I looked at the door and – there were these little black curls – I opened it and this – monster of black smoke hurled itself at me!! OH I – darling could you give me a little room?

CAPE has been sitting too close.

CAPE
Oh. So – sorry. I must – my body odour must–

LOMIA
 It's just that I'm extra sensitive after the fire – and…

CAPE
 You and… smells. Once she stayed in the Four Seasons for a week because they were *painting* next door…

PONY
 (gives blanket to LOMIA) Ma'am…

LOMIA
 It wasn't a week.

PONY
 Sir? *(gives blanket to PASCAL)*

LOMIA
 Oh thank you so much. *(coughs)*

PASCAL
 The fire escape was burning hot, the metal you know, and it didn't even go all the way down!! We were choking and we had to jump more than a storey!

CAPE
 But Mum your hip?

LOMIA
 It's bad – I – that's why I was hoping – well you –you don't mind if – if we – sleep on the couch or – the kitchen table or something, do you?

PONY
 Oh, well ya couldn't go anywhere else now, you–

LOMIA
 Pasc was wanting to sleep in an old Lincoln Continental–

PONY
 Biggest car on the road–

CAPE
 Ummmmmm. Um um um. *(he is upset, but covering it)*

LOMIA
 What's the matter?

CAPE
 Just– *(gestures towards her and PASCAL)*

LOMIA
Oh. Well, I – I think it'll be okay. Your father can handle this sort of thing. They may not have met but they have talked on the phone, and it IS an emergency, and–

CAPE
But – he's ill right now. The shock of having the two of *you*–

LOMIA
God, he's not THAT flimsy, I mean we're still very good friends, and–

CAPE
He's got a bad influenza!

LOMIA
But darling, this is an emergency!

PASCAL
(stays cool) Let's go to Dupras, Lom.

LOMIA
No, Pascy, I don't like his dog!

PASCAL
What's wrong with it–

LOMIA
He sprayed his – what do you call it – white on my leg, at the dinner table. Anyway, there is plenty of room here! Just, Sonny, if you would just go – wake him up and ASK him, I'm sure he wouldn't hear of us leaving. He – don't look at me like *that* – *heavens* – PLEASE, Sonny, if I don't get some sleep right now I will catch tuberculosis, you know my resistance to germs is extremely low.

CAPE
Would you just – keep your VOICE down?

LOMIA
Don't talk to *me* that way GOD I – my mitten! My mitten! I don't believe it! Oh GOD this is the mitten I lost last year, remember? I must have left it here when I dropped off the Christmas gifts – God I missed this mitten so much. I went the whole winter with one hand in a pocket I – Isn't it beautiful?

PONY
That's a very nice mitt.

LOMIA
Oh! Darling, you've forgotten to introduce us to your friend!

CAPE
No I didn't, I wouldn't do that, I oh. Didn't I? Sorry, um – Pony, this is my mother and her slave, Pascal. Just kidding.

LOMIA, in her refusal to see unpleasantness, laughs genuinely.

LOMIA
Ha ha, ha HA.

PASCAL
I've seen you on the streetcar.

PONY
How's it going, Pascal? Please to meet you, Mrs. – sorry, I didn't catch the last name–

LOMIA
I don't have a surname of my own! No woman ever has. I'm Lomia.

PONY
Oh. Boy, that's a handsome name.

LOMIA
Yes, like – LAMINATE – or something. Hee! You – are broad-shouldered – do you – um – throw – shotput or swim or something?

PONY
That is really strange you should ask that 'cause just yesterday I was thinkin I should get back to swimming – see back in Centennial I won five golds–

LOMIA
FIVE GOLDS? You must have very strong – pectorals – or – wait a minute, are you two – no, the two of you aren't–

CAPE
Mother.

LOMIA
And I was starting to think you left Janis because you were – odd – Well I think that is just marvellous. You have my blessings whether you want them or not. *(kisses them both)* Now I'll just go and wake up your father – I think if I explain to him, he'll–

CAPE runs in front of his mother, and makes a grotesque face and noise. This must not be clowny or comic.

LOMIA
You haven't done that since you were seven years old.

CAPE
Yes: I did I just did it now. Ha ha ha!

LOMIA
I really didn't expect you to be so shook up by us –coming here together I – I'm…

CAPE
I'm not shook up.

LOMIA
All right, then let me past so I can wake your father… if you won't let me past, I'll have to call him. Okay, here I go, GLIIIIIIIIDEN, GLIDDDDDENNN, GLLLIIIII…

CAPE runs to PONY, takes her hand.

CAPE
I don't think I can make it, I can *hear* them *grinding*, I don't think I can handle her.

PONY
Don't fret, I'm here.

PASCAL
I'm splitting, Lom. I can't – deal – in – this – shit!

LOMIA
All right, all right, I give up. I surrender. I'll go to sleep like an animal in doorways 'cause my very own son wants me out of his… GLIDDEN!

GLIDDEN, wearing a large bathing suit, walks down a ramp or stairs in time to music, singing the familiar tune.

GLIDDEN
If… I … knew – you – was – comin – I'd – a – BAKED a cake, baked a cake, baked a cake! If I knew you was comin I'd a BAKED A CAAAAAAKE – How'd ya do, how'd ya do how'd ya dooooooooooo…

LOMIA
A… bit ragged, actually, darling. Is this for the – amateur musical?

GLIDDEN
(kisses LOMIA on the cheek) Wh-what a pleasant surprise darl I-I was lying in the sack and I heard your… mellifluous voice – and I said to my-myself… I think a little… en-entertainment is in order but ah – I-I guess nobody's laugh-laughing, eh, LAUGH! Will – will ah anybody have a drink? Piece of toast?

PONY
(pause) I ah – don't eat toast myself, sir.

LOMIA
Gliddy Sonny tells me you're not well, that you're–

GLIDDEN
Nonsense! So, let me take your orders, what'll it be? Darl?

LOMIA
I-I don't think anybody – oh yes, I'll have one, you know, that much water *(indicates lots)* that much gin. *(indicates a little)*

GLIDDEN turns to PONY.

CAPE
Oh. Dad, this is my friend PONY she – she went to law school with me.

GLIDDEN
Go-good to meet you – I-I bet you didn't see much of my son in the law library he – he spent the whole time down with the… pinball machines! Can I get you two barristers a drink?

PONY shakes her head.

CAPE
Not for me.

LOMIA
(drinks) Thank you, pooch. Glidden you don't look well at– *(feels his forehead)* Oh Lord it's a hundred and three at least, poor – here – look, *(takes coat)* wear this–

GLIDDEN
No thanks darl. I'm just fine, I–

LOMIA
No, look, I insist, I–

LOMIA tries to put the coat on GLIDDEN. He runs away, but she slowly pursues him. He trips and almost falls, and she stops.

GLIDDEN
No, no thanks darl.

LOMIA
Please just… okay, if you *really* don't want it, I–

GLIDDEN
Oh. You must be–

PASCAL
Yes. I'm Pascal.

GLIDDEN
Heard you were… slim, yes. Yes…

LOMIA
He's not – that – thin.

GLIDDEN
Well he's not exactly fat, is he?

LOMIA
No. No. I – where are you going?

GLIDDEN
To put – put in the toast, how many pieces you–

LOMIA
NO! Please, please Glidden I have to – tell you something I – look, couldn't everybody please just – leave us – Glid and I alone for a moment.

They all stand still.

PONY
Um. I think the gentleman should take this blanket first.

LOMIA
Yes, yes take mine please.

GLIDDEN
All right, all right. Now you heard what the lady said, go dig a hole to China – SCAT. SCAT!

CAPE
Come on Pony.

He takes her hand, and they go into another room. PASCAL pauses, opens the front door, goes out. LOMIA and GLIDDEN are left alone.

GLIDDEN
Well. I – I see you found your mitten!

LOMIA
Yes! Yes I was sooo happy I – really missed it I – you'll think I'm mad but I liked it so much that I just wore the one the whole winter – I kept my other hand in my... pocket... I... thank you! Thank you for not... throwing it out.

GLIDDEN
Well, I... know how much you... liked those mittens.

LOMIA
Yes... I – did. I do... oh Glid. I'm sorry it's been so long.

GLIDDEN
Ohhh that's all right, I–

LOMIA
And coming at this time, and–

GLIDDEN
Well knowing you I didn't expect you to come at tea time!

LOMIA
No, no, I...

GLIDDEN
And I'm... glad to have met your...

LOMIA
Good. He... wanted to meet you too... I talk about you so much...

Pause.

I... really would have visited more often but I... just – well, I think of you, and it's as if... I'd... seen you. You know?

GLIDDEN
Oh yes. Yes I've... experienced that, all right. Yes...

LOMIA
And the phone is still anathema to me for some reason I just hate using it...

GLIDDEN
I know about you and phones. I guess you got a case of telephonaphobia?! *(laughs)*

LOMIA
Yes.

GLIDDEN
You look like a dream!

LOMIA
Me? No, I'm fat, aren't I?

GLIDDEN
Huh hoo I'm not falling into that trap. If I say you're thin, you'll say that means you were fat before. If I say you look nice, you'll say I mean you look plump, because I like a plump…

LOMIA starts to cry.

Why are you crying?

LOMIA
(upset) Be-be – Oh I didn't want to bother you with it and – and – look I was going to come visit you soon I mean – I mean I certainly never would have come like this with Pascal but they – they torched us, Glid. They – murdered our home. We were almost burnt.

GLIDDEN
What? Who did that–

LOMIA
A little boy he – he spread gasoline round our door when we were sleeping and then – and then – then I woke up and I smelled something and I didn't know what it was, then a rat ran across the floor with his back on fire, screaming, so, so we ran in our nighties down the fire escape and watched, we watched it burn down and – and–

GLIDDEN
Lomia, are you telling me that your – your place has been burnt down?

LOMIA
YES!! I – so we had nowhere to sleep so – oh I feel so BADLY about bringing him here, but I-I don't have any other friends. You are my only other friend. My women friends all loathe me for some reason. They turn their eyes away when I start to talk. *(crying)*

GLIDDEN
Now now – for God's sake stay here as long as you like. You're welcome both of you… *really* you – you're still sharing a place with this fellow, then?

LOMIA
Oh yes.

GLIDDEN
Yes? Well, I'm glad you're not alone. I know you don't like to be alone.

LOMIA
No.

LOMIA strokes her nightgown, smiles, looks away.

GLIDDEN
Oh. I'll bet you could do with a loan to – cover your losses, eh?

LOMIA
Oh. If you could afford it we would be grateful–

GLIDDEN
Who, moneybags? Of course I can af-af-afford it and yes– *(forgets what he is saying)* I'll ah – yuh, and in the meantime you you can bunk down in Cape's old room.

LOMIA
Sonny doesn't want me here. He hates me.

GLIDDEN
I think hate is rather a strong word.

LOMIA
It's true. You should have seen him!! My own son detests me!

GLIDDEN
Oh no, no. He's just – not over his breakdown – poor kid, still right in the thick of it.

LOMIA
Poor… BABY! When I read your letter about him coming back home I – I just cried and cried but then I – thought well, maybe he hated law, I mean it is pretty dull, and I don't think he was ever in love with Janis – maybe a breakdown was the only feasible *escape*, may–

GLIDDEN
You haven't had to live with the drumming.

LOMIA
Drumming? *(sees drums)*

GLIDDEN
Oh yes he's become a… what do you call it… a Beatle. Yes… he just drums and drums. And– *(notices her sadness)* Hey there – don't you worry about him hating you because it's just not… look, I'll call him in. CAAAAAPE, say CAAA–

LOMIA
When did he start using that name?

CAPE enters.

CAPE
When I got sick of the name you named me 'cause your mind was a blank.

LOMIA
Ohhh – sweetie it was just really 'cause your squished little face didn't remind me of anything so I didn't want to BRAND you with–

CAPE
Well I'm Cape now. Okay?

LOMIA
Well I can't call you that.

CAPE
Okay, then. Do you mind if I call you Meatloaf?

GLIDDEN
I'm warning you…

LOMIA
It doesn't matter love.

GLIDDEN
Cape tell your mother you are happy to have her and her friend stay in your old bed for as long as they…

CAPE
Certainly, if they don't mind the mould.

LOMIA
No! No I don't mind mould at all – I – it's just like all the other gunk in the air only bigger, isn't it? I mean they say your eyebrows are just CRAWLING with–

CAPE
My eyebrows aren't crawling with *any*thing.

GLIDDEN
I said tell your mother you are happy.

CAPE
Of course I am. She knows that.

LOMIA
Yes. *(kisses him)* I do. Know it…. Well. I'm glad that's settled. Now let's get the sickie to bed! *(feels GLIDDEN's forehead)* Oh dear you're just burning!

GLIDDEN
Sickie my foot. I'm going to bed because it's way past my bedtime. To hell with the rest of you. Never was sick a day in my life before fifty. Not even a cold.

LOMIA and GLIDDEN exit. PONY enters.

PONY
Is she staying?

CAPE
I guess so.

PONY
Well not much thanks to you!! Jeeps you almost wrecked your chances.

CAPE
I know.

PONY
You can't let your feelings get in the way of the mission!!

CAPE is trembling.

Jeepers. What's wrong?

CAPE
It's it's taking ALL my strength not to *(puts hand up as if to hit)* hurt her.

PONY
I think you're exaggerating.

CAPE
Tell me what I should do.

PONY
Just leave. Once you're finished your mission, just go! You're too old to be living at home anyways. It's nothing. I know a lot of people whose mothers bug 'em.

CAPE
(to himself) I never could leave a room she was in.

PONY
I think you could do a whole lot more than you think you could do. I think—

LOMIA
Fell asleep soon as his head hit the... Sonny! You're looking so saad! *(plays with him)* Don't be sad. Tomorrow we get to throw out a whole hour. Did you know that? The man at the all-night fruit store told me? Or is it we ADD a whole hour. Anyway. *(big clown smile to make him laugh)* Hee hee hee! So! We're gonna take your old room, poop, mould or no mould.

CAPE
How many hours are there in the shortest day?

LOMIA
I don't know, four or five? Where's Pascal? PAAAAAAAAASCAL!

LOMIA opens the front door and looks for PASCAL. He steps in.

PASCAL
I told you not ever to shout.

LOMIA
Shhhhhhhhh!! Everything is fine, they *want* us to stay.

CAPE
I hope I didn't make you feel unwelcome.

LOMIA
We understand, don't we foof? If we have any change in *our* schedule at *all* we're sick for a week!

PASCAL
Sure – well – I wouldn't let us – in, ummmm considering.

CAPE
It's nothing to do with that at all.

Pause.

LOMIA
Yes, well I'd love to stay up with you kids and chatter, but if I don't get this throat to sleep right now it'll pack its tonsils and run away!! Just like you used to, you crumb-bum!

CAPE
I never ran – ran away!

LOMIA
You did so! Don't you remember the time you were away all day? I had the whole fire department out looking for you – and you just appeared at about five with six pieces of bubble gum in a brown paper bag. I don't know where you got them.

CAPE
…And you cut them up, cut 'em up and then we buried 'em in the back 'cause you said that they would grow to dinosaurs under the ground and then step out just in time for my birthday party!! Jesus. Jesus.

PONY
Jeeps. Did you really do that Lomia?

LOMIA
Oh yes. Yes! Did you ever run away, Pony? *(She is stroking herself unknowingly.)*

PONY
Oh I used to be out the door and down the street every chance I got! That's what my mum tells me.

CAPE
Mu-um?!

LOMIA
Yes.

CAPE
Stop doing that–

LOMIA
What? *(realizes what she's doing)* Why?

PASCAL
I – I'm really wasted Lom.

LOMIA
When caveman calls! This way foof, you'll drip over this room!! *(exiting)* I'm sooo happy I found my mitten!

PONY
What a truly beautiful lady!!

CAPE
Is she? All I'm aware of are her nose hairs.

PONY
You are something, you know that? Behind her back you say you hate her like poison, then I see ya with her and it seems like ya really like her!!

CAPE
Well I don't. And it does not really seem like it… does it?

PONY
I can see how ya'd feel strong about her – she's got kinda a profound fume about her.

CAPE
She's estranged. Just like me. *(pause)* We're both – happiest kind of – staring into space! *(mimes exaggerated staring)*

PONY
Well, you must just be a couple of space puppies!!

CAPE is totally absorbed in his own thoughts.

Hey… I was just being sarcastic really – I know what ya mean about staring, I used to sing whenever my mum was giving me heck, just sing right in her face, from the top forty. *(sings)* "Indiana wants me, Lord I can't go back there" and she's yelling… yeah…. Yup…. Um. Hmmmm. Oh, ohhh jeeps I'd better be off–

CAPE
No!!

PONY
But – but I gotta be out at the plaza eight o'clock AM!

CAPE
No! I – want – want you to stay. There's something – I don't know. Most women look right through you, unless you treat them like shit. Not you, not you.

PONY
I – never noticed that.

CAPE
Mmum. Your head smells like–

PONY
Dirty hair?

CAPE
…stale hay, kinda like stale hay, but good, nice, beautiful, you know? In fact, you are – hey, are those acne scars? – just kidding – Why did I say that – I – Christ, I almost – feel something – moving – Pony Pony do you feel it?

PONY
(breathless) I don't really like to say these things out loud.

CAPE
(kisses her) Oh. Oh oh. That was – almost – good. That was…

PONY
(stops) What about your wife Cape?

CAPE
My wife? She – we're not married any more. She's okay. She's okay. *Really.* *(gasps)* What if he dies tonight? *(resolves to take action)* After all this is over, we'll go to Cape Race!

PONY smiles. CAPE goes into his father's room, looks at GLIDDEN sleeping. PONY shyly moves to the couch, sits down, then falls asleep.

Daddy?

GLIDDEN
(*bolts upright*) What's happened what's happened!

CAPE
Nothing–

GLIDDEN
Who who who who who was that on the phone? (*rushes out to landing*)

CAPE
I came up to tell you a secret.

GLIDDEN
A *secret* what, are you stoned again? Been – in-injecting oranges with my vodka again and – and diluting the bottle with water? I can always taste that, you know, I–

CAPE
Dad you're time travelling.

GLIDDEN
What?

CAPE
SHHHHHH. She might hear.

GLIDDEN
Who?

CAPE
Mum.

GLIDDEN
Oh. You mean she WAS here, it WASN'T a–

CAPE
(*whispering*) She's STILL here. She was in a fire, remember–

GLIDDEN
Yes. Yes. Uh oh. My… hair wasn't… up on the one side, was it?

CAPE
You looked dashing.

GLIDDEN
That's a load of crap.

One beat. CAPE does not reply, but continues.

CAPE
: Look I have to tell you – she told me just now that she wants to leave that kid and come back with you!

GLIDDEN
: When – when. When did she… tell you this?

CAPE
: Just now – she was crying in the bathroom and I asked her why and… she told me!

It occurs to GLIDDEN that this could be a function of his son's breakdown.

GLIDDEN
: Why – doesn't she come up and tell me this herself?

CAPE
: 'Cause she wants to break it up with the kid tonight, and then offer herself to you at lunch tomorrow! That's what she said!

GLIDDEN
: No she must be in shock from the fire these things are – look, why don't you just go to bed.

CAPE
: Dad I'm telling you the truth.

GLIDDEN
: If you told her about my illness I'll knock your bloody head off.

CAPE
: No, of course not, although if you want to keep it a secret I wouldn't do your dirt thing in front of her.

GLIDDEN
: Don't be cheeky. Are – are you sure you're telling me the truth?

CAPE
: I swear on my life.

GLIDDEN
: You do? *(beat)* Well – this – certainly will change things…

CAPE
: Yes… I hope it will.

GLIDDEN
: So my wife is coming back to me. I can't believe it you know, I can't believe it.

CAPE
   Tomorrow; sleep well. *(exits)*

GLIDDEN
   Why would she want – to come back to me?

> *CAPE comes downstairs, starts drumming and praying to himself. PONY wakes.*

PONY
   Pardon? What?

CAPE
   Hello.

PONY
   Hi.

CAPE
   You were right.

PONY
   He needs her back? I knew it.

CAPE
   So what do we do?

PONY
   We can't make her do something she doesn't want to do!

CAPE
   Well we just might have to because if we don't, HE *DIES (stops drumming)* and I'm off the BRIDGE. Today. Do you want me to jump off the bridge?

PONY
   Of course not, but – well, to tell you the truth I don't think ya would. I think you'll be able to handle his dying a lot better than you think you can.

CAPE
   You don't believe me! You don't believe how bad my life was!

PONY
   A lot of people live in pain, Cape, and you don't see *them* jumpin off bridges.

CAPE
   YOU DON'T KNOW WHAT THIS WAS LIKE: SUICIDE WAS IMPERATIVE. *(stops drumming)* If we don't get her back, I will – be – dead. Do you – want that?

PONY
>No I – definitely do not.

CAPE
>*(caresses PONY erotically)* Then you're going to stick by me?

PONY
>*(slowly nods, aroused)* I guess I will. Yeah. I will.

CAPE
>*(caresses PONY)* Who said missions were easy? Eh?

PONY
>Nobody.

CAPE
>So help me now. Go into your thing–

PONY
>Okay. Okay, I'm ready if you're ready. Ready?

CAPE
>Ready.

>*CAPE turns out the lights, holds PONY's hand, and drums.*

GO! *(drum)* And – tell us more to catch the *whore*, tell us how to get the *sow*, anything at all we'll give to make my father live oh live oh more the *whore* and how the *sow* and–

>*PONY stands up. She is her twelve-year-old self giving a speech.*

PONY
>Umm – this speech is called the White Biting Dog on account of that's what my dog is. That's Queenie so um – here goes – Linda! We all know you like Randy, you don't have to talk to him – Excuse me Miss Birdsall – anyways, something about that dog. I'm so close with her I almost am her, although I'm not as good a barker, ha ha and um I never bite, just jorshin, I mean – uh oh, that was supposed to come later oh cripe, I did this, Miss, I just oh geep I have to sit down.

CAPE
>*(turns on light)* What was that?

PONY
>Freak – me – right – out!

CAPE
>Who who who was it?

PONY

It was me. Grade Seven public speaking, only I turkeyed it up on account of I had a temperature that day – hundred and three, two before death. Whew. Ever weird.

CAPE

But WHAT THE HELL DOES IT MEAN? Mean?

PONY

I don't know, maybe nothing.

CAPE

Nothing? What are you talking about? It's gotta mean something, you were sent here by the white dog and that was *about* the dog just – *Christ* just please tell me whatever comes into your head, now, anything. ANYTHING!

PONY

Anything?

CAPE

Yes!! *(makes hand gesture meaning "come on")* Yes!

PONY

Well – I – don't know, I – just think you should go tell your mum the whole thing. Go on her human pity, she'll come back.

CAPE

Tell my – mum?

PONY

That's what I – feel is right, yes! That's what I think.

CAPE

I am not going down on my knees to that bitch.

PONY

Did you never see Jason and the Golden Fleece? Come on, you're at least as strong as that guy–

CAPE

(change in attitude) Why are you helping me?

PONY

'Cause you're a good head.

CAPE

I'm not a good head, I'm a creep. I'm using you to *escape*, I'M USING YOU.

PONY
No you're not. You need me. That's all.

CAPE
YOU BORE ME. You're from the lower class "*eh*," "eh" – you're wearing fake wool and desert boots for fuck sake you're laughable!! Just – go home to Kirkland Lake. Just go, you hear me? GO HOME. Go home to *K-K-kirkk to–* (*opens front door*)

PONY
–do you really want me to?

CAPE
Yes!! I want to *flub* this fucking mission it's stu-stupid – why shouldn't I jump off the bridge, I'm a fucking creep. I don't like anything anyway.

PONY
You like me.

CAPE
I – do?

PONY
Yes, I think you do. I think you're fine. Do you really want me to go?

CAPE
No!! No I *don't* – Oh Christ I'm sorry, I'm sorry Pony I – please don't listen to me when I say those things I – I didn't mean it, any of it I – I do do like you, you're right, I – you're the only woman, I've even felt a *spark* with…

PONY
Look. I only want to stay if–

CAPE
If I put my penis in your sweet sweet thing and I rub it up and down till it bursts? AHHHHHHHH! I don't believe I said that. What a fuck, what a dumb look, I – I want you. I'm – I'm even sweating, and I don't ever sweat!

PONY
I don't know why you keep whippin yourself.

CAPE
Pony. How can I beg her?

PONY
YOU CAN. I know ya can. And don't worry, ya won't kill her.

CAPE
I won't?

PONY
　　Nope. You won't. Now go on and ask her… *(steers him)*

CAPE
　　She better say yes. I've told him that she already did.

PONY
　　You did?

CAPE
　　I had to! To keep him– *(holds her face tenderly)* You – you know if we – win – then I'll be able to – love – you.

　　They touch erotically, and he leads her to a bedroom.

　　Would you – wait for me?

　　PONY goes into the room. CAPE shuts the door and runs upstairs.

　　Mother? Mum? *(gags at sound of their lovemaking)*

LOMIA
　　What is it?

CAPE
　　Ah – sorry to bug you but – I must tell you something.

LOMIA
　　Tell me in the morning!

CAPE
　　I have to tell you now!

LOMIA
　　Just – go to bed. I'll see you in the–

　　CAPE throws open the door. LOMIA shrieks.

PASCAL
　　If you really *want* it, man, stay and watch!

CAPE
　　I'm sorry but it's *imperative* that I speak to my mother!

LOMIA
　　Get out this instant.

CAPE
You are coming with *me*. *(pulls her roughly)* And don't you try and stop me, hoodlum.

LOMIA
Let go of me. I'm going back to–

CAPE
You're coming with me whether you like it or not, young lady. *(places her in chair)* Now, in future, you come when I call!

LOMIA
(giggles) You are sooo ridiculous, you haven't changed a bit.

CAPE
Don't say that. *(shakes her)*

PASCAL
Are you – you – okay, lamb?

LOMIA
Just – go to bed, foof.

PASCAL
You sure?

LOMIA
Yes. Go!

PASCAL
You *(points to CAPE)* You are very –conservative – you know that? *(bolts back to bedroom)*

CAPE
Now pay attention. I have something to discuss with you.

LOMIA
Well it just so happens that I am not up to discussion; not only is my whole body trembling with the need for sleep but my baby teeth are screeching in pain! I will not be subject to your abuse, understand? Good. Night. *(starts to exit)*

CAPE
You don't take anything seriously, do you? Do you?

LOMIA
Awww. What would you like to tell me, baby, that Miss Opal said your drawing of a horsey was very bery good? Well I couldn't care less, it looks like a blob to me!!

CAPE
I would like to tell you – that father is dying. *(He has her in his control.)*

LOMIA
–what?

CAPE
They gave him a week to live three months ago. He should be dead now. Dead. Now.

LOMIA
What – what – what is he – dying of?

CAPE
His insides are rotting. It's Latin for that. In – something.

LOMIA
He – is he – he isn't in much pain, is he? Is – he?

CAPE
What do you think?

LOMIA
Oh. Yes, of course.

CAPE
He told me that he would live if you came back. Back to stay.

LOMIA
…Don't. Don't do that to me.

CAPE
(looks at her) If he doesn't know, who does, Mummy? HE WOULD LIVE IF YOU CAME BACK. DO YOU WANT HIM TO DIE?

LOMIA
No!! No of course not but – but it's his pain I'm worried about, not his *death*. His DEATH would be a favour – he can be what he wants then, a red cardinal, or a wrinkle in your sock, even a vowel, on the floor of my mouth, or – he'll be *all right then*, it's his PAIN–

CAPE
It's your *duty* to save his life.

LOMIA
Hah!! Awww when you were little you used to sit in the hallway, playing with your orange truck, and every time I passed you on my way to do something you'd say "Hello Mummy!" as if you hadn't seen me in months, "Hello, Mummy!!" Hah. You are such a *good* son to be so worried about your father –

look. I know it would be – nice – for him to die believing that I loved him the way he wanted. It would be very nice, but I respect him far too much to lie to him. Can you understand that? LOOK. He will be loved more than you can imagine when he's in after-life, I won't matter a bit!! Really! He'll – he'll never have to sleep alone, again, think they'll all sleep together inside a – peach!! Glid and all the dead mothers. Just think, admiring him… and…

CAPE
What creepy bullshit.

LOMIA
No, no it's not–

CAPE
Ha. Where do you reckon you'll go after? Satan's crotch?

LOMIA
No, cheeky, I'll go to Purgatory, and for me, I know exactly what that will be. It will be having to wear itchy itchy wool right next to my skin on a hot humid day with…

CAPE
Cut the *crap*. Are you saying that you won't come back?

LOMIA
Darling, I have to take care of me. I am my caretaker, I – I have nightmares about widows–

CAPE
YOU ARE NO DIFFERENT THAN A SEX KILLER.

LOMIA
What an – ugly and unfair thing to say! You don't–

CAPE
YOU MIGHT AS WELL RAPE AND STRANGLE A LITTLE CHILD.

LOMIA
NO!! NO NO NO!! *(attacking, aggressive)* You don't understand I can't!! *(crying)* I can't come back not to save a *thousand* lives–

CAPE
WHY?

LOMIA
Because I *love* him. *I love him* that is stronger than–

CAPE
WHAT ABOUT DAD? Didn't you love Dad?

LOMIA
Dad – Glid was – codeine. Pascal is–

CAPE
What? What?

LOMIA
He – he spikes my blood. I don't know, it's unsayable.

CAPE
He'll drop you like a hot faggot.

LOMIA
He will NOT, he ADORES me. He lives for my footsteps.

CAPE
You're old. Your arms are like bat's wings.

LOMIA
Sonny, when that boy touches my breasts–

CAPE
You don't feel anything.

LOMIA
What?

CAPE
You've never felt anything! Not on the inside you know that.

LOMIA
I – what a – weird weird thing to say. Of course I feel, I feel intensely, I–

CAPE
No you don't. Not for others, and neither do I. We can't help it. Nothing – gets – in.

LOMIA
Yes it does, it does get in, it, certainly does it – no it doesn't you're right. You're right. *(whispers the next line)* I hate saying it though because saying it – sort of makes it true, no? I want to, I try to feel things – I hate it in here, in this – thick – pitch – everything I do, I do to get OUT. Are you the same?

> *CAPE pulls LOMIA to him and kisses her on the mouth, not sensually but as if he's inhaling her.*

We – we – touched tongues.

CAPE
(holding her closely, starts in a whisper) I'll tell you one thing I feel. I feel – I always feel – I want to take you by the hair *(does so)* and then and then bash and bash and bash and bash and bash your head against the wall till you–

LOMIA
(backs away) What?–

> *There is a knock knock knock at the door. CAPE opens it. It is GLIDDEN, drunk, on all fours with a big bone in his mouth. He drops it, and speaks, a la Churchill.*

GLIDDEN
Rally up, Australia…. There's a great work to be done…. A nation, to be built up – and won… underneath… this… southern… sun… *(to LOMIA)* Eh? How 'bout it, toots? Give a dog a bone, eh? Give a dog a bone!! *(to audience)* Ohhh I *do* like a well-turned ankle!

> *Three beats before blackout.*

ACT TWO

GLIDDEN, dressed up in a tux, has set the table beautifully. He is holding a fork up in each hand, and is very excited.

GLIDDEN
Funny how my – little trick worked. I first learned to do it when I was seven years old and my best buddy Tommy fell out of our tree and the next day I was sent to Ashbury where – where my feet were always cold and I was called "figface" and had to sleep in wet sheets and missing Mummy and Grace so... fiercely – that's when I first learned to – to always – expect the worst. Start – start with little things, see, expect there to be no hot water, not to find your socks, then move up to dinner expect only dog food, expect to have bloody nightmares then a merely "bad" dream, is really quite good! Look forward to nothing, and backward to nothing and it's all... okay. Like a nice train ride. So I... yes, I... expected my wife to leave me, a beautiful woman like that? I used to run home at lunch every day just to see if she was still there. Do you think I expected that heaven to last? That heaven of phoning up from work at five o'clock. And saying "Darl, I'm through! Shall I pick something up on the way home?" And her saying "Yes pooch, a loaf of brown." No no she had to escape that – she had to escape being – bored. I was – boring. Of course she left. I certainly NEVER ever expected her to come back!! That's the – thing of it, eh? It's the way things just work, the fates love to be tricky to give, give you that which you do not expect. Even now, I don't... dare to believe that she *loves* me, not yet, only that perhaps she... likes me – I have made some contribution to my field, after all and... I'll tell you a moment in time like this makes me feel that there really is some spirit of good about... cornball, eh? The one other time I have felt this... spirit... is when my son, my son was young and I watched him eat. I used to... love... to see him eat. *(jumps back into the here and now)* Uh oh!

GLIDDEN sees his forks, places them, and rushes back to the kitchen. PONY and CAPE step out of the bedroom. They have made love. They kiss.

CAPE
I've never even *liked* a woman till I met you, you know.

PONY
No. How come?

CAPE
I'm – ashamed of this but – women to me were just sort of cysts – dermoid cysts? I read about them, they're female hormones, just hair and oil and teeth, all in a – cyst – hah. That's – *all* women were to – me. That's all.

PONY
Jeeps. You musta had a bad experience playin doctor or somethin.

CAPE
Or maybe they were that way. Not you though you are so – good! I want to be like you, you're perfect.

PONY
No I'm not.

CAPE
Yes! Hydra thighs and all! *(slaps her bottom)* Shit. No, really, you are, you're perfect. Per–

PONY
I have bad qualities.

CAPE
What?

PONY
I don't like Jews. There was this family in Kirkland, the Wibbys? They lived out by the shoe factory, eh? So once me and Sherry got this can of rust proofer from her brother and we painted all over their windows with it. Then we grabbed their eleven year old Darlene? She was already havin her period and we didn't yet, so we wanted to see what she was like, eh, so we took her to Sherry's parents' master bedroom. Everything was blue velvet, and we made her strip. Then we cut off all her hair because it was so blonde and we stuck it to their windows.

CAPE laughs through his nose. PONY laughs, shyly, in turn. He laughs harder, so does she. He caresses her, and they start necking.

PONY
Oh. Oh. *(pulls him down to floor, is very passionate, then quickly jumps away)* Oh no – Gol... oh *no*!

CAPE
What's the matter?

PONY
I was right! Like last night – in the middle... it was so... beautiful... I was scared. I was scared 'cause I knew I'd do anything... ANYTHING AT ALL... for that... feeling again... not just sex. It's the thing with you – didn't matter that you're married. It was like we were upside down in one of them big *Nova Scotia waves* – I was scared 'cause I thought I'd do... real... bad for that feeling... ANYTHING, then I thought things'd look different in the morning and they did I thought they did but then just now when you were rubbing me down I got that again, I got that big wash and I know. I know now that I would. That somethin has hatched and – I would... do ANYTHING... for... to get that feelin again. That I got with you. So... I'm no different than when we did that to Darlene, no different at all, see?

CAPE
(grabs her wrists tightly) What we did, it wasn't bad, Pony. It was beautiful like you said. It was *ecstacy*.

PONY
It's... it's probably a sin to like me the way I am now, you know, a sex fiend, a home wrecker, it's probably... *(shaking, teeth chattering)*

CAPE
PONY. Get a grip on yourself. Like you told me – Get a–

PONY
You want me to? You want me to? For you, I will. I will even though knowing what I know about myself hurts worse than sharp sticks shoved up under all my nails, I'm gonna get a grip. Cape. 'Cause I love you. I love you more than anything else on this earth.

GLIDDEN, bringing in a cake, sings Herb Alpert.

GLIDDEN
You say this guy, this guy's in love with you youuuuu – this guy's in looooove... who looks at you the wayyy I do, tell me now...

CAPE
(gasps loudly) Oh no he thinks that Mum is gonna – Dad!! He – he – good morning!

GLIDDEN
How – how does it look?

CAPE
Ace, ace. Is this for–

GLIDDEN
I thought a – a – sense of occasion would be nice.

CAPE
Dad – remember Pony?

GLIDDEN
Yes, yes. You must be starved! Will ya – stay to lunch? *(goes to get another chair)*

CAPE
You look so, so well!

GLIDDEN
I feel – like a young Sequoia – and – your mum always loved me in a tux, so I thought – why the heck not. What've I got to lose? *(whispers)* She's – probably

breaking it off with that fellow now – he'll be *okay*. Your mother always was good with human feelings–

> *LOMIA and PASCAL open the bedroom door. The others hear LOMIA and PASCAL about to come out. CAPE looks desperately at PONY.*

PONY
Uh-uh – pardon my nose sir but as a previous paramedic I don't think you should eat a thing. I think you should go to bed.

GLIDDEN
Pardon? Oh no I feel better than I've felt in twenty years.

> *LOMIA enters with PASCAL. Wearing an old private school sweater of CAPE's, she stretches.*

LOMIA
GOOD morning everybody. Ewww I feel all cakey. GLID! You're up and about! What are you…

GLIDDEN
Your presence, milady, has had a PANACEAN effect.

LOMIA
What a charming thing to say. You look so elegant… what a WONDERFUL set-up what's it–

GLIDDEN
In honour – honour of you–

CAPE
Ready baby? Watch me die.

PONY
Use your brain – make it right.

CAPE
Why? I go down she goes with me.

GLIDDEN
I – thought what the heck let's go to town after all these things only happen once…. Good morning, Pascal. Did you sleep well?

PASCAL
What? Oh – my – eyes are kind of – filmy – um, scratchy, you know, but I can… see–

GLIDDEN
I'm glad of that. Did you sleep well? No, I already said that. I mean are you – ah… no hard feelings, eh?

PASCAL
No hard – oh, about the mould? No – no I'm hon-honoured to be here and – and I just… want to tell you – that um –You – you look just like my old home form teacher and – we really – liked him…. He was a good – human.

GLIDDEN
Good! That's good, would you like to stay to lunch? That is if it's not too painful for you?

PASCAL
Painful? OH! Oh she's told you oh no, my ulcers – shrunk now – I can eat even… pizza so lunch'll be…

GLIDDEN
La? Wouldn't we like Pascal to stay to lunch?

LOMIA has been arranging things, looking in the kitchen.

LOMIA
Of course. As long as he promises not to drool!

GLIDDEN
THAT is a jab at ME, I'm afraid… I always had my elbows on the table.

LOMIA
Pony! Did you have a deep sleep?

PONY
Well, not very, really.

LOMIA
I'm sorry, you must be… tired…

GLIDDEN
(claps hands, puts on party hat) WELL. As master of ceremony, I would like you all ta – get the heck in your seats!! Last one there's a dirty rotten so and so!

CAPE and LOMIA run to the table. CAPE puts on a party hat.

LOMIA
Yes sirreeeee sir!

PASCAL
Oh my stomach is contracting like a snail? When you… touch it…?

PONY
You're not whispering today.

PASCAL
No. No. It wasn't right. I'm re-thinking it.

LOMIA
He's searching, right foof? Gliddie this is CHAMPAGNE!!

GLIDDEN
I trust there are no teetotallers here?

LOMIA
Eeeee. I always feel champagne in my ankles first.

CAPE
So did Janis. My ex–wife.

LOMIA
Janis didn't have ankles, just one long calf! Sorry, that was mean.

PONY
In Hawaii, thick ankles are a sign of great beauty.

GLIDDEN
Well may I be so BOLD as to propose a toast?

LOMIA
Carumba!

GLIDDEN
Lomia!

CAPE
To us.

PONY
Each of us!

PASCAL
Yipyoooooooo! *(trying to show he can have a good time)* Yip – yip *(building)* yip yip – Yipyooooo!

CAPE
Pascal you're the life of the party! Well I'm gonna hork back some of that cake. *(takes some)*

PASCAL
The icing is so white; like the great shark – um – almost mean – um. I mean… in my… personally.

GLIDDEN
Thank you Pascal what a nice head of hair you have. *(to others)* Guess who made it?

LOMIA
YOU?

GLIDDEN
Mrs. Ainsley!!

LOMIA
She still comes? OH I couldn't be in the same room when she was cleaning, what was her perfume? Fermented armpit mixed with SPIC and SPAN?

GLIDDEN
We called her Atom Bomb!!

LOMIA
Oh YES!! And remember her favourite snack was cold chicken fat, right from the pan?! She would–

CAPE
I thought she was cool.

LOMIA
She liked you very much. *(pause)*

PASCAL
Being – being a cleaning lady must be very… hard on the… skin of your knees, I would think.

GLIDDEN
Yes. *(serves himself cake)* Well, since speeches would bore us all to sleep, I'm going to share a little joke.

LOMIA
Joke! I don't believe I've ever heard you tell a joke!

GLIDDEN
(cuffs her playfully) Okay, which's it gonna be, wide-mouthed frog, or horses and coal?

Pause.

PONY
    Ah – horses and coal sounds good!

GLIDDEN
    Then horses and coal it is. Well. There was a horse and his – no – that's not it – there was a – hold on, hold on a second – Hang on a moment, I'll have her in a minute– *(paces)*

CAPE
    Mother you sound like a pig in a slop-trough.

    LOMIA looks up with horror, puts more cake in her mouth, chews it carefully and swallows.

LOMIA
    Do I? *(pause; leaves table, goes to window)*

GLIDDEN
    I've got it! Heh! Look at your mother. I bet she's hoping to see a red cardinal!! Heh heh! SO – there were these two magnificent white palominos, and there they were, both fillies, down in the basement of a beautiful castle counting an enormous pile of coal. One, two *(blanks; rises)* I wonder if you'd excuse me for a moment–

PONY
    (walks over to LOMIA) I – ah – nothing – ah – personal but – ah – may I inquire as to how much you might weigh?

LOMIA
    Pardon?

PONY
    I – didn't mean that I mean – jeesh what's wrong with me I mean – I want to know what it is you have when you walk into a room you – make me feel as though I'm flying in my sleep, you know? Do you – know what that is? Maybe…

LOMIA
    It's because I – *love* being inside of my six layers of skin; it's de-licious in here – everytime I breathe I sort of – breathe out *seeds, seeds*. I feel – I inside I feel like… *(honest)* …like… sewage.

    GLIDDEN re-enters, and immediately speaks.

GLIDDEN
    And a thousand more to go! Well suddenly, just like that, two eggs went flying overhead in the sky, and these prize horses they looked at each other…

LOMIA
    (to PONY) It's true.

GLIDDEN
    …and what in the hell do you think they said? They said, "tsk, tsk, tsk." *(pause)*

PASCAL
    (clapping) Beautiful!! Soooo – *layered* – and – um–

CAPE
    I've never understood it.

GLIDDEN
    Neither have I!

LOMIA
    (lighting up) From over here it sounded wonderful! *(kisses him)* I'm so happy we're friends again, pooch. This is really fun. *(kisses his cheek, puts on party hat)*

GLIDDEN
    (pulls her onto his knee; in funny voice) Get in your place *woman*! That always gets a rise out of her! Well darl, I guess we might as well tell them now, eh?

LOMIA
    Sure! What?

GLIDDEN
    She's playing innocent – WICKED woman– *(whispers to LOMIA)* Don't worry, I'll do it I – seeing as my wife is too shy, I would like to make a little announcement – concerning the both of us concerning our – Mr. and Mrs.-ness – we… are… going to be… living together again… as man and wife and it has made us both… very happy. Hey a real Lucille Ball this one, you know what she told me? She promised, cross her heart and hope to die, that she will never take another book of mine into the bath and get all the pages wet. Now if you have ever seen my wife reading in the bath, and I trust that you haven't, you know that that promise is well let's just say–

LOMIA
    No Glidden. *(takes his hand away)*

    GLIDDEN makes a funny face as if he is about to be hit, then points to LOMIA.

GLIDDEN
    She doesn't like to be teased.

LOMIA
    NO GLIDDEN.

GLIDDEN
(looks at her in a very "couple" way) My– *(points to his hair, to where dandruff would fall and brushes off a bit)* –no?? posture, oh am I – uh oh, by your faces, I've committed quite the stumblebum. I – oh no. Oh NO oh darn I – this is very embarrassing. Mr. Pascal – will you accept my apologies – I just presumed that my wife had – told you I – I don't know what to say I – if there's any way we can make it up to you – I – please feel free to come to our home as often as you – Hey! What are you doing for Christmas next year? Lommy makes a very good hard sauce, it's her specialty, isn't that so, Lom, now what's in it, brandy, icing sugar–

LOMIA
…Glidden…

GLIDDEN
Yes.

LOMIA
What – what gave you the – idea that I was… coming back to you?

Pause. GLIDDEN, in total shock and humiliation, gets up slowly to leave the room. After about three steps, he stops, cocks his head, and shuffles to the window.

GLIDDEN
Goddamn it those dingoes are out best get those sheep in! *(goes towards front door)*

LOMIA
What's happening?

GLIDDEN
Allllright, darl, you can go after them, but for goodness sake if you see an Abbo on walkabout don't run, they're faster than cheetahs, but give him a dollop of cooking fat and he'll be your friend for life. Oh yes, they're big on fat. They… put it on their heads as… decoration. Fat hats! Heh. They're a happy people as a whole, the coloured people, happy… and content… *(pause, a bit woozy)* So. I guess the two of you will want to hop off and see what you can sal-salvage from the blaze! Here, let me give you that cheque now in case you need to buy some new "threads" – ya – can't go around in our honeymoon nightie forever!! Heh. I – trust you'll stay until you find another place?

LOMIA
Oh…. Well. We – we would be very – grateful – are you – sure you don't mind?

GLIDDEN
Mind? Why should I mind? If you can't be good friends with your estranged wife who can you be good friends with?

GLIDDEN exits. CAPE starts to go out to the bridge.

LOMIA
Sonny, speaking of – dingoes, are the kids still in the freezer?

CAPE stops, decides to try one other thing to get his mother back, turns, and puts up his hand as if taking an oath.

CAPE
This spring, I promise, I will bury them this spring. *(stays at door, facing into room)*

LOMIA
It *has* been three years!

PONY
Who are the kids?

LOMIA
Our dachshunds! Erica, Gretchen and Hans – we had them for twelve years and they were all three murdered by a man in a what-do-you-call-it – topless car. The poor things were bacchic, gobbling up each others' viscera, dying all over the road and all – oh GOD all that that man could do was to say "Sorry." Ooooh.

GLIDDEN returns with a cheque, and puts it on the table.

PASCAL
Dogs scare me.

PONY
Ooooh they can probably smell it on you you know, they smell fear; it's a proven fact. They also smell softness and that's exactly what they smell on me. I'd do anything for a dog.

GLIDDEN
(in pain) La! Give us a funny from your Ladies Home Business.

LOMIA
No, Glid, you know I can't tell jokes – anyway I think it's time we– *(knocks over glass)*

Still at the door, CAPE is desperate to rock the boat.

CAPE
Excuse me Mother I wonder if you should consider while searching for apartments what your "roommate" has been – spreading – behind your back?

PASCAL
(stands up, begins small giggle) You… you, you people have a very complicated sense of humour don't you? And I'm beginning to catch on. Oh yeah, oh yeah, you're not leaving me behind 'cause I get it… I get it, see, I–

CAPE
Who's talking humour Pascal? I'm talking… filth.

LOMIA
Lay off him – chit!

PASCAL
(to himself) Who's talking humour Pascal I'm talking… filth. *(quieter)* Who's talking humour Pascal I'm – Oh yeah, *filth*, right! I know what you mean, you mean what I'm telling everybody in town, what I've been spreading around. Yeah I get it you mean about her being the the the the the WHORE OF BABYLON! Yeah, *yeah*, like *my* crowd is all been wondering who it is, eh, and what do you know? It's the lady that lives with *me*, me…

GLIDDEN
This is worse than horses and coal.

CAPE
Mum, I suggest you discuss this with the young man yourself, this is no–

PASCAL
And you guys should have seen the fridge, it was crammed with these jam jars full of blood? Got to be the blood of saints right? And who keeps the blood of saints? – the WHORE OF BABYLON!! GO FOR IT!! St. Sebastian, St. Albans, St. Jude, St. Martin, St. Simeon, St. – I mean there's no room for milk, what's a boy supposed to think?

GLIDDEN
What the hell kind of humour is…

LOMIA
It's the new humour I guess.

CAPE
Except it's no joke is it Pascal? Anyway, chief, don't fret, that's not saint's blood, that's just nosebleeds. Our fridge use to be full of them too except we used to drink them.

LOMIA
Nosebleeds? Beef juice! It's supposed to be very good for you, it said so in the…

PASCAL
So so hey! Is my humour on? Do I get to join the *club* – do I…

CAPE
Mother I know my allegation to be fact.

PASCAL
WHAT, what? That she's the WHORE OF BABYLON?

LOMIA
Well. We will decide whether or not I'm the Whore of Babylon at dinner. Right now, if we want to find an apartment, we have to get started. *(picks up coat)* And Cape, beef juice IS VERY good for you. *(leaving)* They did a study.

GLIDDEN
At least come and have a look at the tiger lilies.

LOMIA
Tiger lilies? I didn't know you'd grown tiger lilies, pooch, I *love* tiger lilies, they always make me sort of want to… sit on them, you know? Come on foofy!! It's okay!

PASCAL
See, I can do the humour too… I can…

Before exiting, PASCAL turns back and takes a step towards CAPE. He is shaking.

I just – you… how did – do… do… you want me to bring you back something? Choc… chocolate? *(takes a deep breath; smiles)* I'm perspiring.

PASCAL exits, leaving CAPE staring after him.

PONY
What is going on, Cape?

CAPE
I'm not… sure.

PONY
Why… why am I so ready to lie with ya and trick and cause trouble between two nice couples and humiliate a good man? Why… what's happened in me that I even *like* doing it?? I get *off* on it, I… *(starts to leave)*

CAPE
You DON'T get off on it! *(grabs her)* Listen. Do you have a worst nightmare? Tell me your worst nightmare!

PONY
Why?

CAPE
> Tell me!

PONY
> Why?

CAPE
> Tell me.

PONY
> *(eyes closed)* Well, I go home, right? And there's these guys, these tough guys drinking Lemon-Lime on the porch, and one of 'em's holding a carp, a great big brown carp, and I look down the mouth, and there are my folks! My parents, movin… their lips for help, all squished in a carp fish. And the guys are *laughin*.

CAPE
> Yes. Well imagine that nightmare, never ending. Not when you wake up, not when you go to the bank, or ride your bike, the intensity never lets up. How long could you stand it?

PONY   Not… very long.

CAPE
> Well neither can I. So help me end it. PONY. I *want* to love you…

PONY
> I believe you do, Cape.

CAPE
> Okay. There is one move we have left.

PONY
> To… ki-kill Pascal?

CAPE
> You wouldn't kill Pascal for me, Pony, and DON'T think you WOULD.

PONY
> I–

LOMIA and PASCAL can be heard, leaving.

LOMIA
> *(off)* 'Bye 'bye, pooch. I'll pick up some broccoli.

PONY
> Do you… want me to go into my fit then?

CAPE

(kisses her hard) Yes. And remember, Queenie is on your side! *(starts drumming)*

PONY

(whistles dog whistle to Queenie) If she hears anything she'll hear that. Okay.

> *PONY bends three times; her breathing becomes faster, she squeezes her eyes shut, and says "mmmmmmmmmmmmm."*

CAPE

Choke choke choke choke choke choke choke.

PONY

(has a coughing fit) I got some cake stuck.

CAPE

(pats her hard on back) It's only wishing Pony – wishing very very hard. Haven't you ever… wished… hard… before?

PONY

It's not just the wishing Cape.

CAPE

Wouldn't you do anything at all to save your father's life? Eh? *(shakes her)* Imagine your father, rotting to death, DECAYING and–

PONY

(screams) YESS! Yes, yes I *would*! I would do anything, anything, to – to to just have him spit, to have him spit on his hanky and clean off my face, have him spit and wipe and I could smell it so strongly and…

> *PONY faints and CAPE hugs her, hard. She is dreaming that her dad is wiping his spit all over her face.*

Ha ha ha Dad! Daddy the spit's on my face, it's on my… *(wakes)* Oh. I guess I fainted.

CAPE

Are you… all right? *(guilty, concerned)* Are you–

PONY

No. No I'm not okay I don't think I'm okay in the least I think I blew a fuse, you know? I blew a fuse on account of I'm scared! I'm scared 'cause the old me is getting killed off by the new me, that hatched after we – This new me – I'm scared – I'm scared that when I say I'd do anything for you that maybe I mean – maybe I'd even – cut my mum and dad! *(crying)* My mum and – my – see – I've never felt two thoughts at once before.

CAPE
(holds her tight) Pony. Why don't you go back to Kirkland Lake?

PONY
Do-do-do – you want me to?

CAPE
No.

PONY
No. So I'm gonna help ya do what ya hafta do, 'cause you're right, I love you. I love you and– *(takes his hand)* Is this okay? I marry you…

CAPE
There's Dad coming back in. Why don't you go for a walk, eh? *(kisses her)* Everything should be all over by tonight… and then we can go to Cape Race… Eh?

> PONY, very moved, smiles. She exits. GLIDDEN comes in through the front door.

GLIDDEN
I just had the most disturbing dream – I was standing by the tiger lilies, checking for ants, and suddenly a white dingo narrowed her eyes and said "Lomia – loves you, Glid, she loves you." I haven't felt such relief since – our Airedale Tommy came back after being lost for three months. Why did you do that?

CAPE
What?

GLIDDEN
You know bloody well what.

CAPE
She – she told me that Daddy, honest, she did. She said she was gonna leave him and stay with you, she–

> GLIDDEN hits CAPE across the face. Peat moss tumbles out.

GLIDDEN
Why are you lying? *(falls backwards)*

CAPE
(crying; cleaning it) I wasn't lying she – she must have – gone crazy – I – you know how she is, just – maybe all the pressure, or – I'm sure by tonight she will have calmed down, you know what she's like when she gets out of bed – tonight – I swear. I swear.

GLIDDEN
But you're having a nervous breakdown! You're a twenty-five-year-old man who had to move home 'cause he couldn't hack it! Why should I believe you?

CAPE
'Cause it's the only thing keeping you alive, Dad.

GLIDDEN
You know NOTHING about what is keeping me alive. Nothing. *(starts to go; stops)* I would be grateful if you would keep your hands off your drums whilst I attempt to have a rest. Thank you.... 'Member what I always told you? 'Member? In the game *tomorrow*, DON'T HANG BACK, GET IN THERE AND PLAY, don't THINK, just get in the bloody game and PLAY!! You never got it, did you? *(exits)*

CAPE
No I didn't.

CAPE hears PASCAL approaching, whistling self-consciously. CAPE gets the three hard balls. PASCAL is drawn back to CAPE. CAPE goes to meet him and throws a fast one at PASCAL, who, surprised, catches it. PONY watches this scene from the watching place.

PASCAL
Owww. That's like a belly flop but – with the hands… *stings*–

CAPE
Give it here. Throw it.

PASCAL
I – I can't. I can't throw, I'm terrible at it. Really you should have seen me in baseball games. I can't throw – hand-eye coordination I guess.

PASCAL puts the ball on the floor. CAPE picks it up.

CAPE
Why don't you try?

CAPE throws. PASCAL catches. CAPE taunts him.

Daddy's little girl!

PASCAL hesitates.

Come onnn – Come on!

PASCAL throws. CAPE throws the ball back, hard and quick. PASCAL misses it, but picks it up and strokes it nervously.

CAPE
You're back early. Where's Mum?

PASCAL
Oh I left her – looking at apartments… I – I hate that kind of shit, you know?

> *CAPE is giving him no response.*

It's dull – looking for apartments, shopping – It makes me so – tired–

CAPE
Is that why you came back? *(long pause)* Hey. Try to hit me in the head.

PASCAL
Why?

CAPE
TRY TO HIT ME IN THE HEAD.

PASCAL
(rolls ball along floor) If you – do a headstand it'll – get you right in the cortex.

> *CAPE, looking at PASCAL, picks up the ball and throws it full force at PASCAL. He does the same with the others. PASCAL falls. CAPE gets him down. PASCAL, fighting tears, surrenders.*

What's the matter, eh?

PASCAL
(whispers) Why do you keep looking at me with that–

CAPE
Why…. Because – I – *know* you. *(lies on top of PASCAL)* Yeah… I know you SO well, the way you looked – what you thought – you thought about me… I know you, and I KNOW that you love me. *(long kiss)*

PASCAL
Oh. *(pushes up)* Oh GOD – Mother fu – Cape. Cape – I-I have to make a confession – I-I have to tell you what I've done…

CAPE
I know what you've done.

> *CAPE is close behind PASCAL.*

PASCAL
Please, please understand, and don't hate me. Oh GOD don't hate me your – well – just like – doing that – after doing that with her, your mother, I felt so – sick, I couldn't help it I – I went to the Rainbow, you know? And I don't know

why, but I showed them, I showed them all how she sucks, how she sucks and sucks her teeth and juts out her jaw when she.... It's not my fault, it was my mouth, my mouth, it yakked and yakked and wouldn't stop yakking and they all laughed so I told them again, I showed them, I showed them the face till they could all make it – now each time anyone says "Lo," or even "woman," everybody in the room sucks their teeth and juts out their jaws – even right behind her back, like – like yesterday at the crosslights– *(pause)* Why? Tell me, tell me why did I do that? Why am I so bad, why?

CAPE

You're not bad, you're wonderful. And I know why you did that. I know you... *(strokes his face)* You're wonderful.... And you need to be taken care of. *(picks him up)* Now. Go to my room, take off your clothes, and lie on your stomach.

> *They go into CAPE's room. PONY has been watching and listening. She softly sings, "You're my dog, my doggie dog." She is just barely hanging together, feels badness coming on, does "see no evil" with hands over eyes, trying to fight badness.*

PONY

No. I'm not turning bad. I can't be, I can't be, 'member? I'm the girl that won the Miss Graciousness award – at Camp Bearmack – in 1963. *(gasp)* The Miss Graciousness award. I won it. I won it. *(whistles)* Queenie – Queenie, oh Queenie I miss you, 'cause *(sings)* You're my dooooog, my doggie dogg, I loved ya soooo I always will – and your eyes do shine so bright and clear my Queenie dear my dear – my–

> *PONY starts to breathe heavily, quickly. She feels a deep, painful hunger, and hears or senses Queenie. She is breaking apart. Blackout. Drums sound. Lights come up on PASCAL standing in the outside area. He takes a ball out of his pocket. Like a cat, he rolls it then falls on it, rolls it. CAPE hides where PONY was earlier in order to watch. We hear the click-clack of LOMIA's heels. PASCAL is alert, nervous. LOMIA runs to PASCAL and hugs him.*

LOMIA

Oh foof I missed you so much!! You were mean not to come with me I-I-I saw a blind man on the bus and the thought of being blind made me feel so dizzy that I had to lie down on the floor of the bus! I was sure I was going to faint! But – I suppose it was good to make me go myself because I *didn't* – faint – and – oh. Everything is burned, or smoked, at least – and – and there are two apartments we have to look at tomorrow.

> *PASCAL is playing with the ball.*

What are you doing? *(kisses his neck)* I'm not in a hurry to go back in *there* either. Noooo – *(changes)* Pascy. Pascy I can hear my food digesting. I can *hear* it! I can hear it being broken by the enzymes and floating along in my bloodstream like cows in a flood in India – oh it's dreadful, Pascal, say something to make it go away – my hands are cold as death of course... Paascy–

PASCAL
You what? You can... hear your food? You know I can't relate to that schizo-shit – just... just... I – wish... that you would just... shut up!

PASCAL walks away gritting his teeth. He speaks under his breath.

Shutup shutupshutupshutupshuchchch...

LOMIA
What's wrong, foofy, what's happened? *(pause)*

PASCAL
Nothing. Nothing has happened. *(not looking at her)*

LOMIA
Look at me, Pascal. Pascal. Pascal, why won't you look at me? LOOK AT ME!! Oh Lord oh my God when I can't look at somebody it's because they repulse me because I... HATE them is... is that what you... feel about me now? Is that what...

PASCAL
...I don't... hate you.

LOMIA
Then what... is it... to – do I have spittle on the corner of my mouth is is – my neck starting to bag – what – please just tell me it's *okay*...

PASCAL
No. It's – not – it's – not okay.

LOMIA
You DO hate me.

PASCAL
Of course I don't, I–

LOMIA
Ohh *(this let-down is familiar)* but you don't... want... me any more?! Wh-why? Why, Pascal, what have I done? I haven't gained weight. Or grown hair on my belly–

PASCAL
STOP. It's not... YOU, Lomia, it's me. Gord, *Gordon; from OAKVILLE*; something's – snapped – I fainted on the way home, I – just blacked out and fell on the sidewalk and when I woke up, a... spell was broken. I'm different I'm Gord, Gord I got... different blood now I'm not I'm not who I – who – who – you–

LOMIA
Poor baby what are you talking about?

PASCAL
PLEASE? *(goes down to floor)*

LOMIA
(gently) What are you talking about?

PASCAL
(biting his hand) Please... just – leave me alone.

LOMIA
But... how could all this have happened so... suddenly just yesterday you said I was your... look *(very close, caressing)* just... turn the clock back! Turn the clock back, yes, here, look it's last night, remember? It's last night and I'm – I'm lying on your stomach counting your breaths, you don't mind, you don't mind at all! You–

> *PASCAL violently throws LOMIA off with a sound like a rabid bear. She attacks him.*

PIG! VILE, POISONOUS PISS FAGGOT PIG I WILL RIP YOUR BLOODY...

> *LOMIA goes for PASCAL's throat. PASCAL stops her hands, holds her.*

PASCAL
You love it Mrs. Race. *(violent, but terrified like a small boy)* You LOVE it and you know it you think it's SEXY.

LOMIA
Take a spoon and pop out my eyeballs, shave off my nipples, you *(highpitched, crouching, incredulous)* sooooooo cruuuuuuuuuuellllll!!

PASCAL
YOU MADE ME CRUEL... "Squeeze me harder limp prick, pretend you hate me that I'm a dirty slut" you you ALWAYS said that and "Tell me, tell me I'm a fat putrid sow but you'll *fuck* me anyways," you you you *made* me cruel *(crying)* I-I-I still went to church when I first met you, I still took the communion *host–*

LOMIA
DON'T... take those... things... out of bed – you *know* I was – *playing* I was just–

PASCAL
You wanted to be treated like shit. YOU WANTED TO BE TREATED LIKE SHIT!

LOMIA
...only because when you treated me like... fecal matter, the pins and needles would start, see? See? I could begin to... I have never... *(looks at him; sighs)* you. You don't... understand me.

PASCAL
No. No, and I don't… want to…. Sorry…. Sorry. You were just a… "neat idea,"
I guess…. Yeah. A neat… something to make me…? HAPPEN – to – glow…
I don't know you, and you don't know me… and… I don't know me… ALL
I know, is that I want to go home. I want to go home… find… the Easy Tree
I could climb it. I had no *trouble* climbing it… I want to find the Easy Tree and
sit in it. Just… sit in it, okay? *(turns to go)*

LOMIA
(quietly) Aren't you going to give me a…. KICK… before you go?

PASCAL
You – really are… enjoying this, aren't you? You're just… bathing in it… you're
LOVING… being… TRASHED!! *(begins to leave)*

LOMIA
PASCALLLL…

PASCAL
There is nothing… I can do for you.

LOMIA
Yes there is. Yes there is, foofy. You can… feed me. You can stuff me! You can
stuff me and stuff me and stuff me till my skin won't hold any more fat and it
bursts. And then, then you can *burn* me!

PASCAL
You're sick.

LOMIA
For wanting to be fed?

PASCAL
See you around.

LOMIA
Where?

PASCAL
Somewhere.

LOMIA
Watch out limp dick, I'm a duststorm!! I am a duststorm and I'm going to tear
out your face and eyes and *(pause, to herself)* I'm not a duststorm, I'm a carrot.
A carrot with its head chopped off. CHOPPED OFF. I can't… hear them, I can't
see them and *I like it* – But… I'm choking. I'm choking and I don't know what
to do! What… do you do when you don't know what to do? You… go home?
Do you go home? Yes, you go where you have to because… the sun has gone
down and our mothers are calling so… no more Kick the Can, I have to be…

home…. Home, yes, even though it's too warm to sleep, with my… husband, my husband, and my son. Yes. I'll *stay here* where I'm supposed to be, and I won't leave again. Here. And it'll all… be okay, won't it? …Won't it?

LOMIA goes into bedroom to have a rest. A percussive sound should cover the blackout. Lights come up on CAPE and GLIDDEN.

GLIDDEN
I… used to be able to eat half a dozen eggs and a pound of bacon at a sitting.

CAPE
And you will again.

GLIDDEN
I'm afraid… not.

CAPE
I was telling you the truth, Dad. She wants to be your wife again. Any minute now, she is going to walk through that–

Sound of skateboard is heard.

GLIDDEN
Oh. Oh there's that lovely… sound again.

CAPE
(yelling, teasing) THAT MAID IS SURE TAKING HER TIME WITH OUR TEAAAA!

GLIDDEN
Don't – don't tease her she's a nice little girl…. She… reminds me of Gravenhurst.

PONY enters with tea tray.

PONY
I didn't take that much time.

CAPE
Awwwwwww.

GLIDDEN
(winks) Don't let him get to you…

CAPE
Look at the way she blushes, in blotches!

PONY
Look, um, I don't like to be teased, okay? At all. I just don't appreciate it, okay?

PONY pours the tea.

GLIDDEN
(tastes it) Oh. Did you… heat the pot first dearie?

PONY
There's nothing the matter with the tea, the tea is fine.

CAPE
Hey sweet, why don't you just get him another cup.

GLIDDEN
Oh no no no, a piece of toast will be fine…

PONY
Okay, okay, there's something the matter with the tea, I poisoned it, okay? Here if there's something the matter with it, I'll get you a new one, okay?

GLIDDEN
Please, don't bother, just sit down and–

PONY
JUST GIVE IT TO ME…. Oh forget it, just forget it, I don't need this any more–

CAPE
PONY…

PONY
YOU just – leave me alone!! Leave me alone, okay? *(exits)*

GLIDDEN
She's not a pothead is she?

CAPE
No. No.

GLIDDEN
She better not be.

CAPE
(gets up) I think she's just – PONY? PONY?

PONY
WHAT?

CAPE
What are you doing?

PONY
    I'm EATING.

CAPE
    WHAT?

PONY
    I SAID I'M EATING. Can't ya see I'm starving? *(comes out with batter all over her face)* I'm starving to death, okay? I NEED TO–

CAPE
    Pony. Pony why don't you just put on the brakes, and go wash your–

PONY
    NO!! NO I WILL NOT WASH MY FACE I AM VERY BUSY EATING!

GLIDDEN
    Have – have you tried Weight Watchers, dear, my wife had a great success with them, they–

PONY
    Weight Watchers? Weight Watchers? Will Weight Watchers give me back my Pony, my–

GLIDDEN
    Look, dearie, my wife used to be an eater too – you'll pull through. Just thank bloody Christ you're not in wartime in a self-dug ditch about to be shot through the temples.

PONY
    Sir, I would give my eye-teeth to be in the war. At least I would know what the hell I was supposed to do.

CAPE
    Pony, one little pig-out is nothing!

PONY
    Look, it's a lot worse than you know, Cape, a lot worse; if you knew the truth you would hate my blankety-blank guts.

GLIDDEN
    Dear oh dear that's rather strong language, isn't it?

CAPE
    We wouldn't Pony–

PONY
    You would HATE MY GUTS you stupid fool! I didn't mean that I like you I love you but I'm not, I'm not a nice girl like you think, see, I'm a pig girl, a slut slutty

slut pig, see? *(snorts three times)* See? I – you know what I did today? You're not gonna believe this but you better 'cause it's true, it's me it's P-I-G me – I didn't go for a walk like you said, I listened and I watched you and it freaked it freaked me right out till I was soo soo hungry I just – I just didn't know what to do – ever been that hungry? Math class used to make me hungry, eh, but not like this, this was E-merg time so so – no listen, listen and don't interrupt. I went to your kitchen – and I go through the cupboards one by one and I see the flour! The Monarch flour so I take it out, see, I take it out and I mix it with water, a whole bunch, and I eat it and eat it and eat it till it's coming up my throat but it's not enough! It wasn't enough, you know that feeling? I needed something else, something to make it perfect, but I didn't know what, I needed help sooo bad like the time I was lost in the snow in – the dark and woulda froze to death if it wasn't for my best helper of all ever my Queenie my dog! My white dead dog that I loved more than anything. She'd save me now even though she was dead. She saved me then and I knew I knew so – I listened and she told me, she told me what to do and I did it, I did it, yeah, I crept down the stairs like a burglar, down to the cellar and over to the freezer and I opened it whew! Cold air! And I took out my Swiss Army knife and I slashed the bags open and – there they were! The dachshunds! Erica, Gretchen, and Hans, her dogs just lying there dead and I did it I did it I sliced off chunks of their fro-frozen flesh and I stuffed 'em here, in the sides of my mouth like a squirrel – yeah, so so I run up the stairs as fast as I can and I get out the cake mix, Dominion brown fudge and I mix in the dogflesh and I put it in my hand I eat it and I eat it and I eat it till I almost faint, till it's coming out my tear ducts but I don't care! I don't care, eh, 'cause I feel good, I feel clean and then you come down and – the sight of you makes me bring up! I bring it all up and it stinks and it's coming and I can't stop it and then the toilet clogs, but it's still coming up, it's burning my throat so what do I do? I gotta put it somewhere, so I-I-throw it up in the – I'm sorry, I really am and forgive me please but if you want to know where I threw up your dogs, smell your smell, smell – smell, smell your cups, suckers!! Smell your cups!! SEE? I told you you would hate me, but I couldn't help it, I... *(pause)* Wanna hear a joke? Fat people practise girth control!! Oh ho ho ho that was a good one, eh? That was cute, I am a funny bunny, eh? Eh you guys? Oh. Oh please don't look like that I – I think I'm okay now, honest – I freaked out 'cause of all that stuff that's been goin on I – really was just joking, don't look so SERIOUS!! I really was sort of kidding I– I don't know what.

PONY freezes for a beat, then exits. CAPE smells his cup, puts it down.

CAPE
I buried the dachshunds last week, Dad. Dad?

GLIDDEN
(feels very dizzy) What is high blood pressure, son? What IS it?

CAPE
I don't know, Dad, too much blood?

GLIDDEN
This young… woman… is she… in love with you, Cape?

CAPE
I… think… so…

GLIDDEN
You could do with what she's got…

CAPE
I guess.

GLIDDEN
…I remember when you couldn't stay up on the rope tow, kept… bell-belly flopping over in the snow – up your wrists, down your shirt, holding everybody up… "Daaaad, daaaad"…

PONY
I heard every word you fuckers said.

GLIDDEN
Good heavens.

CAPE
Pony.

PONY
Oh DON'T say that you know what I mean, for crikey's sake just gimme a break, gimme a break, okay? I miss my dog. I miss my Queenie and my mice just…

CAPE
(embraces PONY) We're not mad at you Pony.

PONY
But… *(sobbing)* I like, get the impression that you think what I did was serious! Like – out of control.

GLIDDEN
We all lose the wheel sometime–

PONY
Oh no! No, I was just joking, I really was. Wow? Did I fool you?

CAPE
Pony, please.

GLIDDEN
Are you on one of those rock concert pills?

PONY
Boy, that's amazing, 'cause like – I didn't think you guys were that gullible – like that was just a comedy show I was planning for shopping centres, like for my job! It's just a show!

CAPE
Pony!

PONY
Don't be mad.

GLIDDEN
We're not "mad," Pony dear, we're…

CAPE
We're *friends*.

PONY
But I'm not just your friend. *Oh no* that's what I was *afraid* you were thinking. I'm–

LOMIA enters. GLIDDEN hides any trace of moss.

GLIDDEN
Lom!! I didn't realize you'd got back from your – jaunt. How – How's the apartment? Is it a total loss or–

LOMIA
Well, almost. Everything's, you know, covered in smoke – I just – when I got back I thought I'd lie down for fifteen minutes and suddenly it's dinner time! Hello, Pony, how nice that you stayed…

CAPE
Um, if you'll excuse us, Pony and I have some – business… Pony?

CAPE and PONY leave. They go outside to the watching place.

GLIDDEN
You – you must be starved. Can I get you something, throw a slice of ham between a couple pieces of toast. Or some po-po-potato salad? Or–

LOMIA
No, no I – oh. I guess I will have a slice of toast. Just. One. Thank you.

GLIDDEN
Just one… *(rushes to kitchen to put toast in, rushes back)*

LOMIA
Thanks again for that lovely… lunch!

GLIDDEN
Yes well, I'm afraid it was... marred by my gullibility...

LOMIA
Oh oh please that was...

GLIDDEN
You must be in a hurry to get out of here.

LOMIA
No.

GLIDDEN
No?

LOMIA
Glidden I have to... tell... ask... you something.

GLIDDEN
You want more cash? Sure thing right a–

LOMIA
NO! No no no it's not that it's... I... I'm too shy to say it.

GLIDDEN
Too shy? Is it medi-physi-medical?

LOMIA
No.

GLIDDEN
Well... if it embarrasses you don't...

LOMIA
But I have to... I – look I just wanted to ask you if I could – I can't. I just can't.

GLIDDEN
Look. Pretend if you DON'T, then a million people will die.

LOMIA
Okay.

GLIDDEN
Go on.

LOMIA
A million... Glid I want to stay here. If you'll... have–me.

GLIDDEN awkwardly kisses LOMIA, a long kiss. She tries as hard as she can to be passionate. He speaks, in a whisper, out of breath. They are face to face.

GLIDDEN
...if you really – want *me*... a... sort of... party hat of a man...

LOMIA
You are not you are not a party hat of a man.

PONY
Wow! That's it! That's it, eh, I guess we did it! Eh?

CAPE
Yeah... yeah, I guess – we did...

PONY
Crikes he looks glad... hey, how come so glum? ...Oh, I know. I know, it's 'cause of what we did to get this – to Pascal and that, eh?

CAPE
What I did, what I did, Pony, not what you did.

PONY
I might as well o' done it 'cause I wished it on... I stood up there and I watched you and I wished it on – for us.

During PONY's speech, GLIDDEN goes to the kitchen.

CAPE
Pony, you don't understand; I did it all for myself – I never thought of you once.

PONY
That's not my opinion.

CAPE
Why? Why don't you see–

PONY
My opinion is that you are forgiven by the Holy Ghost.

CAPE
Why?

PONY
Sorry sinners get *GRACE*, that's what Brother Farney said. Because you're sorry. IT'S ME THAT WON'T BE FORGIVEN, 'CAUSE I'm not sorry. Not at all. So – do you feel the change yet?

CAPE
    What change?

PONY
    The change you said'd come in you if ya saved your dad…. Has it – started?

CAPE
    No.

PONY
    It'll come, it will! Why would Queenie have lied – it'll come when, it'll come when we head off for our holidays.

CAPE
    Holidays?

PONY
    Poor guy you must be bushed! To Cape Race! What we been talkin about the whole time!

CAPE
    No. No, no don't you see?

PONY
    (shocked, shaking all over) Boy, does my hair feel tangly.

> *PONY leaves to fetch brush. GLIDDEN enters carrying toast on a fork. He holds it up then gives it to LOMIA. She holds it up for the duration of the scene.*

GLIDDEN
    I – guess Cape has told you about my darn–

LOMIA
    I think we can beat it, don't you?

GLIDDEN
    I hope so… *(touches her; they look at each other)*

LOMIA
    I am… so – so, so – sorry for having… I *really* am sorry!? *(can't believe it herself)* Me. I – am.

GLIDDEN
    I know you are…

LOMIA
    I don't deserve… your… forgiveness.

GLIDDEN
(covers her mouth with his hand) Shhhhhhh… *(strokes her hair)* I'm the one that… almost… lost faith…

PONY returns to where CAPE is, brush in hand.

PONY
This – this isn't 'cause of that routine I tried out on you guys–

CAPE
No.

PONY
Then… why?

CAPE
Because I'm not – like other men…

PONY
Oh yes you are, you need what other men need.

CAPE
I do?

PONY
I think the word you used was ecstasy.

CAPE
Yes.

PONY
What do you expect me to do?

CAPE
Go back to your fix-it stand. I'm sure there are plenty…

PONY throws the brush on the floor.

Pony, if I could love anybody, I would love you. But it's not going to happen.

PONY
But you said.

CAPE
I know I said, I thought it would. But it hasn't. And it won't. The white dog never existed.

PONY
Oh yes she did. She did so exist! You're just bummed out 'cause of *shame* 'cause you know we did wrong, but ya shouldn't 'cause we're in it together, you and me, we're *bad guys*–

CAPE
NO. We're not in it together. Just go home, please? Go home to your family and you'll be okay, you'll–

PONY
How could I go home, eh? How could I go home to the very people I would have Judas-licked for you? They wouldn't know me anyways 'cause the old Pony's almost squished but – but it was worth it to me for you, anything was, ANYTHING was worth havin YOU and now I don't, I don't have you and oh my Gol – oh my Gol – oh my–

CAPE
YOU NEED TO GET AWAY FROM ME, JUST…

PONY
NO!! No, don't you understand! I got a mission, I got a mission to fulfill, to help you save you and I'm gonna! I'm Crikey well gonna save you and…

PONY crouches down, goes into her concentration. She turns in the crouch, around and around.

PONY
I'VE GOT IT! I got it! Holy OH my feet are buzzing–

CAPE
What?

PONY
You watch, you watch, my darling, I'm gonna swoop down inside myself and pull out the old Pony, and I'm gonna give her over to you. And when she's inside you, you're gonna be saved.

CAPE
Shhhhhhh.

CAPE feels PONY's forehead. When he touches her, she wraps her arms around him.

You feel so hot…. Why do you want me so much?

PONY
'Cause. You're the only husband I ever had.

CAPE hugs PONY very hard. PONY enters the house.

LOMIA
When he first – told me he was leaving I – felt – like a carrot! Headless – cold – I thought I'd lost my power to hold – to – you know, enchant! I haven't, have I? I'm – I mean I'm not just another middle-aged woman–

GLIDDEN
You're a goddess, darl, a sphinx, and the best darn hostess – Hold on a minute, hold on, are you saying that he – left *you*?

LOMIA
He brought it up–

GLIDDEN
If he hadn't – brought it up, then you would still be – with him? *(clutching his stomach)*

LOMIA
Oh Glidden, that's not fair, it's–

GLIDDEN
Just tell me the truth, please.

LOMIA
I wasn't myself when I was with him. I was counterfeit, so it doesn't count.

GLIDDEN
Listen to me, Lomia. I am your husband and I know you. Do you understand that? I *know* about your…

LOMIA
You do?

GLIDDEN
And I love you. Still. Okay? *(starts to go upstairs)* Okay.

LOMIA
Where are you going?

GLIDDEN
Just to get – something – don't – go away.

LOMIA
I won't – *I can't* – are you–?

GLIDDEN
I'm okay. I'm okay, darl, and you'll be okay if you let me in. Will you let me in?

LOMIA
(nods) I'll *try*.

GLIDDEN goes into the bedroom, his body crumpling. He pours peat moss over his head.

"Let me in, let me in, let in IN" WHAT DOES HE MEAN? I know what he means, but I CAN'T, I'm SHUT, I'm JAMMED I – ohh GOD let me let him–

GLIDDEN comes out to the landing with the large bag of peat moss. He falls on it, hugging it to his body.

GLIDDEN
Darl? Darl? I'm sorry I can't hold it off any longer I can't stop it any–

GLIDDEN collapses onto the bag, breathing with great difficulty. He is in a coma.

LOMIA
Dooon't make that death face poochie take it off take it – please, please stop that breathing stop that – Gliddie! Gliddie remember when we were first married you would lie in bed and sing, while I danced to your song? We did that almost every night, remember? Well let me make you better with that dance, watch me, watch me closely and sing the song, you remember it… *(starts up the stairs doing a violent, erotic strip tease)* I'm the LAAAADEEEE who LADDDIES… LOVE to adore, the WOMAN *(dancing up steps to GLIDDEN)* who WOM-BATS DIE longing FOR – CREATED from TIGERS and GOOSE-FEATHER DOWN I'm the LADY BOM BOM DE BOM, the jewel of the town…

LOMIA bends over, rips her nylons from ankle to crotch, and looks at GLIDDEN.

It hasn't worked. Oh no oh help me Glidden–?

Sound of skateboard is heard. GLIDDEN giggles, sits up and says with irony.

GLIDDEN
Oh no, not YOU!! *(looks at audience)* HELP YOURSELVES TO TOAST, EVERYBODY!!

GLIDDEN dies. LOMIA looks, screams a forced scream, then stops, knowing this is fraudulent.

LOMIA
It's no use.

Outside, CAPE gets a flash of danger. He runs around to the back of the house.

Oh Glidden, FOR-give me For– *(her hand on her stomach, she feels some fat)* Faaaat– *(feels a totally unfamiliar feeling; something inside her is cracking)* Oh Gliddie I think… I THINK…

LOMIA takes two deep breaths. LOMIA's face must be very close to GLIDDEN's; her body must look as if a strange chemical has entered it. CAPE enters carrying PONY who has hanged herself. The rope dangles. CAPE sinks down, stunned. He looks up and sees that GLIDDEN is dead.

PONY rises, walks to edge of stage, and directs the following speech to where the projectionist would be if the theatre were a cinema.

PONY
Excuse me, could you call the projectionist, please? He's my Dad – I just have to talk to him for a second – I know – but the thing can run on its own, we both know that – besides, this is an emergency!

Yeah! Thanks, thanks a lot… *(peering)* Dad? I can see the dust-beam but I can't see you oh there you are hi! Hi…. It's me – no, no I'm not back, I'm not even in the Kirk, actually, I'm just – like this is gonna totally weird you out, but I had to appear to you like this 'cause in a couple of hours you're gonna hear that – don't freak out – that I passed myself on and – like – I didn't want you to get too down about it so I thought I'd come and tell you myself that – it's not at all a bad thing. It's quite nice if you just give in to it. You know the feeling when you're falling asleep and ya jump awake 'cause you dreamt you slipped on a stair? Well it's like if you stayed in the slip – if you dove right down into it and held your breath till you came out the other end. I'm in the holding your breath part right now, so I'm not sure what's on the other end, but I feel like I'm so big I'd barely fit into Kirk Community Centre – it's weird, but… Dad? Dad? The main reason I came was to let you know that I didn't… kill myself 'cause I couldn't hack it or because the man I loved couldn't love me back, it was 'cause – I was invaded, Dad, Dad, *filled* by the worst evil… you ever imagined – I guess it happened when I fell in love, on account of I had to open my mouth so wide to let the love in that the evil came in, too… and living with it was just like being skinned alive; worse pain even than your kidney stones, and *we* know how bad *they* were. Now the pain has stopped, and there's still the old Pony to give to my husband: 'cause he needs it, Dad, like a blood transfusion *he* needs it, and just like Mum would give you anything you needed, I'm gonna give myself to him. No, we didn't get papers, but he's my husband all right. His name is Cape Race, like the place, eh? Oh yeah, I told him about your mice and he was really impressed and uh – tell Wade there's a stereo store down here that's looking for someone and Mum – tell Mum not to go into the ditch about this 'cause I know they're gonna let me come visit – to – straighten her fingers and… give her alcohol rubs…. Well… I have to – finish my dive now…. Oh Dad I'm so big now I'd never fit back on earth. Love… Pony.

CAPE, at first in shock, but then thinking that she must be alive, slowly walks up to her, to take her in his arms. She says her last word, "Pony," into his chest. He holds her, then turns and turns with her, making a very high-pitched, mounting sound that breaks into a primal scream. He cries, lies with her on the floor.

CAPE
You didn't have to – *why* for... me?? For *me*?

LOMIA
(in shock, but cognizant of what has happened) Because they... loved... us, I guess.

CAPE
We're not... WORTH...

LOMIA
No!

> *LOMIA looks at CAPE. They both feel, hope, that a change is taking place; deep within them something has cracked. Maybe the only feeling they are experiencing is guilt, but that is something.*

CAPE
Do you think it will make... any... difference?

> *LOMIA looks up. Her hope shows in her eyes. CAPE just does not know.*

> *Blackout.*

> *The end.*

Pink

Pink, the monologue, was commissioned for the Arts Against Apartheid Benefit in Toronto in the spring of 1986.

It was performed by Clare Coulter.

Pink

LUCY, a ten-year-old white girl talking to her dead Black nurse, Nellie, shot in a march, in her open coffin.

LUCY
NELLIE NELLIE NELLIE NELLIE NELLIE NELLIE NELLIE NELLIE NELLIE NELLIE NELLIE NELLIE NELLIE NELLIE NELLIE NELLIE

NELLIE NELLIE NELLIE NELLIE NELLIE NELLIE NELLIE I want you to come back, to shampoo my hair and make a pink cake and we can sit in the back and roll mealie pap in our hands see, I told you not to go in those marches and I told you, I told you that what you people don't understand, what you didn't see, is apartheid's for YOU. IT'S FOR YOUR PEOPLE'S FEELINGS, see, like we got separate washrooms cause you like to spit, and if we said, "Eww yucch, don't spit," it would hurt your feelings and we got separate movies, cause you like to talk back to movie stars and say "amen" and "that's the way" and stuff and that drives us crazy so we might tell you to shut up and then you might cry and we got separate bus stops cause you don't like deodorant cause you say it smells worse than people and we might tell you you stink and the only thing I don't get is how come you get paid less for the same job my Mummy says it's because you people don't like money anyway, you don't like TVs and stereos and all that stuff cause what you really like to do is sing and dance. And you don't need money to sing and dance I just… I don't understand why you weren't happy with us, Mummy let you eat as much sugar as you wanted, and we never said anything to you, some days, Mummy says it was up to a quarter-pound, but we know Blacks like sugar so we didn't mind, and we even let you take a silver spoon, I heard Mummy say to her friends, "there goes another silver spoon to Soweto" but she never called the police… and you had your own little room back there, and we even let your husband come once in a while, and that's against the law, Mummy and Daddy could have gone to jail for that, so how come you weren't grateful? How come you stopped singing those Zulu songs in the morning, those pretty songs like the one that was about love and kissing, you stopped singing, and you stopped shampooing my hair, you said I could do it myself, and and your eyes, your eyes used to look at me when I was little they would look at me like they were tickling me just tickling me all the time, like I was special, but they went out, they went out like a light does and you stopped making my cakes every Tuesday, every Tuesday morning I would ask you to make me a pink cake and you would always say, "you ask your mummy" and then you'd make it, but you stopped making them, you told me I was too old for pink cakes, that the pink wasn't real, it was just food colour anyway and then, and then, you hardly ever came anymore, and when I saw you that day… when I saw you downtown with your husband and four children all… hanging off your arms, I just couldn't stand it! I wanted to yell at your children and tell them you were mine that you were more mine than theirs because you were with me more much more so you were mine and to let go of you to get off you and I hated the way you looked without your uniform, so brown and plain, not neat and nice anymore, you looked so pretty in your uniform, so pretty, but we didn't even mind when you didn't want to wear it.

We didn't mind, but you were still unhappy, and when I saw you in town looking so dusty and you didn't even introduce me to your kids and one of them, one of them did that rude thing that "Amandilia" thing that means Black power I saw you slap his hand but you didn't say anything, so you must have hated me too, I saw that you hated me too and I'd been so nice to you, I told you my nightmares and you changed my bed when I wet it and now you didn't even like me and it wasn't my fault it wasn't my fault it's just when I asked you why that day, you were cleaning the stove and I said Nellie why… don't you like me anymore, and you said, "you're not a child anymore, Lucy, you're a white person now" and it wasn't my fault I couldn't help it I couldn't help yelling

KAFFIR, KAFFIR, DO WHAT YOU'RE TOLD, KAFFIR OR I SLAP YOUR BLACK FACE, I SLAP YOUR BLACK FACE AND I KICK YOUR BLACK BELLY I KICK YOUR BLACK BELLY AND KICK IT TILL IT CAVES RIGHT IN AND IT CAN'T HOLD MORE BABIES EVER AGAIN. NO MORE UGLY BLACK BABIES THAT YOU'LL… that you'll like more than me. Even though I'm ten years old I made you die. I made you go in that march and I made you die. I know that forever. I said I was sorry, I'm sorry, I'm sorry, I'm sorry, I'm sorry, but you never looked at me again. You hated me. But I love you, Nellie, more than Mummy or Daddy and I want you to come back, and sing those songs, and roll mealie pap and be washing the floor in your nice uniform so I can come in and ask you to make a pink cake and your eyes will tickle me. And you will say "yes."

"Yes, I'll make a pink cake…"

I Am Yours

I Am Yours was first produced by the Tarragon Theatre, Toronto in November 1987, with the following company:

TOILANE	Geordie Johnson
DEE	Nancy Palk
MERCY	Clare Coulter
MACK	Peter Donaldson
RAYMOND	William Webster
PEGS	Patricia Hamilton

Directed by Derek Goldby
Sets and lighting designed by Jim Plaxton
Costumes designed by Melanie Huston
Stage managed by Bruce McKinnon.

CHARACTERS

TOILANE
DEE
MERCY: her sister
MACK: Dee's husband
RAYMOND
PEGS: Toilane's mother

I Am Yours

ACT ONE

Scene One

The stage is dark. TOILANE walks slowly toward the audience, on a ramp that juts out into the audience. He is his six-year-old self, in a dream he is hating as an adult. He is walking up to what he sees as a giant door, the door of his own home.

TOILANE
Mum! Muum, I'm home!
Hey, Mum, I'm home!
Where's my mummy?
But this is my house! I live here. *(pause)*
I do so! I do so live here! I do so live here! *(pause)*
I do so! My parents are in there! I do so live here, they're in there! I do live here, I do live here! I do live here! I do live here!

The "door" slams. The audience should serve as the door. Do not bring in a real one.

Scene Two

MERCY, on a bus, on her way to visit DEE, her sister, sitting next to a stranger, is having the same dream, about herself walking up to that door. She startles awake from the slam of the door. DEE, in her apartment, has also been having the same dream, but she can be standing, willing "the creature" that torments her imagination to stay behind the wall, and not enter her being.

MERCY
I knew I shouldnta had that garlic chicken!

DEE
There is nothing behind the wall. There is nothing behind the wall.

MERCY
Did you ever wake up, well not quite wake up and you can't remember where you are? I mean just now, I thought I was in my old room at home, where I grew up, and then I wake up and I'm on this bus, I mean it's weird, on Highway Number One, in this dirty old bus, sitting next to a stinking, sleeping old Italian man who keeps leaning on me.

Scene Three

The same time. An October night, about three AM. DEE is feeling faint, needs air, and rushes downstairs to the courtyard where TOILANE is leaning against the wall. He stares at her.

TOILANE
…Nice night. *(DEE turns away, then starts to go.)* Hey hey do you… do you not know who I am?

DEE
(shakes her head) No…

TOILANE
I'm the new super. You know, like the superintendent? So I'll be looking out for ya, right? Fixin your leaky taps, got a problem with the toilet, whatever! The name's Creese. Toilane Creese *(he extends his hand)* and you go by the name Deirdrena I believe, don't ya?

DEE
Dee.

TOILANE
Oh sure, I can call ya Dee, I'm not formal…

DEE
How do you know my name?

TOILANE
…the lists, the old super give me a list.

DEE
Excuse me. *(She starts to go.)*

TOILANE
Hey! You got the most beautiful feet! I been meaning to tell ya I like the way they're so long… must be size ten, eleven, eh?

DEE runs away.

I like the way they're so long!

Scene Four

MERCY is asleep on the bus. The stranger sitting next to her is an Italian labourer. He is sleeping. MERCY has the dream that follows and in her dream, the stranger becomes RAYMOND, an older man who once picked her up hitchhiking and became her lover. In the blackout before this scene begins,

James Brown's "Prisoner of Love" should play, from the beginning, starting very loud. RAYMOND is bringing a rather guilty fifteen-year-old MERCY to orgasm by manipulating her vagina. She has an orgasm, and then immediately pretends that nothing at all has happened.

MERCY
God. I love that song.

RAYMOND
It's a pleasant one… not like that "headache" music my kids play night and day.

MERCY
(flirting) What's wrong, doncha like rock and roll?

RAYMOND
It gives me… a headache! *(they kiss)* Your lips taste like cough drops.

MERCY
(holds them up) Want one?

RAYMOND
No thank you, no good for the tummy.

MERCY
I'm up to fourteen a day, no kidding, yesterday I had fourteen, in a row!

RAYMOND
In a row!

MERCY
In geography, I mean I was bored almost to death. I mean who cares about the Panama Canal, like who cares that ships can barely get through, like who gives a shit? Anyways, I gotta…

RAYMOND
Mercia,

MERCY
Yo!

RAYMOND
I-I-I – wanted to give you – this.

MERCY
A locket!

RAYMOND
I-I – you'll notice the inscription.

MERCY
An *inscription*; fuck, this musta cost you a mint – what's it say? "*Ich*" – it's German!

RAYMOND
Yes, it's – read it.

MERCY
I can't read German.

RAYMOND
Read it, go on. Try.

MERCY
Okay. "*Ich*" – that's "ich" right? *Ich – bin – dein*? What's it mean?

RAYMOND
It means–

MERCY
SHIT. My garter belt, shit!

RAYMOND
Oh Lord.

MERCY
Now what am I sposeda do?

RAYMOND
I don't know, do you have a safety pin?

MERCY
A safety pin? Are you nuts? You think a safety pin is gonna hold up a pair of nylons? Give me a penny, you got a penny?

RAYMOND
Yes, yes, I'm sure I have.

The school bell rings.

MERCY
Oh God, there's the bell. Hurry, wouldja hurry?

RAYMOND
Yes, yes, I'm sure I saw a whole lot of pennies just…

MERCY
For Christ's sake I got a history test first period, Ray come *onnn*…

RAYMOND
Ahah! Here we are, here–

She grabs it.

Why this is miraculous, you can keep your stockings up with a penny?

MERCY
(sobs) Okay see ya.

RAYMOND
(grabbing her) Wait–

MERCY
I gotta–

RAYMOND
Please, let me… write you a note. I can write you a note!

MERCY
RAYMOND!

RAYMOND
Please I – I've brought prophylactics – I thought today–

MERCY
PROPHYLACTICS! NO! No, no, no!! You're disgusting! You're a disgusting old man and you make me feel like a greasy slut and I hate you for it, I haaaaate you, I hate you, I hate you, I…

RAYMOND turns back into Italian man. The lights should indicate that MERCY wakes up. Please don't use any hats or anything to show the difference between RAYMOND and the Italian; posture, etc. and lighting should be sufficient.

(turning away from him, mumbling) Sorry – I thought you were, I was having this dream, I thought you were this guy I knew before–

Scene Five

MACK, DEIRDRE's husband, after having been asked to leave by DEE about two weeks ago, has decided, in a drunken moment, that he has to see her. MACK stumbles through the courtyard quite drunk.

TOILANE
Hey, chief, gotta light?

MACK
No, sorry man, don't smoke.

TOILANE
Well throw you a fish.

MACK
Hey man, gimme a break I'm just tryin to get home to my…

TOILANE
NO, you give me a break, you give me a break and listen okay, just listen for once.

MACK
Hey, man, I don't know you, what're you–

TOILANE
I just want to tell someone, okay? I just want to tell someone that I just seen the face of the woman that's gonna have my baby. She don't even know me, man but she is gonna have my baby cause ever since I first seen her, in a white skirt with long leather shoes, I felt something. GREEN get it? Like something GREEN like FLASH through our guts, together and I knew that I will spend my life, like inter-gutted with this lady, I KNEW MAN AND I KNOW that when we make love and I don't use the word lightly, it's gonna be like MAJOR WEATHER, LIKE MAJOR WEATHER, I think you know what I mean like MAJOR VIOLENT WEATHER *(very focused on MACK)*

MACK
…Oh

TOILANE
And even tho she don't think I'm SHIT ON HER SHOE NOW I'm gonna git her!

MACK
Well! You got your work cut out for ya man. Good night!

TOILANE
I'm gonna get her and I'm gonna hold her till she's nothing but a warm puddle under my feet.

MACK
Good. Well, nice talking to you.

TOILANE
Thanks for the ear, man.

MACK
RIGHT!

TOILANE
You're alright.

Scene Six

DEE is fingerpainting a large black blob, in a frenzied attempt to depict the "animal" behind the wall that she so fears – on a large canvas. MACK puts his key in the lock, opens the door.

DEE
MACK! What… are you doing here?

MACK
Did I wake you? I didn't wake you up did I?

DEE is silent.

I saw the light on, I was passing by and I saw the light on… I just wanted to get those – books – I called you about.

DEE
At three o'clock in the morning?

MACK
Your light was on.

DEE
Okay, get the books.

MACK
What are you doing up anyway? Painting?

DEE
Yeah.

MACK
So how are you?

DEE
Fine.

MACK
Your… ah… your family… okay?

DEE
Yuh, yes, my aunts are fine and my uncle's fine and my sister's… unstable as ever. How are yours?

MACK
    Fine. My brother and his wife just had a kid.

DEE
    Right. How'd it go.

MACK
    Good, good.

DEE
    Mack. This is all very nice but I really don't feel like chatting right now, maybe we could have lunch or something.

MACK
    Don't ever fucking do that to me. *(He points his finger harder and harder at her.)*

DEE
    Get your finger out of my face.

MACK
    DON'T EVER DO THAT TO ME.

DEE
    IF YOU DON'T GET YOUR FINGER OUT OF MY FACE I'LL FUCKING KILL YOU, I'LL KILL YOU, YOU UNDERSTAND?

MACK
    YOU WANT TO KILL ME? You want to kill me? Okay. OK. Okay. Kill me, come on. Come on, kill me, come onnnnn.

DEE
    Get out of here.

MACK
    NOOO you want to kill me, you kill me, kill me *(He grabs her fist and rams the knuckle into his temple over and over.)* kill me, kill me kill me, kill me kill me kill me…

DEE
    (starts to cry) STOP IT, STOP IT, STOP IT, MAAAAAACKIE.

MACK
    (He stops, walks away. Pause.) I don't… get it. I don't… get… why our marriage broke up. I lie awake all night, all night sometimes I've got a burning hole, and I think, I think and I think, what did I do, what did I do, you never told me what I did?

DEE
    Nothing, you didn't do anything.

MACK
It's not good enough, Dee, you wreck my life, you have to tell me why. WHY DO YOU WANT US APART?

DEE
I fell out of love. That happens. I'm sorry. I just fell out of love.

MACK
I don't believe you.

DEE
I'm sorry.

MACK
I don't believe you because of your eyes. Your eyes have gone dead. Something's happened to you and it's something to do with those nightmares you were having–

DEE
I don't have nightmares, the nightmares mean nothing, I don't have night…

MACK
DEE, you'd wake up and scream for five minutes, five minutes, I'd hold you for five minutes while you… saw some unbelievable thing. *(pointing to blob)* What's that, eh, eh what's that? Come on Dee, I know so much about you. Your mother, your mother. Remember the first time I went up to meet your mother; you were going on about how scared you'd been on the highway, how you would never drive on the highway again and your mother in front of all of us, your mother turned to you and said, "Why? Why do YOU want to live so much?" Remember what you did? Remember what you did?

DEE
Don't.

MACK
Remember how you shook, you shook in the sleeping bag with me all night you shook with your head in my arms?

DEE
No.

MACK
I KNOW YOU.

DEE
No.

MACK
(holds her) You need me.

Long pause.

DEE
I don't love you. I don't–

MACK
Nothing? Is… there's nothing?

DEE
Nothing. Nothing. I'm sorry.

MACK
Okay. I don't believe you, but I guess… if that's what you say, I believe you…

MACK throws her the key and walks off. After a moment DEE screams.

DEE
MAAAAAAAAAACKIE!!! MAAAAAAAAAACKIE!! *(She runs after him.)* Come back, you've got to come back, I'm sorry, I'm sorry, I don't know what, it's like a devil possessed me, I didn't mean any of it, I do love you, I've always loved you, I lied, I don't know why, I'm sorry.

MACK
GETAWAY FROM ME.

DEE
(hanging onto his ankles) Pleeeeease.

MACK
Get… away… from… me.

DEE
Mackie!

MACK
(a cry from the heart) GET AWAY!!

DEE
(crying) You're the only person I ever loved, don't believe me, don't believe me when I say those things I was just cutting my own face, really, I love you, I… please? …Please? Mackie, I am asking you with my whole being, please… stay?

MACK
I want you to promise me.

We can see TOILANE watching them.

DEE
Yes.

MACK
: Never, ever, ever… again, okay?

DEE
: Never, ever, ever again.

MACK
: Once more, and I'm gone, I mean it, forever.

DEE
: Okay… I promise.

MACK
: Boy… boy.

DEE
: Oh God, I'm sorry I'm sorry.

MACK
: I know, I know you are.

> *DEE smiles. They are facing each other. After quite a silence they go to kiss very tenderly, but just as their lips meet, DEE speaks.*

DEE
: Youuuuu sucker, you believe me? I HATE you, I still hate you, I just was scared to be alone, don't you get it, I'm using you I'M USING YOU, YOU WIMP. *(She starts to hit him across the face.)* You suck, you suck, you suck, you suck, get out, get out, get out. *(She pushes him physically.)* Get out! Go!!

MACK
: I'm warning you.

DEE
: I said get out of my life, and I mean it, don't believe the mewling pisshead, in the hall, believe me, I hate you, I hate you, I hate you!!!

> *MACK leaves.*

No, stay! Please stay, please stay! Go! Get out, get out! Stay! Go! *(She puts her head back and wails.)* MAAAAACKIEEEEE MACKKKKIEEEEE MAAACKIEE.

> *As DEE wails "MAAACKIE" we hear a siren, louder and louder. She collapses onto the floor.*

MAACKKKKIE what's happening to me? MAAACKIE MAACKIE MACKIE.

Scene Seven

The siren stops. TOILANE is in his watching position. His mother, PEGGY CREESE, a large, uneducated woman of great power, walks in. TOILANE is a bundle of nerves, after having watched the object of his love go through such a scene. Throughout the scene, PEGS cleans up the messy room.

PEGS
YOU gotta do something about those socks, Toi, all the men in this family have bad feet YOUR FATHER'S socks coulda killed somebody on a bad day. I'm serious, like someone who was infirm or in their eighties.

TOILANE
What are you doing here?

PEGS
I'm talkin about your socks.

TOILANE
Maa.

PEGS
Shoppin bozo, whatja think. Don't look like that, I told ya last night I said I'll come by six or seven-thirty, we'll go for a bite, and then, we'll start our Christmas shopping! …Well it's the third Sarrday in October for buggy's sake, if ya don't start now you'll never get it done.

TOILANE
I don't have no money.

PEGS
Well why not?

TOILANE
I ain't got paid yet.

PEGS
Well that's a fine bed a petunias how're we supposed to go shoppin?

TOILANE
I don't know.

PEGS
Course if you lived home you wouldn't have to worry about money.

TOILANE
If I lived home I'd be a retard.

PEGS
Why do you say that.

TOILANE
Cause anyone who's twenty-eight and still hasn't moved outa home is a retard.

PEGS
You're outa your gourd. Anunciata next door, the Italian, all four of her sons are still at home and they're in their thirties and forties!

TOILANE
Right, and look at em.

PEGS
They're fine boys, that Dominic–

TOILANE
They're retards, mum, the fat one with the small head? I seen him just standing up on the corner, just standing there at night, for hours, the other one, he's got them cataracts, don't even know he's sposda get an operation and the other one's a fag, is that what you want me to be, eh? A fag living with mummy?

PEGS
Oh stop.

TOILANE
You'd just like that wouldn't you?

PEGS
What, if you was a queerbaby?

TOILANE
Yeah, that'd make you happier than a pig in shit.

PEGS
I got nothing against queerbabies, they're good for a laugh.

TOILANE
Or a kick in the teeth.

PEGS
You never.

TOILANE
No.

PEGS
Did you?

TOILANE
Once in a while.

PEGS
Oh that's cute, ya kill any? Eh? EH? I'M ASKIN YOU TOILANE, DID YOU KILL ANY?

TOILANE
NO! I don't know, I don't know he just kept, like we'd kick his head and he'd move again so we'd kick it again and he wouldn't stop moving and I started seein like a monster from the cartoons with all these snake heads and everytime ya kick one off, it grows another one, right? And he kept growin snake heads so I kept kickin them kickin them off and he goes "I think I'm swallowing blood" in this voice… like Gramma or something but he's a guy, he's a guy, right, he's not GRAMMA, he's makin like he's Gramma and he's a GUY.

PEGS
It's the bad fairy.

TOILANE
What are you talkin about?

PEGS
At your christening, Freida Wilkinson, she hated my guts cause she'd been going with your Dad for five years when I come along, she put a curse on you.

TOILANE
What are you talkin about?

PEGS
Just like in the story, the priest pours the water over ya, you wailin your head off, and everybody comes up to give good wishes, eh, well I turn around and there's Freida Wilkinson, starin me eye to eye and she goes "PEGGY CREESE THAT BABY IS IN FOR TROUBLE." I laughed eh, cause I thought she meant your howlin but later that night I got the shakes just thinkin about it, I was so cold nothing could get me warm not fifteen blankets, nothin. She put a curse on you, and you lived it out.

TOILANE
What bullshit.

PEGS
Did you kill the man?

TOILANE
WHY DIDN'T YOU HAVE MORE KIDS?

PEGS
You know damn well why I didn't have more kids, what the heck are you talkin about.

TOILANE
So ya stop buggin me, why didn't you have more kids?

PEGS
Because, BECAUSE, BECAUSE MY SISTER'S CHILD Charlene, if you remember, weighed in at twenty-two pounds at six years of age, SIX YEARS and today that woman owns one-quarter of a pancreas, one kidney and no spleen at all! She HATES my sister for bringin her into this world, she HATES HER. MY BROTHER HAS EPILEPSY THAT'S GOT SO BAD HE HAS TO WALK AROUND WITH A HOCKEY HELMET ON. I was not about to take the chance of givin birth to another family catastrophe and wear that bell around my neck all my life. NO WAY NO WAY JOSE. NOW ASK ME AGAIN WHY I didn't have any more kids.

TOILANE
Okay, okay, okay, okay.

PEGS
ASK ME AGAIN WHY I didn't have no more kids.

TOILANE
Okay why didn't yas.

PEGS
Cause you're the only one I want. *(pause)* You come home, ya'd have all your meals cooked, your shirts washed, ironed, you could come in as late as ya liked.

TOILANE
Maa.

PEGS
I wouldn't wait up for you. Heck, I'm conked out by half-past eight!

TOILANE
Ma.

PEGS
It's easier for me this way, hell I'm livin the life of Riley, sleepin in till half past nine, havin frozen pies for dinner and a bag of Timbits, nobody to worry about but my own sweet self. But think about it. If you had all that stuff taken care of and ya didn't have to worry about nothin you'd have time, time to think, to look in the paper for good jobs, to go back to school, to get trained. Trained to do something you're good at! Something you LIKE.

TOILANE
STOP BUGGIN ME!! JUST STOP BUGGIN ME OKAY? THAT'S WHY I MOVED OUT CAUSE YA KEEP BUGGIN ME BUGGIN ME BUGGIN ME! *(hits something)* FUCK.

PEGS goes to leave, very hurt.

Maa.

PEGS stops with her back to him.

How's your… blood… pressure…

PEGS
High to bursting, in fact I think I feel a bloody nose comin on right now, yup, here it comes. *(lies down, gets out a Kleenex)* See? Oh yah, I go to the doctor after Thanksgiving, he puts me on the scale, I've gained ten pounds, he goes, "Whaja do, eat the whole turkey?" Now I did not eat a lot of that bird. Just a wing, a bit of white meat. Just a bit of soup and a sandwich now and then. I never touch the pies and pastries.

TOILANE
Nope.

PEGS
And he has to go and be so rude.

TOILANE
Bastard.

PEGS
And then, and then, I walk out the door and I see Ginny Richardson down the street, about a hundred yards and that makes me feel sorta better, I mean, I thought we'd have a little chat… then she goes and sees me and she's across the street in two seconds. She crossed the street to avoid me, get it? She was trying to avoid me, Toilane. Now why would she go and do a thing like that?

TOILANE
Cause ya talk too much.

PEGS
How dare you.

TOILANE
Well it's true, no one else is gonna tell you Mum, ya got the talk trots.

PEGS
Don't you be low.

TOILANE
It's true.

PEGS
It is not true. It is in no way true, and if it is, if it is, I don't care. Because I happen to love the sound of my voice. I think it's very nice and I happen to live alone and I happen to need to talk to talk and talk and talk and talk and don't nobody say nothing because I am talking and I am gonna talk and talk till our feet freeze off and our hands get frostbite cause when I am talkin I am swimmin in a *big vat* of English cream – cream – and talk and I want to swim and cream and talk and talk till we all fall over and freeze.

TOILANE
Jesus. You running a fever? Mum? What are you talkin about everybody freezin?

PEGS
Because we'd be standin outside, outside the Dominion, that's where you run into people, that's where they run away!

Scene Eight

TOILANE makes his way up to DEE's apartment. She is lying on the floor. He knocks again and again.

DEE
Yeah yeah yeah. *(She goes to the door.)* Yes?

TOILANE
Uh – superintendent?

DEE
Oh. Yes?

TOILANE
I'd like to talk to you for a minute, if ya don't mind. Please.

TOILANE is silent.

DEE
Is there a problem with the water? *(She leads him into the apartment.)* I've noticed when I turn it on, it starts out dark brown. Come here, look at this. Have other people…

She looks at him. He is looking in an odd direction.

Is something wrong?

TOILANE
No, no, it's not, no.

DEE
Are you okay? Are you feeling okay?

TOILANE
I'm – I have to tell you.

DEE
What.

TOILANE
Like, it's just that I like… I… I've seen you.

DEE
Is this some kind of joke?

TOILANE
I been watchin you, and – I – got this – I don't know.

DEE
What do you mean?

TOILANE
I mean… I mean… I mean that I would lie down on a bed of white hot coals for you to walk over, right on my back. I would fight four Black guys, I'd go to the joint and do sixteen years I mean, I'd lose an eye, a leg… I mean I want like, I want… to be… your knight… like. I'm sweatin! I never said this to nobody before.

DEE
A knight?

TOILANE
A knight, like in the stories except now, modern, now, I'd give ya twenty-four-hour guard if you're nervous of burglars or rapists, I'll, I'll fuckin kill anybody that even… even if they just say somethin that bugs ya, I'll kill em.

DEE
You want to do all this… for me? Me?

TOILANE
I want to be your knight – with no armour.

DEE
Why?

TOILANE
Because – somepin'… you got… somepin'… like ME, somepin YOU know, you KNOW.

DEE
NO, no, I don't, I don't.

TOILANE
Yes, you do, Dee, I SEEN IT, ohhh you do!

DEE
NO.

TOILANE
Let her go, Dee, come on, come on, NOW.

DEE
(whisper) …But I'm sooo scared…

TOILANE
It's okay, I gotcha, it's okay.

DEE
It's… okay?

TOILANE
It's okay. It's okay. It's okay…

She turns her head in such a way to indicate that she is "ready" to "let her go."

Scene Nine

MERCY
You do so remember, you do SO, you say you don't you're lying cause I was there, I was there and you were there: twenty below, twenty below zero running to catch the school bus, all my books fall in the snow, I gotta pick them up, so I miss the bus, have to hitch. Stick my thumb out, this guy pulls over, old English guy in an old blue car, I get in, his name's Raymond, Raymond Brisson, he gives me a smoke, we get talking and like he's really intelligent, he's read *Lord of the Rings*, THREE TIMES, and like, I'm thinking, this guy could be my *boyfriend*!! Like none of the other guys at school would even look at me, but this guy, RAYMOND, he SEES, see? He sees what I always knew… that there's something… like a STAR in me, something, like if they REALLY knew me, even the… truly GREAT would love me… cause I got – something…

So we park at the school, bell goes off, "Oh my God, I gotta go," he looks at me, goes, "You know, you might be quite pretty if you lost some of that poundage…." He said that. He actually… believed me to be… lovely. Lovely.

Not like you you FUCKER DADDY. I HEARD you, I SAW you giving her that locket "for my favourite daughter, *Deirdre*" – that heart with the *ICH BIN DEIN* engraved. What does that mean, anyway, eh? What the hell does that mean?

So he leans over, his eyes going yellow and he kisses me, put his… tongue right in my mouth… like an egg cracking open in my belly pouring out all this like… honey everywhere, GOD I wanted to kiss him again and again. Shit the bell, "I really gotta go, but but, I think I'll hitchhike tomorrow" then I see you guys, leaning up against the wall, having your smoke before class, and I walk by you, almost past you, don't want to be late, when "YOU DROPPED SOMETHING" I feel my face turning red; like Christ, what if something dropped from my body or something but I keep going anyway "HEY WHOREDOG, WE SAID YOU DROPPED SOMETHING." Oh my NO, that word, no, my heart's falling through my chest, SHIT, they saw they SAW your tongue in my mouth, and my underpants, they know, they know, they're all – SHIT I can't move, I can't move cause I know I know that they KNOW that they KNOW that I'm a "HEY WHOREDOG! YA GONNA DO FOR US WHAT YA DID FOR THAT OLD MAN?"

I can't cry, NO please GOD don't let me, I shut my eyes, waiting, just waiting for them to go in, I still can't move, I'm just standing there why can't I move when OWWWW! SOMETHING hit me in the EYE what the OWW!! OWWW! STOP IT what… WHAT – pennies! They're throwing… pennies at me I don't get it, like what should I do? Nobody – told me – how to act how come GOD, OWW please, how could anyone have so much pennies, and why are they throwing them at me, what did I OWW oh no, oh no this is so bad please, Mummy… when poof I know what to do, I know. So I just bend over, I bend over and I… pick up their pennies one by one, all hot and greasy, I pick em up – they're still hitting my back, till my fists… are stuffed, stuffed and I stand up and I walk right to em with my fists out like this *(demonstrates)* right up to em and I go I say, "Here, here's your pennies back." Then they're gone, and I'm standing there… so when I see you you know, even though it's twenty years later, it's today, you know? It's now like no time's passed, all now and I still can't look at a penny, I can't, cause it makes me know, you see, it makes me know that I… am a sick, disgusting whore for letting a guy's tongue in my mouth and especially, especially for letting that… honey pour that… feeling… that I certainly never… ever… had… again.

The OLD ITALIAN MAN kisses her on the eyelids.

Thank you, you… even though you no capiche Inglese, you capiche, eh? My girlfriend Virginia? She told me that you only know a guy loves you if he kisses you on the eyelids. Isn't that stupid? Hey, are you cold?

MAN
Freddo, molto freddo.

MERCY
Here, take my sweater.

Scene Ten

Bus station. MERCY, just arriving in town, runs into MACK, who is just leaving.

MERCY
Maaack! Hi! Howd you know I was coming? How are ya?

MACK
Fine, okay. Look, Mercy? I'm sorry, but… I'm not here to pick you up.

MERCY
Uh oh. Is something wrong between you and Dee?

MACK
I'm just going to visit my brother for a couple of days.

MERCY
Oh no. Oh gee – that's too bad. I was hoping you'd give me a job at your bookstore.

MACK
Sure – maybe – later.

MERCY
Oh. It sounds bad.

MACK
Well, anyway, here's my bus.

MERCY
Mack? Do you think it's for – it's not for good is it?

MACK
I don't know Mercy.

MERCY
Oh. Well, then can I tell you something? I just… you know when we would cut green beans together at the Thanksgiving dinners of Mum's… did you feel… did you ever feel… you know…

MACK smiles.

Why don't you miss the bus. We'll go to the washroom, I'll give you a (*whispers* "*blowjob*")

MACK
Mercia, stop. You don't know what you're saying. I am your sister's husband.

MERCY
You really love her, don't you.

MACK
See you later.

MERCY
Oh God, I'm so embarrassed, you must think I'm a slut, you must think I'm a slut.

MACK
You didn't mean it.

MACK kisses her eyelids. She takes this to have meaning. It doesn't.

Give my best to your sister.

MERCY
Yah. Yah.

MERCY touches her eyelids, rubs them hard.

Scene Eleven

TOILANE is sitting in DEE's living room, smoking. DEE comes out of the bedroom.

TOILANE
Hey, smoke?

DEE is silent.

Hey, what's the matter?

DEE
Just…

TOILANE
You look nice with your hair messed up, pretty. Hey… hey

DEE
Please.

TOILANE
What's the matter?

DEE
I want you to go.

TOILANE
Deedree...

DEE
Please, just...

TOILANE
Are you feelin shamed? You shouldn't feel shamed, you were–

DEE
Please go.

TOILANE
You're beautiful. You're the most beautifullest woman I...

DEE
Listen, I know that you're the superintendent here, but... other than for those kinds of things, I never want to see you. Do you understand?

TOILANE
But... but... what we just been through... you... YOU... can't do that after what we just been through, how can you?

DEE
It was nothing, you understand? NOTHING.

TOILANE
It was so Deedree.

DEE
No!

TOILANE
You showin me your... your animal.

DEE
NO!

TOILANE
You shown me.

DEE
Please go, please

TOILANE
No, I won't go, I won't...

DEE
GOOOOO!! GOOO! GOOO! GOOO! Get out of here! Get out of here!!

> *TOILANE goes to hug her, she pushes him away, she hits him, he stops her, she falls on the ground and bursts into sobs.*

TOILANE
Hey… hey… Jeez, you must be Catholic or somethin, are you Catholic? I used to go out with this Catholic girl, Linda, she'd cry after but… you, you're acting crazy.

DEE
Listen, you said that you would do anything for me. I just… want… you to please…

TOILANE
What?

DEE
Leave, I want–

TOILANE
I think you don't know what you want. I think from what I seen in there, that I'm what you wanted all your life.

> *DEE sobs.*

Okay, okay, okay. I won't talk about it, I won't talk about it and I'll go if you want, but… I'll be there, I'll be right down there waitin for you when you come to your senses… and you know, when I was in high school I broke off with a girl cause she reclined on the first date, like lay down, in the car, but I changed now. I still respect ya! I respect ya.

> *Knock, knock.*

DEE
(to him) Who's that?

> *TOILANE shrugs.*

Who is it?

MERCY
ME!

DEE
Who is me?

MERCY
Me, for God's sake, open the door!

DEE
I'm coming, I'm coming. *(opens door)* …Yes?

MERCY
Dee, it's me!

DEE
I'm sorry, I don't…

MERCY
You don't recognize me?

DEE
I'm sorry – were you at Joan's the other night, or–

MERCY
JOAN'S? Dee, it's me, your sister, Mercy, Jesus, what's wrong with you?

DEE
Merc! Merc! Oh God, God, I'm sorry, I'm sorry. I… guess… I've just been kind of upset – about–

MERCY
Mack.

DEE
(looks at her for a second, wondering how she knows about MACK) Merc, this is Toilane Creese, Toi, this is Mercia, my sister. I haven't seen her in a year and, and…

TOILANE
Nice to meet you.

MERCY
Toilane, I've never heard that name before, is that… foreign?

TOILANE
No, not really, my mum named me after our Chinese landlady's son… Toi… she was really good friends with our landlady, like we used to go to their Chinese New Year's and that, so, you know… it's kinda weird, I know…

MERCY
I think it's nice.

Pause.

DEE
WELL, Toi, I'm sure I'll see you around the building… Toilane is the superintendent.

TOILANE
Good at fixin things… handy.

MERCY
Oh!

TOILANE
Well, I guess I'd better be goin… leave you two long lost sisters to… um… talk… or whatever. *(to DEE)* I'll maybe see you around?

DEE
I'll call you if I need anything fixed.

TOILANE goes to kiss DEE, she avoids him. TOILANE exits.

MERCY
WHAT was THAT.

DEE
How did you know about Mack?

MERCY
Why didn't you recognize me, DEEDEE, your own sister?

DEE
I said how did you know about Mack? Answer me please–

MERCY
NO YOU TELL ME WHY YOU DIDN'T RECOGNIZE ME?!

DEE
Because… I don't know, you're not supposed to be here, you're supposed to be three thousand miles away… what are you doing here?

MERCY
I came to visit.

DEE
How did you know about Mack?

MERCY
I'M YOUR SISTER WHY DIDN'T YOU RECOGNIZE YOUR OWN SISTER?

DEE
What do you want me to do, go down on my knees and bang my head against the floor? I'm sorry, okay? I'm sorry, I'm sorry, I'm sorry– (She falls to her knees.)

MERCY
(crying a little) It just makes me feel you don't want me here.

DEE
Oh come on, I'm just shocked! You just show up after a year – I haven't even heard from you in three months.

MERCY
You don't! You don't want me here!

DEE
Whether or not I want you here is beside the point. I want to know why you have come. Where's Tony? What happened? Did something happen?

MERCY
Do you want to know where I saw Mackie? *(DEE looks.)* The bus station.

DEE
His brother.

MERCY
Yeah, he said something about that.

DEE
How did he seem?

MERCY
Sad. *(DEE nods)* Is it permanent?

DEE
So what happened with Tony? Are you…

MERCY
He came home Wednesday night and said, "I'm moving in with Gina…" She's the slut who works in the store.

DEE
You had no… inkling?

MERCY
No. I mean when I think of it now there were lots of things; the fact that we, we'd go out to a restaurant and go through a whole meal without saying a word.

DEE
Why?

MERCY
What would we say? If I said "Hey look at that lady over there she looks so lonely" he'd say "What are you talking about" so all we'd ever talk about was the food.

He had this thing, you know? Where we could only have sex once a week, every Sunday, between the news and the late movie? And once, I think it was Wednesday or Thursday, after work, I had these white pantyhose on and I was feeling, you know, horny? So he was lying there on the bed watching TV, holding that converter, pushing around the channels, and I you know, climbed on top of him, and… sort of whispered to him that if he felt like fooling around, well he threw me right off him and starts yelling "It's Thursday, it's Thursday you cow, not Sunday, so don't pressure me, don't pressure me, don't ever pressure me again!" So I start crying, you know, just softly and I guess he felt sorry for me, so he says, "Listen, if you can get it up, you can have it, but I'm watching 'The Brady Bunch.'" So "The Brady Bunch" came on and I… rode… him, I took off my panty hose and underpants and I rode him, here I am moaning and groaning while he's chuckling away at something on "The Brady Bunch." Do you… mind… like… if I stay here…? For a while? Dee? What's wrong with you, are you alright? You're shaking like a…

DEE
I'm SO COLD. My body must be in some kind of shock, SHIT.

MERCY
Come here. Put your head on my lap. That's a girl, that's a girl. I was shaking when Tony left too, I swear it's perfectly natural after *ten* years of marriage! Of course you're in shock. Oh boy, it's a good thing I'm here to take care of you kid, you need a nurse!

DEE
Merc, Merc, you know that fear I used to have of an animal?

MERCY
Behind the wall?

DEE
Yeah, well it's like something's happened to me. It's like it got out of the wall. Like a shark banging at the shark cage and sliding out. Out of the wall, and inside me. I feel something taking over. I don't…

MERCY
It's just Mack, really.

DEE
No, no, you don't understand. I have these dreams, I have orgasms, I have orgasms in my sleep, I wake up with my nipples hard but the dream, the dream that carried it was so horrible, so horrible that…

MERCY
How horrible could it be, were you devouring Mummy's brains and spitting out her teeth…

DEE
    I'm afraid. I'm afraid that the dreams will seep into the day. That I'll do things – that I'll…

MERCY
    Is that why you broke up with Mack. Dee? Is it?

DEE
    I don't know. He's the only person I ever wanted. I don't–

MERCY
    Well, sounds to me like you did the right thing.

DEE
    I did?

MERCY
    Well yes. I mean, a man would bring this thing forth, wouldn't he? Or a baby. Dee, you mustn't have a baby.

DEE
    Why?

MERCY
    Who knows what might happen. Who knows what you could do. You could do horrible things. Mum knew that about you – Dee? Knife old ladies in the head. Screw old winos in the park. When people let their animal out they go to the top of tall buildings and shoot forty people.

DEE
    Oh God.

MERCY
    I know you Dee, I'm your sister. Mum knew you. I know what you could do. No, you don't want Mackie. I'm here now. I'll take care of you. I know you. Poor baby, you're really still a baby, aren't you.

DEE
    Sing that song, sing that song you used to sing when I was little and scared of the animal, sing that song.

MERCY
    Weee… are… walking… togetherrr… in the nice weatherrrr
    Ohhh what a lovely dayyyy…
    Weee… are walking… togetherrr… in the nice weatherrr…
    ohhhh what a lot of fuuuunnn…

    DEE joins in; after, she falls asleep.

You know when you have wild sex with a guy like that they stick to you like glue. I mean, I know you probably had to do something wild cause of Mackie, but how are you going to get rid of him?

DEE is asleep. MERCY smiles.

We are… walking… together… in the ni-ice… weather,
oh what a lovely…

Scene Twelve

MACK, addressing the audience.

MACK
When I was nine I was stung by a thousand bees; one hundred fifty-seven stingers in my nine-year-old body, I was on a respirator for three days. I can still feel it, hear it. My mother, Joy, was a cleaning fanatic, obsessed: every time you opened our front door, you'd hear *vroooooom*, she vacuumed twice a day, you'd almost pass out from the fumes of the bleach and the Pine Sol. I always slipped on the over-waxed floor. She'd have done three or four loads of laundry before she woke up my sister and me at seven; she washed the kitchen floor with straight bleach every day.

I remember the first, the first bee, I was about nine and I was having a glass of milk after my soccer game, in the kitchen, she was standing over me waiting to clean it, and there was this buzzing. *Bzzzzzzz bzzzzzz*, my mother looked around, *bzzzzz*, and then it stung her, on the hand. Her hand swelled up badly, she ran the cold water. *Bzzzzz*, I spotted another, by the fridge, and then another on the ceiling, she was frantic. We opened the pantry and although everything was, like, perfectly stored and packaged there were four or five or six of these bees buzzing around. One of them came after me, it actually chased me. I ran to the third floor, it chased me all through the house and then stung me hard on the lip, it hurt so much. My mother, she stood in the pantry like a cat, watching the walls, trying to figure out where they were coming from. I'm watching TV, suddenly *wham bash*, I run to the pantry and there is my mother, my clean mother smashing in the pantry wall with my baseball bat. Down came the plaster, filling the air with dust, and then the lath, and then she's tearing away the pink insulation, sobbing and choking, and I'm trying to see through all this dust. The buzzing sound was deafening like the bass of an electric guitar turned way up, *bzzzzzzz*, and there it was… huge, majestic, a shimmering tower of bees, a six-foot honeycomb, dripping, behind our wall, hundreds, no thousands of bees swarming around it protecting their queen, all for the queen, and they swarmed us, stung us, over and over, the honey poured thick from the hive, into our pantry, into our house, unstoppable over bleached linoleum floor and into the hall, seeped in the carpet…. And since that time I have thought, I have known that there is something deadly, yes, but I don't know really… glorious behind every wall. Deirdre. Her fear of things behind walls? Her eyes?

Scene Thirteen

DEE, at home, is on the phone to the pharmacist. We see her canvas, which she has painted with a black line inside a brilliant yellow circle. Only she and the canvas are lit.

DEE
Hi, I bought a pregnancy test from you this morning, and I seem to have lost the instructions… could you tell me what a black line means? A black line inside a brilliant yellow circle?

TOILANE is watching her, from his glass door. He sits and smokes and watches.

Scene Fourteen

Hospital. DEE, having left her pre-surgery bed and wandered down the halls, in her gown, walks towards the audience as we hear the doctors paged. She has felt the life of the fetus inside her and cannot go through with the abortion. She now walks towards the audience – she addresses the audience as if it is the fetus.

P.A.
Calling Doctor Samuels, Doctor Samuels to Emerg, Doctor Samuels, calling Doctor Rank, Doctor Rank to the OR, Doctor Rank, calling Doctor Johnson, Doctor Deborah Johnson to Maternity, Doctor Deborah Johnson, calling Doctor Roch, Doctor Roch please, calling Doctor Domovitch, Doctor Domovitch, calling Doctor French, Doctor French…

DEE
A feeling like a push; somebody strong, pushing me off the table, it was not a… decision, I was pushed and I felt and I feel and I hear… a breathing… inside me, that is not my own. I do… hear it. A raspy kind of sweet breathing a – a – pulling for breath, for air and kind of a sigh of content. I feel the breath on my face the drops of wet breath, hear a sigh, are you there? A voice not mine, a voice like no other; there you are, in the sighing, and I know I think I know whose voice this is; this is yours, this is yours, this is not a mirage, no, not part of the madness, a moment of clear, oh yes, you are clear, I can taste your sweet breath, a flower, not mine, not mine but inside me I can feel on my hand the press of your hand, fingers, holding my hand, tiny fingernails, not letting go, the impression, the feel of a tiny body lying next to mine, breathing, in the bed, cream sheets. You are showing me, showing me, you are looking at me with your dark blue eyes, staring at me in the dark in the night, smelling my milk, the shininess of your eyes like the moon on the water I see – I see it, too clearly, just as I can hear your voice, too too clear, rising, falling, your eyes, looking at me from across the room, watching me move across the kitchen, watching me; when I hold you and you wrap my hair around your tiny hands, pulling, and your head on my chest rooting for the breast, I can hear, I can feel the rooting.

I am lost, I have heard you, I can feel you drinking of me, you drink my milk and you drink and you drink and oh, I am lost.

Scene Fifteen

DEE, still in her hospital gown, at home with MERCY. On her canvas is the grotesque painting of a ten-week-old fetus.

DEE
I could hear it, Mercy, I could see it, see it, sending these flashes these flashes of life.

MERCY
You're telling me that you were lying on the bed, all ready to be wheeled into the operating room, the poor gynaecologist was putting on his scrubs and you took off? You just left?

DEE
You don't understand!

MERCY
You're not allowed to do that, Dee.

DEE
But I saw it! I SAW THE LIFE that I was about to have SUCKED, VACUUMED–

MERCY
Oh my GOD you haven't gone PRO-LIFE on me!

DEE
IT'S NOT OKAY. It's not okay to take this life this life is LIVING.

MERCY
BULLSHIT, DEE, BULLSHIT, I've been pregnant THREE times, THREE, and I've never felt a thing, the thing is like an INSECT.

DEE
Nooooo.

MERCY
You think I'm some kind of BUTCHER?

DEE
You're asleep, that's all, you don't know what you're doing, this… child… woke me up.

MERCY
>Okay, well what are you going to do then, Pollyanna? What are you going to do? …Could you suckle a baby with Toilane's face? Could you, Dee? Deedee? Aren't you afraid of what your ANIMAL might do? Look at the girl on the news last night who threw her baby into the lake, Dee, what are you going to do?

DEE
>I don't know.

MERCY
>Are you going to give it to him, to Toilane?

>>*DEE stares at MERCY.*

>You have to decide, Dee. You can't just not know. You have to decide.

>>*MERCY shakes her.*

>Deirdre!

DEE
>Leave me alone! Leave me alone! Do you hear me? Leave me–

>>*TOILANE, who has been listening at the door, opens it.*

TOILANE
>It's funny, I sorta knew I madja pregnant. I pictured, you know? While we were doin it. I pictured in my mind, this face, lookin at me, this… face.

DEE
>Listening at people's doors is a criminal offence.

TOILANE
>I want to marry you.

DEE
>It was a one-night stand, Toi.

TOILANE
>Don't be ashamed, please, don't be ashamed. I love you. I want to marry you, I want – our child together, I–

>>*He offers a ring, she kicks it away.*

DEE
>WILL YOU WAKE UP? I'm having this baby and I am giving it away. Get it? Get it?

TOILANE
You're giving my baby away? You're givin my baby away?

DEE
I'm giving your baby away, yes.

There is a long pause. TOILANE goes down to the courtyard to cry.

MERCY
THAT WAS A HIDEOUS thing to do.

DEE
(starts changing) Fuck off.

MERCY
That was a disgusting, cruel, horrific…

DEE
GET OFF MY CASE Mercia.

MERCY
No, no this time I will not get off your case.

DEE
Oh cut the sabre-toothed tiger routine, really.

MERCY
You make me sick you are so smug and beautiful, you have no idea what it is to be me, all the boys looking straight at you, never at me. That time at the dance when you went right up to Stephen Gilroy who you knew was crazy about you and said "Oh dance with Mercy, she loves you so much." And the other time in front of all our friends when you made me pick my nose and eat it; you said I had to, to get in your club that you'd all done it. And then I did it. And you laughed, you laughed. Do you know how much I hated you? Do you know how much?

DEE
Oh come on Mercia.

MERCY
If you're – a woman and you're – born ugly you might as well be born dead.

DEE giggles.

Don't! Don't you laugh!

DEE
Really, Merc, I think you've been watching too much television.

MERCY
 Don't put down television. DON'T YOU FUCKING PUT DOWN TELEVISION, YOU SNOT, TELEVISION HAS SAVED MY LIFE. IT HAS LITERALLY SAVED MY LIFE, WHEN YOU'RE SO LONELY YOU COULD DIE. I MEAN SHRIVEL UP AND DIE BECAUSE NOBODY CARES WHETHER YOU GET UP OR STAY IN BED OR DON'T EAT, WHEN YOU'RE SO LONELY EVERY PORE IN YOUR SKIN IS SCREAMING TO BE TOUCHED, THE TELEVISION IS A SAVIOUR. IT IS A VOICE A WARM VOICE. THERE ARE FUNNY TALK SHOWS WITH HOSTS WHO THINK EXACTLY LIKE I DO. And when the silence in your apartment, the silence is like a big nothing and you're thinking, my God, my God, is this what life is? Years and years and years of this? You turn on the television and you forget about it. Often all I'll think about all day at work is what's on TV that night, especially in the fall, with the new shows, I get really, genuinely excited. I… I love television. I love it. It makes me happy so don't put it down. *(She exits.)*

Scene Sixteen

MACK goes through the courtyard. He sees TOILANE sobbing against the wall. MACK stops, looks at TOILANE.

MACK
 I hope whatever it is… passes.

MACK knocks on DEE's door. The grotesque painting of a three-month fetus is replaced by a beautiful one of a four-month fetus.

DEE
 Hi. Come in. Can I get you some tea?

MACK
 Sure. Okay.

DEE
 It looks like quite the storm out there.

MACK
 Biggest one of the season they say.

DEE
 Yah?

MACK
 Yeah.

DEE
 So, how have you been?

MACK
Oh, oh, you know; okay. Look Dee is this just a visit or–

DEE
I wanted to see you. I've missed you so – I feel it all here. *(puts her hand on her chest)* It's like this great weight here. Do you ever…

MACK
DON'T.

DEE
I try not to think about you but then I dream about you every night. Last night you were holding my – skull in fragments – like a teacup and you held it together – in your hands – you–

MACK
DEE, forget it.

DEE
I know I have no right at all after my terrible behaviour but – every footstep on the stair, Mack, your voice…

MACK
DON'T PLAY WITH ME, PLEASE DON'T.

DEE
I'm serious Mack.

MACK
Yeah, just like my two-year-old nephew says, "I want juice" and then you give it to him and he throws it on the floor.

DEE
NO. NO not like your two-year-old nephew, I'm serious. Look, what I said before, that night, it was like an illness. An infection or something. Encephalitis. I don't know. Whatever it is it's gone. It's gone and it'll never happen again. I wanted to call you for a while now, but I was scared, afraid, really. I've been watching out the window every day in case you–

MACK gets up to go.

Mack, I want you to come back.

MACK
How can I know if you're serious?

DEE
Well for one thing, I'm pregnant.

MACK
So, what, you want me to hold your hand on the way to the clinic, be there when you come out of the anaesthetic?

DEE
I'm keeping this one. I'm already three and a half months. Mack, it – spoke to me – I literally got up off the stretcher and walked out of the *hospital.* Mack – Mack?

MACK
You walked out of the hospital?

Scene Seventeen

PEGS sees TOILANE sobbing on the ground in the courtyard. She approaches him.

PEGS
I don't know if you lost your job or some girl give ya your walking papers, but whatever it is, I don't think you'd want your father to see you take it lying down. Get up Toi. Get up off the ground.

Scene Eighteen

MACK and MERCY are chopping green peppers hard, on a large wooden block. First we hear the chopping sound. MERCY is aroused. We see MACK become aware of this and move away.

MERCY
So uh, I hate to be like nosy, but, like are you guys back together? You spend an awful lot of time in the bedroom.

MACK
How small do you want these things anyway?

MERCY
Oh Mack, stop being such a GUY, are you together or not?

MACK
Yes.

MERCY
What happened?

MACK
You are a sticky beak. *(He puts a vegetable on her nose.)*

MERCY
　I just think it's ridiculous.

MACK
　Awwww.

MERCY
　Well she doesn't love you.

MACK
　Hey, hey, easy.

MERCY
　Well she doesn't. I might as well tell you the truth. She's told me.

MACK
　(*sings*) Here we go a chopping greens, chopping greens, chopping greens…

MERCY
　Are you staying because of the baby?

MACK
　You shut your mouth and keep chopping.

MERCY
　But you're happy about the baby?

　　MACK smiles.

　Why her? Why her Mack? What… does she have?

MACK
　Come on, Merc, don't…

MERCY
　I just want to know, after she treats you like absolute SHIT on her SHOE, what is it you see in her?

MACK
　She doesn't have your nice big bum, that's for sure.

MERCY
　DON'T PATRONIZE ME. I WANT TO KNOW WHAT YOU SEE IN HER.

MACK
　I'm sorry, what can I say?

MERCY
　(*approaching him*) Do you find me at all attractive?

MACK
　　Yes, of course, you're very attractive.

MERCY
　　Would you… kiss me?

MACK
　　Merc…

MERCY
　　Please? Nobody's kissed me in so long. My husband never kissed me not for years, we'd just do it in the dark facing separate directions. Please?

　　MACK walks towards her, kisses her, a nice, long kiss, she wants more, he backs off, pats her on the back in a friendly way.

　　Oh the weight, the weight of a man, you know? I miss that weight. Hey you've got lipstick on your face, really!

　　DEE puts her key in the door, comes in.

DEE
　　I just had the most amazing cab driver! He'd been driving for forty-two years, FORTY-TWO, he was three years in the marines and then he got his hack license, he told me he said, "I hate this city, I hate the other cabbies, I hate the road and most of all, most of all," he says, "I hate the riding public!" Don't you love that, "the riding public?" – Where're you going?

MACK
　　Shit! I have to be at the store in… four minutes ago.

DEE
　　Aren't you eating dinner with us?

MACK
　　Yeah, yeah, yeah, this is just a meeting, I have a meeting, it's one-third my store, I should be there.

DEE
　　(kisses him) Okay. See you soon!

MACK
　　Bye Merc. *(He leaves.)*

DEE
　　(still laughing, putting down bags) "The riding public" I LOVE THAT.

MERCY
　　HOW COULD YOU DO THAT?

DEE
What?

MERCY
Tell him that it's HIS baby, don't you think he'll be suspicious when the kid doesn't look ANYTHING like him.

DEE
I told you, I'm giving it away, the Children's Aid has the *perfect* couple.

MERCY
Does he know that?

DEE
No.

MERCY
Well when are you going to tell him, you have to tell him!

DEE
When I'm sure I have my roots in him.

MERCY
What about your animal or whatever it was. Aren't you TERRIFIED you might–

DEE
Oh that, that was just – I was under a huge amount of pressure at work, it…

MERCY
BULLSHIT, it's not gone, it's taken you over. It is you. You're body-snatched. That's why you're behaving so atrociously.

DEE
How am I behaving?

MERCY
USING MACK, USING…

DEE
FUCK OFF DO YOU HEAR ME? I DON'T WANT TO HEAR ANOTHER FUCKING WORD ABOUT MACK I DON'T WANT TO HEAR…

MERCY begins to freak out, she rips newspaper in DEE's face and screams.

MERCY
I want… to be the centre, I want to be the centre of somebody's life. I haven't been the centre since Mum died, she made me the centre, she sat up when I came in she asked me what I got at the store and how was the bank today and

didn't I think I was overqualified for my work. She said I looked tired and it was too cold for me out there and nobody does that! NOBODY!

You know, I'm so… stupid, so loathsome that I actually, I had this friend in Vancouver, that was dying of a brain tumour? And I wished on my birthday, I wished that I would get one so that I could have that kind of kindness… from people. *(pause)* How can anybody like me, eh? How can you like me? I mean would you like me if I wasn't your sister? Would you?

DEE
You were very kind to me when I was little. You're a very… kind person.

Scene Nineteen

PEGS and Taxi DRIVER.

PEGS
Your children are only loaned to you, that's what Muriel said; they're only loaned to you for a short time…. It comes as quite a shock to us, you know, us girls who been brought up to think family is our whole life and ya grow up and ya get married and ya start havin kids and you are in your prime, man, everybody on the street smiles, they respect ya, you're the most powerful thing there is, a mother, with young kids, and the kids think you're Christmas, they want to sit on your knee, and help ya bake cookies, Mum this, Mum that, and you're tired as hell but you're having the time of your LIFE, right? You're important, you're an important member of society, kids all around you, friend's kids, sister's kids, car pools, Round Robin – you're havin a ball! And then they get older, ya go back to work, and it's their friends, their friends are more important than you, than anything in the world, ya couldn't drag them out on a picnic for a million dollars, and it seems they only talk to you if it's to get money or the car. They whip through their meals in about ten seconds flat, something took you five hours of buying and chopping and mixing and cooking and then they leave the house. And ya never see em, and ya wonder if they hate you. You know they're only there because of the money thing, they'd be gone in a second if there was a chance. Why is that? Why don't they like you anymore? I tried; you know, I tried like hell to listen to the AC-DC and the Led Zepplin and all that, even said I liked it, I did like that "Stairway to Heaven" one, I used to get jokes from the magazines, newspapers, you know, a Mum with a sense of humour? That went over like a lead balloon. I'd drive him to his parties, his roller skatin, his hockey and baseball, we'd go the whole drive silent, not a single word. Only word was at the end, "Pick me up at eight o'clock."
…What happened? What happened to the baby who looked up at me with eyes when the doctor first showed him to me, blackberry eyes, the baby I musta walked ten miles a day in our little apartment, back and forth, back and forth, eyes closin, lookin at me, lookin at me. Why is it that look goes away?

DRIVER
Three seventy-five, please, lady?

PEGS
I know. I know how much it is.

Scene Twenty

MERCY, MACK and DEE are all sitting around having after-dinner drinks.

MACK
So, Dad DIES at the top of the stairs, massive heart attack right on the top stair, well LUCY, our DOG was at the bottom, she goes berserk, howling like a banshee, wouldn't let a soul near him, they had to shoot her with a stun gun; two days later she has a stroke, you'd go into the house, it's pitch dark and there was my mother passed out on the couch with a bottle of Scotch and this DOG with a paralyzed bark.

MACK renders a dog's paralyzed bark.

DEE
She's a sweet dog, golden Labrador.

MERCY
Uh oh, I can feel my boils starting.

DEE
What do you mean?

MERCY
EVERY time I drink red wine I get boils, it's incredible, these huge red things and if I try and squeeze them they just go to twice the size, it's a curse.

MACK
Well when you hear what they put in wine these days…

DEE
Anti-freeze.

MACK
WHAT?

DEE
Whatever the scientific word for anti-freeze is, that's what they put in, I think.

MACK
So, Mercy, you haven't said a word about your new job. Are you bored to death?

MERCY
Apparel can be really interesting you know. I used to work lingerie? And I got so I could tell a girls size as soon as she walked through the door, winter coat and

everything, she'd come in right? and she'd say, "I'd like a 36B please,and I'd go, I'm sorry but you're not gonna need anything bigger than an 'A,'" and she'd get all huffy with me but then she'd try it on and I'd be right! She'd go, "How'd you know?" and I'd go, "I don't know, I just know!" I just knew!

MACK
But... how?

MERCY
Ohh it's a talent, I guess, a creative talent.

MACK
Come on, you're trying to tell me you could guess somebody's bra size under a winter coat?

MERCY
Yes Mack, why, do you think I'm lying? Do you think I would lie about it?

DEE
He's not suggesting you're lying Merc, we're just wondering how you could determine a woman's bra size if she's wearing a coat.

MERCY
...From her face to tell you the truth. Girls of different bra sizes wear different faces, like, if you're a 28, right, you've been that all your life, so you have a certain... you're all looking at me thinking I'm incredibly stupid.

MACK
I know what you mean. I... have the same talent with suit size.

MERCY
...Suitcase!

DEE
What?

MERCY
The word suitcase means suit... case, like case for suits, did you ever think of that? I mean it's amazing, I just never... thought of it...

Knock, knock, knock at the door; repeats.

MACK
(joking) Go away! Go away!

MERCY
I'll get it.

MACK
    No, I'll get it.

MERCY
    No, I'll get it.

MACK
    No I'll get it.

MERCY
    No I'll get it.

MACK
    Okay, you get it.

    MERCY gets it. It is PEGS and TOILANE. PEGS pushes MERCY out of the way.

PEGS
    (*now addressing the room*) THE HECK WITH THIS. THE HECK WITH THIS. (*snaps her fingers*) TOI! Come on, we're gonna have a talk with these people.

DEE
    Pardon me, I don't believe…

PEGS
    Asked or not, we're comin honey and you're sitting down and you're gonna listen up. Sit down.

DEE
    No. I don't have to sit down, what are you…

PEGS
    You know darn well why I'm here now sit down.

MACK
    Sit down Dee, the lady has something to say. Spice things up a little.

DEE
    Mack, I…

MACK
    Come on! We'll all sit down!

DEE
    If you don't leave I'm calling the police.

MACK
: Oh my God there's no need to bring the police into this my dear, let's listen to what the woman has to say.

DEE
: Well, I'm leaving then, you can all stay here.

MACK
: Dee, come on, relax.

PEGS
: Enough of this stupidity. YOU are gonna give my grandchild away over my DEAD BODY. *(terrible pause)* You hear me?

DEE
: I'm sorry, I really don't know what you're talking about.

PEGS
: You know darn well what I'm talking about slut, and you're not gettin away with it. I got the best lawyer in this city workin on the case and we are gonna win hands down. And not only are we gonna get our baby, but you are gonna pay us for damages through the TEETH, understand?

DEE
: I'm sorry, I really think you have the wrong apartment.

MACK
: What is this?

PEGS
: You the husband are ya? How's it feel to be married to a two-timin slut who gives babies away?

MACK
: Look, I'm sure this has all arisen from a misunderstanding, surely we can…

PEGS
: There's no misunderstandin here. Your wife had sexshul relations with my son… on this floor… and made him do funny things. After I spent twenty-three years teaching him to respect a woman. And then she told him herself that she was pregnant with his kid, and that she was gonna give it away – Cause she didn't want her baby with people like us. Am I right?

DEE
: Look, Mrs.…

PEGS
: Creese, Margaret Creese.

DEE
Mrs. Creese, your son came up one day to borrow some milk, or that was the excuse he made, and then he proceeded to assault me; he ripped my blouse and held a knife to my throat and I don't know what else he would have done had my sister not come in.

MACK
What is going on? Did this guy try to…

DEE
It's okay Mack.

TOILANE
(pointing to MERCY) YOU KNOW! YOU KNOW CAUSE YOU HEARD HER *TELL ME* THAT IT WAS MINE. YOU WERE HERE. TELL THEM, TELL THEM WHAT YA HEARD.

DEE
My sister would be only too happy to tell you what she heard, we have nothing to hide.

MERCY
Would you excuse me please? *(She leaves.)*

PEGS
I don't know what that says to the rest of youse, but I sure as hell know what it says to me.

MACK
Dee, what's happening?

DEE
Oh for God's sake, it's just Merc, she's a flake, you know Merc, she's… a flake.

MACK
Dee, I don't understand, what's…

TOILANE
I understand! I understand! I understand that I been used! I been used in her sick fantasies and I been– *(near hysteria, makes terrible noise)* YOU LOVED ME! YOU LOVED ME! YOU SAID THAT YOU LOVED ME! YOU SAID you loved me and you asked me to – YOU SAID THAT YOU WERE HORNIER THAN YOU'D EVER – BEEN, THAT YOU WERE WETTER FOR ME THAN…

DEE slaps him.

You fuck ya fuckin cunt whore fuck. You're giving my baby away! Because you don't want it and I'm not good enough, you throw me away like garbage and throw my baby, now my BABY MY…

TOILANE has been holding DEE by the arm. He throws her off at the end of his speech. MACK, hearing this, realizing that it is genuine, grabs his coat to go.

DEE
MACKIE, FOR GOD'S SAKE, YOU DON'T BELIEVE THE RAVINGS OF THIS…

MACK
He's not raving, he's real…

DEE
No he's not!

MACK
I KNOW YOU DEE, YOU FORGET!! WHAT GAME ARE YOU PLAYING, EH? WHAT FUCKIN GAME? *(He runs out.)*

DEE
Maaaaaaaaaaackieeeee!! *(She turns around and knocks over her easel and a chair.)* GET OUT OF MY HOUSE!! OR I'LL LIGHT YOU ON FIRE I'LL LIGHT YOU ON FIRE, GET OUT OF MY HOUSE.

PEGS
(grabs her) Listen to me. You THINK what is right, I just want you to stop all this bull roar and THINK what is right. Can you do that?

DEE
Get out.

PEGS
We're going. We just wanted to drop by to inform ya that we will have our child. Whatever we have to do, wherever we have to go, we will have our child. Come on, son. And don't try and run away cause well find ya. You better believe we will.

They go.

Scene Twenty-One

MERCY
It's soo lovely outside, the ice on the trees is just… you know, it's like the day that Mummy died, we'd been in that dark hospital room all day, holding her head trying to help her breathe, and then the breath gettin lighter and lighter until I thought we'd all stop breathing… we'd all… rise!! And then it stopped. I opened the door to the hall and a group of doctors were in a huddle and they suddenly laughed, roared like a big audience and I told them to shut up, my mother had just died, and then I walked down the back stairs and stepped out

the door and the snow shone white, and these huge icy trees just... showing... themselves... showing. And I was so startled... to hear my own breath... keep... on... *(pause)* I found this in your drawer. The locket, little silver heart, that Daddy gave you for your special club. "*Ich bin dein*" ...what does that mean?

Scene Twenty-Two

RAYMOND is looking through a book of medieval German poetry and he finds and reads the following poem, translating himself.

RAYMOND
Du bist mein
Ich bin dein
Des sollst du gewiss sein
Du bist verschlossen
In meinem Herzen
Verloren ist das Schlusselein
Du musst immer drinnen sein.

Now, with understanding of the significance of the poem.

...You are locked in my heart
The key is lost
You will always have to stay inside it...
For always.

ACT TWO

Scene Twenty-three

TOILANE'S place, very clean now. PEGS has moved in temporarily. She comes in and lies down on the floor right away with her feet up.

TOILANE
(after waiting for her to speak) WELL?

PEGS
This back is gonna be the death of me.

TOILANE
What'd he say?

PEGS
I got my arthritis puffin up my wrists. My stomach turnin into Mount St. Helens every five minutes. I don't know how I keep on keepin on.

TOILANE
Mum, what'd he say?

PEGS
BLOOD TESTS. IT ALL HINGES ON BLOOD TESTS.

TOILANE
BLOOD TESTS?

PEGS
And even that can't tell us for sure.

TOILANE
But we know! I know it's mine, she told me!

PEGS
Don't stand up in a court of law.

TOILANE
Why not?

PEGS
It's her word against yours. She charge you with assault, who they gonna believe?

TOILANE
Her?

PEGS
: Yes her. Not only will they believe her but they could send you to jail for her. They could, unless we fight with everything we got. I'm serious Toi, this is no laughing matter.

TOILANE
: Oh. Fuck. Shit.

PEGS
: That's right.

TOILANE
: Jail?

PEGS
: That's what I said.

TOILANE
: Jail! Fuck! I'm not doin time again, I… fuck. FUCK! Mum, maybe we should, like, maybe we should just like, forget it… eh? I'm not goin down the river no way, I'm not going down the river again.

PEGS
: IS THAT YOUR BABY?

TOILANE
: Yes.

PEGS
: Are you gonna fight for it?

TOILANE
: I don't know.

PEGS
: Your dad was a quitter, that's how come he spent sixteen years in jail, are you a quitter too?

TOILANE
: No.

PEGS
: All evidence to the contrary, ARE YOU A QUITTER?

TOILANE
: NO!

PEGS
Are you gonna let the high classes chew ya up and spit ya out? Are you gonna let them take your baby? My God I got to hate that class of people cleanin houses. I got to near throw up when I seen them comin; they used to talk to me like ya talk to a dog or a baby; "Hello, Mrs. Creese, how ARE you today?" This one, Mrs. Morrin, I walk in, we're standin on her kitchen floor, so clean you could eat off it, and she says to me, she says: "I don't know what was wrong with that last cleaning woman but she just couldn't get this floor clean!" and I'm thinkin *get me outa here*. One day I'm talkin to her and she up and corrects my grammar. Well I turn around and says "You think I don't know the correct grammar? I know it's 'don't have any' but I say 'don't got none.' I CHOOSE 'don't got none.' I CHOOSE my grammar, cause I'd rather be dead; I'd rather be dead than be anything like you." THEY HAVE US BELIEVIN WE CAN'T TALK WE CAN'T DRESS, AND NOW THEY HAVE YOU BELIEVIN YOU DON'T HAVE A RIGHT TO YOUR CHILD! If you don't fight for your child you're worth even less than they think. Are you listening to me? Are you listening to me? Christ, they've got ya, don't they? They got ya so you don't care about your own blood!! Do ya?

TOILANE
Yes.

PEGS
Do ya?

TOILANE
Yes!

PEGS
Well tell em.

TOILANE
I will.

PEGS
Tell em.

TOILANE
I – will – declare – war!

PEGS
Yeah.

TOILANE
I will… I will… I WILL DE… CLARE… WARRRR!!

> *The siren starts up now, the same siren that sounded when DEE was screaming earlier.*

I... DE... CLARE... WARRRR!!
I... DE... CLARE... WARRRR!!
I... DE... CLARE... WARRRR!!

                    Scene Twenty-four

MERCY and DEE walking hand in hand, singing their childhood song.

MERCY & DEE
We are walking together, in the niice weatherrr, Ohhh what a lovelyyy daaaayy!! We are walking together, in the niice weatherrr...

They laugh because they went off key.

DEE
Now you're not going to falter on the witness stand or walk away like that time at dinner?

MERCY
No, I promised you, I promise.

DEE
You swear on Mummy's grave?

MERCY
Yes, I swear on Mummy's grave.

DEE
Oh thank you!! YOU ARE A GOOD SISTER!!

MERCY
Deirdre, do you love me?

DEE nods.

Say "I LOVE YOU MERCY" – say it.

DEE
(pause) I love you Mercy.

MERCY
More than anything on this earth?

DEE puts locket around MERCY's neck.

Scene Twenty-five

TOILANE and PEGS on their way to court. Dressed up. TOILANE stops at a water fountain, and drinks.

PEGS
What the hell do you think you're doin.

TOILANE
Having a drink of water, what do you think I'm doing?

PEGS
Listen to me, have you ever seen a Chinese have a drink of cold water?

TOILANE
Well… no, I mean, I don't know.

PEGS
Well you never have because they never would because they're smart and because they're smart they live to a hundred and five more often than not. Myrtle Chow told me never EVER to drink a drink of cold water no matter how thirsty you are. Blood goes straight to your stomach to warm ya up and it's game over for your brain. Come to think of it, maybe that's why you're as dumb as you are. Come on, we don't want to be late for court for God's sake.

TOILANE
I'm not dumb.

PEGS
(swings around) DID YOU RAPE HER? DID YOU TRY TO RAPE HER LIKE SHE SAYS YOU DONE?

TOILANE
NOOOOOO!! I TOLD YA NO NO NO NO NO NO NO NO!!!

PEGS
For Christ's sake, you'll get the cops on us. Toilane camm down, camm, down I SAID camm down okay. It's not that I didn't believe you, it's just that when it comes to young boys and sex, there's somethin so big and dark that even a Mum don't know it so I JUST HAD to ask you by surprise, that's what the cops do always ask the accused by surprise, it always reveals the truth. And you said no. So I believe you. I believe you alright. Let's just hope to high heaven they do. Gosh dam all those bloody B and E's and auto thefts on your record from when we was living in Burlington. I knew you was goin with a bad crowd but I just wasn't sure how bad. DAMN THAT Kevin Blanchard, DAMN him.

TOILANE
It's not his fault. Jeez Mum, Kevin's got nothin to do with…

PEGS
Your past, my son, has everything, but everything to do with your present. Every step of the way counts. They don't miss a trick. Boy she thinks she got us over a barrel, eh? Lying bitch. Her own sister won't even back her up. She don't have a hope in hell today.

Scene Twenty-six

MACK addresses the audience.

MACK
When I first saw a girl naked I went into shock. I started shaking, the other kids laughed but I was scared, I was scared. I mean... I knew girls were different but I never imagined... *(pause)* ...there used to be these school dances, and we'd go, a bunch of us and of course the really pretty girls were all taken, and if there were any pretty girls left against the wall, you wouldn't dare ask them, I mean you wouldn't dare because if she turns you down you have to pass her in the halls every day for the rest of the year. NO WAY. So I used to ask this one... I didn't even know her name but she'd always be there, with her friend, all covered in makeup, fat with a short skirt, big barrette in her hair to look prettier, and one time me and the guys had just been walking around all night, going to the washroom for a smoke, you know, the usual shit, and I was gettin sick of it, I wanted, you know, to touch a girl, so this slow dance came up and I tapped her on the shoulder. I didn't even say anything. She looked at me... she had nice eyes... and she came onto the dance floor, I held her so close, so close I swear I could have crushed her, so of course you know, I got an erection and it would be, well, up against her, she would just bury her head in my shoulder and we'd stay in this clutch... we barely moved... for the whole song. Then at the end of the song, I'd just turn around and walk away without looking at her. I never said hello to her in the halls. When my buddies asked me why I was dancing with that "pig" I said she let me dry hump her on the dance floor. If I'm being punished, somehow, for that, now, I guess I deserve it. I guess I do.

Scene Twenty-seven

Court corridor. PEGS comes out after having talked to the lawyer.

PEGS
Toi? Honey? ...we have to drop... the suit.

TOILANE
What?

PEGS
The lawyer believes, is SURE, that with that sister backin her up now those girls will send you up for twenty years. Jail killed your father; it would most certainly kill you. I don't want to lose the both of youse.

TOILANE
But… I thought you said…

PEGS
It doesn't matter what I said… honey, they've brought us to our knees.

MERCY passes. PEGS grabs her.

Hey.

MERCY
Please let me go.

PEGS
We're human beings. We're not animals you know.

MERCY
I didn't say you were an animal.

PEGS
Why are you so AFRAID OF HER?

MERCY
Because… I love her. *(She wriggles free, runs away.)*

Scene Twenty-eight

TOILANE is on the same ramp that he began the play with, apologizing to the judge so that he won't be charged with malicious prosecution. In court, TOILANE on stand.

TOILANE
And I… apol – apulol-o-app – I'm sorry… for makin up lies to the court… I'm… real real real sorry and I'll never do it… again… *(whispers)* I'll never do it again.

Scene Twenty-nine

Same day, after winning in court, DEE and MERCY are in a victory dance. On the canvas is a grotesque painting of a nine-month-old fetus.

MERCY
WHOOOOO! WHOOO HOOOOOO!! Oh God. *(She flops down on the couch.)* We won.

DEE
Yes. *(pause)* We did the right thing didn't we? Don't you think?

MERCY
(takes off shoes) I'm just glad they don't live here anymore. *(She prepares tea.)*

DEE
He couldn't have handled a child, I mean there's no way.

MERCY
…Do you want some tea?

DEE
Merc? Don't you think?

> *MERCY goes out to make the tea.*

Uh!

MERCY
What's that, a kick?

DEE
BIG kick in the ribs. Hey, little one?! You getting restless? You want out, to the Johnsons? Hey Merc, don't you LOVE the Johnsons?

MERCY
They seem nice.

DEE
They're *fabulous, fabulous* people, Merc, the kid will thank me on its KNEES in twenty years. For sure! Oogh!

MERCY
What's wrong, did something happen?

DEE
(checking under her skirt) No no it's just… a leak, I think a trickle – amniotic fluid, a… oh, there's the mucus plug… *(wraps it in Kleenex)*

MERCY
Does that mean…

DEE
No, no, I told you, it's just a leak, a trickle of water, it means there's a tear in one of the sacs, that's all, a little tear… it could have torn it with its… fingernail.

MERCY
Are you sure we shouldn't go to hospital?

DEE
No, I'm fine, I'd just like that tea I think.

MERCY
Sure, Sure, *(brings it)* here. Do you want something to eat? (DEE *almost swoons.*) Dee? Are you alright?

DEE
Ohh. Nooo! Ohhh! Oh my God, oh my God, a Lion a Lion, I can… see – a – a – lion, a lion, breaking through the wall a lion roaring all the stones breaking, flying, roaring. Stop!

MERCY
What do you mean, you see this in your mind?

DEE
Ahon! …stop it! Stop it!

MERCY
Let's go to hospital, Dee, come on.

DEE
AAAAAHH!!

MERCY
Let's go to hospital!

DEE
No, no, no it's just lack of sleep… it's lack of sleep, it's lack of sleep.

MERCY
I know, I'll make you some hot milk, that'll make you feel better, let me make you some hot milk.

DEE
It's lack of sleep.

> *DEE lies down on the couch, shudders. Knock at the door. MERCY gets the door.*

PEGS
We just… my son just wanted to make an apology to youse, he feels bad for what he done, and…

MERCY
Oh there's no need for that.

PEGS
Oh, yes there is. We caused you people a lot of trouble and expense, and we want to apologize. Do you mind…

MERCY
Well…

DEE
No, Merc, I'm going to bed I…. Really, there's no need for an apology, I…

PEGS
Oh certainly there is, we'll just sit down and have a cup of tea with ya… and ya see we want to be friends, we want to put all this mess behind us, and you know what I mean?

DEE
It's just that I was about to go to bed, and–

PEGS
For God's sake give us this, girl, you had us evicted you made my son lie in court, for God's sake, let us be your friends. For his sake, not for mine, believe me if it was up to me…

DEE
Okay, I'm sorry, please, have a seat. Mercy? Would you like to give these people some tea?

MERCY
Okay. What do you take?

TOILANE
No milk, two sugar please.

PEGS
Just clear for me, thanks.

MERCY
One clear, one double clear.

DEE
So… how do you like your new place?

PEGS
Oh we like it fine. We'd been wanting to get outa here anyway, so really, you done us a favour.

DEE
It wasn't anything to do with me whatever you may think, really, I hardly know the landlord.

PEGS
 Oh that's okay.

DEE
 Really!

PEGS
 I believe ya! That's a nice picture.

DEE
 Thank you, a friend did it.

PEGS
 Oh? What's it supposed to be?

DEE
 It's uh… whatever you like…

PEGS
 Oh I get it.

MERCY
 Some biscuits?

PEGS
 Oh not for me, got to watch the old waistline.

MERCY
 You don't have a weight problem.

PEGS
 Oh that's very kind but I do. I weighed ninety pounds when I married Toi's father. *(to DEE)* NOW you certainly don't have a weight problem… how much you gained with the baby?

DEE
 Oh… I don't know, I guess about twenty-five pounds. I don't really keep track.

PEGS
 No more than twenty, my doctor said. He said if I gained more than twenty he'd hang me.

DEE
 (pause) Did you?

PEGS
 Seventy-five pounds and I lived on chicken noodle soup. I'm serious.

> As PEGS talks, DEE starts to go into mild labour. Of course, we have to speed things up: every half minute or so.

MERCY
Here's the tea… double sugar for you and clear for you.

PEGS
Thanks dear. Yes, as I say, he's going into retail management, what's the name of the store Toilane?

TOILANE
Jones Work Warehouse, it's just like work clothes, sort of, and I'm just at the till, Ma, it's not management.

PEGS
But darlin, nobody stays at the till certainly no son of mine, oh no you're far too smart to stay at the till.

MERCY
I worked in retail for a while.

PEGS
Did you now dear? Well did you get managerial?

MERCY
No, no, I didn't.

PEGS
Good tea, what kind is it? *(starts to notice DEE is in pain)*

DEE
Darjeeling, I think, isn't it Merc?

PEGS
That's Indian isn't it?

DEE
I'm not sure.

PEGS
You okay dear? You look a little uncomfortable.

DEE
Oh, I'm fine, it's just… the baby's foot sticks in my ribs… I… think I am gonna have to go lie down, actually.

PEGS
Little tightness in the chest?

DEE
   Yuh, I just…

PEGS
   Here, lie down here, here, we'll sit in chairs, Toi can sit on the floor, well just finish our tea and we'll go.

DEE
   Really I–

PEGS
   There, there, just lie yourself down, I was a RNA I know what I'm talking about a little company's not gonna kill you.

DEE
   (lies down) Okay, just a few minutes, though.

PEGS
   Comfy now? You'll be okay. Well! This is like a reunion after so long! Eh? Just a bunch of friends, after all that's happened? Who would've thought it… Toilane knows he mighta made a mistake… I do, however, think it would be a nice gesture if you… admit, just for me bein his mum, that my son did not assault you.

DEE
   Oh listen, if I thought you were going to…

PEGS
   No no no now don't get het up. I just want you to tell me whether or not my son assaulted you.

DEE
   I withdrew the charge. What does it matter.

PEGS
   It matters to me, I'm his mother.

DEE
   He knows the truth.

PEGS
   I think we all know the truth.

DEE
   Would you please leave?

PEGS
   No. I'm enjoying the reunion; and after what you done to us I think we gotta right…

DEE reaches for phone.

Toi.

TOILANE cuts the phone. DEE gets up.

DEE
What is this?

MERCY runs to door. TOILANE blocks the door.

PEGS
We want… to be treated… *hospitable* by you! We want the respect… we deserve! Now sit down and talk nice.

They sit down nervously. DEE's waters break.

DEE
AGHHHHH.

PEGS
Your waters!

MERCY
Deedee are you okay?

DEE
It's nothing, nothing.

PEGS
Nothing! My dear your waters broke!

MERCY
I really think we ought to be going. Dee I'll get your coat.

PEGS
YOU'RE NOT GOING ANYWHERE TILL WE'VE HAD OUR VISIT NOW SIT DOWN.

MERCY
You're crazy. YOU'RE A CRAZY LADY!

PEGS
You try to leave and my son will do whatever he has to do to stop you. So sit down.

MERCY
Just… a short visit, then, please?

PEGS
I WANT MY REUNION!

DEE contracts, bad labour pain throughout this speech.

Huh, speakin of reunions, I got a story. We had our high school reunion last year and of course I didn't want to go, I'd got so old, fat, you know, but my girlfriend, Janis, she said, oh come on, we're all old and fat, we'll have a ball, get out the rum and cokes, and the taco chips… play a little bingo, have a blast! So finally I thought, oh alright, so I trudged on over with Janis, and I had a pretty good time, and I was sittin at a table havin a pie and coffee with a few girls when one of em says, well she says, "I've had such a nice time, but I just wish to heaven that Peggy Lane had come," Lane's my maiden name, "she's always such a laugh." Well I musta turned three shades a red, I could hardly speak but I did, like a fool, I turned to her and I said, "But Marjorie, here I am, I'm Peggy! Didn't you see me?" Well then SHE turned three shades of red and she SAID, "Well, yes, I did, but I wouldn't have known you… your FACE!" My face, had got so… it's true I guess, I don't look nothing like my wedding pictures. Toi don't believe me when I tell him how pretty I was.

TOILANE
Yes I do.

PEGS
Isn't that a funny one? You okay, dear? Looks like you're gonna have a baby in a day or so! Toi? I guess we'd better be goin.

PEGS gets up, TOILANE is still.

Toi?

TOILANE
I don't want to go.

PEGS
Toi, the lady is going to have a baby, good God.

TOILANE
I want… my baby.

PEGS
But Toi, the courts ruled.

TOILANE
I don't care what the courts ruled. I want my baby.

PEGS
Well you can have another one, there are plenty of girls out there.

TOILANE
 I want my baby with the woman I love.

PEGS
 Toi, you don't love her you had a silly crush, now–

TOILANE
 I love her and she loves me. I love you. You love me and you are going to have my baby and I… want it. I want to take care of it. Mum, you know you said if there was anything I really needed you would be there for me, you'd help me out.

PEGS
 Toi.

TOILANE
 You said to trust you, you said you'd come through, are you gonna help me?

PEGS
 Help you what?

TOILANE
 Deliver the baby.

PEGS
 Toi for God's sake, what if there's complications?

TOILANE
 What?

PEGS
 If that baby won't come out, she might have to have a Caesarian you know, be cut out.

TOILANE
 Well you done that, you done them things you said, when you worked in the hospital.

PEGS
 Toi, this is… against the law, this is…

DEE is about to vomit.

Do you need to throw up dear? *(She gets something.)* Here, if you want to throw up.

DEE does.

DEE
 I want to go to hospital, I want…

TOILANE
 I WANT MY CHILD. I'M GONNA HAVE MY CHILD.

DEE
 You can't do this, this is sick, this is…

PEGS
 My son wants his child and he got a right and you know he does. Now nobody's gonna hurt you. We're just gonna take what is rightfully ours.

DEE
 Just for Christ's sake, can't you just leave. MERCEEEEE!!

MERCY stands up. Stands on her tiptoes. Lifts her hands high in the air. Eyes wide, turns around and walks out.

TOILANE
 Hey.

PEGS
 It's okay, let her go.

TOILANE
 But what if she drops a dime, Ma?

PEGS
 She won't.

TOILANE
 She won't?

PEGS
 She won't.

DEE
 Oh no oh nooo it's coming again it's coming again the big lion is coming *down to* crush me to crush me oh no oh no ohhh I can't stand it I can't stand it uhhh-hhhhh Mackie, Mackie, please, please, take me to hospital, I think I'm gonna die, I really think I'm gonna die.

PEGS
 That's what they all say dear, the schoolyards are full.

TOILANE
 I'm your husband now. I'll help ya through it.

DEE
Oh God, oh God, I must be in hell, that's what it is. I died and I'm in hell, or I know! It's a dream, that's what it is, a terrible nightmare, oh God, oh AGHHHHH. LET ME WAKE UP PLEASE LET ME WAKE UP.

PEGS
(to TOILANE) I think it's time we brought her into the bedroom, Toi, she'll be more comfortable there.

DEE
NOOOOO!!!

TOILANE helps DEE into the bedroom.

(to TOILANE) YOU… you won't let me die will you? Will you?

TOILANE
I love you, Dee, I'd never let you die.

DEE, crying, collapses into his arms.

Scene Thirty

This could be a dream. MERCY, stunned in courtyard. RAYMOND walks by. She is just staring.

RAYMOND
(after looking several times) Excuse me, excuse me but your name wouldn't happen to be… Mercia… would it?

MERCY
Yes. Who are you?

RAYMOND
Raymond. Raymond Brisson from… I used to drive you to school when you were… a schoolgirl… in Montreal… you were about fifteen, I believe – St. Francis.

MERCY
Raymond.

RAYMOND
Yes, that's right – Raymond…. How strange to see you here, do you live… in one of these apartments?

MERCY
Yes. Do you?

RAYMOND
Well I keep a small flat here… you see I teach here twice a week, so I go back and forth from the country.

MERCY
It's… funny to see you, like seeing the house I grew up in with different people living in it, it's funny.

RAYMOND
Yes, it's that way seeing you too. As if – a – light – switched.

MERCY
Oh Raymond, I love the way you touched me.

RAYMOND
(blushes deeply) …Are you alright? You seem to be…

MERCY
What, what do I seem?

RAYMOND
Well, it looks as if you've had a bit of a shock.

MERCY
It's just that I see you, and all I want, all I really want is for you to touch me again.

RAYMOND
It's lovely to see you.

MERCY
Oh Raymond, I've had so many… dreams about you, you know nobody's touched me in the same… way, made the honey – pour–

RAYMOND
Say, would you like a cup of tea, why don't you come up to my flat and I'll get you a cup of tea and a – a – biscuit.

MERCY
Yeah, I'd like to come up to your flat, I'll come up to your flat and have a nice cup of tea and then I'm going to take off my clothes and I'm going to spread my legs and you're going to… make love to me. We never went all the way, you know, in the car, we only ever did everything but.

RAYMOND
(clearly aroused) Well, let's just see about that tea first of all and sitting you down…

MERCY
I dreamed about you all the time.

RAYMOND and MERCY hold position.

Scene Thirty-one

TOILANE and PEGS and baby on a bus in the night. TOILANE goes to light a cigarette.

PEGS
No smokin, with the baby, Toi, you should know that!

TOILANE
Oh right. How is she?

PEGS
Oh Tracy Meg is just fine, sleepin like a baby.

TOILANE
Ever cute! You sure you brought enough formula?

PEGS
I brought you up didn't I? Trust me for God's sake.

TOILANE
I do, I do, I'm just... nervous, you know. What if they catch up with us? *(pause)* Ma, do you think she's okay?

PEGS
Who?

TOILANE
Deedree.

PEGS
Sure she's okay. She never wanted a baby and now she doesn't have one.

TOILANE
I love her though Mum you know, I still love her.

PEGS
Don't be a sap.

TOILANE
I'll love her till the day I die! Hey. Do you think she looks like me?

PEGS
I think she looks like your father, if you want to know the truth.

TOILANE
But she looks like our side, like, you can definitely see it's mine.

PEGS
Oh no question about it, the minute I saw her.

TOILANE
It's like there's a well, you know and when I seen her, Tracy? Something pumped that water up and it filled my whole head, you know, it filled my whole head!

Scene Thirty-two

Waiting room. MERCY and MACK.

MERCY
But I betrayed her, I betrayed my own sister. I thought, you know, I thought it was the right thing. I wanted to do the right thing for once in my life. I'm sorry you know but I'm not at the same time. Do you know what I mean? I mean I'm sorry but I'm not sorry I'm not I'm sorry I'm not I'm sorry I'm not I'm not I'm sorry.

They go into the hospital room. DEE is in bed, breasts bandaged. She wakes up.

DEE
Mercy.

She reaches for her. MERCY goes and hugs DEE.

Mercy. Where's the baby?

MERCY
Dee, she's... she's in the nursery. She's in the nursery with the other babies. She's fine.

DEE
A girl? She's a girl?

MERCY
Yes, a little girl.

DEE
And they didn't get her? Him and his mother, they didn't get her?

MERCY
No Dee, they left. They left and we went to the hospital and you had the baby. You just had a very rough time. You had a very rough birth.

DEE
Then it was a dream? You mean it was a dream? But I was so sure it was real, no it couldn't have been a dream, you're lying to me, you're lying...

MERCY
Mackie–

DEE
You're lying, where's my baby, where's my...

MACK
She's here, I told you Dee. She's... okay, really.

DEE
She is? She is?

MACK
The baby is just fine. The nurses are taking care of her in the nursery – she's in the nursery.

DEE
But I was sure that it wasn't a dream. Mackie? Mackie?

MACK
You're okay Dee, you're gonna be okay.

DEE
Are you gonna stay with me? You aren't going to leave?

MACK
No, I'm not going to leave.

DEE
Cause, cause I want to keep our baby now, Mack, I want to keep her. The Johnsons aren't here, are they, get them away, get them away.

MACK
I just think you ought to get some rest now Deirdre.

DEE
But I want to see my baby, show me my baby, show me my baby. My God, you're on fire, your eyes are on fire. Your eyes are on fire!

MACK interjects throughout the speech with "Shh" and "No, no."

Mercy, Mercy, your face your face is burning, burning burning, white. I want to talk to my mother. I want to talk to my mother.

MERCY
But Dee, Mummy's dead, she's dead.

MACK
DEE.

DEE
I know, I know she's dead, I know she's dead but I want to talk to her, I want to... talk to her, I want... to tell her that I'm... sorry! I want to say I'm sorrry!! I'm sorrry!! I'm sorrrry!! I'm sorrrry!!

Scene Thirty-three

RAYMOND speaking to MERCY, but it doesn't matter if she is on stage or not. He should NOT be speaking directly to her.

RAYMOND
I dreamed about you too, you know, several times a year every time the season changed. Swimming, swimming in cold blue water, clear; striped fish and dark, inky seals jumping around us, and I turn, and look at you and your eyes, your eyes are toooo... blue.... And then I'd wake up, look out the window and see the first snowfall, or the leaves had turned... overnight...

Scene Thirty-four

PEGS and TOILANE in hotel room. Light flashing outside.

TOILANE
Sudbury on a Saturday night eh?

PEGS
Sssshh shhh. I think she's down.

TOILANE
(sits down) Mum.

PEGS
Yuh.

TOILANE
I wanted to tell you... that... like... I wanted to apologize.

PEGS
What for?

TOILANE
For that time… when I was in grade four that time, and… we were having the goodbye thing… party or something for Mrs. Lamb.

PEGS
She was your favourite teacher.

TOILANE
And you came to get me just when I's gonna give my present to her, I was just giving it to her and there you were and I was so embarrassed you looked so… bright or something, too bright or too big… so… I said for you to get out. I said, "Get out of here mother," and you did, you ran, crying down the hill, and broke your high heel. I felt so bad about that high heel, about you breakin it on that hill cause of me. Okay.

PEGS
It was damn stupid of me, I knew how much that teacher meant to you, I shouldn't have come.

TOILANE
Mum, how come she breathes so fast?

PEGS
Babies do, they breathe fast… look at her little face, will ya?

TOILANE
Mum? What… do you think she's dreamin? Do you think she's dreamin?

PEGS
I don't know. Little rose.

TOILANE
Little rose.

PEGS
Ohhhh. Boy. I'm gonna have to sit down I'm not feelin too good.

TOILANE
What's the matter?

PEGS should not be sitting on bed, but on a chair beside the bed.

PEGS
I think it was that sandwich, the Toasted Western, I think it musta been bad.

TOILANE
Yah? What… is it your stomach or–

PEGS
No, my head, it feels like my heads on fire, like white…

Scene Thirty-five

DEE opens a door. A light blinds the audience. She walks forward on the ramp towards the audience. The audience, to her, is the nursery. She is looking for her baby.

DEE
Ohhhh! Which one are you, baby? Which…. Oh! I see you! I see you now! Oh! You are so beautiful. Yes! Yes! I want you baby I want you forever because I… love you. I LOVE you. Oh! Your eyes are opening…. Hello! Hello! Hello! Hello!

Scene Thirty-six

We cross-fade to TOILANE. In the hotel room, hotel light still flashing. PEGS passed out or maybe dead in chair. TOILANE stands there, holding the baby, bewildered.

TOILANE
Mum??

The end.

Lion In The Streets

Lion in the Streets was first produced as the inaugural Public Workshop Project at Tarragon Theatre in Toronto, in May 1990. It received its world premiere at the duMaurier Theatre Centre as part of the duMaurier World Stage Theatre Festival in Toronto, in June 1990.

Lion in the Streets subsequently was remounted with a revised text by Tarragon Theatre in Toronto, in November 1990, with the following company:

ISOBEL	Tracy Wright
NELLIE, LAURA, CHRISTINE, SHERRY	Jane Spidell
RACHEL, LILY, RHONDA, ELLEN, SCARLETT	Ann Holloway
MARTIN, ISOBEL'S FATHER, GEORGE, MARIA, DAVID, MAN, RODNEY, BEN	Robert Persichini
SCALATO, TIMMY, BILL, RON, FATHER HAYES, MICHAEL, EDWARD	Julian Richings
SUE, JILL, JOANNE	Clare Coulter

Directed by Judith Thompson
Set and Costumes Designed by Sue LePage
Lighting Designed by Steven Hawkins
Music Composed and Performed by Bill Thompson
Sound Designed by Evan Turner
Stage Managed by Nancy Dryden
Apprentice A.S.M. & Dance Captain: Nancy Katsof
Electrician: Patrick Hales
Sound Operated by John Alderman
Set Construction by George Vasiliou & Will Sutton
Scenic Painting by Gabriele Schnutgen & David Rayfield
Properties by Kate Hemblen
Wardrobe by Cheryl Mills & Sue Ward
Assistant Lighting Design by Paul Mathiesen
Waltz Coached by Viv Moore

This published text includes sections rewritten since the Tarragon premiere.

CHARACTERS

ISOBEL
NELLIE
LAURA
CHRISTINE
SHERRY
RACHEL
LILY
RHONDA
ELLEN
SCARLETT
MARTIN
ISOBEL'S FATHER
GEORGE
MARIA
DAVID
MAN
RODNEY
BEN
SCALATO
TIMMY
BILL
RON
FATHER HAYES
MICHAEL
EDWARD
SUE
JILL
JOANNE

Lion In The Streets

ACT ONE

The ghost of ISOBEL, a deranged and very ragged looking nine-year-old Portuguese girl, runs around and around in a large circle, to music, terrified of a remembered pursuer, in fact, the man who killed her in this playground seventeen years before the action of the play. There are autumn leaves all over the playground, and the kids who approach her all have large handfuls of leaves, which they throw at her. At this point ISOBEL does not know she is a ghost, but she knows that something is terribly wrong. She is terrified.

ISOBEL
Doan be scare. Doan be scare. *(turns to audience)* Doan be scare of this pickshur! This pickshur is niiiice, nice! I looove this pickshur, this pickshur is mine! *(gesturing behind her)* Is my house, is my street, is my park, is my people! You know me, you know me very hard! I live next house to you, with my brother and sisters, Maria, Luig, Carla and Romeo we play, we play with your girl, your boy, you know me, you know me very hard. But… when did tha be? Tha not be now! Tha not be today! I think tha be very long years ago I think I be old. I think I be very old. Is my house but is not my house is my street but is not my street my people is gone I am lost. I am lost. I AM LOOOOOOOOOST!!

Four children—two girls and two boys—laugh and approach ISOBEL.

NELLIE
Take a bird why doncha?

RACHEL
Go back with the nutties to the nuttyhouse!

SCALATO
She looks like a crazy dog!

MARTIN
(barks) Hey!

All bark.

ISOBEL
Peoples! Peoples, little boy little girl peoples! Hey!

ISOBEL walks towards them.

MARTIN
What's she doin?

NELLIE
  She's coming over here!

RACHEL
  She's gonna get us!

ISOBEL
  You, girl, you help to me. I am lost you see! You help!

NELLIE
  She smells.

RACHEL
  You should dial 911 so the police could help you.

SCALATO
  Where do you live?

MARTIN
  With all the other pork and cheese west of Christie Street?

RACHEL
  Martin that's not nice.

ISOBEL
  (overlapping) Portuguese, Portuguese, yes… I catch a bus! Is there a bus, bus maybe? To take me to my home? You know a bus?

SCALATO
  No buses here.

ISOBEL
  Yah, bus right here, bus right here, number ten, eleven, I take with my mother to cleaning job, where this bus?

SCALATO
  I said there's no buses here you ugly little SNOT.

ISOBEL
  (points) You! YOU bad boy you bad boy say Isobel, BAD.

SCALATO
  Why don't you get your ugly little face outa here, snot?

MARTIN
  Snotface!

ISOBEL
  Shut up boy, shut up, I kill you I kill you boy.

SCALATO
Hey she's gonna kill me!

RACHEL
She's a witch.

ISOBEL tosses rocks at them.

MARTIN
She's throwin rocks! Hey she's throwin rocks!

NELLIE
STOP IT.

RACHEL
Stop throwin rocks or we'll tell the police!

ISOBEL
You BAD boy you BAD I will kill you!

SCALATO
(jumping off and attacking her) You just try it you goddamned faggot!! Faggot! Faggot!! *(hitting her)*

ISOBEL
(growling like a dog) G-r-r-r-r-r. G-r-r-r-r-r.

They circle one another.

MARTIN
What's she doing?

NELLIE
I don't like her.

ISOBEL and SCALATO scrap and the others join in. SUE, a thirty-eight-year-old woman in a grey sweatsuit, walking home from a meeting, spies the fight and rushes up.

SUE
Hey! Hey hey hey stop that right now! *(she pries them apart)* HEY! Listen! What is going on??

ISOBEL
I KILL YOU BOY!

SCALATO
She started it!

MARTIN
She was throwing rocks at us!

ROSE
She's crazy.

ISOBEL leaps towards SCALATO. SUE catches her, she falls to the ground.

SUE
Little girl? Little girl!

ISOBEL
(overlapping) I kill that stupid boy.

SCALATO
She started it, lady.

MARTIN
I'm getting out of here.

SCALATO
Me too.

NELLIE & ROSE
Wait for me!!

SCALATO
You chicken, Martin! You suck!

ISOBEL
I kill that stupid boy! *(beat)* I no like those boys.

SUE
I'm sorry if they hurt you.

ISOBEL
They no want play with me. Why they no want play with me? Why all the kids no want play with Isobel? Ha?

SUE
Ohhh… sometimes kids are just… mean, that way, Isobel, when I was little kids were mean like that to me once.

ISOBEL
Kids? Mean no play to you?

SUE
> That's right. We had just moved to a new town, Cornwall actually, near Montreal? Well my sisters and I went for a walk around the neighbourhood and these big boys on bikes started firing arrows at us.

ISOBEL
> Boys on bikes?

SUE
> That's right, just like those nasty boys!

ISOBEL
> Nasty boys, to you, too! Mean to you!!

SUE
> That's right. And those arrows, they hurt! They really hurt!! And I was the oldest so I told my sisters, "Just cry, just start to cry and then maybe they'll feel sorry for us," so we all started to cry.

ISOBEL
> Cry.

SUE
> But you know what? It didn't work! They kept shooting those arrows anyways. They were just mean.

ISOBEL
> Mean boys shoot arrows. Haaah!

SUE
> AND suddenly, a bigger boy, about sixteen, came along and made them stop, and you know, he was like an angel, to us, an angel who came down from the sky on his big blue bicycle I've never forgotten that.

ISOBEL
> Never forgetting.

SUE
> Nope. I guess I'm your helper today.

ISOBEL
> Helper.

ISOBEL'S FATHER
> *(on porch)* Hey! Is-o-bel.

SUE
> Isobel is that your father?

ISOBEL
Father. My father. *Eu pensava que té tinha perdedo!*

ISOBEL'S FATHER
(ordering ISOBEL to go around to the back door) *Vai pela porta das traseiras.*

SUE
Hello.

ISOBEL'S FATHER grunts.

My name is Sue Winters and I don't know if you're aware of it, but some of the boys in the neighbourhood have been well I'd say doing some not very nice teasing of your daughter. I just… thought… you might…

ISOBEL'S FATHER goes in, slamming the door.

Poor man probably works all day in construction and then all night as a janitor in some Bay Street office building. What a life. *(she exits)*

ISOBEL
My father? My father is not there. My father is dead. Yes, was killed by a subway many many years; it it breathed very hard push push over my father; push over to God. Hi my father.

Music. Lights come up just a bit. SUE is in her son TIMMY'S room, in the dark. TIMMY is in bed. ISOBEL watches.

SUE
And so the giant starfish saved the drowning boy.

TIMMY
What was the starfish's name?

SUE
The starfish's name? Uh… Joey. It was Joey.

TIMMY
Mummy? Why isn't magic true? I want magic to be true.

SUE
Well. It is true, in a way, it…

TIMMY
Not it's not. It's not true. And ya know what else?

SUE
What, darling?

TIMMY
　I think tonight's the night.

SUE
　That what, Tim?

TIMMY
　That we're all gonna die. Tonight's the night we're gonna die.

Music. A dinner party, around a table. ISOBEL is there, invisible. The conversation is simultaneous.

LAURA
　There was nothing to do! Nothing to bloody do but sing in the church choir!! And go to baked-bean suppers!! The snow at one point was actually up to the second-floor window.

BILL
　No, she had the gall to ask my male students to, "Please leave the room," for her senior seminar. She did "not wish to be dominated by men." Where did that leave me, I asked her?

LILY
　No, no no, you have to pat the dough, pat it for ohh a good five minutes then put it in the microwave for one, then take it out, then pat it again.

GEORGE
　St. Paul said, "We are as vapour," what is it? Like "vapour vanisheth" or – something. "We are no more." So I got up this notion of Martians – being these – wisps of vapour… no, you see your problem is you want the aliens to be like you, you are anthropomorphizing, you…

LAURA
　That's so boring. That's so knee-jerk boring.

BILL
　And she launched into the most savage tirade–

SUE rushes in, dressed in her sweatsuit and sneakers. Everyone turns and freezes, except BILL, who continues to talk until SUE's third "Bill."

SUE
　Bill… Bill… Bill!! We have to talk!

BILL
　Sue! Hi! Who's with the boys?

SUE
　Mum came over, Bill I need to talk, NOW.

LAURA
  Would you like a drink, Sue? We have…

GEORGE
  Yeah, come in and sit down…

SUE
  No, no thank you, I just… want to talk to my husband.

ISOBEL
  My helper, Suuuuusan!

BILL
  Oh – okay, Sue, I'll just finish this conversation. Anyway–

SUE
  He thinks he's going to die.

BILL
  Who?

SUE
  Timmy! Your son! He–

BILL
  What, did he say that tonight? Oh, that's just kids, he's–

SUE
  BILL, come home, your son is very depressed his father is never there, why are you never never…

BILL
  Sue PLEASE, we'll talk about it later, okay? So as I was saying, Laura…

SUE
  Come with me.

BILL
  I'll come in a while. I'll just finish this conversation, and then I'll come, okay?

SUE
  YOU COME WITH ME NOW!

BILL
  Sue.

SUE
  Bill, I need you, please, why won't you come?

BILL
Why won't I come? Why won't I come? Because... *(he walks over to the others)* I'm... not... I am not coming home tonight.

SUE
Bill! Stop it, this is private–

BILL
It is not private, Sue, nothing we do is private for Christ's sake, you tell your friends everything, they all – know everything – about us, don't they? How many times we had sex in the last month.

LAURA
I don't think that's true, Bill.

GEORGE
I haven't heard anything.

SUE
Bill, I think you're being very unreasonable.

There is an awkward pause in which BILL and SUE lock eyes.

LAURA
(to LILY and GEORGE) Well, it's a lovely night out there. Why don't the three of us go for a walk?

BILL
No.

SUE
You stay and finish up that wonderful looking chocolate paté, Laura, I'm sure you spent a lot of time on it. I'll just get Bill's coat and we'll go on home.

BILL
There is... somebody else, Sue. And I will be going home with her.

GEORGE
I think we've all had a little too much to drink, why don't we just...

SUE
Don't worry guys this isn't real. He's just drunk he's just trying to scare me because we had this argument about the new sofa – Come on honey, let's go home. Who is it. Who is it, Bill? She's not here, is she? You didn't, you didn't bring her to my neighbours', OUR friends' dinner party, to which I was invited. Laura! Laura for God's sake.

LILY
It's me.

SUE laughs.

Why do you think I'm joking?

SUE looks at LILY, then looks at BILL.

Bill??

BILL
This is – Lily.

LILY
How do you do, Susan?

SUE
Don't you call me by my name you FAT!! Please, I don't think you know what you're doing. This is not just me, this is a family, a family, we have two children.

LILY
I'm sorry.

SUE
Bill you are not leaving your children.

BILL
Sue, please.

SUE
YOU TOOK A VOW! In a CHURCH in front of a priest and my mother and your mother and your father and you swore to LOVE and honour and cherish till DEATH US DO PART till DEATH US DO PART BILL, it's your WORD your WORD.

BILL
I am breaking my word.

SUE
No!

BILL
YOU turned your back on me!! You you – look at you in that... sweatsuit thing you're not – I mean look at her, really, you're you're you're a kind of... cartoon now, a... cartoon mum a... with your day-care meetings and neighbourhood fairs, you know what I mean Laura! Your face is a drawing your body, lines. The only time, the only time you are alive, electric again is... when you talk on the phone, to the other mums, there's a flush in your face, excitement, something rushing through your body, you laugh, loudly, you make all those wonderful female noises, you cry, your voice, like... music, or in the park, with Timmy and John, while they cavort with the other children at the drinking fountain,

spraying the water and you talking and talking with all the mothers, storming, storming together your words like crazy swallows, swooping and pivots and… landing… softly on a branch, a husband, one of us husbands walk in and it's like walking into… a large group of…

LILY
You see, I love… his body, Sue. I mean, I really love it. I love to suck it. I love to kiss it his body is my God, okay? His body–

SUE slaps LILY twice.

SUE
YOU… DON'T LIVE ON THIS STREET. You don't belong in this neighbourhood.

LILY contains herself from slapping SUE back.

Where did you meet this… woman? On the street?

BILL starts to try to answer.

In a house of prostitution? I demand to know–

LILY
I fucked him on the telephone, Susan, many many times.

SUE
That is a disgusting… lie.

LILY
Come on Suzy, don't you remember? You caught him a couple of times, on the downstairs phone with his pyjamas around his ankles, he told me!

SUE
(the wind totally out of her) I thought he was making… obscene phone calls.

BILL
Hello.

LILY
Hi there.

BILL
You got back to me quickly.

LILY
Fucking right.

BILL
: Fucking right.

LILY
: Your voice makes me crazy.

BILL
: My voice.

LILY
: I'm wet, Bill, wet just from hearing your voice.

BILL
: What are you wearing?

LILY
: Black silk underwear, red spiked heels, black lace bra.

BILL
: Yeah? And what do you want? What do you want?

LILY
: I want to suck your big cock, Bill, would you like me to do that? Would you like me to suck your big cock?

BILL
: Oh baby, baby.

LILY
: And then I want you to fuck me from behind all night long, can you do that? Can you do that for me, Bill?

BILL
: Yes, yes, oh yes! Yes! Yes!

LILY
: Oh, Bill!

SUE
: BILLLLLLLLLLLLLLLLLLLL!!!!!!! *(she physically attacks LILY)* Aghhhh! Listen, you, if you take my husband away from me and my children I will… kill you, I will I will… come when you are sleeping and I will pull your filthy tongue out of your filthy mouth. And then I will… feed it to our cat.

BILL
: Susan.

SUE
(forced laugh) I didn't mean that, I really didn't. I'm sorry everybody, this is all just so ridiculous and embarrassing and I'm sure we'll all laugh about it someday I KNOW we will, but um… Bill? Won't you just… give me a chance? To show you? That I can? Be sexy? Cause I can, you know, much much more so than THAT creepy shit… don't you remember? Don't you remember before we were married how you loved to watch me dance? Come on, you did! Remember remember that wedding, Kevin and Leslie's? I wore that peach silk that you loved so much that dress drove you crazy! And after after the wedding we were in that room in the Ramada Inn over the water and I danced? You lay on the bed and you just… watched me you loved it I… whooshed whooshed in that dress, back and forth to this thing on the radio back and oooh and back and you were laughing and and *(laughs)* and whoosh.

Music beats louder, filling the room, and SUE begins a slow striptease.

And whoosh… and… close to you, you're hard… and far away and… turn… and whooosh… and… let… my… hair… down… you – love my hair whoosh and… zipppper… whoooo down so slowwwww turn and turn… you watching lying on the bed and ease… off my shoulders you love my shoulders, elegant ohhh Billy, and down. Over my body the soft silky down and whooooooooo-ooooooo whooOOOOOOOO Billy. Take me home, Billy, take me home and let's make mad passionate love! Please.

BILL and LILY leave. GEORGE and LAURA pick up SUE's clothing and bring it to her. LAURA dresses her.

LAURA
Honey, I'm sorry.

SUE
Aghh don't feel sorry for me it's fine, everything will be fine because… his colon cancer's gonna come back, don't you think? Dr. Neville said he had a sixty-forty chance, it will. And she'll drop him, for sure, don't you think? And he will let me nurse him I will… feed him broth, with a spoon, like I did my mum, and I will hold, I will hold his sweet head in my chest till till his lips are black and his eyes… like bright dead stars and he is dead and I will stay I will stay with his body, in the hospital room because I did love that body… oh I did *love – that – body* once.

ISOBEL
Susan, Susan, Susan. The boy with the arrow ha *killed* you, ha? Where's your helper now? Oh Susan, you can't help me now you can't take me home. *(to the audience)* Hey! Who gonna take me home? You? You gotta car? What kinda car you got? Trans-Am? What about bus tickets? You gotta bus tickets? C'mon. Come on. COME ON. SOMEBODY. What I'm sposed to do, ha? Who gonna take me home? Who gonna take me home?

ISOBEL finds a watching place. A few hours later, at LAURA and GEORGE's, LAURA clears the table.

LAURA
Poor Suzy. Poor poor Suzy.

GEORGE
(half asleep) Yeahh. Chee.

LAURA
God, that is the worst thing I have ever seen happen to anybody.

GEORGE and LAURA laugh hysterically and imitate SUE in the previous scene.

GEORGE
Whoosh! That peach silk, oh baby take me home.

LAURA
Take me home, Bill. Let's make mad passionate love. *(stops imitating SUE)* I don't know, I mean I know she needs a friend badly, I am her friend I mean I love her. George, how can you laugh? This is important. If she calls me tomorrow, what should I say? I'm just going to say, I'm going to say, "SUZY? I feel really badly for you and I think you're a wonderful person but you will have to look somewhere else for–"

GEORGE
Nice.

LAURA
GEORGE, you KNOW–

GEORGE
You always say she's your best friend, Laura, "my BEST–"

LAURA
She is! But George, are you forgetting Maria? I had a nervous breakdown because of that woman and her problem how could you FORGET?

GEORGE
I was on the book tour, Loo.

LAURA
I told you about it a hundred times, how could you forget?

GEORGE
I was on the book tour – Loo.

LAURA
George, you are so insensitive, I can't believe this. I told you about it one hundred times. How can you forget?

GEORGE grabs a tablecloth and wraps it around his head, like a shawl, speaking in a Portuguese accent.

GEORGE
How could I forget, how could I forget?

LAURA
George.

GEORGE
Looka this. Me? I donta forget nothing.

LAURA
George I'm going to bed, Molly gets up in two hours and it's always me that gets up with her of course.

She walks around the circle.

GEORGE/MARIA
LAURA.

Now he speaks as MARIA, ISOBEL'S mother. ISOBEL recognizes her.

LAURA
George! Come to bed.

GEORGE/MARIA
LAURA.

LAURA
Maria.

MARIA
I am… so sorry to be coming to your house, maybe you busy, I don't know–

LAURA
No, no, please come in Maria, I'm just – reading the paper the kids are at school and–

MARIA starts shaking violently and keening. She looks like she is in shock.

Maria?… uh… Maria? Are you alright? You look – why don't you sit down. Here. Sit down. Can I get you a drink of water?

MARIA starts to keen with grief, quite quietly.

MARIA
Eeeeeeee

LAURA
Maria? Maria… are you alright? Maria, Maria please tell me… what's…

MARIA
…I think… I think… Antonio–

LAURA
Your husband? Something happened to your husband?

MARIA continues to keen.

It's okay, Maria, you don't have to tell me if you don't–

MARIA
Five o'clock in the morning I cook: smelt and three scramble eggs, nice bread, coffee. For Antony must work long day, construction on highway, long day in the sun, he come from his shower to kitchen, but he don't want. He gotta rat in his stomach that day he say, make a joke, don't want my cooking eat a little bitta bread and just small glass of milk and he go, catch his subway. I fold. I fold clothes one pile for Antony, one pile for me, one for Maria, Romeo, ISOBEL and Luig, my hands fold the clothes but my… *(gesture indicating self or soul)*

LAURA
Sure, you go on automatic – I–

MARIA
Like I fold myself too, and I go in his body, maybe, you know, his… hand to, wipe off his face when he hot and too sweat I am there;

She walks operatically down-stage and delivers the rest of the speech, which should be like an aria.

I am foldin a light sheet of blue then and sudden, I can see through his eye, am at subway, in him, he stands on the platform, is empty, empty and I am his head, circles and circles like red birds flying around and around I am his throat, tight, cannot breathe enough air in my body the floor the floor move, and sink in, rise up rise like a wall like a killin wave turn turn me in circles with teeth in circles and under and over I fall!

ISOBEL falls on an imaginary track in front of her mother.

I fall on the silver track nobody move I hearing the sound. The sound of the rats in the tunnel their breath like a basement these dark rats running running towards me I am stone I am earth cannot scream cannot move the rats tramp… trample my body flat-ten and every bone splinter like…

We hear the sound of a strong wind as the "Sugar Meeting" is being set up on the stage. By the end of the wind, LAURA is at her table, addressing the meeting.

LAURA
Good evening everybody.

GEORGE
Good evening.

RON
Hi Laura.

LAURA
I uh might as well get straight down to business. As head and sole member of the menu research committee, I have spent some three weeks doing... a great deal... of... research, and even a little detective work...

RON and GEORGE are talking to one another.

...and I would like to make my presentation tonight without too much interruption, thank you.

GEORGE
Go for it.

RON
No problem.

LAURA
POINT ONE. Sugar: I strongly recommend that we make a concerted effort to eradicate all sugar from the children's diet. Sugar is an overstimulant, sugar is empty calories, sugar rots...

RON
Uh, I have to say, that, while I agree, sure, too much sugar is not a good thing, that once in a while...

LAURA
Would you let your four-year-old smoke "once in a while?"

A murmur from the crowd.

RON
(with a little laugh) I don't really think you can equate...

ISOBEL rises and walks into the meeting.

LAURA
Sugar is a known carcinogen, Ron, I have a study right here...

JILL
Lettuce is a known carcinogen, for God's sake!

ISOBEL
Hey! Boys! Girls! Looka this! I think tha they can't see me! They no see Isobel! Wha happen? Wha happen?

JILL
Okay as chairperson, I say – let's cut the comments and raise our hands for questions. Laura? You want to go ahead?

LAURA
Yes, thank you, Jill. Uh. *(clears her throat)* It has come to my attention...

GEORGE groans.

Excuse me, I have to ask you why you groaned like that, George, did I say something wrong?

JILL
George, penalty for groaning out of turn, just kidding.

GEORGE
No, no, I'm sorry, I just, I don't know, I just... have a kind of a hard time with "meeting... talk... it has come to my attention."

LAURA
Well, I'm very sorry, George, if you have a better way of–

JILL
That was uncalled for George, really.

RON
George, your mother's calling you.

General laughter.

JILL
Let's let Laura continue please, so we can get out of here...

ISOBEL
I think I invisible!

LAURA
Thank you Jill. I have NOTICED, if you don't like "it has come to my attention," I have noticed that in this nursery school they are… subtly, and I'm sure unwittingly, encouraging an addiction to sugar in our children.

RHONDA
Hey, that's not true.

LAURA
Rhonda, I'm SAYING it's not intentional…

RHONDA
The kids are not…

LAURA
PLEASE LET ME TALK.

JILL
Go ahead, Laura, please.

LAURA
I have noticed that sugar is used as a reward. If you're good we'll make cookies tomorrow. If you tidy up you get chocolate cake as a reward. You are creating… unwittingly, I concede, you are creating TOMORROW'S COKE ADDICTS… TO–

RHONDA
EXCUSE ME I HAVE TO SAY THAT, AS THE CAREGIVER, I RESENT THIS.

LAURA
Rhonda, I'm not accusing just you, I think you are fabulous with the kids, it's our whole society…

RHONDA
I am not creating drug addicts.

JILL
Rhonda, Laura does not mean any of this personally, I think that's…

LAURA
I'm saying it's a small step from sugar addiction to–

RON
Excuse me, I have to say, all food is sugar…

LAURA
REFINED SUGAR IS FAST-ACTING, RON, IT BURDENS THE PANCREAS.

GEORGE
I think you are taking this a little too seriously, Laura, we're just talking about a few cookies now and then for heaven's sake.

LAURA
WE ARE TALKING ABOUT A LIFETIME ADDICTION AND I DON'T THINK IT SHOULD BE TAKEN LIGHTLY.

JILL
Laura, are you willing to listen to a response from Rhonda?

LAURA
Sure.

RHONDA
I would just… like to say that I, also have done… a great deal of studying diet and menu and that, and I fully agree with Laura that sugar is… something to be avoided, IF YOU CAN. Listen, if I'm giving the kids yogurt, they won't eat it without honey they won't, so I figure, a bit of honey is worth getting the yogurt down em…

LAURA
BULLSHIT THAT IS ABSOLUTE UNADULTERATED BULLSHIT.

RHONDA
I beg your pardon, Laura?

LAURA
You don't know what you're saying, Rhonda.

RHONDA
If you don't trust me, Laura…

LAURA
Rhonda…

RHONDA
I do not encourage sugar, I do not hold it up as a reward, ever, I have never done that.

LAURA
You re lying, Rhonda.

RON
WAIT A MINUTE HOLD ON JUST A…

LAURA
SHUT UP RON. LISTEN. LISTEN TO ME RHONDA. I FOUND OUT THAT JUST LAST FRIDAY, LAST FRIDAY, AS A REWARD, YOU TOOK SIX KIDS,

INCLUDING MY TWINS, TO A DONUT SHOP. YOU TOOK THEM TO A DONUT SHOP AND BOUGHT THEM EACH A JELLY DONUT. I think I screamed for five minutes when the twins told me that I just couldn't believe it they started harassing me every five minutes, "Mum, if we're good, can we have a jelly donut?" I don't think they'd ever HEARD OF JELLY DONUTS BEFORE THAT!! I find it unconscionable, UNCONSCIONABLE that a jelly donut would be the sole purpose of an excursion.

RHONDA
Um, I can explain that. It was a Friday, right, and I happen to get severe cramps with my period, right? And I was very sick that day and the kids had bad bad cabin fever, well...

LAURA
(overlapping) And the Friday before that it was popsicles, Rhonda, I'm not blaming you I'm saying you need to be re-educated, we all do, smelling the flowers is a reason to go for a walk, not getting a poisonous body-destroying drug...

RHONDA
LET MEEEEE TALLLLLK. LET ME TALK LET ME TALLLLLLLLLLLK!! I feel... nailed to the wall by you lady, nailed right to the fucking wall. I have to say and something else I have to say is that I think you are... are very... inconsiderate... of feelings! I brought up two kids on what I feed your kids, and they turned out just fine, are you telling me what I feed my kids isn't good enough for your kids? You know the funny thing is, Laura, you may be a bitch on wheels, but lookin at all the rest of you, Laura? at least you're honest you are. Youse others, what you're thinkin is... it really doesn't matter what they get at the day care the real learning is at home, that's where youse teach your kids to become – huh. Here I am saying "youse" I haven't said that since I was a kid! that's how flustered I am – at home you teach your kids... to be... higher kind of people, higher kind of people don't eat Kraft slices and tuna casserole, I've seen that kinda laugh in your voices, all of you, when you say, "Oh, they had *tuna casserole*," I seen, I have seen the roll in your eyes at the grace before meals, or the tidy-up song, or the stars we give out for citizen of the week, you think, oh well the kid is happy, well cared for, we can undo all that and we can make the kids high people like ourselves better people, more better people than the poor little teacher who reads ROMANCE, yes, yes, JILL MATHINS, I saw you showin my book, my novel to RON there and Cathy and havin a big giggle, you think I didn't see that? You think the books you read are deeper more... higher, well it's the same story, don't you see that? What's makin me cry in my book is, when ya come right down to it, is exactly the same thing that's makin you cry in your book, oh yes, oh yes and I'll tell you something, I'll tell all of you I GREW UP ON THAT. I grew up on jelly donuts and butter tarts, and chocolate ice-cream, and I happen to think they're a wonderful thing. I happen to agree with the mice and the cockroaches and the horses and birds that treats are a wonderful thing, you need treats, you need treats in this life, each bit of a treat can wipe out a nasty word, every bite of a jelly donut cleans out your soul it is a gift from GOD, a wonderful gift from GOD and I for one... I for one... I...

for… your eyes, eh? Your eyes are all the same colour and shape like a picture, a… freaky art picture all the same in a row like dark soldiers raisin your…

ISOBEL shoots everybody there except RHONDA with her finger. There are real shot sounds although ISOBEL is imagining this.

ISOBEL
(big laugh, then struts) Rho-HONDA! Bebbe! Beautiful belle! I have killed those dirty bastards, babe, I have killed them dirty dead. I am your harmy, Rhohonda! And you! You gonna take me home!

ISOBEL falls and wraps herself around RHONDA's feet. Music. A restaurant. DAVID takes his place behind the bar, another person is sitting alone at a table. RHONDA and her friend JOANNE meet for drinks. They are laughing. ISOBEL watches.

RHONDA
Oh man is this Singapore Sling fantastic.

JOANNE
My Fuzzy Navel is warm. Hot!

RHONDA
SEND it back! We're paying through the teeth for these drinks. Waiter, take this thing back!

JOANNE
No, I like it this way, honest, Rhonda, I do.

DAVID
Is there a problem with your cocktail?

JOANNE
No no no no please…

DAVID
I could take it back–

JOANNE
No.

RHONDA
Are you sure?

JOANNE
I'm sure.

DAVID
Okaaay.

RHONDA
Ohhh Christ, I'd like to just sit and drink all afternoon to tell you the truth.

JOANNE
I thought you quit heavy drinkin.

RHONDA
I did. I'm just… down in the dumps.

JOANNE
Why, ya on your time?

ISOBEL
Is this my home? This is not my home!

RHONDA
No no no, I get happy then, no, it's just… work.

JOANNE
Yeah, Jeez I'm glad I'm not workin it made me crazy, what's goin on? The kids at the day care gettin to ya?

RHONDA
No no it's not the kids, the kids are great, it's the parents.

JOANNE
Uh oh. That same B-I-T-C-H?

RHONDA
No, she was quite good this time, strangely enough, it's another one.

JOANNE
They all look like bitches to me in their leather pants. Stuck up, puttin their kids in forty-five-dollar shoes, I looked at the price of them REEboks for kids – the other day when I picked you up I saw three of those kids had those shoes on I couldn't believe my eyes.

RHONDA
Yeah, well, they're pretty well-off, but I don't hold that against them, I mean, who wouldn't be if they had the chance, right?

JOANNE
Well that's a good point SO…

RHONDA
We had this meeting, okay?

JOANNE
RHONDA. Excuse me!

RHONDA
  What?

JOANNE
  (intake of breath) …I don't know.

RHONDA
  What do you mean?

JOANNE
  I mean… no, I don't know.

RHONDA
  Joanne.

JOANNE
  I mean… oh God, I wasn't going to tell nobody–

RHONDA
  You're pregnant again?

JOANNE
  No no no no, if only, I…

RHONDA
  JOANNE, I'M YOUR BEST FRIEND.

JOANNE
  YOU'RE MY BEST FRIEND?

RHONDA
  Yes, you know that!

JOANNE
  THEN SWEAR ON YOUR MOTHER'S LIFE.

RHONDA
  What?

JOANNE
  That you will do what I'm gonna ask you.

RHONDA
  Joanne, what is this?

JOANNE
  Just… swear.

RHONDA
I'm not swearing on my mother's life without knowing what it is, she's got enough problems…

JOANNE
Okay, your husband's life.

RHONDA
Okay, I swear on the asshole's life. There. Now what?

JOANNE
You remember… I had this pain in my back?

RHONDA
Yeah, for the last few months, every time ya bend down.

JOANNE
SEARING pain, every time I moved…

RHONDA
…Okay…

JOANNE
Well remember I told you I went to that specialist and he said he was gonna do some tests?

RHONDA
Right, uh-huh.

JOANNE
Well–

RHONDA
You gotta go in and have an operation and you want me to take your kids, no problem of COURSE I'll take them Jo, for God's–

JOANNE
(overlapping) No. No, I mean, you might have to take the kids but that's only… part of it.

RHONDA
Joanne, I really don't like guessing games.

JOANNE
Shadows… that's what they call them, and… it is… the very worst thing it could be, and the… kind, the kind is of the bone.

RHONDA
Oh boy.

JOANNE
Yeah.

RHONDA
(whispers) Jo...

JOANNE
Don't... don't touch me. I'll go hysterical please.

RHONDA
YOU... want a cigarette?

JOANNE
Yeah.

RHONDA lights one and gives it to her.

Ya know, I have to go to the bathroom, like, real bad but I'm not gonna go, ya know why? Cause every time... I sit down to pee I feel my whole life drainin out of me, just draining out with the pee, goin... outa me, into the water down in the pipes, and under the... friggin... GROUND. That's where I'll be, Rho, that's where I'm gonna... *(fights to regain her composure)* I'll come home with the groceries? Like after dark? and I'll see Frank and the kids through the window, in the livin-room, right? Watchin TV, or drawing on paper, cuttin out stuff, whatever, and I'll stand on the porch and watch em, just... playing... on the floor, and I think... that's life, that's life goin on without me, it'll be just like that, only I won't be here with the groceries, I'll be under the ground under the ground with my flesh fallin off a my face and I just can't take it. You know in that picture? That picture I had in my bedroom growing up?

RHONDA
UHH–

JOANNE
My aunt and uncle sent me that from England, the poster it's OPHELIA, from this play by Shakespeare, right? And she she – got all these flowers, tropical flowers, wild flowers, white roses, violets and buttercups, everything she loved and she kinda weaved them all together. Then she got the heaviest dress she could find... you know how dresses in the olden days were so long and heavy, with petticoats and that? And she got this heavy heavy blue dress, real... blue and then she wrapped all these pretty pretty flowers round and round her body, round her head, and her hair, she had this golden, wavy hair, long, and then she steps down the bank, and she lies, on her back, in the stream. She lies there, but the stream runs so fast she's on her back and she goes. It pulls her along so fast and she's lookin at the sky and the clouds, and she's singing little songs "I'm lookin over a four-leaf clover" – and being pulled so fast by a clear cold water pulled along and she's not scared, she's not scared at all, she's calm, so happy! And just ever so slowly her dress, gets heavier, right? Then, then, she gets caught on a stick, like a branch, of a willow tree, and her dress pulls her down, soft,

she's still singin down deep deep deep to the bottom of the stream and with all
these "fantastic garlands," these beautiful flowers all around her – "one's for the
roses that blew down the lane" – she dies, Rhon, she dies… good. She dies good.

RHONDA
That's… something.

JOANNE
I want to die like that. But… I don't… want to do it all alone, I mean, I want
you to help me, with the flowers, and with the dress, and my hair, I want you to
make sure the willow branch is there, and the stream is right, and maybe…
maybe that… Frank… sees I… wouldn't mind him seein… me in that stream,
with the flowers, and the heavy blue dress… I wouldn't mind if you took maybe
some pictures of me like that and then you could have them printed and given
out at the funeral, something like that… just, you know, two by four, colour,
whatever, it's the one thing that would make it alright – it's the one thing…

RHONDA
I just… I don't know, Jo, you know I'd do anything to make it alright…

JOANNE
Well this is what I want, Rhonda, it's really really really what I want. Are you
going to help me?

RHONDA
I uh – think you need to see a counsellor, Jo, you know they have counsellors
that… specialize in these… situations I'm surprised your doctor didn't…

JOANNE
You think I'm crazy.

RHONDA
No no, Joanne, I just think that… your situation is so hard that you are not
quite yourself, I mean this is not… you, the Joanne I know is practical she…
you should believe in the treatments, Jo, they do work sometimes, they really
do, and the Joanne I know would never ask a friend to help… her… is one of
the most thoughtful people that I know, of other people and how the hell, how
the hell do you think that I could live with that after, eh? I mean it's all very
lovely and that, your picture, in your room but that's a picture, that's a picture,
you dimwit! The real of it would be awful, the stalks of the flowers would be
chokin you, and the smells of them would make you sick, all those smells comin
at you when you're feelin so sick to begin with, and the stream, well if you're
talking about the Humber River or any stream in this country you're talkin
filth, in the Humber River you're even talkin sewage, Jo, you're talkin cigarette
packages and used condoms and old tampons floating by you're talking freezin,
you'd start shakin from head to toe you're talkin rocks gashin your head you're
talkin a bunch of longhairs and goofs on the banks yellin at you callin you
whorebag sayin what they'd like to do to you, you're talkin… and where would
you get a dress like that, eh? You'd never find the one in the picture, Jo, it'd be

too tight at the neck and the waist, it'd be a kind of material that itches your skin, even worse wet, drives you nut-crazy, the blue would be off, wouldn't look right your shoes wouldn't match you could never find the same colour, Joanne. You can't become a picture, do you know what I mean? I mean you can't… BE… a picture, okay?

They freeze. ISOBEL runs from her watching place, around the circle screaming; she has realized, listening to JOANNE, that she is not lost, but dead, murdered seventeen years before.

ISOBEL

AAHHHHHHHHHHH!! I am dead! I have been bones for seventeen years, missing, missing, my face in the TV and newspapers, posters, everybody lookin for, nobody find, I am gone, I am dead, I AM DEADLY DEAD! Down! It was night, was a lion, roar!! With red eyes: he come closer *(silent scream)* come closer *(silent scream)* ROAR tear my throat out ROAR tear my eyes out… ROAR I am kill! I am kill! I am no more!

Music.

(to JOANNE) We are both pictures now. WHO WILL TAKE US? WHO WILL TAKE US TO HEAVEN, HA?

Lights down. Cathedral bells ring. DAVID is outside, walking down the street.

DAVID
God, that customer dying of bone cancer. I didn't even want to touch her glass. I don't know she had that look, that dead look. I mean I almost felt hostile.

ISOBEL
(inside the cathedral) I WANT TO GO TO HEAVEN NOW!

She sees a life-size statue of the Virgin Mary and approaches it.

Holy Mary Mother of God. Will you take Isobel to heaven now, please?

She lies at the base of the statue, her hand touching the statue's foot.

DAVID
God that cathedral is beautiful, funny, I've passed it every day on my way out from work and I've never really looked at it. Look at the stonework, those spires–

He opens the church doors and enters. The doors slam behind him.

Oh I love this it's so… the air is s … holy it IS, look at those bird-bath things full of holy water, I love it it's so primitive. *(He splashes some on his face.)* In the name of the Father… the Son, and the Holy–

FATHER HAYES
Good evening.

DAVID shrieks, startled. His shriek echoes.

It's alright, it's alright. Have you come for…

DAVID
Confession. I've come for confession, 8:30, yes? I'm not too late, am I, see, I just finished work, and…

FATHER HAYES
Not too late, of course not.

FATHER HAYES goes into his part of the confessional.

DAVID
(to himself) I guess just – God I don't remember a THING about what to do!!

We hear the wooden barrier being opened, and the priest begins the Latin prayer.

FATHER HAYES
In the name of the Father, and the Son, and the Holy Spirit.

DAVID
(overlapping) Oh God he's saying something–

FATHER HAYES
May the Lord be in your heart and help you to confess your sins with true sorrow. Let us listen to the Lord as he speaks to us: I will give them a new heart and put a new spirit within them; I will remove the strong heart from their bodies and replace it with a natural heart, so that they will live according to my statutes, and observe and carry out my ordinances; thus they shall be my people and I will be their God.

DAVID
(overlapping) I think it's Latin, isn't that against Papal Law? I should report him to the Vatican and have him defrocked here goes nothing–

FATHER HAYES finishes the prayer.

AHH – FORGIVE ME FATHER FOR I have sinned. It has been… four weeks since my last confession. These are my sins?… OKAY, told Barb I'd be there last night for dinner with her and the niece and nephew – didn't show up didn't phone nothing, was in a mad PASH with my hockey player. I was very cruel to Daniel Thursday, saw him at Billy's – the club? And I don't know, the way he was looking at me drove me CRAZY CRAZY he was mooning! Well I walked up to him and told him to "quit mooning I'd rather see your hairy ass than that pathetic face, face it!" I said, "Face it you old fag, you have been dumped, DUMPED!" That was really mean, that's gotta be more than a venial sin, AND THEN, then, yesterday, I walked through a park? And I saw a large group of poor children playing, and I just thought they were trouble; I wondered why God had put them in the world, really, isn't that unkind? THEN today I saw a fat lady eating an ice-cream cone and I said, I think quite audibly I said "disgusting" oh AND I did not stand up in the subway the incredibly packed subway, for a hugely pregnant lady and her kid, I just didn't feel like it. Quite the catalogue, eh? Oh and another thing, I've lied to you already. I haven't been to confession in fifteen years, haven't stepped in a church in fifteen years, just... did it on a whim, don't ask me why I was passing by on my way...

FATHER HAYES
AND you felt the hand of GOD?

DAVID
Well... it was just a whim – really...

FATHER HAYES
David.

DAVID
How do you know my name?

FATHER HAYES
David I know your name better than I know my own.

DAVID
Wait a minute, wait a minute, I think maybe this is some odd coincidence because although my name is DAVID, I don't actually know you at all, so...

FATHER HAYES
There's nothing odd about it, David, you were an altar boy for me, two years, for two years you served, in 1957 and 1958 at St. Bernard's in Moncton, New Brunswick. Remember?

DAVID
Moncton? We were around there for a couple of years–

FATHER HAYES
You were a believer, David, the other boys were just forced into it by their parents, you believed in every statue every–

DAVID
Father Hayes? You – are Father Hayes?

FATHER HAYES
I am.

DAVID
You're still alive?

FATHER HAYES
I think.

DAVID
But you were so old even way back then!

FATHER HAYES
Not really.

DAVID
I remember you now. I remember you did look old, because you stooped, and you had white hair already didn't you?

FATHER HAYES
Indeed, I was prematurely white...

DAVID
White hair and... and... red eyes.

FATHER HAYES
I... suffered from allergies, hay fever. I'm sorry if it frightened you.

DAVID
I guess maybe it did frighten me a bit, Father, but you know how young boys are–

FATHER HAYES
I am sorry, but, but...

DAVID
No no, I... look, I uh–

FATHER HAYES
David, I want...

DAVID
...don't mean to be impolite but I'd like you to be honest with me, sort of man to man I... I always got the impression that you were looking at me much more than you looked at the other boys am I right?

FATHER HAYES
Well...

DAVID
I felt... I felt as though your eyes were devouring me.

FATHER HAYES
 No, no, no…

DAVID
 No?? I'm gay, Father, you can be honest with me. I'll forgive you, I mean you never actually did anything, you never even touched me, you just… looked. You kept looking at me – tell me, tell me the truth.

FATHER HAYES
 It was not what you think, no, no please–

DAVID
 Confess to me Father, come on, come on…

FATHER HAYES
 I make my confessions on a regular…

DAVID
 Have you confessed this sin?

FATHER HAYES
 No, no I haven't, but–

DAVID
 God loves sinners who confess, Father, you taught me that, as long as you speak up and you're sorry as hell, you're okay, you still got your ticket to heaven, but you won't you won't Father, if you don't tell me, you'll wither in LIMBO! I suffered, I need you to tell me! CONFESS…

FATHER HAYES
 I'm due to a christening. I have to shave first, there's a big party, I–

DAVID
 You would christen a baby with this sin, bobbing on the surface, bobbing? Confess, you son of a bitch. Con–

FATHER HAYES
 Forgive me Father for I have sinned.

DAVID
 Alright.

FATHER HAYES
 I looked at you, David, because… I… because… I wanted… to… remember… you.

DAVID
 Remember me?

FATHER HAYES
Because… of what was to happen, in the water: oh OH when the day arrived, when the picnic came round, in July, that Canada Day picnic? I had a bad feeling, I had… a very bad feeling indeed. We all piled out of the cars: families, priests, nuns, altar boys, piled out and lugged all those picnic baskets to tables under trees. The grownups all fussed with food and drink while the kids, all of you children, ran ran in your white bare feet to the water, throwing stones and balls, and a warning sound a terrible, the sound of deep nausea filled my ears and I looked up and saw you, dancing on the water, and I saw a red circle, a red, almost electric circle, dazzling round and round like waves, spinning round your head and body. I thought watch, watch that boy, on this day he will surely drown, he *will*. David, *I knew that you would die*. And all because of the chicken. The twenty-nine-pound chicken brought there by Mrs. Henry grown on her brother's farm, everyone had talked and talked about that chicken, who would carve that chicken, Mrs. Henry took it out you skipped along the shore, she laid it on the table, "FATHER HAYES, YOU GO AHEAD AND CARVE, AND DON'T MAKE A MESS OF IT OR YOU WON'T SEE ME AT MASS NEXT SUNDAY." Everyone laughed laughed the men, the men drinking beer, watching me, sure they're thinking, "Watch him carve like a woman," most men hate priests, you know this is a fact, I could see them thinking cruel thoughts under hooded eyes and practised grins; my sin was the sin of pride! The sin of pride David, I started to carve, didn't want to look up, lest I wreck the bird. You see at that moment that chicken was worth more, indeed worth more… than your LIFE, David I SHUT OUT the warning voice and I – carved. I carved and carved and ran into trouble, real trouble I remember thinking, "Damn how does any person do it, it's a terrible job," people behave as if it's nothing, but it's terrible, I kept at it, I wouldn't give up, I wouldn't look up till I'd finished, and I finished carving, and I had made a massacre. The men turned away the women… murmured comfort, and before I looked up I had a hope, a hard hope, that you were still skipping on the rocks and shouting insults to your pals all hands reached for chicken and bread, potato salad, chocolate cake I looked I looked up and your hand from the sea, your hand, far away, was reaching, reaching for me far away… oh no! I ran, and tripped, fell on my face ran again, I could not speak ran to the water and shouted as loud as I could but my voice was so tiny; I saw your hand, ran to the fisherman close, he wasn't home his fat daughter and I, in the skiff, not enough wind no wind, paddling paddling, you a small spot nothing then nothing the sun burns our faces our red red faces.

DAVID
And I… was… never found?

FATHER HAYES
And now… you have come!! You have finally come!!

DAVID
And what have I come for?

FATHER HAYES is sleeping.

DAVID
    Uh… Father? Uh – listen… I'm sorry. I'm sorry but I never died. You got the wrong guy I knew you… some other time – I mean, shit, I wish I had died, I only wish, it would have made my life so much more interesting… I grew up, I grew up. Listen if I had drowned in the sea, in Moncton, New Brunswick a beautiful perfect young boy, if I was… pulled by the sea if I reached and was lost, and all those people felt this loss, a loss all their lives, mother father brothers and sister friends a dark ache, somewhere in their chest for what could have been, they could all imagine, you see, what could have been Father Father? I forgive you, I forgive you Father, it was nice on the water, you know? It was neat, so calm, as I slipped underneath I wasn't scared, I'll tell ya. I wasn't scared a bit. The water was so… nice!!

    Music. ISOBEL dances joined by the cast one by one until they are all dancing fully. Cast dance off one by one leaving ISOBEL, who freezes. Blackout.

ACT TWO

Sounds of kids playing in a park, a group of mothers chat. ISOBEL watches.

CHRISTINE
How's your pregnancy going, dear?

Lion roar.

ISOBEL
I hear the LION, I hear the Lion ROAR!!

ELLEN
Wonderful! I finally feel… good for something. LEO, SHARE IT. Share it please.

CHRISTINE
Not me NOT me when I was pregnant I felt as useful as a cow. A large, stupid…

ELLEN
Christine!!

CHRISTINE
EMMA! Five more minutes honey! Mummy's got to go to work! Well, considering I despised the man whose child I was carrying–

ELLEN
I suppose that would… alter things – GOOD CATCH, Leo!

SUE
Hi guys. Timmy, just five minutes. Remember, your father's coming to get you at five.

CHRISTINE
Sue, I love that blouse! Really suits you!

ELLEN
Gorgeous!

SUE
Thank you, I'm organizing a bake sale, if you can believe it, for the community centre over on Ash Street. PLEASE say you'll bake, or sell tickets, even a promise to buy–

ISOBEL
I must tell these peoples, I must tell them now!

ELLEN
Forget me, I'm a diabetic! I can't even look at the stuff.

SUE
Tim! Why don't you try the swing? You love swings.

CHRISTINE
Okay, put me down for fudge brownies, if my kids don't eat them first.

GEORGE enters with a kid's bicycle.

George! How's the book going?

GEORGE
Well, well, very well indeed!! And how's the busiest freelancer in town? Bradley, don't push so hard!

CHRISTINE
Overworked and underpaid.

GEORGE
What else is new?

RON enters.

Ron! Why aren't you at your office?

ELLEN
We're telling!

GEORGE
Good. Bradley!

SUE
Tim? Why don't you try the swing?

CHRISTINE
RON did you get my note? EMMA PUT IT BACK!

RON
Yes, I did, I – I – I–

ISOBEL
(hitting them) Shut up Boy! Shut up Girl! I say I say it's time!! He's in the streets get them out he's in the streets save your children take their hand take their leg.

SUE
Isobel! I saw this girl before, she–

ISOBEL
I say shut up! I say LISTEN TO ME NOW! Can you no hear? Listen! Can you nooo–

All freeze except SUE, who crosses slowly towards the children.

SUE
Timmy?

ISOBEL
(goes to her) The lion is here, in your streets. He is trying to kill you, to kill all of your children. He really really is.

She picks up a great crooked stick which she will carry until she says "I love you" to BEN in the final scene.

Watch me! *(laughs)* I am your HARMY! *(laughs)* I am your SAINT! I am your HARMY! Watch me, watch me, *(a war cry)* I WILL KILL THE LION NOW!!

Thunderstorm as SUE shouts "TIMMMYY!!" and the others ad lib to their children, e.g., "Quick, you don't want to get wet!" All exit. A kid's bike is left on stage. Blackout. Lights up on CHRISTINE walking towards SCARLETT'S basement apartment, "tracked" by ISOBEL.

ISOBEL
This girl, Christine, Christine, this girl, SHE will take me to the lion, yes, for she… she is very hard. Harrrrd. HARRRRRRRD!!

CHRISTINE
116 Carlisle. Lord what a stench. What could that be? *(knocks)*

SCARLETT
Come in!

CHRISTINE
Scarlett Deer?

SCARLETT
That's my name, don't wear it out, has to last a lifetime!!

CHRISTINE
I'm Christine Pierce from the *Telegraph*. We talked on the phone.

SCARLETT
Have a seat.

CHRISTINE
Thank you. Nice place.

SCARLETT
What, this hole? Sorry if it stinks, I cooked chicken today an ever since I ate it I been fartin up a storm. Dead chicken farts, that's what my brother always said.

CHRISTINE
Scarlett, I don't have a lot of time, so is it all right if I ask you some questions?

SCARLETT
Sure, How does it feel to be an ugly geek? Fine thank you, fuck you very much.

CHRISTINE
Scarlett, advanced cerebral palsy is a serious handicap. Don't you feel that living on your own is dangerous?

SCARLETT
Would you like to live in a freakhouse?

CHRISTINE
Well, Scarlett, I–

SCARLETT
Freedom, freedom girl, I'd rather fuckin rot on the floor of my own home than be well-fed and cared for in a freakhouse.

CHRISTINE
What you're saying, then, is that above all things, you cherish freedom. That you would rather risk–

SCARLETT
Once when my volunteers were sick? All of em were sick, right? And I just wanted to see what the hell I would do? I lay in my own shit and piss for three days.

CHRISTINE
Good Lord, what–

SCARLETT
I coulda phoned somebody, my parents live down the street, but I just wanted to see… I wanted to see how long I'd survive, I wanted to see if I could do it.

CHRISTINE
Well, who did you eventually–

SCARLETT
My mother, my poor mother. And it makes me sick, sick, because what will I do when they die? They're old you know, they're gonna die soon.

CHRISTINE
What will you do?

SCARLETT
I'll die on the floor in my shit and piss.

CHRISTINE
    Scarlett, do you have any hobbies; that is, what do you do between volunteers, do you have favourite soap operas or game shows, or–

SCARLETT
    I screw my brains out.

CHRISTINE
    (a weak laugh) No, seriously, Scarlett.

SCARLETT
    You think I'm kiddin? You think I sit around and watch game shows and uh stare out the window waitin for the next volunteer? No way, girlie, I git it ONNN.

CHRISTINE
    You're... sexually active, then?

SCARLETT
    Shocked, aren't you, pretty pea?

CHRISTINE
    No.

SCARLETT
    YOU ARE TOO YOU LYING BITCH!!

CHRISTINE
    Alright, I will admit, I am... surprised. I suppose the public perception of handicapped people is somewhat – skewered.

SCARLETT
    You think you're bettern me, dontcha?

CHRISTINE
    Oh Scarlett, really I...

SCARLETT
    Well I'll tell you somethin, Christine, my boyfriend wouldn't rub your tittie. And you think he's handicapped? No way, babe, I'm not fucking a freak.

CHRISTINE
    Well, I'm very happy for you, really Scarlett.

SCARLETT
    Bullshit, you think it's sick.

CHRISTINE
No, honestly Scarlett, I don't! I think everybody deserves to have a happy sex life.

SCARLETT
Yeah? Wanna hear more?

CHRISTINE
Sure!

SCARLETT
But don't print this part in your article, right, just the crap about how noble I am copin on my own and that shit, and how good the United Church is helpin me out, all that shit right?

CHRISTINE
Scarlett, I won't print anything that you don't want me to. I despise journalists that do that kind of thing. I want you to think of me as a friend. Maybe we could even go out sometime, catch a movie, or go to dinner…

SCARLETT
Sure, if you like.

CHRISTINE
So! How did it all start with your boyfriend?

SCARLETT
It all started one night, I'd just been watching TV for sixteen hours straight, from eight in the morning, right? And that's hard on the eyes, I was bone tired. So I go to bed, I look out the window and there's no moon, right? And I lie there for hours, can't sleep, itchy, bored, just wishin I was dead, as usual, when I hear, my door open.

CHRISTINE
Were you frightened?

SCARLETT
I couldnta cared. I thought it was, you know, a guy with a knife, come to carve me up. I thought good, great, what a way to go. I laughed thinkin a Monica, she's my morning volunteer, thinkin a her comin in findin me dead – so I wait to be cut, but I don't hear nothin, nothin, I figure he's in his socks, not a sound then… he sits on the edge of my bed, and and and, and then he start… he start… he start… touchin my foot just touchin my foot so soft, and nice, and I… laugh. I laugh and laugh, and Christine, I don't think I ever laughed so long and so long in my life.

CHRISTINE
Who was it?

SCARLETT
That's the question, isn't it Chris? Who the hell is it?

CHRISTINE
Did he… ever come again?

SCARLETT
He come every time there isn't no moon, in like a big cat sit on the bed, and me, like a big piece of fruit,

Dance music starts. SCARLETT gets up.

explodin in the heat, exploding up and out the whole night, I can MOVE when my boy comes, *(she twirls)* I am movin, I know I am, I am turnin and swishin and holdin,

A MAN enters. He and SCARLETT dance romantically around the set. He leaves her back in her chair, immobile, and exits.

like eels, you ever seen eels? Lamprey eels, brilliant light moving fast fast they swim from the Saint John River down to Montego Bay to spurt their young, I swim like that coloured-up, bright and fast when my boy comes, swirlin and movin in the dark no moon…

CHRISTINE
Hey, is he handsome?

SCARLETT
I tole you there's no moon.

CHRISTINE
You mean you haven't–

SCARLETT
He's my midnight man, you dick! My midnight man he is my midnight man, get it? You can't SEE night, you can't SEE when there's no moon why? Why do you think it's so big to see your boyfriend two eyes, nose, a mouth, what the diff, what the hell is the–

CHRISTINE
I must go, I… have an appointment.

SCARLETT
You're not gonna print that.

CHRISTINE
I have a job, Scarlett, I have a child to support…

SCARLETT
I'll slit your throat if ya print that.

CHRISTINE
Goodbye.

SCARLETT grabs CHRISTINE's clothing.

SCARLETT
PLEASE!! PLEASE!! Please, Christine, my old lady and old man, they're old, my mum's had a stroke, my dad's got MS, this'd kill em, please!!

CHRISTINE
That is not my business, Scarlett, Scarlett, let go of me, LET GO!

SCARLETT
Reverend Pete and everybody down the church, they'd think I was a slut, they'd send me to the freakhouse.

They struggle.

CHRISTINE
Let me go!!

SCARLETT falls on top of CHRISTINE.

SCARLETT
You're gonna kill me, you're gonna kill me.

CHRISTINE rolls her off and onto the floor.

CHRISTINE
You are trying to obstruct the freedom of the press, lady.

SCARLETT
You can't do this you can't do this!

CHRISTINE
(frees herself and gets away) I'm sorry. I'm doing it.

SCARLETT
I'll see you in hell!!

This stops CHRISTINE.

CHRISTINE
What?

SCARLETT
I said you'll go right to hell for this!!

CHRISTINE
I don't believe in hell.

SCARLETT
Joke's on you, girl, cause I'm in it, right now, live from hell, and if you do this, you're gonna be burning here with me, maybe not today, maybe not tomorrow but soon, soon, you'll be whizzing down the highway with a large group of handsome friends to some ski resort or other, and your male driver will decide to pass on the right, you will turn over and over, knocking into each other's skulls breaking each other's necks like eggs in a bag, falling through windshields it's gonna rain blood and I will open my big jaws and swallow youuuu! YOU will spend the rest of eternity inside me. Inside my… body and ooooh time goes slowwwww…

CHRISTINE
You're crazy.

SCARLETT
I am waiting for you Chrissy, I'm waiting for you Chrissy, I am waiting for you Chrissy, I am…

CHRISTINE
STOP THAT. Stop that craziness NOW there is no such thing, there is no such thing as any of that ANY of it. You live and you die in your own body and you go up to heaven or just nowhere.

SCARLETT
Into the middle of Scarlett…

CHRISTINE
You don't know ANYTHING.

SCARLETT
Inside my big wet behind…

CHRISTINE
Stop it. Stop saying those things.

SCARLETT
In the bummy of a big dead fish…

CHRISTINE
Stop it, I said stop it now.

SCARLETT
Your left arm and your head too, Chrissy, gonna be severed you'll be all over the highway and your mean little soul will…

CHRISTINE
(*beats SCARLETT to the ground, screaming*) STOP IT! STOP IT! (*kicking her*) STOP IT! STOP IT! (*CHRISTINE collapses*)

SCARLETT breathes with difficulty.

Oh no. Oh no. Scarlett, are you okay? You're okay. You're okay. Your mother will be by soon or a volunteer and, and I'll call, I, I, I'll call an ambulance. You shouldn't have made me do that, Scarlett. You shouldn't have made me kick you like that. The way you, you, you talked to me like that. Like, like, like you belong. In the world. As if you belong. Where did you get that feeling? I want it. I need it. (*pause, about to exit*) I need it.

SCARLETT
OOOOOOH! Come down and kiss me, put your tongue in my mouth!! Come on, NOW, RIGHT now, there's no one around, right now, on the ground, do me, kiss me, come down and kiss me, like a lion, so hot right here right now, swirl, swirl me twirl, twirl me, make me light, light exploding into… (*laughs*)

CHRISTINE returns, swooping down like a condor, gives SCARLETT the kiss of death. SCARLETT, thinking it is her lover, responds passionately and then, without air, dies.

ISOBEL
(*to CHRISTINE, touching her*) SLAVE! You are a slave of the lion! You lie with him you laugh you let him bite your neck, you spread your legs. You will take me to him now.

Music, blackout. Lights up on CHRISTINE's office. She is moving things in an angry way.

ISOBEL
Shhh. I wait for the lion!!

RODNEY, an early-middle-aged man with a stoop, CHRISTINE's research assistant, comes in and waits until she addresses him. He has an armload of papers.

CHRISTINE
Yes, Rodney, what is it?

RODNEY
I've… uh… brought the research material you asked for.

CHRISTINE
Good. Great. Thank you… how was your weekend?

RODNEY
Quiet.

CHRISTINE
Rodney. Rodney – Rodney I told you I wanted stats on CP, cerebral palsy, not just "handicapped people." I wanted information on cerebral palsy!

RODNEY
You did NOT specify cerebral palsy, Christine.

CHRISTINE
Oh yes I most certainly did, I said–

RODNEY
I have it on tape, Christine!

CHRISTINE
Rodney! Are you or are you not a professional researcher?

RODNEY
Yes.

CHRISTINE
Well then start doing professional work! NOW! Or you are out. Is that understood? IS THAT UNDERSTOOD?

RODNEY
…of… course…

CHRISTINE exits. RODNEY is at his desk.

You will NOT EVER SPEAK TO ME THAT WAY AGAIN CHRISTINE YOU WILL NOT TREAT ME AS AN OBJECT DO YOU UNDERSTAND? Is that understood? IS THAT UNDERSTOOD??

Knock on the door.

Yes? Hello. May I help you?

MICHAEL
Yes, I'm looking for a Rodney LeHavre – I was directed to this office.

RODNEY
I… am… Mr. LeHavre.

MICHAEL
Rodney?

RODNEY
Do I know you?

MICHAEL
Michael… Lind… from St. George's, '60 to '64. How are you? You remember me, don't you?

RODNEY
Michael… Lind? No. No, I'm afraid I don't, I'm sorry. Were you in my class?

MICHAEL
Yeah, yeah, we were good friends for a while even; don't you remember? Come on. We played chess. You were a great player. You taught me… how to play. You must remember.

RODNEY
Chess.

MICHAEL
I guess you don't remember. I'm sorry. I was sure that you'd remember. I… I… *(backing out)*

RODNEY
Would you like to come in and sit down? I can take ten minutes I think. Would you like to sit down?

MICHAEL
Oh, oh, okay, if you don't mind…

RODNEY
No. A cup of coffee… I could – get the secretary Sherry – to–

MICHAEL
(laughs) You've got to remember the fly collection. It was really hot. July, I think. We caught it must have been fifty house flies, and, and we stuck them with Elmer's glue, to a piece of Bristol board. To a big piece of Bristol board. And labelled them in Latin. Don't you remember? You must remember.

RODNEY
Wait a minute… wait a minute… yeah, yeah, and we even named them, didn't we? Didn't we name each one?

MICHAEL
Yeah, yeah… I'll never forget. You even named one Clarence. I thought it was brilliant.

RODNEY
Right! And yours were all names like Fred, Joe, Cindy, weren't they? Right!

MICHAEL
And yours were all royalty – Elizabeth, Margaret, Clarence. God!

RODNEY
God. A fly collection. So what did we *do* with it?

MICHAEL
I think... we had it arranged... to show someone. A colleague of my father's. Someone in insect...

RODNEY
Entomology.

MICHAEL
Yeah, that's it. And it was raining or something...

RODNEY
Pouring, yes, pouring, and all the flies–

RODNEY & MICHAEL
–FELL OFF THE BRISTOL BOARD!

RODNEY
God. Michael Lind. Michael LIND! I'm sorry.

CHRISTINE
(off) Rodney I need that material as SOON as possible, please!

MICHAEL
Well I see that you have to get back to work, I'd better go... ahhh... just before I go, there's one thing. I uh... this is going to sound strange, but... I've been having... sort of... dreams... about... back then, I... have them a lot–

RODNEY
Oh?

MICHAEL
Yes, only... I always wake up at the same spot, fairly distressed, actually, and... I just... wondered... if you could... help me... remember... what actually happened. Back then... when we were... kids. Do you think you could–

RODNEY
Sure, I could try...

MICHAEL
Okay, let's start at the beginning. It was something to do with chess.

RODNEY
Chess.

MICHAEL
You loved to play chess you… brought me to your house after school, it was a Tuesday, I think, cold, we went through a short cut it said "Pedestrians Only" I thought it said "Protestants Only" and I was terrified.

RODNEY laughs.

And we went to your room, with all the paper airplanes hanging from the ceiling all over the room! And we lay on the floor. Do you remember? You remember lying on the floor? Rodney, your carpet. Your carpet was brown and orange, sort of circles or something. There was the sound of a snowblower outside. My queen. You took my queen. And then, and then, Rodney, didn't we laugh, or or or or… some touch some touch Rodney and you made a strange sound. What was that sound. Please help me! I need to go back there. I need to go back there, you see? You were the only – friend that I – we saw the world the same way. Remember? We saw the world the same way. I want to go back there. *(caresses his shoulder)* I want to go back there…

RODNEY
I want to go back there, too. I want to go back there, too.

MICHAEL and RODNEY embrace. RODNEY makes the sound. MICHAEL pulls him back and throws him to the ground.

MICHAEL
QUEER!! Queer queer queer queer queer queer QUEER! FAIRY SISSY LITTLE CREEP!! DON'T YOU EVER ever remember again. YOU have WRECKED my life, your slimy memory, using me over and over and over again like an old porno magazine you will RELINQUISH that memory you will wipe it OUT, YOU understand?

RODNEY
You're crazy, you need psychiatric…

MICHAEL
You will NOT remember me again because if you do, if you do, I will feel it, oh yes, and I will come and I will kill you. I could feel you remembering, almost daily, I would be in the middle, the middle of a crucial business meeting all the way in Vancouver and suddenly I would feel you… holding my memory, turning it over and over, folding it, caressing it, reliving it, SPEWING, spewing your filth all over me. How how I always wondered how could you do it in the middle of the day? Did you do it here, at work, at this desk is this where you–

RODNEY
Anywhere I can, Michael. You see, my life has been terribly disappointing.

MICHAEL
You will... free me–

RODNEY
Of course. I'll try, but memory... does seem to have a will of its own, I can't really help what–

MICHAEL hits him, they fight, rolling and punching, and end up on the floor. Very, very slowly MICHAEL raises his head, extends his tongue, RODNEY does the same. They come together and their tongues touch. It is an ecstatic moment for both of them. MICHAEL pulls out a knife, RODNEY takes it from him and cuts his throat. MICHAEL dies. Music. The actor playing MICHAEL gets up and exits. ISOBEL goes to RODNEY and touches him, then RODNEY gets up and straightens himself.

RODNEY
"Hello, welcome to St. George's. My name is Rodney LeHavre, grade seven, and you're...? Michael Lind! Welcome! You just came from Vancouver? I have a cousin there! Do you play chess?" Chess, every day... chess, Monday, Tuesday, Wednesday, Thursday, chess, with... Michael... at school, at my house at his house in his room, lying on our stomachs staring at the chess board, he sticks his tongue out at me because he had just captured my queen and then I stuck my tongue out back at him and he moved forward just a bit till his tongue was touching mine, and my whole life jumped into my tongue we didn't move just lay there touching tongues, "Would you boys like some tuna sandwiches?" his mother the best mother in the world with her red bangles and bourbon sour at six, "Okay Mrs. Lind, thanks!" And we had a secret, an atomic secret nobody else in the whole entire world knew that we had touched tongues oh OH wrote his name, MICHAEL, over and over one thousand times one thousand times; on the fifth day, the fifth day after, I'm at the blackboard doing math, very good at math, superb mind for mathematics the other boys jealous, always been jealous of my superior brain throwing spitballs, used to that, yelling "Froggy, froggy frog" because of my francophone name, used to that, I turn, I catch his face white darkened so quickly like a sky, he caught, he knew, suddenly he knew, Michael, that he had been playing chess with the loser "FROGGY, HEY FROGGY" they scream "HEY FROG." He stands up! They look expectantly, is the new kid going to defend his friend? What's he going to say, I to myself, "Oh thank you, Michael, thank you thank you the first to ever defend me oh what what are you going to say to defend me?" He takes a breath, I'm holding mine, he smiles he speaks he says: "Is he a frog... OR A TOAD!!" They laugh and laugh and laugh screaming their laughter slapping their desks shaking their fists triumphing a new member of the PACK!! Is he a frog, or a toad – Am I a frog or am I a toad?

SHERRY enters.

SHERRY
RODDEE! RODDEEE!! Baby Bunny.

ISOBEL
   She!

SHERRY
   You'll never guess what I have! Milk chocolate bar with lots of gushy cream in it. Two squares for you, and two squares for me.

ISOBEL
   She!

SHERRY
   One hundred and forty calories a square who gives a shit. I heard Christine chewin ya out, what a fuckin cow.

ISOBEL
   She… I see, I smell the spray, the Lion's spray…

SHERRY
   (notices that RODNEY is very upset) What happened?

   SHERRY runs from RODNEY's office back home to the apartment she shares with her boyfriend of two years, EDWARD, an out-of-work actor. When she comes in he is practising a tap routine for an audition. Newspapers are all over the floor.

SHERRY
   JeSUS I'm peed off – I'm standing on the escalator, right? Goin down to the subway? My back hurts, I don't feel like takin the stairs? So I'm standin there when this woman shoves by me right into the wall and goes, "Can't *you* move? Some people are in a hurry!" And I just STAND there like a fucking WETWIPE with my mouth open FUCK if I see that bitch again–

EDWARD
   That's very interesting, Sherry.

SHERRY
   Whatcha workin on that dance try-out thing?

EDWARD
   Uh, no. I'm fixing the faulty wiring with my feet, it's magic, Sherry, really! Right through the–

SHERRY
   Ah Jeez, you're not mad at me again are ya? Whad I do now?

EDWARD
   I don't know, Sherry, what did you do now?

SHERRY
I get off work at five-thirty, Ed, it's ten to six what the hell am I supposed to do? Fly home?

EDWARD
I phoned work at four o'clock, Sherry, and Arlene said that you had left for the day.

SHERRY
Oh well THAT – I was havin a coffee and a piece of cake with Rodney, he–

EDWARD
Don't lie, please.

SHERRY
I was, Eddie, ask Rodney, ask–

EDWARD
You've rehearsed them all.

SHERRY
Listen to me! Rodney had some kind of fit today, Christine just about called the cops he was yelling and screaming at nobody all afternoon – he's right nuts.

EDWARD
It is a skillful liar it is.

SHERRY
Don't call me "it."

EDWARD
I beg your pardon?

SHERRY
Have you been drinking? Or doin coke or some shit? You have, haven't you? You–

EDWARD
We're out of toilet paper.

SHERRY
No, there's more right under the–

EDWARD
No there's NOT!

SHERRY
Alright, I'll go and get some now–

EDWARD
YOU'LL stay right where you are, Sherry. Please. PLEASE I'm asking you. Don't leave me alone – here – I don't want to be alone.

SHERRY
Aww Eddie, you know I love you, don't you.

EDWARD
If – if you're not happy with my performance in bed… I wish you'd just… tell me and – and–

SHERRY
Honey, I love your performance in bed.

EDWARD
You don't really, do you?

SHERRY
Listen I was just tellin Arlene today you got the best hands of I bet any guy there is on the whole fuckin planet!

EDWARD
You were?

SHERRY
The way you touch me, Eddie, Christ, I feel like a whole bouquet, you know? A bouquet of red flowers just… poppin open, poppop pop pop pop just like on one of them nature specials. I love makin love with you, I think about it all day, half the time my pants are wet thinkin about you.

EDWARD
They're not, really?

SHERRY
They are. Feel… feel that *(puts his hand under her dress)* Oh honey I want you to make love to me. Please?

EDWARD
(kissing her) Oh! Oh! I've been thinking about you too, all day, every day.

SHERRY
Oh Eddie, I want you.

EDWARD
You want me…?

SHERRY
Did you not get that part in the TV series? About the runaway kid or whatever? Is that why you're – Eddie what's wrong? Did I say something wrong?

EDWARD
YOU ARE A FLAMING ASSHOLE!

SHERRY
Eddie!

EDWARD
Who are you dreaming about every night?

SHERRY
What?

EDWARD
Every night you're moaning like an animal in heat, who?

SHERRY
What?

EDWARD
Who are you dreaming about, Sherry?

SHERRY
Nobody! I'm not dreaming about – nobody.

EDWARD
WHO ARE YOU DREAMING ABOUT?

SHERRY
Just forget it, I'm going over to Arlene's, I'll see you later.

EDWARD
You tell me who you are dreaming about or I will cancel the wedding.

SHERRY
Eddie.

EDWARD
I will… TODAY, if you don't stop lying to me treating me like a fucking maggot–

SHERRY
I'm not lying to you Ed, please, just–

EDWARD
I'll cancel the wedding! I'll phone up Father Hayes and I'll cancel the whole fucking thing.

SHERRY
I paid nine hundred dollars for that dress, Eddie.

EDWARD
I don't give a flying fuck what you paid for it.

SHERRY
EDDIE my mum's got her ticket from Florida, my sisters–

EDWARD
I don't give a hot damn miss–

SHERRY
OKAY OKAY OKAY OKAY you're right, you're right. There is someone I'm dreaming about… it's… uh… it's…

EDWARD
Now we are cookin with GAS, Sherry. This is what I always knew in my heart never DARED with all this feminist shit going down. Come on, come on tell me if I'm going to be your husband I want to know it all.

SHERRY
Tell you. Tell… you…?

EDWARD
You were walking home from the subway, yes?

SHERRY
Yes.

EDWARD
About one thirty in the morning, yes?

SHERRY
Yes. Well. I had been at my great aunts doin'–

EDWARD
I don't give a fuck where you were Sherry you were walking home, one-thirty in the morning, right?

SHERRY
Right.

EDWARD
And you hear steps behind you.

SHERRY
Steps.

EDWARD
Clack clack clack like cowboy boots.

SHERRY
  Clack. Clack.

EDWARD
  And a voice…

SHERRY
  Like a housefly.

EDWARD
  A VOICE.

SHERRY
  Asks me if I had been seein that… porno show down the street.

EDWARD
  And you said…

SHERRY
  I didn't say, Ed, I walked faster.

EDWARD
  But your heels, were so high, so provocative, that you turned on your ankle.

SHERRY
  I sprained my ankle.

EDWARD
  And he grabbed you.

SHERRY
  By the arm!

EDWARD
  He was all man.

SHERRY
  Oh no! No!

EDWARD
  And then what happened, Sherry? What happened then?

SHERRY
  You know what happened Ed.

EDWARD
  I forget, Sherry. Tell me again. Tell me again, come on, come ON or I… cancel…

SHERRY
You know what happened.

EDWARD
OR I CANCEL…

SHERRY
He threw me between two houses, Ed.

EDWARD
And you are breathing fast. And hot.

SHERRY
And he smashed my head against the fire wall, Ed.

EDWARD
You dream about that, don't you Sherry?

SHERRY
And he told me he was going to kill me.

EDWARD
His voice. MASTERFUL…

SHERRY
And he held my throat and he…

EDWARD
And he…

SHERRY
Please, Eddie. Please please, I am asking you… I can't do this again, I can not go through it for you, Eddie. I'm tired, I'm…

EDWARD
And? And?

SHERRY
And I fought like a cat, Ed, you know that! I scratched him and bit him and twisted and screamed but he–

EDWARD
But he…?

SHERRY
He–

EDWARD
He–

SHERRY
　　Eddie please…

EDWARD
　　Say it!!!

SHERRY
　　NO!

EDWARD
　　Say it now Sherry.

SHERRY
　　Eddie!

EDWARD
　　You *are* the snake.

SHERRY
　　No.

EDWARD
　　Because the snake tempts others to sin, uh huh? SATAN tempts others to sin. Say it Sherry. Come on, "I am the snake," come on, "I am the snake," "I am the snake" come on COMEON.

SHERRY
　　I… am… the snake.

EDWARD
　　With the diamond back, glittering.

SHERRY
　　Yeah. I am. The snake. With the back.

EDWARD
　　Oh yes!! You ARE the snake, baby, come on, "I am the snake!"

SHERRY
　　I am. The snake! I am the snake! I am the snake! I AM THE SNAKE I AM THE SNAKE I AM THE SNAKE I AM THE SNAAAAAAAAKE!

　　SHERRY breaks down in tears. She collapses on the floor. EDWARD cleans up and then sits down.

Eddie? Will you come with me tomorrow then to Ashley's to pick out a pattern? Like I've made the appointment and everything Ed, and after all, you are going to have to live with the dishes. I mean, I know guys hate goin in there, all guys do, but everyone that gets married goes to Ashley's, everyone that gets married–

EDWARD
Alright. But nothing with flowers on it. I just want something clean, maybe – white, with a black stripe.

She thinks, changes her mind, then turns away.

ISOBEL enters the room, and offers her hand to SHERRY, who takes it, gratefully. Arm in arm, they walk away from SHERRY and EDWARD's apartment to a graveyard. At first ISOBEL is helping SHERRY, but by the time they reach the graveyard, it is SHERRY who helps ISOBEL find her grave, and gently lays her down, and disappears.

NOTE: The next section has two scene options

SCENE OPTION 1:

In the graveyard, sitting on another tombstone, is BEN, the man who killed ISOBEL seventeen years before.

BEN
There's one thing, you know. There's one thing that I always... wanted to tell somebody and that is that... I done her a favour. I was – kindly – yeah, see, I pull her outa the car and throw her on the cement in front of the warehouse there's a streetlight and... and she says to me she says, "Please," she says, "Please no strangle, I so... scared of strangle," in this voice of breath just... purely of breath so I stopped, eh? I did. I stepped out of the twister cause that's what it's like, when you're doin something like that, you're inside a twister and to step out, is like... liftin a dishwasher, eh, but I did. So I go back of the warehouse and I picked up a brick and I hit her – cause she touched me okay? She touched me, right?

ISOBEL approaches with her weapon.

SCENE OPTION 1 CONTINUES ON Page 324.

SCENE OPTION 2:

In the graveyard, a group of mourners exit, leaving BEN and his mother alone.

JOAN
Dear, you're looking quite uncomfortable, shall we go?

BEN
Yeah, yeah, let's go. No. No. Let's stay here. Here, sit on a tombstone why dontcha? *(reading)* "Harvey J. Walker, 1920-1973." What's that make him?

JOAN
Dear, it's getting quite chilly, don't you think?

BEN
It's summer, Joanie!

JOAN
Yes dear, but there is a wind! I'm afraid my silly old hair will just–

BEN
JOAN! I wanna siddown and pay my respects. SIDDOWN! SIT DOWN!

JOAN
(sitting down awkwardly) All right. Somebody hasn't watered these Impatiens in a very long time. Poor old Father Hayes, I will miss him.

BEN
He was an old fruit.

JOAN
Benny he was not, how can you say that about Father Hayes?

BEN
Because he talked like a fruit; he walked like one too.

JOAN
Now now, you don't mean that.

BEN
I sure as hell do.

JOAN
BEN PLEASE your language!!

BEN
So, whatdya been up to, Joan, lots a charity work, what?

JOAN
Yes, I'm still working in the shop, at the hospital.

BEN
What about bridge, you still play bridge?

JOAN
Oh yes, every week, heavens, I guess it's been every week for the last... fifteen years. Ben I wish you would call me Mum.

BEN
I can't. I told you that before.

JOAN
You are my son. We've had you since you were three weeks old for heaven's sake.

BEN
I don't give a shit. You're Joan, I like you, you're just not my mother.

JOAN
You break my heart, Christine still calls me Mum.

BEN
Christine's different.

JOAN
How? How is Christine different?

BEN
Cause… she's… like you, see; she's the same. Her mother was some kinda student or something, her father a professor or some shit, me, I wasn't from nothin, I'm different, I'm different from you, see?

JOAN
I love you Ben, I hope you…

BEN
Don't say that word.

JOAN
I'm sorry, but it's true, I love every hair on your sweet head…

BEN
Joan.

JOAN
And I will till the day I die.

BEN
DO YOU LOVE ME?

JOAN
Well yes, I just–

BEN
Do you love me?

JOAN
Terribly.

BEN
Well then gimme some money.

JOAN
I beg your pardon?

BEN
I need a loan. About sixty thousand bucks. And I need it tonight.

JOAN
Oh so that's why you agreed to come with me to Father Hayes' funeral, stupid me, I actually thought…

BEN
Shutup, I came because I knew it meant something for you, I hadn't seen you in a while–

JOAN
Eight months.

BEN
Yeah well I was busy.

JOAN
You're only seeing me because you want money.

BEN
Shutup, don't give me that shit…

JOAN
It's obviously true, Ben.

BEN
Okay, it's true. Can you get the money?

JOAN
What do you need it for?

BEN
I said can you get it?

JOAN
I don't know, Ben, I don't know until you tell me what you need it for.

BEN
Okay I'm leaving.

JOAN
Ben WAIT, WAIT. *(crying)* I'm sorry.

BEN
WELL don't cry, I hate it when an old woman cries, it's friggin gross youse are ugly enough to begin with but when you start with the water…

JOAN
Ben that's enough.

BEN
I'm just being straight, Joan, come on, the old "visage" is NOT what it used to be, HEY, you can take a little tease can't ya?

JOAN
Well I know I've aged, dear, but I didn't think–

BEN
You're old and ugly. But you're okay. Wanta smoke?

JOAN
No thank you Ben, you know I don't.

BEN
The cancer thing, right, right, well I don't give a shit myself, so I'm gonna smoke myself sick.

JOAN
Ben, why do you say you don't care?

BEN
Cause I'm a sittin duck. Unless you give me that cash money now, I'll be dead news anyways, so what do I care.

JOAN
I don't follow you, Ben.

BEN
I'm saying that there's people after me, Joanie, bad bad dudes, these jokers don't think nothin, nothin of blowin a guy's head off and stickin him in a trunk.

JOAN
Oh Benny how did you get involved with these…

BEN
Don't ask questions, Joanie, for crying out loud, I did time in a federal penitentiary, I did twenty years in friggin Collins Bay the place is crawlin with creeps they follow you out…

JOAN
Why are they… after you?

BEN
Why are they after me? Why are they after me? You are askin me why they are after me? Why do you think?

JOAN
Well goodness anybody who knows anything knows you did not kill that little girl, all the magazines wrote about the suppressed evidence, and impossibility of the time factor, everybody knows it was a miscarriage of justice–

BEN
I know that you know that, butcha think the turkeys know that? Hey, they just gotta feel upper than somebody, right? They're the lowest on the social ladder they gotta have somebody lower, that's me, scum of the earth.

JOAN
Oh Benny.

BEN
You never thought I done it.

JOAN
Not for a second.

BEN
May I ask why?

JOAN
Because – because – you would fall asleep only in my arms till you were six years old.

BEN
ONLY IN YOUR ARMS.

JOAN
And you brushed my hair, your favourite pastime in the world was for us to lie on the bed and you would brush and brush my hair, my hair was long then black…

BEN
I still like brushin chicks' hair.

JOAN
I always knew, I always knew it wasn't you.

BEN
I know. I know you always knew that.

JOAN
I am your mother…

BEN
NO!

JOAN
    I AM.

BEN
    You are not! You are... my guardian, LIKE a mother to me not my mother. My mother is probably some whore living outa Dominion bags now.

JOAN
    Oh Benny.

BEN
    Are you gonna give me the cash?

JOAN
    Just... please, please tell me what it's for? Please darling?

BEN
    Surgery. Changin my face so those jokers won't know me, then I'm gonna start in on the pasta, the milkshakes, gain fifty pounds, then dye the hair red.

JOAN
    But surely that won't cost–

BEN
    LET ME FINISH, Christ, did ya ever let anybody finish anything?

JOAN
    I'm sorry.

BEN
    You better be. Now where was I...

JOAN
    About why you need so much–

BEN
    Okay, after the looks change, I go into business I gotta idea for a business gonna make me a millionaire. Alls I gotta do, is have some cash up front.

JOAN
    Ben, dear, I don't mean to be discouraging, but I've watched so many of these schemes of yours–

BEN
    What?

JOAN
    Fail!!

BEN
>They didn't fail! They didn't fail they just didn't work cause of people rippin me off cause my heart was too big!! Well this time I learned my lesson I know I know to be ruthless, okay?

JOAN
>Well I don't think you have to be "ruthless," I mean Walter was a brilliant business man, but he was never never–

BEN
>*(spits)* HE WAS A SON OF A BITCH.

JOAN
>Walter loved you, Benny.

BEN
>Don't you mention that man's name the man was a pig.

JOAN
>Ben you are talking about your father, my husband.

BEN
>NOT MY FATHER NOT MY FATHER YOU only saw one face, Joanie one WALTER face, the other face was secret, between him and me, only I saw the…

JOAN
>Oh Ben how can you–

BEN
>He he he he he used to force me…

JOAN
>He forced you to do what?

BEN
>Well… forget it.

JOAN
>Ben, please, I don't understand what you–

BEN
>WHY DO YOU THINK THIS BOY IS HELL, I was hell for you from the time I was seven, killin the cats, wrecking the car, sellin your stereo WHY? Cause my mother was a fifteen-year-old kid from Gerrard and Parliament with stringy hair… who couldn't say her alphabet? You think it's that? Why do you think it is, Joanie, why do you think I am hell?

JOAN
I think that when we told you that you were adopted, you were crushed and we were never able to help you.

BEN
No. So whaddya think it is, Joan?

JOAN
...Something... Walter...?

BEN
Yeah. Yeah. Yeah...something Walter said.

JOAN
You are saying that he... did something to you – he struck you?

BEN
Joanie bein hit, I wouldn'ta minded, hell it was a relief when it was that. It's... the other...

JOAN
It's not true.

BEN
You never noticed anything, NOTHIN strange? Whyd'ja think, whyd'ja think he left the bed every night?

JOAN
To have a snack, he... always said that he had had a... snack.

BEN
(laughs) Yeah right.

JOAN
I'm... really in a state of shock.

BEN
Believe me, Joan.

JOAN
I thought I knew Walter so well...

BEN
Yeah.

JOAN
OH GOD. My little boy, my poor little...

BEN
    Poor Joanie, no one told her. No one ever told her that ninety-five percent of the human population is maggots. You got fooled into thinkin life was nice tea parties and hot cocoa after skatin and tuckin your kids in and singing a pretty song about the fuckin moon…. Member that rabbit I used to have?

JOAN
    Honey.

BEN
    Yeah Honey, well, Honey always made me think of you, you know, with those big wide apart eyes, believe everything thinkin everything is nice, so trusting, she was so trustin it made me mad, you know? Like why do you trust me don't you know I could pull your eyes out? You should hop away when my hands are in your cage, hop away, you stupid pest, don't just stand there. With those eyes.

JOAN
    Is that why you–

BEN
    I DON'T LIKE STUPIDITY.

JOAN
    Oh dear.

BEN
    Look, Joan, I'm short on time here, so do we have a deal?

JOAN
    Sixty… thousand…?

BEN
    You got it.

JOAN
    Oh Ben. Oh Ben. Walter. I am shattered to know that my Walter–

BEN
    Hey. Would I lie to you Joanie? Just to score some cash? Come on…

JOAN
    Now I know, Ben, I know…

BEN
    Whaddya know.

JOAN
    Her picture, in the papers on all those posters, that picture, her eyes, she had unusually trusting, wide apart–

BEN
   Back off, I'm tellin ya Joanie–

JOAN
   YOU HATE TRUSTING EYES because – they reminded you of me and how… I trusted Walter, how I let it go on, how dumb I was how dumb I was, you were killing me, killing – WALTER! It's all my fault!! That little girl's death is all my fault!

BEN
   There's one thing, you know. There's one thing that I always… wanted to tell somebody and that is that… I done her a favour. I was – kindly – yeah, see, I pull her outa the car and throw her on the cement in front of the warehouse there, and… I put my hands around her neck and she says to me she says "Please," she says, "please no strangle, I so… scared of strangle" in this… voice of breath just… purely of breath and I stopped, eh? I stepped out of the twister cause that's what it's like, Joanie, when you're doin somethin like that you're inside a twister and to step out, is like… liftin two hundred pounds but I did cause she touched me, okay? She touched me right – she was me, right? She was me, under Walter, asking him askin him please Daddy, please, please, Daddy so I done what I always wanted Walter to do, what I always wished what I wished every night, I got a brick a plain red brick, yeah, killed her with a brick, smashed her little face in. To this day I can't watch them Brick commercials, you know, the furniture warehouse? No money down – turn the set right off, right off for the night. Hey! Did I really used to brush your hair?

   He puts his head in her lap. She extricates herself and backs off in horror. ISOBEL approaches with her weapon.

SCENE OPTION 1 AND SCENE OPTION 2 BOTH
RESUME AT THIS POINT IN THE PLAY:

ISOBEL
   BEN… ja.. men.

   He looks.

ISOBEL
   BEN ja men BEN ja men.

BEN
   Who are you?

ISOBEL
   Is… o… bel.

BEN
　Isobel.

ISOBEL
　July. Isobel in July July the one, remember? Don't you remember? CANADA day day for CANADA Birthday. I selling tickets tickets on a Chrysler car, for boys' and girls' club, one dollar fifty for a ticket. I have five tickets left. Don't you remember? I see you in park. It is raining. In my park I ask you "you want to buy ticket on a Chrysler car?" You say "yes, yes, I buy all five all five tickets. Come into my car, come into my silver car with dark red seats, come into my car. I will give you the money for the tickets I have the money in my car" you said…

BEN
　I'm hallucinatin.

ISOBEL
　I'm Isobel.

BEN
　You're a picture.

ISOBEL
　I'm Isobel.

BEN
　What… do you want?

ISOBEL
　I have come.

BEN
　What do you want?

ISOBEL
　I am here.

BEN
　WELL GO AWAY! You hear me? GO AWAY.

ISOBEL
　(*she is about to kill him with the stick, the forces of vengeance and forgiveness warring inside her – forgiveness wins*) I love you.

BEN
　NO!!

ISOBEL
　You took my last breath!

BEN
    Christ I'm sick, I'm so sick.

ISOBEL
    I want back my life. Give me back my life!

> *Players enter singing a religious-sounding chorale with a sense of sadness and triumph. They place a veil on ISOBEL's head, the actor playing BEN joining them.*

ISOBEL
    (an adult now) I want to tell you now a secret. I was dead, was killed by lion in long silver car, starving lion, maul maul maul me to dead, with killing claws over and over my little young face and chest, over my chest my blood running out he take my heart with. He take my heart with, in his pocket deep, but my heart talk. Talk and talk and never be quiet never be quiet. I came back.

    I take my life. I want you all to take your life. I want you all to have your life.

> *Players sing a second, joyful chorale, walking off. ISOBEL ascends, in her mind, into heaven. The last thing we see is her veil.*

    The end.

Sled

Sled was first produced by Tarragon Theatre, Toronto, February 1997, with the following cast:

ANNIE DELANEY	Nancy Palk
JACK	Ron White
JOE	J.W. Carroll
EVANGELINE	Pamela Matthews
KEVIN	Michael Mahonen
VOLKER, MIKE, JASON, M.C.	Derwin Jordan
MOTHER, MARSHA, CARMELLA	Ann Holloway

Directed by Duncan McIntosh
Music composed by Bill Thompson
Annie's songs: music by Bill Thompson, lyrics by Judith Thompson
Evangeline's songs: music by Pamela Matthews
Set & lighting by John Jenkins
Costumes designed by Sue Lepage
Stage managed by Brian Scott

CHARACTERS

ANNIE DELANEY
JACK
JOE
EVANGELINE
KEVIN
VOLKER
MIKE
JASON
M.C.
MOTHER
MARSHA
CARMELLA

SETTING

The present, Toronto; a lodge in Northern Ontario and its snowmobile trails; a wilderness farther north.

PRODUCTION NOTES

The play should run no longer than 2 hours and 15 minutes (not counting two 15-minute intermissions). The audience should be out by no later than 10:50 PM, given an 8:00 PM curtain. The key to a good pace, other than in the playing, is in the transitions between scenes which should, in almost every case, be instantaneous – the last word of one scene immediately followed by the first word of the next. The designer, of course, can faciliate the speedy transitions.

MUSIC

Transcripts for the songs in this play may be obtained through Playwrights Canada Press? Shain Jaffe, Great North Artists?

Sled

ACT ONE

Scene One

White birches, snow, a Great Snowy owl, and a trail, with a hill, running around behind or through the audience. ANNIE appears walking fast and hard, out of breath through deep snow and birches. The music is mounting, ominous like a heart beating harder and faster but moving towards a dark euphoria; ANNIE, walks the trail around or through the audience and climbs the hill. At the top of the hill, she looks down over the scene. The music for "Oh heavenly time of day" plays. She sings:

ANNIE
Oh heavenly time of day
the snow and the quiet
the birch
white pine
so high and so high
Shall I sink in the snow and just lie there for hours alone there for hours
till dark night
erases me?

Oh heavenly time of day

ANNIE breathes in the air. There is the sound of a wolf howling. She sings.

lie on the white snow and
stare at the dark sky
the sky full of stars
who are people who died
maybe people I know

hello Maeve O'Hara
my mother's mother's
mother's mother's
motherrrr... hello!

A wolf howls. She makes her way down the hill.

Scene Two

A residential street, with mostly red brick houses with high pointed roofs, some three storey, but most two-storey workers' houses. The houses, however, look as though they are in the middle of a forest. The birches remain.

JOE
"*America Bella! Si abbandonare a me!*" That's what she used to say whenever things were – fallin apart. My mother. I don't think she ever said the word "Canada." It was always "America." "*America bella.*" This here used to be a cow path. The whole of what you see now, of Clinton Street, wasn't nothin but a cow path. My mother and father and the nine of us kids we were livin south of College, that was about 1918, my dad workin at the slaughterhouse at Clinton and Bloor. It's still there to this day, they won't move it; we'd come up here to the pastures and we'd watch as the cows walked down the cow path to the slaughterhouse, to become ground meat. Led always by the great black bull. Course we'd never see the meat, nor the milk, never saw milk till I went in the Air Force. But I loved sittin on the fence and watchin all these cows walkin down. And all the Italian ladies, they would chase after these cows, to catch the manure they dropped on the way. For their gardens. And my mother, Carmella? She would be the first. She would always be first.

Scene Three

The Lounge Dining Room at Pickerel and Jack Lake Lodge. A warm fire crackles in the fireplace. There is a trophy on the wall. A deer with antlers. VOLKER, the proprietor, has a German accent.

VOLKER
Good evening everybody. My name is Volker, and this is my lovely wife Marsha. Welcome to Pickerel and Jack Lake Lodge: The snowmobiling mecca of North America. Marsha and me hope you are really enjoying your stay and that you have seen the 500 kilometres of snowmobile trails out there, and have wind-burned faces, but now it's time to warm up, yes? So we have brought for your entertainment tonight a great honour, a beautiful diva, the sexy singer of Toronto nightclubs, the very interesting and I think such a good singer, the great Annie Delaney. Let's give her a warm hand, yes?

ANNIE Delaney steps out of the shadows in a beautiful red dress with long red velvet gloves and performs a simple transformation or act of magic, as she sings:

ANNIE
Oh heavenly time of day… the fog and the quiet…
the mist
no sun
I move out of my dream and into this day as the fog it clears so slowly away
to reveal…
to reveal…
to reveal…

KEVIN enters, interrupting. An awkward silence. He sits down.

VOLKER
   Isn't she fantastic?

ANNIE
   I saw a fox this morning. On the green trail. The long one? Early this morning. I was walking along, thinking: there's still snow here. It's all melting down there, in the city. Mud rivers running everywhere. But here: snow, spruce, evergreens. I was walking toward a heart-stopping stand of birch, and I saw a fox. A red fox. We looked at each other, for a moment. A wonder. At dawn; a secret time of day.

   My son, Jason, was born at dawn; that time of day gives me hope. Whereas, the hour *before* dawn? In the winter? The job that degraded day after day, that picked at my being. It was dark when I rose and I walked down the empty cold street and I am nauseous just before dawn I wake up, with dread. My heart beating very fast. I know I will die just before dawn.

   She sings once again: "Thursday in November."

Thursday in November
at that duskish time of day
Walking west on Bloor Street. Past Italian groceries, Korean fruit and flowers, Hungarian deli… I feel a sharp pain in my knee a red dog, no, a fox, has bitten me…

(spoken) It's a fox.

(sung) At Bloor and Bathurst my downtown
in the rushing
A red fox
Is here and
has bitten my knee and it stands and it stares back at me.
And we all
go down on our – knees on the spit covered sidewalk and say
Oh heavenly time of day
ohhh heavenly time of day
A fox on the street
the geese in the V twisting this way and that
The lights through the dark clouds the blues and the indigos, breathe in the chatter, the down to the subway and buses to homes
See the fox on the street
grab a paper, a Mars bar, a *People*, and rest your head
Let the thoughts drift like I did on Pickerel Lake.
Just drift
Oh Heavenly time of day
Gives me some hope
And I do, believe that I'll stay
For a while
With this fox

On this street
A red coat
For a while
with its dusk
With its eyes

Scene Four

Lodge dining room lounge: MIKE Head and KEVIN Dorner are eating dinner at one table. ANNIE sits down and immediately JACK praises her.

JACK
Beautiful. That was beautiful. Never heard that one before. It's something.

ANNIE rests for a moment.

ANNIE
How's the dinner? Are you enjoying it?

JACK
Beautiful roast of beef.

He offers her a bite, she turns her head away.

ANNIE
What did you mean "something."

JACK
What?

ANNIE
You said "It's something." My song. As if it was deranged.

JACK
I liked it. It was good.

ANNIE
But…?

JACK
You're not gonna get a fox on Bloor Street.

ANNIE
Well. I saw a fox in Trinity Bellwoods park once. Early in the morning.

JACK
You did?

ANNIE
> Yes. I did. I told you about that–

JACK
> Shit. Shit I forgot to cancel the paper. What a fucking idiot I am.

ANNIE
> Shhhh, don't worry, Joe will do it.

JACK
> Joe?

ANNIE
> Old Joe from across the street.

JACK
> Oh yeah, Joe. Ace.

ANNIE
> He'll pick them up for us. He knows we're going away. He's my pal.

JACK
> Why does he sit there watchin everybody all day? Doesn't he have anything better to do?

ANNIE
> Give him a break, he worked like a dog for fifty years, he's earned his rest. Besides, it's great for us: He never misses a thing on that street.

> *He touches her knee under the table. She enjoys it.*

ANNIE
> Jack.

> *He takes her hand.*

JACK
> So I never asked you, what'd you do Thursday, did you swim?

ANNIE
> Seventy three lengths.

JACK
> You're amazing. But you like that, don't you, just thinkin your thoughts.

ANNIE
> Actually I don't think at all. I just don't have a thought in all that green water.

JACK
You are looking incredibly beautiful tonight.

ANNIE
To your eyes only.

JACK
You're the most beautiful woman in this room.

ANNIE
You look very handsome yourself. That jacket does look nice on you.

JACK
It better for thirteen-hundred bucks. Hey. That was very wonderful last night. Last night you were all…

ANNIE
Shhhh.

JACK
I did pretty good with the hand last night, eh? You had, how many, four fireworks last night, didn't you? You are so unpredictable. My quiet woman.

He touches her. She looks at his fingers on her arm.

ANNIE
Jack? How long do someone's fingerprints… last? Say, in a house?

JACK
Ten years. Give or take. Less they're wiped off.

ANNIE
So if I don't clean, if I don't polish, my mother and father; their fingerprints will stay with us for ten more years after they…

JACK
(*nods*) Annie. I won't talk about hockey. If you don't talk about death. Deal?

ANNIE
"Behold I shall tell you a mystery. We shall not all sleep but we shall all be changed." I wish I believed that. For even a minute.

JACK
Hey. Look at the fire. You love fires.

At the other table, KEVIN and MIKE are getting rowdy.

KEVIN
Sunday roast beef dinner, eh? Just like my old lady used to make.

MIKE
Right. Sunday my old lady would open a box of potato flakes. Throw some boiling water on 'em. There's Sunday dinner. I'm not fucking kidding.

KEVIN
Look at that waitress. Fuck, man, looks like she swallowed the Skydome.

MIKE
This beef is fine, man.

KEVIN
But where's the Yorkshire pudding? I want my fuckin Yorkshire pudding.

MIKE
Yeah. Yorkshire fucking pudding.

On the other side of the room:

ANNIE
Is it working, Jack? This weekend? You think things are going to be alright? With us?

JACK
It's working. I haven't seen you like this in months. Maybe it's the nature, the snow, whatever. You're actually, I don't know, happy.

ANNIE
Yes. I am, aren't I.

JACK
Yes. You are.

KEVIN
HEY. WAITRESS.

MARSHA
Were you born in a barn? Or was it a sewer?

KEVIN
Sewer. That's good, that's good. You're Big Marsha aren't ya? Didn't you used to work at The Keg in Huntsville?

MARSHA
Yes I worked at The Keg. I think I tossed you out a couple of times, did I not? What can I get for you boys?

KEVIN
I was just wondering… um, like… did I fuck you?

MARSHA
That's not funny. I don't think that's funny at all. You're out of here.

MARSHA leaves their table.

KEVIN
I'm sorry.

MIKE
We didn't mean nothin.

MARSHA
Everything okay here, folks?

ANNIE
Yes, thank you, wonderful.

JACK
My compliments to the chef. The roast is excellent.

MARSHA
Well thank you. I made the roast myself tonight. Chef was off sick, he's got some kinda kidney trouble. So Volker says "Marsha you're doin the roast beef." And I don't cook, eh, generally, so I said, "Volker I can't cook a roast of beef." Volker hands me some garlic and some paprika and says "Rub it on, Marsha, like lotion on a baby's bottom." So there you are, it's not so bad.

ANNIE
Look's very good.

MARSHA
It's very good, I know. Hey. I meant to tell you, I like your singing. It's unusual. Different.

ANNIE
Thank you.

KEVIN
Waitress. Excuse me, not to bother you or anything, but like, we were wondering. Like where's our Yorkshire pudding. It says on the menu "Yorkshire pudding." Pardon my French.

MARSHA
That is Yorkshire pudding.

MIKE
Where? Am I like, buh-lind?

MARSHA
　　On your plate. There.

　　KEVIN points to the Yorkshire pudding.

KEVIN
　　THAT? You are tellin me that THAT is Yorkshire pudding?

MIKE
　　No fuckin way.

MARSHA
　　Yes, that is Yorkshire pudding. I made it myself.

KEVIN
　　Looks like my grandmothers tit, man.

MIKE
　　Looks like my grandmother's snatch.

MARSHA
　　That is it.

　　MARSHA exits. They laugh hysterically. JACK and ANNIE exchange a look. ANNIE is pleading with him silently not to do anything.

KEVIN
　　Look at those two, they are pissed.

MIKE
　　Excuse me, miss? No, you, big guy's woman.

ANNIE
　　Are you talking to me?

MIKE
　　Like, how did you get so tall and skinny anyways? Did you, like, eat the CN Tower?

　　(Note: if the actress does not fit this physical description, replace the lines with "How'd you get so homely lookin anyways? Did you, like, eat Yonge Street?") They laugh even harder. JACK stands up, furious.

KEVIN
　　And that guy over there, he ate Exhibition Stadium, man.

　　They laugh some more, knocking over some plates etc. JACK walks over.

JACK
  Before we go any further, I would like you both to go down on your knees and apologize, to my wife, NOW.

ANNIE
  It doesn't matter, Jack. Let's go.

JACK
  You are going to get an apology. Do it boys. Do it now.

  Silence.

KEVIN
  It's a free country, sir, I believe. And I would like to keep eatin my supper.

MIKE
  I'm really enjoying these green beans. Delicioooooso.

JACK
  You are going to apologize to my wife and to every other diner in this establishment, or I will make you sorry.

MIKE
  What the fuck? Is this, like, a Sylvester Stallone movie or something?

KEVIN
  He's a cop, man. I see it in the whites of his fuckin eyes. He's one of those, that shoves ya up against the car and bangs your head over and over.

JACK
  Diablo.

KEVIN
  What?

JACK
  Just do what I told you to do.

ANNIE
  Jack.

JACK
  Everything's gonna be just fine. Annie. Just stay where you are.

  There is a long pause. KEVIN and MIKE laugh and start eating again.

KEVIN
So as I was saying, Mike, I wouldn't fuck that wife of his if you paid me a fuckin million, like fuckin the railroad tracks, right? She likely smells down there, anyways, right? Like a fuckin can of sardines.

MIKE is laughing like a kid, snorting. JACK slams MIKE's head into the table, knocking him out.

JACK
I have had just about enough out of you, you piece of fucking trash – you fucking apologize NOW.

JACK drags KEVIN to his table, forces him to his knees and into a bow. KEVIN goes for his hunting knife strapped to his belt but JACK pins KEVIN's arm behind him, pressing hard.

Now learn some goddamned respect.

Scene Five

JOE sits, rocks on the porch.

JOE
I used to have the satellite. Because I enjoyed the television quite a bit. Because I was a TV salesman at Eaton's for forty-three years. That was my profession. So I enjoyed my television. But since Essie got sick, I can't watch it no more. I turn it on, and I just can't watch it. Because I got to watch the street. That is what I am here for. Now that my kids are grown and gone. To watch the street. Trouble is, a kind of strange thing is happening to me. I'll sit here, sippin on my coffee, and instead of watchin out for how things are, right now, like if little Claire and Joshua two doors up come home from school on time, or if too many people seem to be livin in the house on the corner, instead of those urgent things, I keep seeing what has already happened.

Scene Six

Hotel room. MUSIC: sexy like Santana. Presumably coming from radio. JACK and ANNIE. They start at some distance from each other and move slowly together dancing in response to the music.

Scene Seven

KEVIN and MIKE in enclosed shack getting ready to go out sledding. KEVIN loads his gun.

KEVIN
Fuckin cocksucker. I'll kill that cocksucker.

MIKE
Forget it, man, you know what cops are like.

KEVIN
Nobody does that to me. NOBODY.

MIKE
Well somebody did. A fuckin psycho cop did. And it could have been a hell of a lot worse, we coulda been dead, he'd get away with it. Now let's get over it and go man. Let's go do what we're here for, we fuckin risked our necks gettin this sled, let's shoot us a moose!

KEVIN
MOOSE!

MIKE
Whooo!

They whoop and bark like dogs as they run out.

Scene Eight

ANNIE and JACK's room. He is asleep. She is lying next to him, looking out the window. An owl hoots. She sees the owl and the owl sees her.

ANNIE
Ohhh.

She turns, excited.

Jack? Are you awake? It's an owl, a Great Snowy owl. I'm going to go for a walk. I'm gonna go and walk until dawn. Wait for the light. Sweet dreams.

Scene Nine

It is a dark night lit only by a mass of stars. A night bird sings ominously. We are looking at a snowmobile trail in Northern Ontario. A green or pink neon sign in handwriting overhead says: "Pickerel and Jack Lake Lodge: Snowmobiling Mecca of North America!" And then in small letters, underneath, in a different colour of neon, it says: "50 KM of Pristine X-country ski trails!" The cross-country ski trail is zig-zagging through a stand of birches. ANNIE walks by the sign and heads down a steep hill. It is very steep. She edges down it, grabbing onto trees occasionally, slipping.

ANNIE
All alone, in the woods, in the dark. In the middle of Northern Ontario by myself at night. I've never swam across Lake Ontario. I've never run across the 401. I've never driven across the frozen ice. But I am here.

She sings briefly in Gaelic. A shimmering, strange music. She sees a vision in the distance.

I see her again. The girl. On the ship. A dark, battered, dying ship. In Gaelic, my blood tongue, say: *Long an bhais*. [pronounced: Long on vache] Big holes in the mast. The crashing of fifty foot waves. Maeve. The raining. Maeve O'Hara, born in Connemara, December 6th, 1791. Praying. Standing on the mast of the ship. Praying to our Lord Jesus Christ. And everybody else down under, is dead. Of fever. Babies, and mothers, and fathers and families, all dead, piled together. They threw them overboard, one by one, wrapped up in sheets, until there was nobody left to throw them. Only Maeve, to say prayers for the dead. And she looks out to sea. For land, or whales, or fairies of the sea. In Gaelic, say: *Si na farraige*. And a cold wind comes up, cold and strong and she hangs on she doesn't fall but her hair, her hair stands straight up.

I know this is true. I know this girl is my great great grandmother. I know this girl is me.

She hears the sound of breaking branches. The shadow of a moose appears. They stare at one another for a moment. She reaches up to touch the moose.

Oh. God. What is it? It couldn't be. Oh my God it is. A moose. I don't believe it. Hello. You are so big. Hey I'm not going to hurt you. Wait!

The moose runs. A snowmobile approaches. ANNIE stands, terrified in the moonlight.

Oh my God. This is all I need.

The snowmobile's light beams on her. There are birches between her and the snowmobile. There is a stand of birches blocking their view of her.

KEVIN
Hey hey shut off shut off. I see somethin through those trees.

He shuts it off.

ANNIE
Hello. Hello.

KEVIN motions MIKE to stay back. MIKE keeps his sunglasses and headphones on. He is drunk. KEVIN moves in.

KEVIN
Well look at that. We got ourselves a she moose.

MIKE
Moose. Fuck.

ANNIE
Hey, fellows! It's not a moose. It's me from the lodge. The singer. Hey. Can you hear me!

MIKE
Shoot her, man, before she takes off.

KEVIN
Right cornered she is.

MIKE
Fuckin shoot it.

ANNIE
No! No! Please answer me, guys. Hello! I'm here, through the bushes. What, are you wearing headphones? Take off your headphones.

KEVIN
Let's cut open her belly, and if there's a calf there, we pull out the calf.

MIKE
Where is she man, I can't fuckin see her.

ANNIE gasps and goes into shock.

ANNIE
This is not funny. Will you answer me please. Please. PULL OUT YOUR HEADPHONES.

KEVIN
Let's pull out the calf. Just shoot her, cut her open, and pull out the calf. Take it to a vet, leave it on the steps, whatever.

MIKE
Did you shoot it?

KEVIN
Just pull the calf right out. Alright.

KEVIN moves through the brush until he has quite a clear view of ANNIE.

ANNIE
My husband will kill you.

KEVIN
   I want the antlers.

ANNIE
   I'm sorry about the thing at the lodge, my husband went too far. He will apologize to you.

KEVIN
   We split the meat. Shove it in the freezer, that's supper all winter. Moose and chips, moose and fries, moose and rice, moose and Yorkshire pudding.

ANNIE
   Please.

MIKE
   Why isn't she movin', man? What's wrong with her?

KEVIN
   She's froze; in the light of the sled. She's froze.

MIKE
   I can't fuckin see her!

KEVIN
   Ek skal skjota ther huortu i gegnum. [This is Norse and pronounced: Yeg skal skeeota tear hertu ee gagnum.] Let's shoot her man. Right through the heart.

   Two shots. Blackout.

Scene Ten

EVANGELINE comes out on her porch and looks around with great expectation. She is looking for another neighbour's tame pigeons. She sees them, flying in circles. She follows them with her eyes. They make quite a racket.

EVANGELINE
   Morning Joe.

JOE
   Morning.

EVANGELINE
   See the pigeons?

JOE
   Where? Oh yeah. A whole flock of 'em.

EVANGELINE
Have you noticed they do this every day at this time? Fly around in a circle, from here to the Loblaws over to the Food City, and down to Fiesta Farms and back.

JOE
Now that you mention it. I do see 'em flying around every day. I didn't think nothing of it. Don't care for pigeons.

EVANGELINE
They belong to a guy over on Grace. 'Parently he races them, down in the States every spring. They're in training.

JOE
Training?

EVANGELINE
For the races.

JOE
Well well.

EVANGELINE
How's Essie today, Joe?

JOE
I tried to cut her toenails for her and I couldn't. They're too hard. And yellow. Don't know what that means. I'm gonna have to give the doctor a call. Get that mobile foot clinic over here.

EVANGELINE
I could come do them later Joe. Before I go to work.

JOE
It's a nasty job, Ev.

EVANGELINE
Agh.

EVANGELINE looks at ANNIE and JACK's house. The house looks ominous to her.

EVANGELINE
Ooooh. That house give me the shivers today. Looks empty.

JOE
Workin holiday for Annie up north. Singin in a lodge up there. She's a lounge singer. The two of them went for the weekend.

EVANGELINE
You know I don't think I've ever seen him.

JOE
Long hours. He's a police detective. 14th Division.

EVANGELINE
So they're way up north.

JOE
Don't tell nobody though. 'Specially that nosy check-out, over at Fiesta Farms.

EVANGELINE
Hah. She's always askin me when I'm getting married. Next time, I'm gonna just tell her "It's none of your business, you potato-faced grocery girl." HAH. That'd be funny.

JOE
I'd like to see that.

EVANGELINE
Joe.

JOE
Yeah.

EVANGELINE
Will you think I'm crazy?

JOE
No.

EVANGELINE
I heard footsteps last night. And the night before that. On the street. Real clear, like it was summer. And I thought I heard someone climbing the steps and coming up on the porch. When I looked out the window, I didn't see anyone.

JOE
Maybe you should get a dog. Although they do shed something terrible. Our Dory she was a piece of work; she would get up on the couch soon as we went up to bed. One night my stomach was bad, I come down for a Brio, I'm half asleep and I think I see my mother sittin on our couch. I go "now what are you doin comin back from the dead and sittin on my couch in my parlour when you never let me so much as touch that precious couch of yours" and Dory she kinda whimpers and jumps off. Ha. Oh, I felt a fool.

EVANGELINE
Joe? Do you think, maybe, I mean, don't you think, there is some possibility that it might be him?

JOE
> Who?

EVANGELINE
> You know. Kevin. My brother. Joe? Do you think?

JOE
> Oh dear.

EVANGELINE
> Well, it's possible.

JOE
> I don't see how, Evangeline. It's been 20 years.

EVANGELINE
> But maybe he – found out somehow, about who he was. That he belongs right here. On Clinton Street. Like maybe she got sick and she wanted to just tell him the truth, people do that, you know, they get tired of keepin somethin buried.

JOE
> Even if he did know the truth, Ev, what makes you think he's gonna come back here? This is not home to him no more, not since he was took. He was only four years old, remember. He's got a life there, wherever that woman stole him to, could be Australia for all we know, he likely has a job, a girlfriend–

EVANGELINE
> But don't you think he'd want to come and find his real sister? And mother? I mean everyone wants to know their real family.

JOE
> I don't know about that.

EVANGELINE
> He'll be real disappointed when I tell him Mama's dead.

JOE
> Evangeline, dear. Please don't count on him comin'.

EVANGELINE
> I heard those footsteps. Joe? I know I did. Are you sure you didn't hear nothing?

JOE
> Well…

EVANGELINE
> You did? You did Joe? You heard them too?

JOE
> More than likely it's just some drunkard comin home from the Tasty's Tavern.

EVANGELINE
> I'm going to stay awake all night tonight, and watch out the window. Then I'll be sure not to miss him.

JOE
> Evy, there's no point in you losing a good night's sleep.

EVANGELINE
> He's gonna want to know everything about Mama, about our life before he was took. I gotta be ready. Tell me, Joe. Tell me about like, how she used to keep the house so nice. Before. Before she got sick.

JOE
> She made apple crisp. That's the mother you should remember.

EVANGELINE
> She made apple crisp? With brown sugar on top? With what kind of apple, Joe?

JOE
> I'm not so sure about that..

EVANGELINE
> But what kind do you think… like… McIntosh?

JOE
> Yes, that's what it was. It was McIntosh.

EVANGELINE
> Oh. McIntosh!

Scene Eleven

Trail at night. ANNIE, in her red dress, lies in the snow before a towering tree. Sound of an owl hooting. ANNIE slowly wakes up looks up at the owl.

ANNIE
> This is very strange. This is very very strange. My heart is not beating, the blood is pouring, gushing out of me – In my Gaelic, *Vee a mer egg foil vache*. [this is the phonetic spelling] I am dying. I will be buried. Deep, unmoving inside a box under the ground, eyes never moving my tongue curling up mouldy inside my mouth these hands folded, living only in dreams, and thoughts, and hurried conversations in front of Steven's Milk, with dogs pulling at the leash and kids dancing round, "Did you hear who died?" or at the skating rink, flirting, buying hot dogs, "Did you hear?" less and less, and less, present only in my recycled clothes, hanging at the Goodwill, in the hairs I have left in the brushes all over

the house, in my fingerprints which will fade in ten years, she disappeared; then the neighbours they will go on and on for years Valerie Pratt rushing her three children out the door at two minutes to nine, every day, for years and years to come, Joe will sit on his porch the Sikh men will deliver flyers to our door every Sunday and the kids will play road hockey and I will have left so little; I wish to leave more on this earth, more than I have, *(big raspy breath)* oh let me go back, to lie naked in the wet cement, to spray paint my name in blue all over my city, *(another big breath)* to French kiss the men lying in doorways and stinking of urine, to run from rooftop to steeple, to stand on a speeding train and r-r-r-rave *(breathing becomes more difficult and shallower)* I have made such a faint impression in the world a bird alighting on a branch *(breath)* I want to go back and resume my life and just be be be *(breath)* with my son, my husband, just walk, breathe just breathe again in the leaves in the snow, walk *(breath)* and the snow can cover my footprints the blue light of the snow dropping bare feet on burning sand *(breath)* the August humidity wrapping around me, diving into murky lakes with weeds the rough of my husband's cheek *(breath)* the smell of his neck in the summer the breath of my child, with a cold, *(breath)* the smell of his head his head in the night oh!
let me resume—

Final breath. She lies, still. The owl hoots.

Scene Twelve

JACK in the hotel room.

JACK
Annie? You in the bath? You enjoy your bath, I won't bother you. I know how you love your long bath. I was thinking about what you were talking about, my temper. Like my… anger. The local punks callin me "*Diablo.*" What I did to those kids tonight and that thing with Pochinshky on Eglinton. I was thinking – I have to tell you something I haven't told you yet.

Remember, we ran into that – Jemma? The legal secretary from Brantford, blonde with the moussed hair – in February. Remember? At Yorkdale Mall? And remember how uncomfortable you said you felt? The way she looked at you? You said you thought there was something…

I used to…get very pissed at Jemma.

Sometimes I think it was because she was blonde. And she was so big breasted. I, like, I wanted to own her. I would leave you at home reading in your nightgown, tellin you I had to work all night and I would drive to Brantford to see Jemma, to have sex with her four, five times every which way I did things to her that… and then I would drive home and slide into bed next to you and we would talk that sweet night talk and you were so trusting – I was an animal. I was out of control. I still don't get it. I don't get why it happened. I didn't tell you before because I was afraid you wouldn't forgive me; maybe you won't forgive me, maybe you'll get outta the bath and say you want a separation, I wouldn't blame you. But I love you so much I wanted to tell you the whole truth. I was good as golden right up till I was nine. You know? The perfect kid. I would give my dad the paper, ask him if he wanted a beer, go get it for him, help my Mama with the table, change my baby sister. Sundays, I would put on the little suit, and we'd go to church. My sister and I would get under a blanket on the couch and watch cartoons all morning. I'd talk French with my gramma, sing songs with her; I played every sport goin', hockey, baseball, soccer, everything. I slept with my football. And then this kid, at school, he started to pick on me. Take off my hat, in the winter, throw it around. Say I was cheating in ball hockey. I never cheated. But he was a grade older, bigger, and said I couldn't play ball hockey. And I would sit there, on the side, and hope to be asked.

It was around then, I got – angry at home. I put holes in the walls with my fists. I wouldn't talk French wouldn't eat French, if my mother put *tortière* and sugar pie on the table I would throw 'em on the floor, "You stupid bitch, I want a hamburger and a fuckin popsicle not this frog shit, not this..." I never kissed a woman till you, Annie. I would turn away. I would say, I'm not one for kissing. Because kissing meant... I don't know. Being there. Goin inside like an underwater cave with someone, swimmin in, hand in hand, and you're under the water, inside the cave, with this person, and so much so much could go wrong. You're not the first woman I slept with, as you know, and maybe not the last, as you also know, but you are the first, and the last woman I will ever kiss.

Annie?

Scene Thirteen

EVANGELINE's house. She is in a slip, about to get dressed for her job at Fran's. The ghost of her mother stands behind her.

MOTHER
Evangeline. My lovely girl.

EVANGELINE
Oh Mama, I am so lonely. I am missing you so much.

MOTHER
I'm all around you, Vange.

EVANGELINE
I've been waitin so long for Kevy I've forgotten how to make friends.

MOTHER
I can see him coming, like a storm, my love.

EVANGELINE
My Kevin? My brother? Is coming back?

MOTHER
Oh. My lovely child. Just…

MOTHER is trying to warn her.

Scene Fourteen

The two snowmobilers walk through the brush towards ANNIE's fallen body. They do not see her yet.

MIKE
Wait'll my dad sees all this moose meat in his freezer. He's always after me sayin I never bring home nothin he will go freaky when he sees a pair of antlers sittin on his kitchen table.

KEVIN
Hey. I'm gettin the antlers. I'm the one that…

MIKE sees ANNIE lying in the snow.

MIKE
Oh my God. Oh my fucking God.

KEVIN
The lady from the lodge.

MIKE throws up and throws down the earphones.

MIKE
I told you we shouldn't wear these fucking things. Fuck. I'm blind in one eye, man, I didn't fuckin see her through all them trees. What's your fuckin excuse? Eh? Eh? Why didn't you see her?

KEVIN
I did see her. And so did you, Mike.

MIKE
What? What do you mean you did see her? What are you talking about?

KEVIN
Mike.

MIKE
What do you mean "Mike." WHAT THE HELL?

KEVIN
We were gettin back at the cop, right?

MIKE
You are saying you knew it was her? You saw it was a lady, man? Why didn't you tell me?

KEVIN
I thought you were jokin around, man. I thought you could see.

MIKE
No!

KEVIN
We messed him up good, man.

MIKE
I don't give a fuck about that, Kevin.

KEVIN
You know and I know we followed her here. Mike.

MIKE
I'm tellin you I didn't see her. I can't see without my glasses, man. I thought she was an animal.

KEVIN
We only meant to scare her, Mike. We didn't mean to kill her.

MIKE
But we did kill her. We shot her. YOU shot her.

KEVIN
We shot her. Right through the heart.

MIKE
(*pushes KEVIN to ground*) Why didn't you say nothin', asshole. Why didn't you fuckin say nothin'? You want to end up in fucking Millhaven? Do you know what that fuckin place is like? It's a rat's fuckin asshole, man, it's worse than any fuckin hell in any fuckin bible. I heard stories, man, see what happened to Kendal? Kendal got knifed in three days man, the place is a fuckin hellhole. I'll kill you man, I'll fuckin kill you if we get sent down. (*MIKE unpins KEVIN*)

KEVIN
Mike.

MIKE
What?

KEVIN
    Do you feel it?

MIKE
    What?

KEVIN
    The rush.

MIKE
    That's the devil, Kevin. That's the devil, shakin your hand.

                        Scene Fifteen

        JACK walks along the trail, pointing the flashlight in various directions.

JACK
    (passing close by ANNIE) Annie? Annie? Annie?

                        Scene Sixteen

        EVANGELINE is getting into her waitress uniform.

EVANGELINE
    I like working the graveyard shift at Fran's. Because it's quiet. And people who come in, mostly just want to think. They have scrambled eggs and toast with butter, ice cream and chocolate sauce, macaroni and cheese. And always coffee. They always have their coffee. With cream. With sugar. They are very much alone. I can see it in their eyes. Looking down. Smoking.

    Lately I been thinkin about things. Last things.

    Many people say they don't believe in God or life after death or heaven or hell but I have seen God. I have seen God in the deep brown eyes of the smoking people who ask for rice pudding at three forty-five in the morning. The Indians, teasing me, "Hey Apple," whatever that means, watching me. And I have seen hell in their raw dirty hands. The boy prostitutes from Grosvenor Street. Talking. Together. Lookin around the room, never resting. Smoking. Joking around with me. Want fries. Jesus Christ. In their voices. The way their voices sing. In the way their hair falls over their eyes. Sons of God. I touch their shoulders, sometimes. And in those times, I know… I know… that… I have seen…

        KEVIN starts taking ANNIE's dress off.

    I hope Patty's working tonight she always has the best stories. She's got this great big family out in Etobicoke, like six brothers and sisters and fourteen cousins and her mother and father and they have these big, funny dinners. And the way she tells it, she keeps saying everything is "so fabulous" and "so hideous" and she is just so funny.

And every time after she tells me a story I think it's that much more possible that when I get home…

Scene Seventeen

Night trail with KEVIN beside ANNIE's body. MIKE is watching in shock as KEVIN takes dress off the body.

MIKE
I don't fuckin know you man.

MIKE picks up his gun and exits. KEVIN finishes and stuffs the dress into his jacket. Sound of owl. JACK walks into clearing.

JACK
(*off, shouting*) Annie?

KEVIN hears him, takes off, and hides.

Annie. Oh my God.

He walks over to her. He kneels, he shakes her. He tries to give her the kiss of life, sees she is dead. He sees the bullet holes. He puts his coat over her. He picks her up.

Annie!

Scene Eighteen

JOE
I was there. At the table, in the kitchen. Sittin on the boarder's knee. About to eat my pepper and egg. When I saw my father killed by his own brother. Shot through the heart. With the gun from the garden. They'd had to dig up my mother's climbing yellow roses to get it, it was hid, ya see, under the roses. They had dug it up from the ground to scare some Irish fellows that were botherin them at all hours, askin for whores and for whisky. My uncle, he was sittin at one head of the table, across from my father, and he was cleaning the gun. My mother, she says "get the *pistola* offa my table." My father he tells her, "be quiet" and he and my uncle they are joking around about this and that and boom. My father falls back. Blood. Spraying out of him. Over the walls. Over me. Her face. She falls to her knees. And she cries: "*America Bella, se abbandonare ah meeeeeeeee!*" I still hear her sometimes, just outta nowhere, I'll be bringing home a bag of groceries from Fiesta Farms, or walkin to the bus up on Dupont.

Scene Nineteen

On the trail. Dawn. MIKE is sitting, drinking. We hear the sound of KEVIN's snowmobile and we see the beams of its headlights. KEVIN enters, the headlights lighting his way.

KEVIN
Beautiful night. Clear.

MIKE
Kev?

KEVIN
Yeah, Mike.

MIKE
What was that... shit you said... before you... shot her? That fuckin... "*Ek skal...*" what was that?

KEVIN laughs.

KEVIN
English teacher back home. Fag. Used to buy me cigarettes, CD's, down jackets whatever I fuckin wanted. Knew all these, like, ancient languages. Said I woulda been Norse, like a thousand years ago. Took me hunting. Deer. Taught me how to say "*Ek skal skjota ther huorti geognum*" "Let's shoot her man, right through the heart." You like that?

MIKE
I'm turning myself in.

KEVIN
What?

MIKE
To the OPP. First for the stolen sled. And then for the manslaughter.

KEVIN
WHAT?

MIKE
You can't stop me, man.

KEVIN
I'll fuckin stop you, Mike.

MIKE
Kev, look. It was an accident. These things happen all the time up here. My uncle, he got shot in the Kap – I'm gettin married for Christ sake, Kevin.

I don't want this on my conscience. Kev. Come with me. If we own up we get manslaughter at the worst. That's nothin'.

KEVIN
You're not gettin out of these woods, Mike. I got things goin on, things – waitin on me–

MIKE
Don't play asshole with me, Kev. I can beat your ass.

KEVIN
Oh yeah?

MIKE moves to KEVIN who then points his rifle at MIKE.

KEVIN
I couldn't take the green paint, man. In the jail. All the jail's a kind of green to make you sick to your stomach, never seen another green like that to make you feel less than a piece of shit crawlin with maggots, they'll put me in with the Jamaicans again man, cause they hate me, the cops already hate me; living with that green, a kind of green that gets into your mouth, turns all your food rancid, I'm not livin in the green again, not because of your fuckin conscience.

KEVIN shoots him. MIKE is felled. As he dies, KEVIN talks to him. During the following speech, the Northern Lights appear in the sky, lighting up KEVIN and darkening him, flashing across his face and body.

KEVIN
Mike, I'm gonna tell you about the greatest sled of my life. My ride through the Northwest Territories. It was this friendship thing I was hired on: promotional. I replaced the guy who owned the Bombardier dealership I was workin in Thunder Bay, you know Pierre, he was sick, right, he knew I was keen and he seen how I handle a sled, so he sends me on this fuckin ride. First off, everything you have heard about the toughness of pullin off a ride in the interior of NWT is totally true. On the other hand, it happens to be the most beautiful place on this earth. From the Bering Strait to the Tundra there it's like nothing you've ever seen, Mike. And all that wind, and snow and nothin like nothin for miles and miles and no trees and you are, well, very much alone. But you're not, Michael, you're not really alone, right? Cause come nightfall, you'll be sittin there, and… Mike? *(pulling out his hunting knife)*

have you ever seen…?
the lights?

You know, *(drawing his knife across MIKE's throat)* the Northern Lights?

Northern Lights on KEVIN, as MIKE dies.

Blackout.

ACT TWO

Scene One

The North. Under music, KEVIN is running, breathless, away from the scene of his crime, on the trail.

A light and music change. KEVIN, with his bag, is in Toronto, walking up Clinton Street, searching for his house. The ghost of his mother appears, full of sadness, for she senses what horror is to come.

MOTHER
Kevin. Oh Kevin. I remember the day you were born. My water broke on the Bathurst streetcar, goin down Bathurst to Queen, and there I was, stretched over the back seat; my waters gushing out of me, pouring out, like a fast stream, over everybody's boots and shopping bags. Well when the car stopped at Queen I somehow got off, crossed the street, everyone staring, staring at me and into Galaxy Donuts. The front of my dress is soaked and I'm there with the donuts. The chocolate sprinkle, the sugared, the iced, and smell of coffee overpowering and BOOM I pass out and the next thing I know you're crowning and the nurse said she said she said "would you like to feel your baby's head?" and I reached down and then I pushed and I pushed and whoooooooo there you were, Kevin, all wet and blue and bloody and they put you on my tummy and oh my goodness you had such a wise little face. I have never forgotten your wise little face. Kevin? Ohhhhhh Kevin. Please– *(disappearing)*

KEVIN walks up the street and stops in front of her house. He stares at the house. He looks at the next house. EVANGELINE calls out.

EVANGELINE
Um Excuse me? Hello?

He turns.

Are you looking for somebody in particular? I uh – know the neighbourhood pretty well.

KEVIN
Yeah. Yeah I am.

He searches in his bag for a notebook with the particulars written on it. He finds it and reads her name.

I'm lookin for a – uh – a woman called Evangeline Melnyk? The street number got blurred, right? But the name, I can read. Is there anyone of that name who lives around here? Or did? With her mother, name of – Crystal–? But, then, the mother, I was told she passed away sometime last year, so this Evangeline, she would be livin alone now. If she was still here.

She is in shock so he doesn't see a response in her face.

KEVIN
It must be other side of Bloor then. Okay, *thanks* for your *help*, have a good day!

He heads down the road. She lets him go till he is almost out of sight.

EVANGELINE
Kevin?

He turns, slowly. They look at one another. They know. During JOE's speech, they slowly make their way inside.

Scene Two

JOE is at the grocery store. We see the fruit and vegetable stand. He calls in to the owner, and then walks home.

JOE
Grazie, Vincente! Ciao! *(he starts his walk home)* I don't read Italian and I don't write Italian. But I can speak it. Pretty well. I grew up speakin it. To my mother. To the fella who ran this store. To a couple of neighbours. To everyone else, I spoke English. You have to bury all that. Once you're here. In Canada. My father, Carlo, he arrived at Union Station in 1909, all by himself. He gets off the train and he leaves the station and he walks up Yonge Street. What else is he gonna do? He sees a man selling bananas, he goes up to him he says *"Paesano,* can you tell me where I might get a room, and a job." The guy sellin bananas he's Calabrese, and he tells him he can work on the railroad for 7 cents an hour, or sell bananas, then he asks my father if he has a gun, a *pistola*, and my father says "Yeah," and then the guy says to him "Bury your gun." Like, in the garden. He tells him if the cops catch you with a gun, you're on the next boat back.

I speak Italian when I get together with my brothers and sisters, you know, a mix of Italian and Canadian, I speak it to old Annunciata, down the street, but to tell you the truth, I'm always behind, translating, back into English in my head. So I guess I don't really speak it. My children, they don't speak it at all.

Scene Three

In the sitting room.

KEVIN
Until a few months ago, I thought I'd never been to Toronto. I thought I was born in North Bay and I thought Diane was my true mother.

EVANGELINE
Kevin. Oh Kevin.

KEVIN
So she's in hospital with cancer last year and she calls me to her bedside and she tells me that she's not my mother at all. She says she had been my babysitter and she had stole me away from my home in Toronto when I was four years old. At first I thought she was delirious, right? With the morphine, eh? I didn't think nothin of it.

EVANGELINE
It's true. She stole you away from us Kevin. We nearly died of it, the whole city was lookin for you, flowers on our porch every day, hundreds and hundreds of cards, the police, the whole city–

KEVIN goes into his backpack and pulls out a wind-up music box from home.

KEVIN
(winding the music box) Then I had to be in TO on business. And… I found the name and address she gave me, right? So I thought I'd check it out.

He gives it to her. It plays.

EVANGELINE
Oh Kevin. I've been waiting for you for so long.

KEVIN
I'd forgotten about you. And my real mother. Everything. Because I was so young… when she… fuck. This is fucking…

An awkward silence.

EVANGELINE
And Diane, did she – Was she–?

He sees EVANGELINE is wondering if he was ill treated. He was, so he can't answer.

KEVIN
Huh? Yeah…. What are the – uh – balloons and that for?

He is starting to get edgy, looking through the curtain out into the street, nervous that cops might have followed him.

EVANGELINE
Just – your birthday.

KEVIN
It's not – Oh yeah?

EVANGELINE
March 27th. Didn't–?

KEVIN
No. She didn't.

EVANGELINE
You're twenty-four, right?

KEVIN
Yeah. Today. I guess.

EVANGELINE
I always wished you happy birthday. Every year.

KEVIN
Cool.

EVANGELINE
You're shaking. Kevin? What's the matter?

KEVIN
Crashed. Snowmobile. White snow, dark, and–

EVANGELINE
What, a moose? A deer? Kev? You crashed into a moose?

Scene Four

JOE is working in his garden. Sound of a car driving up to the back. Door slamming. JACK walks along the side path to the front of the house, with luggage. He ignores JOE and carries the luggage up the front steps.

JOE
Jack. How was your holiday? Still got snow up there?

JACK just stares.

JOE
Everything okay? Jack?

JACK appears frozen. He tries to get his keys.

JOE
I got your papers, if you want 'em. You forgot to cancel. I know what that's like, I'm forgetful too. Where's Annie?

Sound of robins.

JOE
Oh listen to that. First robin. First robin of the year.

JACK
There uh… there was…

> *Silence.*

I didn't know how to give her the kiss. If I'd known how to give her the kiss, she would be alive today.

JOE
Oh my God.

JACK
They go into the woods. For deer meat. They're jittery, they been drinking, they been there for days, nights, seen nothing. They see a shape. They shoot. Guy told me it happens a lot up there. People get shot. Mistaken for deer, usually. Should never go walking at night. I told Volker, he should have put up a sign. It's very dangerous in the woods up there. Annie thought, people think it's like a… conservation area so they are safe. They think because they are in the woods, in their own country, and there is a warm fire back at the lodge, they are safe. They're not safe.

> *JOE nods.*

There was… the poacher, he has something of hers, her dress, her red… I am going to find him, if I have to spend the rest of my life doing it, Joe. I am going to find him and I am going to tear him apart.

JOE
Si abbandonare ah me.

JACK
What?

JOE
I said if there's anything we can do, please, just let us know. I mean that, Jack.

JACK
Yeah uh thanks. I don't exactly…

> *Silence. JACK goes into the house.*

JOE
(an echo of CARMELLA) Si abbandonare ah me.

Scene Five

> *EVANGELINE's house: KEVIN crouched on the floor of his room stares at ANNIE's dress hanging there. In his underwear, he sits on a diagonal from the*

dress in the corner, shivering. He puts on the dress. EVANGELINE is calling to him while she makes dinner:

EVANGELINE
You know what guess what? I was thinkin we could start like a business?

ANNIE's ghost appears. She is a little wonky, as this is her first visit back to her home and neighbourhood since her death. She moves slowly. She stares at her home with longing, and she turns and sees EVANGELINE. She sees the horror EVANGELINE faces, and she reaches for her to give her the strength on her journey.

Cause like I know the ladies at the Bank of Montreal up at Christie and Dupont really well they're really really nice to me, especially Gloria. *(EVANGELINE becomes aware of ANNIE's presence and stops talking for a moment)* I think if we saved up my tips from Fran's, and you start workin soon, we could save up and then go and ask 'em for a loan and then just start up our own business. I was thinking maybe a bed and breakfast. After all we have the house, it's paid for. It's got the six bedrooms. Alls it needs is well, quite a bit of work, but we could do a lot of it ourselves, hire some students, and…

EVANGELINE looks directly at ANNIE's ghost, and she knows something has happened. She is deeply shaken. In his room, KEVIN is putting on ANNIE's dress. It is very clingy, sexy. He looks in the mirror, terrified. EVANGELINE walks almost in a trance outside to JOE, who is standing on his porch.

What happened? Did something happen? To Annie Delaney?

JOE
A poacher. In the woods. Shootin after deer. A terrible accident.

She stands, leaning against the porch, in shock. ANNIE's ghost appears as KEVIN's reflection in the mirror.

Scene Six

JACK's place: He makes some calls.

JACK
Yeah, Hello, is this The Bay credit office? I'm calling about my payment? Just to let you know that my cheque is in the mail, I put it in Friday. Yes, okay.

He lays out some clothes for ANNIE in her coffin. He lays out a red dress and shoes in the image of her body on the floor. Meanwhile, KEVIN has heard from EVANGELINE about ANNIE. He looks out his window at JACK's house. He initially thinks of leaving, but decides he would like to stay. In the danger.

Yeah, can I have the number of the Bank of Montreal on Dupont and Christie. Hello. Yeah is Gloria there. Gloria. It's Jack Prevost. Fine fine how are you. Yeah. I was phoning about locking money in that high yielding account because my wife she she is in the morgue, on a cold in a cold her body is on / her heart isn't beating / a slab they are cutting / the coroner / her blood isn't running / is cutting to see the insides how the insides she isn't even thinking her quiet thoughts her quiet quiet–

He drops the phone.

Scene Seven

JOE
(to audience) I ran; when he was shot and I ran out the door and for blocks and blocks all the way over to Yonge Street, where I found myself by the movie theatre, with the celluloid they used to throw out, after the show, I picked it up, rolls and rolls of it, put it in my pocket and I held it to the sun, so I could watch it burst into flames, it always calmed me, doin that, I sat on the curb and held it and I watched as the fire flamed and then travelled around and around and into my pocket and fwoof I was fire, burning, red, my father, blood, spraying hot, hot and like it was like it – snowed, and white, holy white surrounded me, and it was white and it was quiet and there was only the smell of sweet bread. And then I passed out. In and out, in a cloud of white flour. Because the baker next door, he had seen me, on fire, from his window, where he was pounding dough, and he had run with a giant bag of flour and emptied it over me, over the fire, and surrounded me with his sweet-smelling arms.

Scene Eight

EVANGELINE with a candle lit for ANNIE. She prays and cries. KEVIN watches her silently.

KEVIN
I know what you're goin through. I lost people too. Blurry snowfall, can't see too well. I'm walkin towards this figure I seen, on the ice, on the lake, hearing the wind, the figure don't move. I get closer and I see it's a man. It's a frozen man. His hand, like, out. Stretched. He doesn't look human any more I'm tellin you. And I'm just starin at him and then I hear, like a breath. And his one of his eyes, like was lookin'. At me. He's alive. And I look over into the bush and I see his sled crashed, and I walked up real close and I breathed my hot breath onto his face, to try to… he breathed in some air one more time and then his eye went dead like the other one and he was just froze. He was the frozen man.

EVANGELINE
When someone's dead they're dead forever. So long…

KEVIN goes to her and comforts her.

KEVIN
Hey now, don't cry. Don't cry.

His actions become sexual. EVANGELINE breaks away.

EVANGELINE
What are you doing? Kevin, what are you doing?

KEVIN
Givin you some brotherly love.

EVANGELINE
It's not right.

KEVIN
Uncut nine inches, babe.

EVANGELINE throws him across the room. She is very strong.

EVANGELINE
You are my brother. And you're in shock. That's all. You're not right because of your crash. So I will forgive you this once. But you must never ever ever do this again. You mustn't ever.

KEVIN
Harsh me out why don't ya.

EVANGELINE
We're brother and sister.

KEVIN approaches her.

EVANGELINE
No!

She slaps him. KEVIN moves away from her and sits down, crying.

It's not right. It's not right for you to talk to me like that.

KEVIN
Not right, not right. Nothing's been right since she took me away from you, my whole life, nothing. I should just go and fuckin die. That's what I'm gonna do, I'm gonna fuckin walk right down Bathurst Street into the lake and I'll be outta your way and bother you no more.

KEVIN puts on his coat and goes to leave. She tries to stop him.

EVANGELINE
Kevin please.

He goes to leave again.

Kevin.

He comes back in. He undoes his jeans and rubs himself against her breasts until he ejaculates. [Whether this is seen or not is optional.] He then holds her tightly. She is confused. KEVIN moves away.

KEVIN
Anyways, don't worry about it. It's not like we have the same father.

She looks at him amazed.

Well, look at your hair. Look at your hair, and then look at my hair. Oh, by the way, I been lookin over our accounts? And we gotta get you makin some cash.

Scene Nine

The North. ANNIE walks very close to EVANGELINE, and gives her solace with a touch or a look. The following speech is in reaction to what has happened.

ANNIE
I am a silent woman. That is what they say about me. When they have to say something about me. Oh, Annie, she's… quiet. When she's not on stage, singing her quirky songs or telling her strange stories she is… quiet. Jack, he really liked my silences. That's why he married me.
When I was a child, I would lie in my bed and hear the voices of my parents fighting, underneath me, night after night.
All their words like a claw in my chest;
I would go for days without talking, days and nights and days and there was only one place I found peace and that was… under my dear grandmother's skirts. A kind of chapel, there. Blossom was her name, her real name was Catherine but they called her Blossom. It was dark and fragrant under there, 4711 I think, lemonish scent, and I loved to look at her veiny legs. Beautiful blue worms. Tea and toast. Sweet wine. Falling asleep, together. She lived with us, she spent her time looking out the window, and doing watercolours of birds, and my mother was always exasperated with her. "Mother, will you just get OUT of my kitchen?" "Mother, do you need to go to the toilet?" When she fell and broke her hip, she was moved to a home for the aged. It smelled of Phisohex and creamed corn. The look on her face, when we left her there, on a cold autumn morning, sitting on her designated bed. She held onto her coat her brown coat and the look of… there is no word; I stood there, treachery, looking at the floor. A few weeks later, my grandmother walked out of the home with a razor blade she had stolen from one of the old men and into the Rosedale ravine and she cut her wrists and she walked and walked through the brown and yellow leaves and she turned in circles and then bowed, deeply, I think.

ANNIE grabs the curtain behind her, or an imaginary dress and wraps herself in it.

Ahhhhhhh! Ohhh there she is. Waiting for me. Huge. With her big skirt…
This silence is perfect.
This is silence exquisite.
This is…

Scene Ten

EVANGELINE in a nightie, remembering. Her mother's ghost is there, and speaks, slightly drunkenly.

MOTHER
Oh babe you woulda loved Nathan. He was a dreamer, like you, always… tellin me his funny stories in that deep sexy voice, wearing that tall black hat, with his black glossy hair, long. Him and me we made this seafood soup with the, the shrimp and the whitefish and after we lay in the backyard under the lilac tree…

EVANGELINE walks over to JOE's porch and checks to find him rocking in his chair:

JOE
Everything okay?

EVANGELINE
I couldn't sleep.

JOE
Nope. Me neither.

EVANGELINE
Joe. Do you mind if I ask you something?

JOE
Go right ahead.

EVANGELINE
Did you know my father?

JOE
Sure, I knew Bert, when he was around. Worked up at the TTC. Nice fella. Till he took to the bottle. But that's not his fault, really.

EVANGELINE
And Bert was my father. My real and natural father.

JOE is silent.

Joe? Do you know anything that I don't know?

Silence

Joe? I always knew I looked well not like my mother and father but I figured I must be some you know, genetic throwback to like an Indian or Spanish great grandmother somethin like that; my mother when she was drinking she used to say something about… a man named Nathan?

Silence.

Joe?

JOE
There was a guy. Used to come around. Before she married Bert.

Silence.

EVANGELINE
Did she have me before she married Bert? Joe, please, just tell me the truth.

JOE
Bert, he didn't seem to mind. I always figured she had told you.

EVANGELINE
No.

JOE
I don't think she told the guy neither.

EVANGELINE
His name was Nathan?

JOE
Yes, yes I think it was. He was a nice enough fellow. Tall, with the long hair, an Indian fellow I believe. You know, Canadian Indian.

EVANGELINE
Indian? Oh my goodness. Indian?

JOE
He said… somethin about he was teaching book writing at George Brown. He had a couple of books you could buy in the bookstores. And your Mom she was going for the cooking, to become a chef. She brought him home one night. I could hear the two of them laughing from two blocks away. Your mom told me they stayed up all night cooking and laughing. Oh he brought out the woman's laugh. She stopped laughing when she married Bert.

EVANGELINE
Nathan was my father.

JOE
I think that's what your mom told Essie.

EVANGELINE
(touching her hair) And you say he was Indian? Joe?

They sit in silence

Scene Eleven

JOE
After he was killed, my mother became nervous. She was nervous of me. Second son. Because she blamed me. Second son. For the shooting. She thought my playing with the pepper and egg distracted my uncle, caused him to shoot off the gun. And kill my father. Second son. The way she looked at me when he fell… it is a look – I wish I had never…

Scene Twelve

EVANGELINE and KEVIN walking down the street. She wears spiked high heels that he has given her.

KEVIN
Beautiful. Remember: smile, talk nice.

EVANGELINE
I don't know what to say.

KEVIN
Don't say nothin. I'll say.

EVANGELINE
Only for a couple weeks, right? Just till we get up the money for the roof.

KEVIN
You're wobbling.

EVANGELINE
I am not.

KEVIN
Don't fucking wobble. If you wobble you won't get the fucking job.

EVANGELINE
Well maybe I don't want the job, you bad-breath pimp. Whoremonger. *(as KEVIN walks away)* I'm sorry. I'm sorry okay, your breath is fine, I didn't mean it.

KEVIN
You're tryin to make me feel bad, aren't you?

EVANGELINE
No.

KEVIN
Don't try to make me feel bad, Evangeline, I'm just tryin to keep us alive here. Okay? Let me tell you something: There is only one thing in this world I ever ever did that I feel bad about and that is–

JOE appears on his porch.

EVANGELINE
(cutting him off) Kevin. C'mere, I want you to meet somebody.

They move to JOE's porch

JOE
Hello. Good morning.

EVANGELINE
Joe? I would like you to meet my brother Kevin. Again.

JOE
Kevin. It's a huge pleasure. And a very big surprise. Ev told me this morning on the phone and I almost fell to the floor! I remember you very well indeed. You would climb up our stairs and you would stand in front of the door and say "Open." "Open." Curly blonde hair. Essie would say "That kid is too cute for words." She'd laugh.

KEVIN
A long time ago.

JOE
"Even the fox must sleep," that's what Essie would say when we seen you sleepin on the porch.

KEVIN
Oh yeah?

JOE
Well you've made your sister very happy.

KEVIN
That's nice.

JOE
Gonna stay for a while? Get some work?

> *JACK enters onto his porch for a breath of air.*

KEVIN
I'll stay for a while.

JOE
It's good to have you back.

KEVIN
Even the fox must sleep.

> *JOE waves to JACK. When KEVIN sees him we hear the sound of the bullet that killed ANNIE.*

KEVIN
C'mon we gotta go.

> *EVANGELINE and KEVIN leave.*

JOE
Bye now.

> *JOE watches EVANGELINE wobble up the road. This reminds him of the past. JOE's mother, CARMELLA, comes up the road with a shoe in her hand and a broom.*

CARMELLA
Joe.

JOE
Mama!

CARMELLA
I told you not to go climbing fences and playing rough. We can't afford another pair of shoes. What are you trying to do?

JOE
Ya can't get me a pair of shoes?

CARMELLA
We can't afford nothing. We can't afford a loaf of bread for the ten of us, Joe. You know that. You do this on purpose, to make me cry, don't you, you bad, bad…

She hits him with her broom.

JOE
Ask the priest, Mama. The priest always helps us.

CARMELLA
I canno go that priest again, Joey. I canno do that.

JOE
Mama. Please. What am I going to wear?

She is silent.

JOE
Mama.

CARMELLA takes off her Depression-era widow shoes and presents them.

CARMELLA
You will wear my shoes to school.

JOE
But Mama, I can't. I can't wear your shoes.

CARMELLA
If you want shoes so bad, you wear my shoes. Put them on.

JOE
No.

CARMELLA
Put them on.

JOE
NO.

CARMELLA hits him hard. He cries and slowly puts the shoes on. He is totally humiliated. They are way too big. He walks, with difficulty, across the stage. His mother is very upset for him, but cannot show it.

Scene Thirteen

JACK dusts the house for fingerprints. They come up very clear. He spots ANNIE's, and puts his hand on her prints. (If the theatre is unable to do this just drop it.)

Scene Fourteen

Funeral music.

JACK
Thank you all very much for coming. Annie and I used to place bets who'd get a bigger turn out at their funeral. It's clear she's the winner. Annie, I'll pay you later. Ummm, Annie, she was afraid of getting old. And now she never will be getting old. *(long pause)* I don't know if you heard this already or not. Anyway, I wanted to play it.

ANNIE appears. Song: "My mother and father."

ANNIE
my father and mother
are getting old
I and my brother
were sad when they sold
our old house
with it's sagging porch
and kitchen mouse
and view of the forks
of the Credit River
we were puppies biting at their heels
now they are old
don't finish their meals

They were big bright so perfect
now they are old
not as happy somehow
not as quick
not as clean
can't sleep very long
they get up before dawn
sit in the dark
Watch the dew
on the grass
My mother and father are old
When I say good-bye after Thanksgiving dinner
They have tears in their eyes
so do I.
for something lost
Something lost. And gone.
Am I saying good-bye to ghosts

(spoken) oh no.

(sung) my mother and father
Are getting old.

Scene Fifteen

JOE's house

JOE
My older sister, Annabella, married young, seventeen, very young, to get away from my mother. Niko, her husband, he was older, in his forties, but he was good to her. The problem was that he couldn't see. He couldn't see. And it was the depression. Who had money for glasses? And when she was crying in pain, with her menstrual cramps, eh? Niko goes to get her medicine. And he thinks he's gettin like a Alka-Seltzer and he puts the tablet in water and he gives it to her. It was athlete's foot medicine. It killed her in two days. I'm playin ball in the schoolyard, I refused to go see her in hospital. I didn't like hospitals. Her body looked so stiff. In the coffin. The ring on her finger. Her face… with the terrible makeup… her lips and fingernails inky blue. God forgive me, Annabella. *(seeing a ball land on his lawn)* GET THAT BALL OFFA MY LAWN. I'M GOING TO CUT IT INTO LITTLE BITS NEXT TIME THAT BALL LANDS ON MY LAWN, YOU HEAR ME? DO YOU HEAR WHAT I'M SAYING?

Scene Sixteen

ZANZIBAR strip club. EVANGELINE as a Mother Superior. JACK walks in mid-dance and stands at the back, electrified by her. She directs most of her dance to him. She throws her garter to him. Back stage, KEVIN, in the dressing room, waiting, watches her and notices she is dancing for JACK, and is enraged. She comes in and covers herself with a bathrobe.

M.C.
Let's have a big hand, gents, for Sister Fantastia, our Lady of Perpetual Love!

EVANGELINE gives KEVIN six twenties.

KEVIN
Seen you flashin that cop out there. I told you to stay away from him, Evangeline.

EVANGELINE
Are you coming home tonight?

KEVIN
If I see you lookin at him again you know what I'm gonna do.

EVANGELINE
Shall I thaw the chicken? Make some chicken curry?

KEVIN
And another thing. You're not bringing back enough cash. You gotta show more pussy, I tole ya. Flash a little candy floss.

EVANGELINE
Go to hell.

KEVIN
The house is fallin down, Evy, we need the money. If we don't start workin on it, we may have to leave it.

EVANGELINE
(after a silence, loud) Ha! Ha! Ha! Ha! Ha! Ha!

KEVIN
What's do funny?

EVANGELINE
This. It's – it's – it's – it's like something out of Charles Dickens. *Little Dorrit.*

KEVIN
What?

EVANGELINE
You know, you comin back here, forcing me into a life of… ill-repute… but you know what? To tell you the truth I love it. I love fancy dancing. EXOTIC DANCING. Takin my clothes off. I *love* the griminess of the place and the men's *hungry* faces I love watching them jack off to the sight of my swaying hips. I'm Lucifer, I'm bringing them light, and I just think it's so funny that you think you're this bad dude and I'm this poor little–

M.C.
And coming up in a few minutes, the pure and lovely Fantasia, guys, she is just getting herself ready for you as we speak…

KEVIN
Are you makin fun of me?

She looks at him, kisses him. Aroused, he pursues it.

M.C.
And now… the temperature rises, the temperature soars. What's happening? Are we moving closer to the sun? Oh no, my friends, we have a furnace here. A furnace named FANTASIA. Gentlemen, please will you put your filthy hands together for Fantasia.

KEVIN
Now you get out there. And remember, only your brother loves you.

She leaves. KEVIN watches her dance towards JACK and shouts.

ALWAYS!!

Blackout.

ACT THREE

Scene One

JACK, in his dressing gown, remembers. He enters his and ANNIE's living room. She is reading on the couch.

JACK
I got us a movie.

ANNIE
Oh. What did you get?

JACK
A special movie. You know. Romantic.

ANNIE
Oh.

JACK
I think you'll like this one. The girl… is very good.

ANNIE
Ohhhkay. If you say so.

JACK
Listen, if you don't want me to put it on, just say so. I just thought something… erotic might be fun. Help me forget the shitty day I had.

ANNIE
No, no, it's okay. Actually I'm kind of interested.

JACK puts in the videotape. The porno type of music starts up. They watch. ANNIE is amused at first. JACK is also amused but the amusement turns to arousal.

JACK
Look at that one. The blonde.

ANNIE
You like her?

JACK
I just think she's good. She's a good actress. I don't know. She really seems to be liking… all the guys at once. I don't think she's acting. Do you know what I mean?

ANNIE
Hmm.

They both become aroused. JACK begins to kiss her. They begin to make love in an almost violent way. JACK cannot keep his eyes off the screen, and both times he looks at it he is more violent with her. Suddenly, ANNIE gets up and covers herself.

JACK
What's wrong, you okay?

ANNIE
I just… I just don't feel so well.

JACK
Yeah? What is it.

The porno music blares.

Is it the movie?

ANNIE
No, no, I think I'm getting sick that's all. I had a headache before.

JACK
Are you sure it's not the movie?

ANNIE
Yeah.

JACK
Okay. Do you want me to get you something? An Alka Seltzer?

ANNIE shakes her head. He turns back to the movie.

ANNIE
Would you mind, turning down the volume?

He turns down the volume but still looks at the screen.

Would you… take it out, please? Take it out of the machine. Take it out of the machine.

He does so. He puts it down on the table.

JACK
I thought you were enjoying it.

Silence.

ANNIE
All those men, crowding around her…

JACK
You shoulda said something. How come you didn't say nothing?

ANNIE
Their faces: dogs.

JACK
Oh come on. You were enjoying it at first. I know you were.

ANNIE
Crowding her.

JACK
But honey, it was what she wanted. She was the one that asked them all…

ANNIE
No.

JACK
Annie.

ANNIE
No.

JACK
Would you relax? It's just a movie. A sexy movie. Sex between consenting adults. What's the big deal?

ANNIE is silent. She is deeply distressed, JACK doesn't know what to do.

JACK
There was no violence, I made sure of that. I just thought, something different…

ANNIE begins an activity she always begins when she goes into one of her silences.

Please. Don't go into one of your silences. This is not a good time for me.

ANNIE
I'm going to go – for a walk.

JACK
A walk? At this time of night?

ANNIE
I need a walk. When I return I want it to be out of our house.

JACK
I'll put it out with the garbage tomorrow.

ANNIE
Tonight. Take it out of our house tonight. I'm not coming back till it's out of the house. I'll walk the streets all night if I have to.

JACK
Oh for God's sake.

ANNIE
Out of our house!

JACK
Alright. You go for your walk and I will take the movie out of the house. I'll take it right out of the neighbourhood. Will that make you happy?

ANNIE slams the door.

ANNIE
OUT OF MY HOUSE!

JACK
I want to make you happy, Annie.

Scene Two

The North. KEVIN is in the dark. In the woods. In the spot where he killed MIKE. MIKE is frozen there, like a statue. KEVIN has driven all the way up north. He approaches MIKE's frozen body.

KEVIN
Two and a half hours, 120 all the way, Mike. You shoulda seen these bozo's from Quebec playin chicken with me I pushed em off the road man, they're still waitin for a tow.

KEVIN covers MIKE's body with evergreen boughs as he speaks.

I can't believe they didn't find ya, Mike, fuckin search party probably walked right by you I'm sittin there down in Toronto thinkin I gotta bury Mike. He's my best friend in the whole world and I will not have his body torn apart by wolves. Goodnight Michael, I'll be thinkin about you.

He covers him up. ANNIE appears behind him, in the same position as she was when he shot her. He faces her. He runs away from ANNIE.

Scene Three

JOE and EVANGELINE on JOE's porch

EVANGELINE
Tell me more about my father?

JOE
Well, like I said, he was funny.

EVANGELINE
Funny? How? How was he funny?

JOE
Like TV. Very funny. Make ya laugh out loud kind of funny.

EVANGELINE
Did he talk much about… his people?

JOE
He never said. Well, once he said somethin about he could never do the sun dance. He didn't have the patience. And he said his mother lived out at some reserve in Manitoba. He'd go out to see her once in a while. I think he said he was of the Cree nation. I think.

EVANGELINE
Cree. So that's why I've always felt so – apart from… Cree? Will I ever know him, Joe?

JOE
You may. You may not.

EVANGELINE
I just feel things are going in a certain way. And there's nothin I can do to stop them. Like I'm in a sled, right? In a runaway sled goin down a mountain of ice, faster and faster and if I tip over I will break my neck and bones for sure but if I keep going, what's at the bottom, what's at the bottom Joe is the lake. I'll crack through the foot-thick ice in a moment and down into the frigid waters, stopping my heart and my breath…

JOE
I know the feeling.

EVANGELINE
My very life is shaken, Joe. If you know what I mean.

JOE
Yeah. I know what you mean.

Scene Four

EVANGELINE's house. KEVIN goes into the bedroom and looks out the window. She wakes.

KEVIN
Hold me, baby. Please hold me.

She moves to the window and puts her arms around him.

I missed you so much. I missed you so fuckin much.

EVANGELINE
Hardly seen ya in the last few weeks, Kevin. I was gettin worried.

KEVIN
That cop from across the street – has he been around?

EVANGELINE
Haven't noticed, really.

KEVIN
Just hold me.

EVANGELINE
Steer escaped from the slaughterhouse today. Ran right up the street.

KEVIN
Yeah? Fuck. What… happened?

EVANGELINE
They shot it through the head and dragged it back down the street. Blood all over the street.

KEVIN opens the window.

KEVIN
Fucking – dogs.

EVANGELINE
You know what he was sayin'? The guy that runs the video store?

KEVIN
What?

EVANGELINE
That the earth is gonna get hit by a comet. Like, soon.

KEVIN
How does he know?

EVANGELINE
The scientists, the astronomers have said, soon. What will we do when that happens? What will we do, Kev?

KEVIN
We fill up a needle. And we shoot ourselves into deep dark space.

EVANGELINE
So we won't feel the quaking. The fires.

KEVIN
We don't feel sweet nothin'. Just like that steer. He's not afraid any more. He's not anything.

Scene Five

JACK's house. He is sitting in the dark, in his dressing gown. He walks over to a table where ANNIE is sitting, doing some translating.

ANNIE
(Gaelic) Bhiomar ag fail bhais den ocras in Eirinn. [Pronounced: Vee a mer egg foil vagh den ocras in Airinn] We – were – getting death – of the hunger – in Ireland. I want to go to Ireland. To Connemara, to look at the graves.

JACK
Why? What for?

ANNIE
I want to know–

JACK
Who you are.

ANNIE
Yes.

JACK
You and about three hundred thousand American tourists a year.

ANNIE
Jack, I want to hear my natural language.

JACK
They hate you over there. They have no interest in you whatsoever. They don't see you as family, they see you as American.

ANNIE
I don't believe it. If I were to meet a Delaney I know it would be… a very beautiful… it would help me, Jack.

JACK
I have absolutely no desire ever to visit France, or even Quebec. Just because my name is Prevost? And my grandfather grew up in Rimouski? I have nothing to do with those people. *Oh tabernac, je me souviens je suis tres* fuckin *triste* and pissed off that Wolfe *il triumph de Montcalm* on the fuckin Plains of Abraham and *je suis triste vive le Québec libre vive le Québec libre* that was my ancestors, on both sides, two generations ago, but that is not me do you ever see me watch the French station? No! No! I am this now, THIS.

ANNIE
I am going to Ireland. In the spring.

JACK
And leave me alone?

ANNIE
I need to go.

JACK
And if I ask you not to?

ANNIE is silent.

If I ask you not to?

ANNIE
And why would you do that, Jack?

JACK
Because… I would worry about you, over there all by yourself. The IRA is everywhere–

ANNIE
The IRA? Why are you LYING Jack you are a LIAR you are not worried about me being shot by the IRISH REPUBLICAN ARMY you are worried about me doing something that has nothing to do with you; the way you were with your girlfriend Jemma; *(She prods and hits him.)* you gonna hit me too? Throw me up against the wall and then fuck me up the ass and piss on me the way you did with her?

JACK
(breathless) Annie.

ANNIE
You are just like the pathetic husband in the story of the selkie, the half-woman half-seal, terrified his beautiful wife he stole from the sea would find her seal skin, her true skin because he knows if she finds it then nothing, not children, not love, not any amount of pleading, will keep her from the sea. YOU WANT TO KEEP ME FROM THE SEA.

She collapses.

JACK
(in the present) Annie, you didn't know about Jemma then, I hadn't told you, this isn't fair, this isn't…

ANNIE weeps.

ANNIE
But of course I knew, I knew in – here.

She pounds her gut.

JACK
I even said I'd go, I said if you feel that strongly about it, let's just… wait till my holidays in August, and we'll go together. What about that? Do one of those walking tour things you like.

ANNIE
No.

JACK
Why not for God's sake? Hey it's quite a sacrifice for me even goin there, you know I like Trinidad and Tobago, or St. Lucia, I love to lie in the sun I HATE the rain. I mean Annie, Ireland is just like fuckin New Brunswick. And who wants to go there?

ANNIE glares at him.

ANNIE
You don't understand at all, do you?

He looks at her.

JACK
I'm trying to, Annie. I'm really really trying to. I just thought if we went together, maybe–

ANNIE
I need to go alone. And you will have to accept that.

JACK
How long have you been sleeping with him?

ANNIE
WHO?

JACK
Whoever it is you are meeting there, Annie. This is classic–

She laughs.

A lot of things are making sense now.

ANNIE
What are you talking about?

JACK
You're coldness. In the last few months.

ANNIE
What?

JACK
Like making love to a fucking corpse.

ANNIE
Go to hell. And fucking burn there.

JACK
You don't make a sound, you don't move. I don't remember the last time you gave me a back massage.

ANNIE turns away.

What is his name? Annie? Who is it? Do you do for him what you haven't done for me in five years?

ANNIE
Jack. First of all, I swear on my life there is nobody else. And secondly, I am your wife not your concubine. NOT your concubine! If I am like a – corpse–

JACK
Worse than a corpse because you lie there and you send out these waves, these waves of like, hatred.

ANNIE
And that hasn't stopped you, has it? Maybe you like that, maybe you like – fucking a dead woman.

JACK
: Get the fuck out of here. Go to fucking Ireland and suck your boyfriend's dick dry.

ANNIE
: Aghhhhhhhh! *(She attacks, they struggle.)*

JACK
: Please don't lie to me. If you have any respect for me.

ANNIE
: There is no one else. But I have been cold. I've been feeling – very – cold. I feel as though I may never get warm again.

JACK
: And may I ask why?

ANNIE
: I don't… know. I don't know.

JACK
: Okay. Can I take a guess? You've ah… fallen out of – love with me. After twenty years. It's okay, I mean it happens. And I'm not exactly any great catch. You always much preferred the company of your son to my company, the two of you ignore me when he's here, home from college, maybe you're longing for his Daddy, your one night stand from where was it? The El Mocambo? I would just like to know for certain, okay? And once I know, I would appreciate the chance to to to…

ANNIE
: Jack, Jack, it's it's listen. It's just sometimes I'm not sure who you are. I hear these rumours about you being a brutal cop, being called *Diablo* by the local kids and–

JACK
: So you're saying I'm like a stranger. Like someone you might brush past on the subway. Twenty years wiped out, like that.

ANNIE
: I'm going to work on it, I promise, I don't know, maybe if we go away, north to the country–

JACK
: My brothers said this would happen. They said you were too good for me, too educated, too – swish. I'm a cop from Mississauga with a grade twelve education. They would go "What the hell is she doin with you?"

ANNIE
No Jack, it's not any of that, believe me, our differences, I love, they kept things electric for so long.

JACK
So what's happened? WHAT has happened?

ANNIE
I have been having this dream. For the last year or so. And I am having it more and more. In the dream, you are walking towards me with an aluminum bucket in your hand. And in that bucket is a rattlesnake. *(makes rattle sound)* And I'm saying "Please, Jack, please don't come closer," *(makes rattle sound)* and you are humming to yourself and you keep approaching… you have this rattlesnake in this bucket and I think the dream it is something to do with I don't know, with me sensing or my body sensing that you have…

JACK
Secrets.

ANNIE nods. JACK is silent. He does some cleaning.

JACK
Well we all have secrets. Don't we? *(exiting)*

Scene Six

Zanzibar. Music: EVANGELINE does a table dance for JACK. Their eyes meet. They have connected in a way that transcends the grotty environment. She gives him a bracelet.

Scene Seven

JOE's porch.

JOE
I risked my life for this country! That's the thing. I was a belly gunner. In a Lancaster. Seventeen missions. It's cold, man, on your belly, you better believe it at 20,000 feet. They were always shooting at us, I shit my pants twice. It's the coldest I ever was in the belly there. Most belly gunners didn't last three missions. Because the Messhershmitt, they wiped us out. And the Night Fighters. I remember this one. We're moving along. And there's a Messhershmitt coming that way, and the other way. Well soon enough the pilot's dead, the second dicky's dead, he was a boy of nineteen on his second mission, and the nose gunner's dead. *(taking a moment to recover from the memory)* When the war was over I come back to Toronto. And Eatons, they got signs up everywhere "We want vets." "Vets please apply." Well I went down to apply, with a few of my buddies, other vets. We filled out the application. And under religion, I put

Catholic. Because I was. Well all the other vets I knew, they were Protestant. They all got the job, right off. They were called the next day. I didn't get any calls, nothing. I said to one, "I wonder how come I never got called." He looked at me, he says, "You didn't say you were Catholic?" "Well, yes," I says. He says "You'll never get a job if you're Catholic. Not in Toronto. Not in Ontario." So I went to an Anglican priest and I told him my predicament. I told him I wanted to change religions and he was very accommodating. He made me an Anglican. So I went back down, and I filled out the form again. And this time where it said "Religion" I wrote down Anglican. And I got the job the next day. But to tell you the truth, although I was an Anglican, I was still a Catholic. You always are.

Scene Eight

A piano bar at night with cocktails.

JACK
How how did you think up a dance like that? 'Cause that is really exotic.

EVANGELINE
Oh. I don't know. I just got bored with the same old thing.

JACK
So you came up with this?

EVANGELINE
You think it's okay?

JACK
It's… enchanting.

EVANGELINE
It's a kind of a…

JACK
What?

EVANGELINE
Nothing.

JACK
No, what were you going to say?

EVANGELINE
Prayer. In a way. You think I'm crazy.

JACK
No, I don't. I think that's cool. I pray too. By driving fast. Seriously. In a chase. Chasin some guy who's just robbed a bank, or knocked down a kid, hit and run. It's like a prayer.

EVANGELINE
Because the other kind of prayer, on your knees and putting your palms together? And repeating words you learned in Sunday school? Those don't work.

JACK
I know, I used to try it. Please GOD make my brother get run over by a truck so my dad and I can get Swiss Chalet Christmas dinner. Please GOD let the guy not have a gun on him, please GOD let my wife have a heartbeat. It never–

EVANGELINE
You okay? You're trembling, aren't you? Here, let me–

She puts her jacket on him.

JACK
They should turn the goddamn heat up in here. What are they trying to do, freeze us out?

She is silent.

So how do you like the boss, is he okay? I heard this one he doesn't treat the girls so well.

EVANGELINE
No.

JACK
Well… do you… like working there?

EVANGELINE laughs.

EVANGELINE
You're asking me if I like working there?

JACK
Isn't there… isn't there… anything else that you wanted to do? With your life?

She turns to him. There is so much to say that there is not much point in saying anything.

So why do you stay there?

EVANGELINE
You don't understand.

EVANGELINE smiles.

I've seen you. You live in my neighbourhood.

JACK
Where do you live?

EVANGELINE
Clinton just south of Dupont.

JACK
Oh. That's close to me. I'm closer to Follis.

EVANGELINE
You're a policeman.

JACK
Is that bad?

EVANGELINE
Your wife. Annie Delaney. The singer.

JACK
Yeah.

EVANGELINE
"As a heart yearns for channels of water, so my soul yearns for thee."

JACK
Oh you've heard Annie's– *(EVANGELINE nods.)* It's hard at night. *(ANNIE's ghost enters.)* Sometimes I just get up, go out, for a walk. Sit in some all-night donut place. Keep away the thoughts.

EVANGELINE
I know what that's like.

JACK
At work, and at the bar, I can almost forget, you know, distracted. But as soon as I get home.

EVANGELINE
Yeah.

JACK
Get into bed. That bed. It's like… I swear to God I've seen her. In the house.

EVANGELINE
　　I've seen my mother.

JACK
　　Yeah?

EVANGELINE
　　You loved her. Annie Delaney.

　　Silence. EVANGELINE nods, smiles.

JACK
　　Annie would have liked you. She would have liked you a lot.

EVANGELINE
　　I said "Hi." to her a few times on the sidewalk. We even talked about the weather. Our gardens. You think so?

JACK
　　Yeah.

　　EVANGELINE caresses his face.

EVANGELINE
　　I like those lines from the ends of your eyes.

JACK
　　You do? I hate them. Reminds me I'm getting old. Hey. Am I too old for you?

　　EVANGELINE is embarrassed.

　　Because I would like to, I don't know. Hang out with you. Go to the Botanical Gardens, you ever been to the Botanical Gardens?

　　EVANGELINE shakes her head.

　　Oh you'll love the Botanical Gardens.

　　EVANGELINE kisses him. He kisses her back.

　　Do you mind if I tell you, I find you very beautiful?

EVANGELINE
　　Me?

JACK
　　And mysterious. A forest. In winter.

EVANGELINE
   No.

JACK
   Would you like to dance?

   He touches her, caresses her. The ghost ANNIE sings. They dance to ANNIE's music. They dance politely, and then more and more sensually.

Scene Nine

Song: "morning in bright fall."

ANNIE
   A morning in bright fall
   In Caledon Hills

   Maple leaves my bouquet
   I had chills

   On my day *(pause)*
   from my lips to my knees
   Love *(small pause)*
   You were stung by a bumblebee
   the ringing of bells
   Your cheek swelled
   as you said *(pause)*

   Till death us do part
   Clear eyes and clean consciences
   Oh when did this start
   This painful infection *(pause)*
   Of our strong our red heart?

   Oh when did this start?
   Are, *(tiny pause)* we so far apart? *(pause)*

   That morning in bright fall
   Maple leaves – my bouquet
   You were my prince
   And now what you say
   Makes me sad *(pause)*
   Makes me fear

   You said you were the sun dear
   And I was the sky
   But are you the gun dear
   I carry inside?

Waiting to fire
To kill your tall bride

Oh when did this start
Are we so far apart
Are we so far apart?

Scene Ten

Dawn breaks. JACK and EVANGELINE are on Clinton Street, looking at the stars.

JACK
You see that there? That's the North Star.

EVANGELINE
Keeweetinok Atchak. In Cree. I'm half Cree.

JACK
Yeah?

EVANGELINE
That star stays still. The other stars, they swirl around but that one stays just still.

JACK
You know it.

EVANGELINE
I studied the stars. The stars and some Cree. Songs, a few phrases. I got books from the library.

JACK
Wow. I like that, I like it that you studied the stars, and the Cree, that's elegant.

EVANGELINE
Your eyes – like a sea of glass.

She laughs, and kisses him. From inside, KEVIN sees, and, drunk, wanders out.

KEVIN
What the hell are you doing, Evangeline?

They start and turn.

EVANGELINE
You'd better go.

JACK
Who are you? Are you the brother?

KEVIN
Who the fuck are you?

EVANGELINE
Kev, please.

JACK
Jack, pleased to meet you. I'm just walking Evangeline home.

KEVIN
You come near her again and I'll kill you. Now get the fuck off my property.

JACK
Is this your house?

EVANGELINE
Kevy please don't talk to my friend that way. He's been very nice to me.

KEVIN
Get offa my property. Fuckin now.

JACK
Evangeline is an adult, Kevin. And what she does is none of your business.

KEVIN
Evy, get inside.

EVANGELINE
I can do what I want to do, Kev. You can't stop me anymore.

KEVIN
I said GET INSIDE.

JACK
Hey you don't–

> *KEVIN hits her. JACK hits him. They fight. KEVIN is trying to escape JACK and the fight moves inside, and towards KEVIN's bedroom. EVANGELINE tries to stop them, crying "Please." "Stop it." and "Don't." They are there, squaring off, when JACK sees the red dress hanging in KEVIN's room. He looks back at KEVIN, and back again at the dress. He touches the dress. They freeze.*

JACK
Annie!

He turns to KEVIN. KEVIN laughs.

KEVIN
We thought she was an animal, man.

EVANGELINE
Kevin?

KEVIN
We couldn't see through the branches. In the dark. It happens.

JACK attacks KEVIN hard.

EVANGELINE
No. Stop it. Stop it you two, I'll call the cops. Stop it, You're hurting him.

They are fighting, JACK is about to kill KEVIN, by strangling him. EVANGELINE grabs the gun.

Stop it or I'll shoot. I swear to God I'll shoot.

EVANGELINE has a moment of terrible indecision, but then her need for her brother, for family, wins out and she kills JACK. The sound of the bullet is naturalistic this time, to avoid comic melodrama. He falls to the ground. MUSIC should come in right away.

KEVIN gets up, takes the gun, then steals the money out of JACK's pockets and takes off.

EVANGELINE has blood all over her hands. She is in shock. She puts on the red dress. She sings a Cree song of lamentation over JACK's body (see music for "Evangeline's Lament" at end of play. She walks outside. JOE sees her.

Help me.

JOE
What happened? What happened child?

EVANGELINE staggers down Clinton Street.

Scene Eleven

Night. KEVIN appears out of JOE's front door, rifling through ESSIE's purse and throwing it away. JOE is on the porch.

JOE
Who's that? Who's there?

KEVIN
Cover your face. Cover your face or I fuckin kill you.

JOE
My wife is not well. Please don't hurt her. You can have anything you want.

KEVIN
Shut the fuck up, Joe.

JOE
Kevin. What are you doing here? Where's Evangeline?

KEVIN
Where's your wallet? Where is your fuckin wallet, old man.

JOE
It's okay. Now calm down Kevin, you're welcome to anything you want. It's right here, in my jacket.

KEVIN
Okay, now what's your PIN number? Tell me the wrong one, I come back and shoot your fuckin head off.

JOE
Okay. It's – uh… 6?

KEVIN
NOW. NOW!

JOE
6… 5, no 4… no, 5, 7, 9. Yes, that's it.

KEVIN
6579.

JOE
Kevin? It's not too late to give yourself up.

KEVIN
Are you tellin me what to fuckin do? YOU, who sat on your fuckin porch and watched as I was dragged away from my home only four years old? You sat and you rocked and you didn't do nothing. You didn't do nothing.

JOE
Kevin.

KEVIN
I remember the sound of the chair. The sound of the rocking I remember it, man, I have nightmares.

JOE
I thought she was takin you down to Christie Pits, to play on the big airplane. You loved that big airplane.

KEVIN
Bullshit.

JOE
It's God's truth.

KEVIN
Bullshit.

KEVIN goes to leave.

JOE
Kevin. May God forgive you.

KEVIN
Fuck that.

KEVIN leaves.

Scene Twelve

Night. Bloor Street. Fruit and vegetable stand. Streetlight shines on it. EVANGELINE is standing still among the fruit and vegetables. We can see Honest Ed's neon signs flashing across the street.

EVANGELINE
(whispers) Hail Oh Hail Annie full of Grace we are soaked we are soaked in our neighbour's blood my brother and I the Law the Law is with thee. Come to me I wait here, behind the apples and avocados and oranges sweet I will wait for you to guide me are you here? Are you—

ANNIE appears.

Annie. Hey. Have you come to smote me down? I wouldn't blame you. I am murder see my hands? *Geen-sa. Ni nipbo.* [I have killed somebody. I am death] Soaked in blood His blood—

ANNIE
Evangeline, walk.

EVANGELINE
Walk?

ANNIE swings around and points north.

ANNIE
Keeweetinok Atchak. The North Star to the northern star walk you'll reach the dark forest where the air is clear you lie on the moss you will have your baby on moss not a grimy jail floor; clean your baby with clear water not infected jail water you go, and walk and disappear. It happens in Canada all the time, a disappearing woman, nobody minds. Just walk. Disappear.

EVANGELINE
Oh. Annie. Will you ever sing to me again?

ANNIE disappears.

You know my baby? I'm callin her after you, Annie.

EVANGELINE fills her bag with oranges and apples. KEVIN, meanwhile, is all over the neighbourhood looking for her.

KEVIN
We gotta take off, babe, cause they're comin after us. There's buses every hour we can be outta here in twenty minutes.

She starts to walk up the street.

EVANGELINE
We are walking.

KEVIN
Walking? *(pausing and watching her walk)* Walking.

They walk together into the horizon, up Yonge Street.

We see JOE's rocking chair, a yellow police ribbon around EVANGELINE's house. About halfway through the speech we see KEVIN and EVANGELINE, in the woods, in a sled or on a stump. He seems to be sleeping, in a sleeping bag beside her. She is heavily pregnant.

EVANGELINE
Tansi niskneeksqueem [hello my daughter] dear my darling daughter.

Happy eighth birthday Annie Northstar. *Kisageetin ooma* that means I love you, baby, in Cree; the language of your blood I hope this finds you happy and strong. My dear friend Patty is giving you this letter. Patty is your mother now and I know she is tellin you funny stories and bringing home rice pudding from Fran's for ya, and taking real good care of you. I wanted more than life itself to keep you, love, but I had to send you down to Patty to keep you safe, because I am doomed to walk, forever. And that's no way for you to live. Your feet would get tired. I want you to have school, and friends, and gymnastic classes and all of that I do not know what lies ahead, on my travels. I know one thing only, and that is that you will see me, in the North Star, because, the North Star, in Cree: "*kewe tinok atchak,*" is always there in the sky, Annie, and guides us.

Nell, whatever people may tell you about your father, I want you to know that what you are is a long summer evening, Nell, Clinton Street, kids playing outside our window my friend Joe cutting his roses, talking with the neighbours, and we lined up barefoot for soft ice cream and Kevin he got a vanilla with the hot chocolate dip and I got the warm butterscotch and we brought them inside and we sat in the dark and we licked them faster and as the ice cream melted his face melted too, melted along with the ice cream we had no fans, Nell our house was so hot, and the laughing boy was there underneath, that boy who said park and I saw him again and he was gentle and sweet and your father, my love, was not the man but the sweet heavenly child.

Kisageetin ooma, I love you so, *kisageetin ooma.*

Scene Thirteen

EVANGELINE
Oh I wish I could be near you, Annie, while you read this, touching the lights in your soft hair, wish it were possible but I know that it isn't, for the bone in the air it has broke I am doomed to walk till I cannot walk more till I fall on my knees to the ground till I fall on my–

Kisageetin ooma, I love you so, *kisageetin ooma kisageetin ooma kisageetin ooma*

daughter

Kev? Kev, come on, wake up.

KEVIN
Leave me alone. I gotta sleep.

EVANGELINE
Kevin it's time. We have to walk.

KEVIN
Fuckin cold, fuckin wolves, howlin in my ear–

EVANGELINE
You're going to be fine. Come on.

They walk together for a while along the trail. They struggle.

KEVIN
My foot is killin me, Ev. I can't fuckin walk no more. Don't make me, don't–

He falls.

EVANGELINE
No resting, Kevin. If we rest we fall into the fires! We burn. Forever. Now come on. You can do it. Come on. Stand. Up. Now. One foot in front of the other. Come on.

She tries to make him walk, like a puppet.

KEVIN
Have some mercy, woman. Mer-cy. Can't you see I'm dyin here? I'm goin blind. Left eye is worse. Everything's startin to look shimmery. Just the way it happened with the right one.

He buckles.

EVANGELINE
Keeeevin!!

KEVIN
And the cold. Ev. I can't take the cold no more, I never felt such cold. This fuckin country. How come you don't feel the cold?

EVANGELINE
Come on.

KEVIN
Take me home. I want to go home.

EVANGELINE
We have no home! You know that.

KEVIN
Then I'll go to fucking Millhaven. At least there's television there. Regular food.

EVANGELINE
Kevin. Kevin look at me.

KEVIN
(he laughs) What are you going to do, have the baby out here? In the bush? And then keep walkin with her? What do you do when it's time to put her in school?

EVANGELINE
I have plans for Annie, Kevin. Annie will be just fine. Now can you please try to walk?

EVANGELINE decides to carry him. She lifts him over her shoulder. She sings to him, a Cree lullaby "Evangeline Carries Kevin." She lifts him onto her back and they climb the hill where ANNIE was killed. KEVIN wakes, a final burst of energy before dying. He hears wolves. The Northern Lights light up the sky.

KEVIN
Wha's that sound? 'Vangeline, it's the wolves. Oh yes. There they are. In the blizzard, can you see them?

EVANGELINE
Oh, no, my little brother. No! It's something else. Something kind. Yes. *Cheepyuk Neemeetowuk*. They've finally come for us. Oh. Dancing spirits. Yes. They're every bit as lovely as you said, Kev.

His breathing has become shallow, quick, as breathing often does before death. The Northern Lights surround them. ANNIE sings:

ANNIE
Oh heavenly time of day…
the fog and the quiet.
The mist, no sun. I move out of my dream and into this day as the fog it clears so slowly away to reveal… to reveal…

The Snowy Owl hoots.

The end.

Perfect Pie

Perfect Pie was first produced at Tarragon Theatre, Toronto, in January 2000, with the following company:

PATSY   Nancy Palk
FRANCESCA   Sonja Smits
MARIE   Liisa Repo-Martell
PATSY (young)   Tara Rosling

Directed by Judith Thompson
Set and Costumes designed by Sue LePage
Lighting designed by Andrea Lundy
Composition/Sound designed by Bill Thompson
Stage Management by Winston Morgan
Assistant Directed by Caroline Azar

CHARACTERS

PATSY
FRANCESCA
MARIE
PATSY (young)

Perfect Pie

ACT ONE

Scene One

Darkness. PATSY Willet is in the kitchen of her farmhouse, at an old wooden table, making dough for a rhubarb pie. Moonlight illuminates a perfect ball of dough, a pot of tea and a teacup. There is a small tape recorder in front of her on the table. She is preparing to send a letter by tape to her old estranged friend, MARIE. She kneads the dough for a while. A train whistle sounds. She looks up at the window to glimpse the train. The train approaches, and passes.

PATSY
"I will not forget you, you are carved in the palm of my hand."

Dawn breaks. She presses "Record" on the tape recorder.

Marie? Are you sitting down? 'Cause if you're not I think you better cause you might just get the dizzies when you find out who I am. Now don't turn me off thinkin I'm some kinda crazy stranger like one of your fans. Because although I am a fan, I am not crazy I don't think, and I'm not a stranger that is for sure... I am... it's funny I feel a little shy to say, because I'm sure you know who I am at this point, at least I hope you know: that I am Patsy. *(pause)* Willet. Now Patsy McAnn but you would know me as Willet. You know? Of course you do: big red face, hash brown hair? We hung around together near Marmora, Ontario like Siamese Twins till you left town when you were about fifteen or sixteen? Well Marie I have followed your career of course; and I am proud... to have known you, Marie. And, well, the reason that I am gettin in touch with you after all this time, Marie, this thirty some years is I have been... yearning.

Lights up on YOUNG PATSY and MARIE.

To... behold you, I suppose. Because I'll be honest with you, when I have been having a hard day and I'm very tired and it's the end of the day and I'm makin supper or doin the dishes and the room fills with oh orange light and I hear the train, the low whistle at the back of our property and I stare out the window and I see – just the glimpse of it, of the train speeding on to Montreal, the crash... does flash out, in my mind; like a sheet; of lightning, and when the flash is over, and all is dark again, I know you did not survive. I know in my heart you did not survive, Marie. So how is it? How is it that I see you there, out there, in the world?

PATSY goes to get rhubarb fruit pie filling from fridge and fills the pie shell.

Light on FRANCESCA, in her own dark apartment in the Big City, a great view of the city at night behind her. She remembers...

Scene Two

As PATSY finishes her last line in Scene One, MARIE and YOUNG PATSY, in white, sing the 1ˢᵗ verse of "Abide with Me."

MARIE & YOUNG PATSY
Abide with Me... Fast falls the eventide
The darkness deepness; *(pause)*
Lord
with me abide:
When other helpers fail, and comforts
flee,
Help of the helpless...

Scene Three

FRANCESCA stares out into the darkness. She smells the pie and takes a fingerfull and eats it.

PATSY
Well, Marie, I got all my chickens waitin to be fed and the damn cows to take care of – they been gorging on crabapples so they're in agony with the gas, eh, bloated up just terrible so I better let you go; Oh I almost forgot. Hope the pie's not too crushed out; it's a fresh rhubarb, Marie; grown in my own garden. My prize winner at the Northumberland County Pie Contest. Makes a really nice light dessert. So just heat it up and serve it to your man, if you have one of those in your life, which I am sure you likely do. Marie, I'll let you go now, if you haven't turned me off already, and ahh listen: if you do happen to be drivin east, to Ottawa or Montreal... please... go on to highway seven. You know the way from there; past the Big Red Apple and down the road a few miles and just show up at my door. I'll put the kettle on and we'll have a visit. So I know you're still... here. In the world. Would you? Would you ever think of doin that?

All best, Your old friend, Patsy.

PATSY presses the stop button on the recorder.

Scene Four

The two GIRLS sing the second verse of "Abide with Me".

MARIE & YOUNG PATSY
Swift to it's close
ebbs out life's little day;
Earth's joys grow dim,
it's glories pass away;

5   Change and decay
    in all around I see…

                        Scene Five

        *Marie, now FRANCESCA on railroad tracks. She is re-visiting the site;
        perhaps in reality, before she goes to see PATSY, perhaps in her imagination.
        When PATSY speaks, she speaks from her kitchen. They are in an abstract
        dialogue: actually PATSY is listening to FRANCESCA's tape, sent some time
        before the visit. PATSY completes her pie and puts it in the oven.*

FRANCESCA
Patsy? It's me… yeahhh. Well… Helloooooo – doesn't seem a big enough
word… does it…? After all this time. Hearing your voice… made something
inside me… I don't know, bloom; like the crabapples on your farm; I somehow
always, but never… expected… to hear your voice again. I have thought about
you so much over the years, Patsy. It's funny, as I… erased more and more of   5
Marmora I remembered… more and more of you. The tips of your eyelashes.
Every freckle on your arm. Your face: so clear to me! And I would have known
your voice anywhere. Anywhere. I've often listened for it, you know, and even
thought I've heard it, not just in Toronto, but in far away places: in the Munich
Train station once I was SURE I heard your voice I turned and of course, not   10
you and I – oh I *yearn*, Patsy, to see you again.

PATSY
Course I've seen you a few times on the TV, and in the newspaper but it's not
the same. As face to face. And although you are lookin well in the sense of, very
attractive for your age, Marie, you are lookin'–

FRANCESCA
–It was very strange to hear the name "Marie" you know, "Marie… Begg"   15
…feels to me like a reproach somehow; a weird sister I have dog-chained in
the attic…

PATSY
–Not – well – in the face somehow, and I am very concerned about this Marie–

FRANCESCA
–Thank you so so much for the prize-winning pie. It was inexpressibly
delicious; I ate the whole thing myself, in the dark. I gorged on that delicious   20
pastry while listening to your voice. Every bite was perfect; I could almost
taste your hands in the pastry. But you always did make good pastry. I can
just imagine you kneading the dough the way you used to. With that almost
ferocious look…

        In unison.

On your – face

PATSY
Because I care about your face.

I see it, sometimes, in the kitchen window, early in the morning when I get up to make my dough.

FRANCESCA
I'm ashamed of how little I remember… of my life in Marmora. It's like one of those vast intrinsicate dreams.

PATSY
—And it's always while I'm makin my dough I get thinkin of things you know, I'm looking out at the roseate dawn and the mist… *(the following lines are somewhat overlapped)*

And I think of the time

FRANCESCA
that all but disappears

PATSY
We woke up.

FRANCESCA
when you wake up…

PATSY
We were both in these softy soft flannel pajamees and you woke me up and you said, "look" and I look out the window and I saw all this…

FRANCESCA
Ice.

PATSY
Glistening, shimmering, crystalline–

FRANCESCA
Ice.

PATSY
Glazing the trees, the bushes, the barn roof, and the fields all the way down to the dark blue lake.

FRANCESCA
Yes, I remember, and all the icicles…

PATSY
And I would like…. Grab your hand and we shove on the rubber boots and we are out the door and we go! We slide, all over the farm in our boots and our nighties laughin and–

FRANCESCA
–Sliding, across the fields, sliding and shrieking!

PATSY
And the AIR!

FRANCESCA
Oh, the air!

PATSY
I think of those times.

FRANCESCA
I think of those times–

PATSY
Early in the morning.

FRANCESCA
Late at night

PATSY
When I get up to make my dough…
So if you are comin over this way…

FRANCESCA
And my heart races.

PATSY
You might want to see your old friend.

FRANCESCA
I am… somewhat shy of Marmora. But I would like very much to see you, Patsy.

PATSY
I won't go in to Toronto. I went once to see "The Phantom." Ric took me for my birthday but I did not care for it at all. No. You're gonna have to come to me, Marie.

FRANCESCA has arrived in PATSY's domain.

FRANCESCA
Yes.

Scene Six

FRANCESCA is now in PATSY's kitchen, late morning. They have a moment, which is the first moment they encounter each other.

FRANCESCA
Oh yes. It is exactly the same…. As I remember. This wallpaper. Those little bluebirds, and the vines.

FRANCESCA runs her hands along the wallpaper. PATSY watches her.

PATSY
Right in style in 1929. If ya try to scrape it off the whole wall comes down. Hah. I'd like to gut the kitchen but Ric keeps puttin it off.

FRANCESCA
Oh but the… history is wonderful, don't you think?

PATSY
You sound like my Mum. I say, "Tear the history down, and give it a nice coat of paint." See that Peanuts comic strip? Over there? That was up before you left, I am talkin thirty-five years. I said to Mum, I said, "Mum, if you care about the strip, take it down, and put it inside the family photo album for Pete's sake." She said "no," she liked it on the wall it reminded her of Dad. Because he had found it funny. It was one of the few times he laughed right out loud, ever. She said if she put it in a photo album she wouldn't never get it out. So I haven't had the heart to take it down. If I touch it, it will turn to dust.

FRANCESCA
When did your father die?

PATSY
Ahhhh… I guess it was about – five or no, six years ago. He was seventy-eight years old. Still working the farm every day. He'd been raking leaves. Just out front there. My mother was right here, scrapin egg off a fry pan, when it happened.

FRANCESCA
Heart?

PATSY nods.

PATSY
He just fell over the bag of leaves.

FRANCESCA
It must have been very hard on your mother.

PATSY
They'd been married for fifty years, eh? She tried, right? To keep going with her church work and that, you know the kind of person she was, always doin for others, but you could see the strain. Little things. Like she didn't wipe down her counters the same.

Scene Seven

Past.

FRANCESCA as MARIE, about eight, standing in the schoolyard, against a wall. Her head is very itchy, as she has lice. PATSY, with jumping rope approaches. She is very interested in the new, "poor" girl. She stares at her. MARIE does not look at PATSY.

PATSY
Hullo. *(MARIE does not respond.)*

What's your name again? I didn't really hear ya when you said it in class.

MARIE
Marie Begg.

PATSY
Pardon? You're talkin so softy soft.

MARIE
Marie. Begg.

PATSY
Oh! That's a beautiful name. Like olden days.

MARIE
I hate it.

PATSY
(gasp) You shouldn't say you hate your name.

MARIE
Why not?

PATSY
Because if you say you hate your name you're saying you hate your mother because your mother gave you that name and you shouldn't say you hate your mother. MARIE BEGGS.

MARIE
Begg. Marie Begg.

PATSY
Oh. I still think it's a beautiful name.

MARIE finally turns to look at PATSY.

Scene Eight

Present.

FRANCESCA
I always loved this house. I always felt… comfortable here.

PATSY
Ric's been fixing it up, slowly. He's handy, you know, but he is a real procrastinator, I mean there is so much…

FRANCESCA
Oh I think it's wonderful just the way it is. Perfect.

PATSY
Oh but it's falling down, Marie. It has been for the last thirty years. Dad, he just didn't have the time–

FRANCESCA
Your Dad was a lovely man. I remember he used to tell jokes in that gentle voice while he was milking the cows by hand. He would lay his cheek against the cow and then he would look right at you and…

PATSY plugs the kettle in for tea.

PATSY
We were one of the last to get in the machinery, about 1963.

FRANCESCA
He was… traditional.

PATSY
He was cheap!

FRANCESCA
And his hands, were so… strong, remember? Remember he would pick us both up and…. Didn't he used to… slice open the cows? To relieve their gas? When you mentioned on the tape about the cows being bloated with gas I had a flash… of your dad with a very sharp tool, slicing….

PATSY
Oh yes, we still do it in emergencies, Marie. See, the poor things are in agony from the overeating. Every spring it happens, after the long winter in the barn,

eh? They start gorgin on the alfalfa. The gas'll kill em you know. Oh yeah, you have to know exactly where to slice, which stomach, and with a clean knife.

FRANCESCA looks at a laminated picture on the fridge of Ric and the boys and PATSY.

FRANCESCA
What a beautiful family you are. The boys have your eyes, Patsy. Oh he looks adorable.

PATSY
(She gets up, bustles.) They should be back from the fair in Dundee around suppertime if you can stay that long; Ric's dying to see you again, I been talkin about you so much…

FRANCESCA
Well…

PATSY
And I think Kevy may be coming home with a red ribbon for Blossom, she's the Jersey we gave to him for his 4H eh, he's done very well with her. You will like Kevin, he is the image of my father…. And Ry is shy, you know reserved, but once you get to know him? He is the funniest, I'm serious, the wittiest boy. He could do very well in the stand-up comedy.

FRANCESCA
I'm sorry, I really do have to be off by six or so.

PATSY
Oh right, your big "gala" in Montreal. I'm sorry, I forgot. Stupid.

An awkward moment.

FRANCESCA
I would absolutely love to stay and meet your family. I never enjoy these events, but… it's kind of in my honour.

PATSY
Stupid of me to forget.

FRANCESCA
No no no. I just wish… well…

PATSY
So what time did you say you need to be there?

FRANCESCA
If I'm there by 9 or so… that should be fine.

PATSY
Well it's a good four hours. So if I were you, I would leave by 5:00 sharp. But then I like to be punctual. Now you, you used to be late for everything. Always marked tardy on your report cards, remember? Are you still that way?

FRANCESCA
Well–

PATSY
–It really is too bad you won't meet the boys.

FRANCESCA
Yes. I would really love to… sometime.

PATSY
Maybe on the way back.

FRANCESCA
Sure. Yes, maybe.

Uncomfortable silence. Music.

PATSY
Well…

PATSY pours tea. Music over awkward moment. The baking bell goes off.

Oh. There's my baking.

FRANCESCA
Smells wonderful.

PATSY
Well, you know what that is, eh?

Scene Nine

Past.

Schoolyard. MARIE scratches her head while looking at the ground.

PATSY
Where you come from anyways?

MARIE
Detroit.

PATSY
In the States? You come from the States? Oh my gosh I love the States. The States is fancy!

MARIE
No…. NO. Like we're from here. My dad he grew up here but then they lost the farm, cause our well run dry and so he went to work makin cars in Detroit like his cousins but he hurt his back and my Gramma took a stroke an left us the house so we come back that's all. He's workin as a hand over at Penny's cattle ranch near Tweed but he grew up here. We're from here.

PATSY
So what's it like in the States? Is it really fun?

MARIE
Their chocolate bars are better.

PATSY
Really? What's your favourite?

MARIE
Zagnut.

PATSY
"Zagnut." Cool. ZAGNUT. How old are you?

MARIE
Nine. My birthday was in August. August 23rd. We went to the Dairy Queen.

PATSY
Oh my GOSH mine is January 23rd! That's amazing. Maybe you could come to my birthday party. We'll be going skating on the river. Would you like to? Would you like to come? Marie? Cuz we're gonna do lots of other fun stuff too like um musical chairs? We'll play musical chairs and my mother, she plays the piano? And sings like this really cool song about this pretty girl who is on her way to a party? And it's like really cold like a hundred below zero and so she like falls asleep in the snow and she freezes in her Sleighride thing? And my mother? She's singin and then when she stops? Like you have to sit in a chair, and…

PATSY jumps into a "freeze" position. MARIE expresses acceptance, joy.

Scene Ten

Present.

Kitchen: PATSY transfers the cookies to a plate to cool.

FRANCESCA
Gumdrop cookies!

PATSY
Your favourite! Soon as we walked in the house it was, "Did your mom make those gumdrop cookies?" "Do you think we could have one?" Or two? Or three? And you would take as many as you could get in your little hands–

FRANCESCA
–Oh oh. Ohhhh. There is nothing, nothing like the smell of gumdrop cookies in your kitchen. I could honestly give up everything for it…. It's what I want to smell as I lay dying, you know, in a nursing home or on the 401 or a wet field after a lightning storm. I remember sometimes your mother would let us hand her the gumdrops, to rest in the cookie batter. "I'd like a yellow drop now please." she would say.

PATSY
Poor Mum. After Dad passed away she was dead within 16 months eh? Cancer of the kidneys. She used to lie on that divan right there, all day. It was my Grandmother's.

FRANCESCA
Yeah, I remember it.

Pause.

PATSY
Dark green bile coming out of her mouth and the morphine didn't touch that pain Marie it was like hyena dogs eating her body, eating her alive, day after day, night after night and there is nothing we can do. Well one day the pain seems to have subsided, eh. And we're feelin kinda hopeful, we are all in her hospital room, 'cept Wayne and Roger of course, eatin her chocolates, readin the paper, I'm changin the water in her vases thinkin how rancid that smells when she takes, like a convulsion. Her face like twists like rubber and her body goes rigid and I start screamin'. Marie, they had to strong-arm me out of the room. This was my mother. I kneeled down in the waiting room and I prayed. I prayed so hard to God I went purple. I was certain that she would pull through because I had always believed in the power of prayer and I felt the presence of God, I felt His breath on my face and I was sure… I was sure he would breathe her to LIFE and there's people running in and out and then my Aunt Nancy, with a line down her face and her black coat over her arm… she is standing there and at first I thought she was gonna say "Mum is fine, she is okay and and we're gonna take her home" and I thought thank you God thank you for this and then I saw her face. Her eyes, like her pupils these large black holes; and then I knew; I knew I was stupid, simple to think Mum would make it out of there alive and in that moment, I wondered, Marie, if there is any God at all "See I will not forget you are carved in the palm of my hand." That's what the minister said at her funeral. I liked that, I liked that very much.

Scene Eleven

Past.

School bell. MARIE crouches. She is afraid to go back into school, past the taunting children.

PATSY
Are you scared cause they were teasin you before?

MARIE
I'm not goin back.

PATSY
Don't mind them they're just ignorant.

MARIE
Not going back there.

PATSY
You go back in with me and they won't dare say nothing more. They say something? I report them to Mr. Eaves. You know the principal? With the glass eye? He's really really nice. *(pause)* And if I report them? They'll get the strap. Cause Mr. Eaves comes to our house for Christmas dinner. Always has seconds of stuffing. And oh my goodness, you should see that strap. Gerry d'Entremont got it for blowin his nose on his desk? And he said Mr. Eaves smiled the whole time he was strapping him. And you know what he was smilin at?

PATSY looks up at imaginary picture. MARIE also looks.

The picture of the Queen.

MARIE
The Queen? Of England? She's hardly pretty.

PATSY
I know. My mother even met her. In Belleville? She curtseyed to her.

School bell rings again.

MARIE
Your mother met the Queen?

Scene Twelve

Present.

FRANCESCA
I knew that my mother was dying. My Aunt Trudy tracked me down. Begged me to come. Back here. To Marmora. I stayed on my bed for days; didn't leave my apartment until I knew she was dead.

PATSY
I still go to church, you know, I sit there, I even sing in the choir, but I don't really believe anymore. Not after that.

Silence.

FRANCESCA
No. I don't know. Sometimes I do.

PATSY
When? When do ya?

FRANCESCA
After a stomach flu. You know… that moment when you've been – sitting up all night in bed with the pain, running to the bathroom, throwing up bile, passing out while you throw up, drinking almost a whole bottle of antacid and endless cups of hot water, and just trying to bear it and just when I think I really cannot stand it any longer, when I think I will just decompose with the pain, the pain… lifts. And I believe in God again.

PATSY
Oh to me that's just the devil playin with you. Because you know that stomach flu is comin back. And you also know it may turn to stomach cancer one day, right? And then it will go on for months like that till you die! Stomach flu's just a preview, right?

FRANCESCA
(laughs) Patsy. You haven't changed at all.

PATSY
No. I'm exactly the same. On the other hand, I'm totally different. Like you. Hey. Have a cookie. Go on. Gorgeous.

FRANCESCA
Thank you. Oh. Patsy. They are heaven. *Heaven.*

PATSY
Hm. You talk so… different. Than you did. I mean, of course, that's to be expected.

FRANCESCA
Sorry. Am I sounding very–

PATSY
I'm listening for Marie, right?

FRANCESCA
And… have you heard her yet?

PATSY
(long pause) In the… *(PATSY illustrates with her hands)* undertow.

Scene Thirteen

Past.

Both girls on swing, having big fun. They jump off in a thrill of laughter.

PATSY
Are you poor?

MARIE
No.

PATSY
You look poor.

MARIE
No I don't.

PATSY
I mean only a little. Just the scabs on your legs. That IS a nice dress. I like the zipper. Is that what they're wearing in the States? Is that what's in style?

MARIE shrugs.

Scene Fourteen

Present.

Kitchen: PATSY wraps the remaining cookies, and starts making lunch.

PATSY
You know my brother Wayne, right? You remember what a sweet kid he was? He comes for my mum's funeral with the town whore on his arm.

FRANCESCA
You have a "Town Whore?"

PATSY
Well. She is very loose. And what is she got around her dirty little neck but my mother's cultured pearl necklace.

FRANCESCA
I remember that necklace.

PATSY
He just went into the house and into her dresser and put mum's pearls round this little whore's neck. I don't know what he was trying to pull.

FRANCESCA
Well coming to your mother's funeral with the "Town Whore" is better than not coming at all.

Pause as she puzzles at her selfishness.

PATSY
Maybe you just weren't ready for this place. You know, didn't dare to look back. Afraid you'd turn to stone like what's her name in the Greek Mythology. That's what I been tellin myself all these years, anyways, about you.

FRANCESCA is puzzled.

Why you woulda done… what you did.

FRANCESCA
Patsy. You understand why I had to – you were there–

PATSY
You took off and you never even GLANCED back, Marie. Not a phone call, not a card, I was in a coma for six weeks broke every bone in my body you didn't even… bother to.

PATSY is breathless with emotion.

FRANCESCA
I wanted to, every day. Every day.

PATSY
You could have – picked up the phone.

FRANCESCA
I could NOT Patsy, honestly, I tried and my hand would not…

PATSY
Oh garbage, Marie.

FRANCESCA
I'm sorry. I am truly sorry, Patsy – I…

PATSY
…My God when I woke up from a coma first thing I say, I go "where's Marie? Where's Marie?" I mean I didn't know if you were even alive until I read about you in the paper, ten years later.

Past.

FRANCESCA remembers. MARIE, her hands high in the air, concentrates and speaks, sending her thoughts to PATSY.

MARIE
Dear dear dear dear dearest friend Patsy, I am sending you this letter by thought because I do not want to contaminate you with my scabby voice or my messy handwriting. I am sending you this letter by thought to tell you that I will not be bothering you ever again. Not you, nor anyone in Marmora, so fear not, my friend. You will not even see my shadow again. I know that it is not possible that you would ever ever ever accept my apology so I say "I am Sorry" for the train with no expectation that you will forgive. For what I did, was unforgivable. I will love and cherish you always forever till the very end of time, which has no end anyways, anyone knows that.

Your very best friend, soon to be someone else altogether… Marie.

Present.

I prayed for you, thinkin you were dead or being tortured somewhere. Sitting in calculus, feeding the chickens, lying in my bed at night, I prayed – did you pray for me?

Francesca is silent, ashamed.

PATSY
I mean ya come back here for your own reasons, re-visiting your past, whatever – and I see you lookin at me like I am your nightmare, the one who stayed, the quaint country–

FRANCESCA
Would you like me to go, Patsy?

PATSY
I mean why, really, why are you here?

FRANCESCA
Patsy! Don't you remember? Something… happened – Before the train; I these flashes – through my head – like like…

PATSY begins to remember herself – images.

PATSY
You were talkin so wild, turning in circles…

FRANCESCA is remembering.

…with your dress all torn, I didn't understand what you were sayin–

FRANCESCA
I wake up in the middle of the night screaming, Patsy – these faces–

PATSY
(starts to remember) I – I thought you were doped up on drugs or or–

FRANCESCA
I didn't even want to come back. Ever. If you knew how… hard it was for me to…

PATSY
Every once in a while I would get this terrible feeling, you know? About what you had been sayin', but then I would think no, no way.

FRANCESCA listens.

I would talk myself out of it; are you saying…?

FRANCESCA is not ready to go there yet. PATSY nods, understanding that FRANCESCA is not ready, and they embrace.

Like mum always said, "less said, soonest mended." Let's just…. Oh my God. You know? I cannot believe you are sittin in my kitchen. It's like I cannot believe my eyes.

Scene Fifteen

Past.

The girls are playing by the swings, practicing ballet moves.

PATSY
Are you on welfare?

MARIE
: No.

PATSY
: Are you sure?

MARIE
: Yes. Who told you that?

PATSY
: Patty Hagerty.

MARIE
: She's full of shit.

PATSY
: I'm telling.

MARIE
: What?

PATSY
: You said the "F" word.

MARIE
: That's not the "F" word.

PATSY
: I told them that was not a nice thing to say. "If you can't say anything nice don't say anything at all." That's what my mother always says.

MARIE
: I am not on welfare.

PATSY
: I believe you.

Scene Sixteen

Present.

FRANCESCA
: It's nice that you can keep this house. That your mother left it to you.

PATSY
: Been in the family since 1816.

FRANCESCA
1816! Over a hundred and eighty years. About eight full generations, eh?

PATSY
I belong in this house.

Wayne and Roger they were very upset, when Mum left the house to me they were gonna take it to court but I said to them, I said: "Listen, it was us who looked after her, me Ric and… Kevy and Ry, we were on call 24 hours a day for the last year, it was me who held her while she died, who gave her the sponge baths daily and emptied her bed pan while the two of you were busy with your "Sports Bar" in BC. They didn't even come for the last week, the final week of the woman's life. When I called 'em and I go: "she's dying and she's been askin for you." Oh no they're too busy with the sports bar puttin in the wide-screen TV's and that. Well in that last week before she passed on, Francesca, she was so very weak but she would sit up every now and then straight up and look at the door with these wide eyes, expecting her sons. I had to tell her they were on their way, I go "They just called and said they were on their way, Hon." That's what I said, I told her they were comin so at least she died thinkin her sons were on their way.

FRANCESCA
I bet my mother did that. Looked at the door. For me. With her one blue eye and her brown eye.

PATSY
Oh Marie. You can't know that.

FRANCESCA
She used to cry. When she was drinking. Say she was no good to me.

PATSY
She also used to knock you to the floor when she didn't like the look on your face.

FRANCESCA
Well…

PATSY
Well. *(She points to cookies.)* Go on. Have another. Lunch'll be a little while.

FRANCESCA tries to eat a cookie. Puts it down.

Hah. When you were a kid, you couldn't get enough of them.

FRANCESCA
I had a sweet tooth?

PATSY
What? Every chance you had you'd be down at Becky's gettin your Tootsie Roll Pops. Hah. Remember Becky's? That cat with the infected eye walkin all over the candy? And you never saw Becky, only her daughters. She had seven daughters, remember?

FRANCESCA
All of them had names starting with "B" and you never could tell them apart. "Oh hello Bettina, or is it Belinda? Nope, oh my God it's Barbara." "No, miss, I'm Betsy". Aghhhh!

PATSY
Now me, I don't have a sweet tooth. I go for the chips and the cheesies. But it just seems to go right through me. You, you have the perfect figure. Well I guess you'd have to, it's your bread and butter.

FRANCESCA
I think you look wonderful, Patsy.

PATSY
Oh I do not, Marie, I'm a scarecrow. *(or "I'm fat")* No shape on me. But it don't really matter around here. All the women are shapeless. *(or fat)* Except the ones who are shapely. *(or "scrawny", scrawny by nature)* Shapely by nature.

PATSY
Oh my Godfather I've been calling you Marie the whole time you've been here. I am sorry. Oh you must want to clobber me.

FRANCESCA
No.

PATSY
But you would... rather... I call you by Francesca, right? Your stage name?

FRANCESCA
Well, it has been my name for twenty years. A very good friend of mine picked it for me. He died and... I don't know. I haven't been called "Marie Begg" in a very long time. And when I hear "Marie"–

PATSY
You feel like Marie?

FRANCESCA
Uh... yes.

PATSY
And?

Scene Seventeen

Past.

The girls are by the swing, each playing with a large yellow grapefruit.

PATSY
Do you have lice?

MARIE
No.

PATSY
Yes you do.

MARIE
No I don't.

PATSY
I saw one. Crawling on your head. This morning. Cause you were sittin in front of me.

MARIE
You did not.

PATSY
Honest. I did. I know what they look like 'cause my brother had them once. The Welfares brought them into the school.

MARIE
I do not have lice.

PATSY
I won't tell anybody, I swear, Marie. I swear on my very own life.

MARIE
I don't have lice, alright?

Pause.

PATSY
I could show you a special way to get rid of them. Then they would be all gone.

MARIE
My mother won't buy the shampoo. She says they're not lice they're bedbugs.

PATSY
That's okay. Don't you worry 'bout a THING. I'll get rid of 'em for you. I know this REALLY special way.

MARIE
What's that?

PATSY
I'll show you. You come over to my house, after school, okay? and I'll get rid of every single lice on your head. *(pause)* You just come with me, after school.

Okay?

MARIE
Okay.

Scene Eighteen

Present.

PATSY watches FRANCESCA's hands run over the wallpaper.

PATSY
You still have those elegant hands, Francesca. You always did. Have you ever done any hand modelling?

FRANCESCA
Well no, actually–

PATSY
–Oh, you should go down for it. I hear you could make a fortune.

FRANCESCA
Oh. Hah. Maybe I will.

PATSY
You know, for the "Sunlight" commercials.

FRANCESCA
Right.

PATSY
We enjoyed seeing you in that commercial for the flavoured coffees.

FRANCESCA
Oh that was a long time ago. I haven't done a commercial for fifteen years, Patsy.

PATSY
Oh. Why is that…?

FRANCESCA
Well, it's not very gratifying work and…

PATSY
Looks like easy money to me.

FRANCESCA
Yes. Yes it is. But…

Pause.

You're not taken very seriously… if you…

PATSY
Oh well you're so famous now, though.

FRANCESCA
Oh, I'm not famous. Believe me.

PATSY
You won all those awards. I saw it in the paper.

FRANCESCA
Oh a few junky statues, yes, but they're just… for the stage, Patsy. It's the movies. Movies make you famous. And I have only made a couple of very very tiny films that about three people saw.

PATSY looks at her, unbelieving, full of faith in her fame.

PATSY
You are being overly modest.

FRANCESCA
Oh no. No. My career is definitely not what it seems to be, Patsy.

FRANCESCA wipes the kitchen table.

PATSY
Well. I liked that commercial. I even went out and bought the coffee.

Pause.

I mean, I know you have done much more serious things than the commercial. I saw that one play you were in that they filmed for television. What was that?

FRANCESCA
Oh. *Hedda Gabler*!

PATSY
Yes. I liked it. Although I have to admit I did fall asleep. Well I was very tired. *(cough)* Well now why don't I start our lunch? I have a nice chicken pot-pie and what about a Patsy salad, would you like a Patsy salad?

FRANCESCA
I would love a Patsy salad.

PATSY
Ric named it that he loves to tease. BIG TEASER.

PATSY begins to make lunch. There is a pie all ready to go, it has been warming in the oven. She opens some wine and sets about making a huge salad for the two of them.

Care for some ice wine?

FRANCESCA
Sure. Why not?

PATSY
Ric makes it himself. He is crazy about wines, got his own vintner, in Ottawa, even.

PATSY pours FRANCESCA and herself some ice wine.

And... here is to...

FRANCESCA
Here's to–

FRANCESCA approaches PATSY and kisses her on the cheek.

Past.

Girls in PATSY's bedroom singing Verse #1 of "Dark end of the Street".

PATSY & MARIE
At the dark end of the Street
That is where we always meet
Hiding in shadows–

Present.

Women finally clink glasses. with arms crossed.

Scene Nineteen

Past.

First sleepover, PATSY is standing behind MARIE, picking nits. She wears gloves.

PATSY
Seventy-nine.

MARIE
Jeez.

PATSY wipes off her fingers.

PATSY
Eighty.

PATSY finds another.

MARIE
Holy Crow. Don't tell nobody, eh?

PATSY
Eighty-one.

MARIE
My mother won't do this. She says no child of hers has lice.

PATSY
I don't mind doin it. *I like it!* Eighty-two.

MARIE
Sometimes, at night? I'm lyin in bed and the itchiness is so bad I think I'm just gonna jump out a window and run down the street screaming.

PATSY looks through her hair for more nits.

PATSY
And that's it for the nits. Looks pretty good. Yup. Now. Close your eyes real tight.

PATSY opens a tub of margarine.

MARIE
What are you going to do? What is that?

PATSY
Shhhh. It's margarine. *(mar–ja–reen)* It suffocates them.

MARIE
Wait. Wait. Aren't ya gonna get in trouble for takin the margarine?

PATSY
Nope.

MARIE
Are you sure… this is what ya do?

PATSY
Yup.

MARIE
Is it going to feel yucky?

PATSY
No.

MARIE
Am I going to look stupid?

PATSY
No.

MARIE
How long will I have to have it for?

PATSY
Just till tomorrow. When we wake up. Then they'll all be dead. And then we comb 'em out.

MARIE
Oh the smell!

PATSY
And you'll never have them again.

MARIE
Never?

PATSY
Never.

MARIE
Never.

Scene Twenty

Present.

PATSY continues making lunch. FRANCESCA is drinking her ice wine.

PATSY
So. I've been dying to ask you. I hope you won't think I'm nosy. Those magazines say that you have been married three times. Now I know they are always tellin terrible lies…

FRANCESCA
It's true!

PATSY
No way.

FRANCESCA
I know. It seems like a lot. But it just… happened that way.

PATSY
Round here nobody gets divorced even. Well, Sherry Bryden, she left Norm but he was beating on her and the kids, nobody thought the less of her. And come to think of it, the Andrews. Well let's just say its not common.

FRANCESCA
I thought each one was going to be forever. Except the third, which was just to help my friend Paulo get into the country.

PATSY
Well now that's interesting. That you thought they were going to be forever.

FRANCESCA
Hey, once a Catholic, always a Catholic. With the first, Douglas, we were so young. We had no money, we led this crazy downtown existence, living on mocha cake and jumbo Martinis, running out of restaurants without paying, making terrible scenes in gay dance clubs, slapping people in the face, stealing lingerie from Holt Renfrew, and then being chased down Yonge Street by security, hiding in the bathroom of the Papaya Hut, gossiping viciously about everybody, passing rumours, destroying reputations. It was a lot of fun.

PATSY
So what happened?

FRANCESCA
Oh nothing. He turned out to be gay. I went back to school.

PATSY
Gay?

FRANCESCA
Uh huh.

PATSY
I don't think I've ever met anyone who's gay. I mean I've seen them, on television, and in movies.

FRANCESCA
Oh sure you have, Patsy.

PATSY
Oh no, there's nobody gay in Marmora. I would know if there was.

Awkward moment, PATSY knows FRANCESCA thinks she is backward.

FRANCESCA
Well, people can be secretive, you know. When they know they will be… hated…. After all, no one wants to be another Marie Begg.

PATSY
Oh you weren't hated.

FRANCESCA
Yes I was.

PATSY
I mean, it wasn't personal. You were just the scapegoat. Because you were… arty.

FRANCESCA laughs. Awkward pause.

I've often wondered, you know, if it still bothers you, ever, when you think about it. Like, the way you were treated here, as a kid.

FRANCESCA
Sometimes in a flash I am eleven years old again and they're throwing stones at me. Calling me those names and coughing. Remember? They used to cough when they saw me.

PATSY
Ignorant dogs.

FRANCESCA
On my bad days I think it was something in me. Something they detected? Something that is… still there. You know? There was a reason they picked on me, and not, say, Darlene Rowan, who was also poor.

PATSY
Because Darlene, she knew her place, right? She never raised her head!

FRANCESCA
So I walk out of my beautiful penthouse on the twentieth floor feeling this big kind of Dirty Yellow Stain all over me. The Marie Begg Stain. I go to openings, dinner parties, book launches, and I feel that people are avoiding the Stain, when they do talk to me I can feel them wanting to get away from the Stain, I see their eyes wandering and I feel the others are whispering about me, all over the room, and then I think I hear them coughing, they are coughing about me. And again, I am the girl with the running sores and the scabby legs, the lice and the dark circles under her eyes and the crooked teeth. I am Marie Begg. With the Stain.

PATSY
Well you look pretty clean to me, if it's any comfort.

FRANCESCA
You know it's funny, I stand backstage sometimes and conjure… their faces and I am filled with a kind of electric energy, you know? And then I go out, like a lightning bolt; I guess it's revenge. I take my revenge on the stage somehow. *(pause)* Where are all those… people? Are they still… around?

Scene Twenty-One

Past.

MARIE has the rain bonnet on to keep the margarine in.

MARIE
Are you sure it's alright for me to sleepover?

PATSY
Yeah! You heard my mum.

MARIE
She is so nice. And so pretty. This is the first time I ever been on a sleepover.

PATSY
Really? How come?

MARIE
Because.

PATSY
I'm glad your mom said yes.

MARIE
I think she was drunk. Don't tell nobody I said that. What are we having for breakfast?

PATSY
French toast. With our own maple syrup.

MARIE makes the sign of the cross in gratefulness. PATSY notices.

Um Marie? I have to ask you something. Are you… um… Catholic?

MARIE
What is French toast? Exactly.

PATSY
I like Catholics. It's okay.

MARIE
Like I know what French is. And I know what toast is.

PATSY
If you're Catholic, how come you don't go to St. Mike's?

MARIE
My mom said Father Duchene touched her tittie.

PATSY
Shhhh.

MARIE
I mean… breast. Chest.

PATSY
My mom says to stay away from Catholic kids. She says they're tough. But I'll tell her you're nice… I'll tell her you don't say bad words.

MARIE
I won't say no more.

PATSY
Thank you.

MARIE
That's why we don't have a farm anymore.

PATSY
Why?

MARIE
Because. We're Catholic.

PATSY
Oh. That's too bad.

MARIE
Because the Catholics got all the bad land. That's what my Dad says. On the other side of the 401.

PATSY
So why don't you change to Protestant?

MARIE
I would but I can't, you know why? Because my gramma's last words, when she was dyin on the bed and she held on to my hand so tight I couldn't let go? Her last words to me were "Keep the Faith." And that means "Stay Catholic." And then her eyes rolled up in her head.

PATSY
Ewww.

MARIE
I know.

Scene Twenty-Two

Present.

PATSY
So number one was "that way" who was the next husband?

FRANCESCA
Oh… Paul… handsome Paul… I met him at McGill.

PATSY
So what happened?

FRANCESCA
We used to meet in his carrel, his study carrel? He was at the law school there. And the sex was indescribable. It even felt important, as if we were working for the French Resistance or something; he was by far the most passionate man I had ever met but as soon as we got married, the DAY we got married he started… to… raise his voice, no, yell at me.

PATSY
No way.

FRANCESCA
Just bellowed. All the time, about anything. A sock left on the floor. My dress being improper. My kissing, too hungry. And then one day, he threw a chair out the window.

PATSY
Oh my God if there had been someone walkin by with a baby in a stroller that chair coulda killed the baby.

FRANCESCA
That's exactly what I told him. And then I left. Didn't want my mother all over again.

PATSY
No, no ya wouldn't. *(pause)* What was he so damn mad about anyways?

PATSY finishes off her Patsy salad.

FRANCESCA
You really want to know? That time, specifically? I cut the banana cream pie with a spoon. He found that... careless.

PATSY
Hah! You used to do that around here too!

FRANCESCA
I did?

PATSY
Yes! Oh my Godfather, my mother would just shake her head.

FRANCESCA
I don't know why I did it. I just liked to use a spoon.

PATSY laughs. FRANCESCA laughs.

I just liked it!!

They laugh harder. FRANCESCA helps with the placing of the cutlery.

I still do!! But I realized something, you know. I realized that in that moment, he saw Marie. When I did that. Because that is something Marie would do. Not Francesca. And he certainly did not want to be married to Marie. Who would?

PATSY
Well I happen to like Marie, myself. I was disappointed when you threw away your name. Like you were throwin my friend away, you know? I was disappointed... when you left. Did you know that?

FRANCESCA
...Lying in that hospital bed for all those weeks, with broken bones, I stared at the ceiling and I knew how I would end up if I stayed. I would end up the way they all thought of me because you can't keep fighting the way people think of you, eventually, you have to give into it, and become it: I would be the strange

schoolteacher living alone. Riding a bicycle with long hair and torn stockings, being called a witch by the schoolchildren; grandchildren of the people who had thrown rocks at me, and smeared dog shit all over my coat, and thrown my books all over the yard. And that's when I decided that I was going to leave, and leave Marie behind like the Thousand Island Rat Snake leaves behind his skin, and I was never ever going to come back.

Scene Twenty-Three

Past.

Girls (12), by their lockers at school.

MARIE
I was in the washroom today? And ya know what happened?

PATSY
What?

MARIE
Patty Hagerty and Jane Howard started bangin on the door. They're bangin on the door going, "We're going to kill you, you shitty arse face, you Catholic whore, we're going to beat you till you shit your pants!" And I go, "My mom already does that ANYWAYS!" I hadda stay in there the whole lunch hour.

PATSY
I'm reporting them to Mr. Eaves. He'll give them the strap.

MARIE
No, Patsy, don't.

PATSY
But they can't keep bullying you.

MARIE
Don't worry, one of these days I'm gonna come out and I'll beat their fucking faces in.

PATSY
Marie. Do not use that language, please. It degrades the human body.

MARIE
I'm sorry. I'm sorry Patsy, I just get so mad. I promise I won't use it anymore.

PATSY
You always promise and then you–

MARIE
Patsy?

PATSY
Listen, Marie. I can't hang around with you if you use that kind of language. I promised my mother.

MARIE
Okay. I really really won't use it again. Patsy? Patsy? Patsy?

PATSY doesn't answer. And then she suddenly turns around and hugs MARIE.

PATSY
Patty and Jane? They're gonna end up workin at the Lipton's Soup factory in Belleville, and you know that smell of powdered chicken soup? You can't get that off. Not ever.

Scene Twenty-Four

Present.

PATSY and FRANCESCA eating the meal with wine.

FRANCESCA
Oh. This pastry is sublime

PATSY
Actually I was kinda worried about the pastry. Thought I over-kneaded the dough.

FRANCESCA
NO! And the filling…

PATSY
Chicken Dijon with the red port wine, shallots and garlic, cilantro and bay leaf all grown in my garden.

FRANCESCA
It's incomparable.

PATSY
Gee. Alls Ric ever says is "Not bad." That is, like the height of a compliment comin from Ric.

FRANCESCA
Well he needs a shake.

PATSY
Ric? Oh no, he means well.

FRANCESCA
But that's not good enough. He should lavish you with praise, Patsy, you deserve it. You are his wife and he should adore you.

PATSY
He likes me well enough.

FRANCESCA
Likes you?

PATSY
He's just not the type to say it, if you know what I mean.

FRANCESCA
Patsy. Don't you get… tired? Living with the same person year after year?

PATSY
No.

FRANCESCA
Come on. I won't tell. I promise.

PATSY
When I hear Ric's truck pullin up? To be totally honest? I get excited, like a kid. I mix up the sound of the engine with the sound of his voice. And the truck with his body, I don't know. I like hearin his voice, it's like warm tea goin down my throat, and seeing like the way he rolls up his sleeves those big forearms, you know? And washes his hands, with the nails bit down, the way he sits in the chair and reads the paper while I'm makin supper. I just like… havin him near. It's the nearness, you know?

FRANCESCA
But does he challenge you? Intellectually?

PATSY
Well… he doesn't love to read the way I do, but Ric is a very smart man, Francesca.

FRANCESCA
And you are equal partners?

PATSY
Well of course we are. But he is the man, Francesca. And they don't tend to compromise. You know that. It's the women who tend to compromise.

FRANCESCA
　Patsy.

PATSY
　I mean I have my opinions and he listens to them, but he is the man of the household. He does usually have the final... Marie I am not one of these strident feminists who who hates men.

FRANCESCA
　I have never known a feminist who hates men.

PATSY
　Are you trying to tell me there is something wrong with my marriage?

FRANCESCA
　No.

PATSY
　Yes.

FRANCESCA
　Patsy. Is there any... passion left?

PATSY
　Passion?

FRANCESCA
　Yes passion. You know.

PATSY
　Oh! That. Yeah. Sometimes. When the lights are out. Nosy.

FRANCESCA
　But, I'm talking about, you know, ecstasy? Do you find... ecstasy?

PATSY
　In sex?

FRANCESCA
　Well...

PATSY
　Not really.

FRANCESCA
　Then where, Patsy? Where do you find it?

PATSY
　I don't know. Here and there. *(pause)* Where do you find it?

FRANCESCA
I haven't.

Scene Twenty-Five

Past.

Music. Girls run out both holding either end of a white sheet. Pretending to be in a sleigh.

PATSY
I am the beautiful Annabel Lee.

MARIE
And I am the dancer, Miss Bon bon McFee.

PATSY
I am wearing golden silk organza and a red rose in my hair…

MARIE
And I am wearing a snow queen's dress, with the white rabbit fur and the deep blue-velvet Lake Ontario blue.

PATSY
And we are on our silver sleigh…

MARIE
Our sterling silver sleigh…

PATSY
Going to the winter ball…

MARIE
At the Marmora Castle on Marmora Hill…

PATSY
And only the beautiful, the rich–

MARIE
And the famous and their dogs–

PATSY
There are six white horses pulling this sleigh…

MARIE
And we are sipping warm hot chocolate…

PATSY
With marshmallows.

MARIE
The snow is deep...

PATSY
And high...

MARIE
Snowflakes swirl around us...

PATSY
Oh!! I think it's a snowstorm, Bon bon!! Oh my heavens!

MARIE
It is! It is a snowstorm! The horses are scared. *(They neigh.)* And they have lost their way.

PATSY
Hours and hours and hours of cold...

MARIE
The horses go way far way way WAY.

PATSY
And leave us alone...

MARIE
In the snow.

PATSY
And I am feeling sleepy...

MARIE
My eyes are getting heavy...

PATSY
And I sleep...

MARIE
And I sleep...

PATSY
And I sleep...

MARIE
And I cough... *(cough)*

PATSY
And I cough… *(cough)*

MARIE
And I freeze…

PATSY
And I freeze

MARIE
And they find us two days later.

PATSY
Frozen stiff.

MARIE
The beautiful Annabel Lee…

PATSY
And BON BON McFEE.

Scene Twenty-Six

Present.

PATSY feels too warm. She gets up and looks out. She holds her head. She backs up, and looks dizzy. She leans over and breathes deeply.

PATSY
Jeez, I'm finding it warm in here. Are you?

FRANCESCA
Not really.

PATSY
Maybe it's the stove. *(She sticks her head near an open window.)* Get some air. I hope it's not the menopause. You know, with the hot flashes and that? Or maybe…. You know we been tryin'… for a daughter for our old age, eh? If if if…. Come to think of it I am kinda late and…. Uh oh. Uh oh.

PATSY sees the stalker, walks backward.

FRANCESCA
Patsy? Are you alright?

PATSY
(staring at the stalker) I think so I'll just lie down. *(She lies on the kitchen chaise.)* You still know how to treat a seizure, eh?

FRANCESCA
Seizure?

PATSY
I know. I stole your disease on ya.

FRANCESCA
Patsy? You have…

FRANCESCA gets her a drink of water.

(overlaps PATSY's next line) Seizures?

PATSY
Oh about once a month. The grand mals, just like you had…. Flailin around, screamin like an animal bein slaughtered…. Last time I had one was at Kevy's Christmas recital. That was really pleasant. Oh yeah, ever since–

FRANCESCA
The crash.

PATSY
(overlaps) The crash.

I was in a coma for eight weeks, Francesca. Nothing was the same when I come out.

FRANCESCA
I came, you know… to see you. Before I disappeared.

PATSY
I know ya did.

FRANCESCA
You knew? You knew that I was there?

PATSY nods.

PATSY
I knew that you were there but I couldn't open my eyes, or my mouth. And there was something I wanted to tell you, Marie.

FRANCESCA waits.

I wanted to tell you to scratch my head. My head, my head's so itchy can you imagine an itch like the end of the world and there you were and I could not lift my hand or my arm to scratch my head and I could not move my lips or my tongue to say "Scratch" to say, "Please scratch my head" and you're standing there and I just want to sit up and scream "WILL YOU SCRATCH MY DAMN HEAD PLEASE?"

Four months in a trauma ward with angry foul-talking teenage boys who had dived off cliffs or had head-on collisions!

FRANCESCA holds her.

FRANCESCA
I should have stayed and helped your mother look after you, Patsy. I will never forgive myself for–

PATSY, feeling a seizure is imminent, moves away.

PATSY
You should have stayed and helped my mother what? What… are you saying? To help my mother look after you? I'm sorry, I just… don't… think my mother… my…

FRANCESCA
Patsy? What are you looking at, is… Patsy?

PATSY looks very frightened, and then she goes into a full epileptic seizure, hitting the floor, and convulsing. FRANCESCA at first is paralyzed, recalling her own seizures with terror. Then she goes to PATSY and holds her as she jerks. As she seizes, the lights flicker as a lightning storm, and we move to the past.

Scene Twenty-Seven

Past.

Lightning storm. The 12-year-old girls are in a closet. Lightning and thunder.

MARIE
Patsy, my knees are killing me. How long is your mom gonna make us stay in the closet?

PATSY
Oh. Just till the lightning has passed.

MARIE
How long will that be? Till the lightning passes?

PATSY
I don't know. Sometimes it's all night.

MARIE
Can't we just hide under the covers? In your bed? It's much more comfortable in your bed.

PATSY
Marie. Kevin Creaser's aunt got killed in her bed by lightning last year. It came in the window, lightning comes in the window, get it? And do you see any windows in here? Do you?

BIG BOOM/lightning, thunder. The lightning strikes, the thunder claps, the girls scream. ADULT PATSY screams along as her seizure has subsided.

Scene Twenty-Eight

Present.

PATSY continues screaming. Finally, she calms.

FRANCESCA
Patsy? It's okay. You had a seizure.

PATSY looks around…

PATSY
Oh God, I'm sorry. I'm so sorry. Here you finally come for a visit and I have to go and do that.

FRANCESCA
Please, don't apologize. The important thing is that you're alright. Is there someone you would like me to call, or…?

PATSY
(feels and sees the wetness on her clothing) OH my God how embarrassing. I'm sorry. I'm so sorry. I won't be long.

FRANCESCA
Would you like some help, or…?

PATSY
Oh God no, you know what it's like. Once it passes it's gone. You know that. Just I – uh could really do with some fresh air, you know? Would it be okay if we took a walk?

FRANCESCA
Oh yes. Please, I would love a walk.

PATSY
Good!

PATSY exits to change and shower.

FRANCESCA
You know I haven't had an attack since I left here.

PATSY
(from offstage) Oh. That was your goin away present, was it?

FRANCESCA looks around the room slowly. She feels dizzy herself. She falls to her knees. Music.

Scene Twenty-Nine

The two girls (12), lie on the train tracks.

PATSY
Hey. I got an idea. Let's go swimmin'!

MARIE
Where?

PATSY
In the RIVER, silly…. Look, you can see it if you really try. See? Isn't it beautiful?

MARIE
Yeah. *(She does not look.)*

PATSY
Well what are we waitin for? Let's go! *(pause)* Well come on, Slowpokey.

MARIE
I can't.

PATSY
Why not?

MARIE
Cause. There's eels in there. They could strangulate you.

PATSY
No. No, there's no eels, just carp, ya goofus. Great big carp we feed em bread crumbs they're hardly cute! My Uncle Willy even kissed one on the lips once.

MARIE
Can't go swimmin'.

PATSY
  Marie, I tolja…!

MARIE
  Don't matter bout the eels. I was just makin that up.

PATSY
  Well then what then? Marie?

MARIE
  Promise you won't tell?

PATSY
  Yeah, what?

MARIE
  It's because uh my… secret.

PATSY
  What secret?

MARIE
  I – take… spells.

PATSY
  What?

MARIE
  Fits.

PATSY
  Like Darlene Rowan's brother?

MARIE
  Worser.

PATSY
  Worser?

MARIE
  And if, like, I did it in water I could get drownded. So, that's why I don't want to go swimmin'.

PATSY
  Oh boy. Can ya do it right now?

MARIE
  No. They just come on whenever they want to. Like a storm.

PATSY
Well what are they from?

MARIE
My mother hittin me on the back of the head.

Pause.

PATSY
Let's go swimmin'. Let's go swimmin anyways.

Scene Thirty

Present.

PATSY comes back in fresh clothes. She grabs two jackets from an outer room.

PATSY
I was lookin up on the Internet about it, eh? And did you know they used to think it was contagious? Like the common cold?

FRANCESCA
Only for you and me I guess.

PATSY laughs.

PATSY
Here. Put this on, you don't want to get your nice outfit covered in burrs. *(PATSY hands FRANCESCA a coat, she herself puts on Ric's coat.)* And one of the cures? Was you had to drink blood flowin fresh from a wound! Like some kind of vampire! I actually gave a talk about it at the Northumberland Epilepsy Association.

FRANCESCA
Are you sure you don't want to lie down for a while before we go out?

PATSY
And they used to cut off your privates! Like, genital mutilation. Thinkin it was from bein oversexed! Men and women, can you believe it?

FRANCESCA
Patsy, are you sure you're alright? I know I used to feel very strange for *hours* afterwards. As if I were underwater. Not real.

PATSY
Oh, me? I'm fine. A little embarrassed. In front of a famous person like you.

FRANCESCA
Oh stop, you don't need to be embarrassed in front of me. You've seen me in seizure. I had long ones, too, twenty, thirty minutes. I remember waking up, looking into your face.

PATSY
I remember your face turning purple. Like an eggplant.

FRANCESCA
Cyanosis.

PATSY
Right before death. That's what I always thought when I saw your face lookin like that. That it was right before death.

FRANCESCA
It was.

PATSY
I know, I was holding you. Darlene Rowan's brother he did die of it. He died in the bath one Sunday, when everyone else was at church.

FRANCESCA
It's funny you should mention blood because I always used to think I smelled blood before mine. This thick, dark sweet and very personal smell... you know when you wake someone up in the morning, and the smell underneath the sheets? It's the essence of the person, that smell; I guess that's why I like to sleep alone. What are they like for you, Patsy? Do you remember them at all? *(long pause)*

PATSY
What are they like what are they like I would like to say they're like going to sleep in fact that is what I tell people, don't want to worry them, but Marie I live in fear. I live in fear of the next seizure it's like there's a stalker. And he's always there, parked in the driveway, in his old car, waiting. I come down to turn out the lights his face, in the window, his eyes, goin through me, I am out in the fields on the tractor, there he is, behind the tree, with his knife and his dirty long fingernails all for me, waiting, and sometimes, if I've had too much wine, or not enough sleep, he will walk towards me. Last week, in the Kingston Shopping Centre, there he was comin out of the Cotton Ginny Plus store, smiling, smoking and he comes towards me and the floor starts moving and I'm lookin around I'm saying oh my God no, no, somebody help me my God and the walls are shifting and my stomach is turning I'm about to throw up and he keeps walking towards me, he is going to kill me.... Now everybody, people are staring, I put my head between my knees, "Are you alright, lady? Can I get you a glass of water?" And they don't seem to see him he is right on top of me, his scrawny arms around me his breath like vomit in my face his eyes burning me and he holds me so close like constricting, and crushing and I'm trying to yell but they can't hear my voice because he's over my face and he is pulling and

pullin me closer... can't breathe.... Can't breathe now and the people are so far away it's like he is moving me under the floor, the linoleum-marble floor and under the mall and the people and into the dark the pipes and the loneliness and they are all so far away and I will die under this floor like a cockroach all my life over, all over and he will be filled up with me and then, then, suddenly, the way someone whose been underwater just kinda pops out and the water falls off them I am there, on the floor of the mall, and the air, and the people around me, and the ambulance guys, and I sit up, I tell em it's okay, just a seizure, but I got these needles in my head, and I drink a Sprite someone's got for me, and I tell the nice lady who's a nurse that I'm okay, and the staring children, and I get myself up, and I'm shakin', yes, and wobbly, but I gotta do my shopping, gotta get it done, only come to Kingston once a month and I walk down the mall, and into the Grand and Toy, got to get supplies for the books, and he is there. There he is, behind the paper, just staring, oh he wants me back. Could be another seizure, see, that's the thing, the more you have them, the more you have them, your brain remembers that's what my doctor said, so he knows, Stalker knows he could get me again. He stands there, Marie, he stands there lickin his dry lips, waiting, waiting with his dirty fingers to hold me too close and move me under and he knows; he knows that he can get me any time he wants.

ACT TWO

Scene One

Past.

The girls, 15, at the edge of the pond. They have been skating. They unlace their skates and put on their shoes.

MARIE
My hands are so cold I can't feel 'em.

PATSY
Mine too.

MARIE
And I'm sure I have frostbite on my left ear. I don't care though. It's so nice out here.

PATSY
The air.

MARIE & PATSY
The air… *(laughter)*

MARIE
The ice…

PATSY
Yeah…

MARIE
Patsy?

PATSY
Yeah.

MARIE
Why do you hang around with me?

PATSY
Because. You are my friend.

MARIE
But what's the reason? Like…

PATSY
Marie. You're always looking for reasons. Sometimes there is no reason. The only reason is that you are my friend.

MARIE
But how come when you look at me, you don't see what they see? That makes them cough, and call me all those unspeakable… names.

PATSY
Because, well, I didn't catch the sickness.

MARIE
What sickness?

PATSY
The "hate-Marie Begg" sickness. I figure it's contagious, like a cold, eh, for stupid people. It's like, in the air and they catch it.

MARIE
How come you didn't catch it.

PATSY
Because.

MARIE
You know, you could be a lot more popular if you didn't hang around with me. I heard that Mark Brant even thought you were cute.

PATSY
Look! A falling star, look!

MARIE
Quick. Say what you want to be. It'll come true if you say it on a falling star.

PATSY
Ahhhhhhhhh…. Wife and mother. On the farm. Except I wouldn't have to feed the chickens. Or have anything to do with the barn.

MARIE
Patsy get real. A WIFE and MOTHER?

PATSY
But Marie. That's what I want.

MARIE
What about a mountain climber? Or a movie star? Or a medical researcher?

PATSY
Marie, you wish what YOU want. I want to be a wife and mother. That is what I want.

MARIE
I don't believe you. You lost your chance.

PATSY
My chance to what?

MARIE
To get out of Marmora. Don't you want to get out of Marmora?

PATSY looks at her blankly.

Patsy. Do you not want to get out of Marmora? Do you want to be here for the rest of your life?

Scene Two

Present.

The women are outside, up in the hay maw.

FRANCESCA
My favourite place in the whole world. Ohhh the smell is glorious.

PATSY
You like that? Can't stand it. Dries my sinuses right out.

They sit and look out at the farm.

FRANCESCA
Patsy. I'm scared to ask.... Is there anything else.... Besides the attacks...?

PATSY
Oh the crash left me with a big bag of bothers. Still can't move my left hand well. They call that a-taxia, can't walk fast, can't run at all, I dream about running; and you know the weirdest thing?

FRANCESCA listens.

Can't cry. Haven't cried since before the crash. Not even when Ry lost his arm, or when my Annabel was stillborn, I just cannot cry. Doctor says it's just one of those things.

FRANCESCA
Oh Patsy, you had a stillborn baby?

PATSY
I held her. For over a full day. I just held her, wrapped in the soft pink blanket my Mother had made, and I kissed her sweet little face with the white down, her toes, like Lily Of the Valley.... But I did not cry.

FRANCESCA
And your son?

PATSY
Yeah, well it happens, on farms. All the machinery. He was three. But he does really well with the prosthesis now, you would never know if ya saw him.... Now stop lookin like my dog after she ate the roast offa the table. As my son says, "Shit happens."

FRANCESCA
I have been so… favoured.

PATSY
Favoured?

FRANCESCA
For me, it was a… resurrection, Patsy. Another chance. But knowing what it has done to you… I would give anything to–

PATSY
–Oh God, no, I wouldn't trade places with you for the world. NOT for the WORLD in a straw basket.

Awkward pause – FRANCESCA doesn't get it.

I mean seizures are one thing but to be haunted; the way you must be I mean I would far rather have a seizure than wake up in the night and see THEIR eyes starin at me outa the dark. I always remember people's eyes, don't you?

FRANCESCA has a flashback of the eyes. This is very unsettling for her.

Scene Three

Past.

The girls are drinking parent's liquor with AM *radio in the background. Groovy* AM *pop music. They are laughing hysterically.*

MARIE
You know what I hate?

PATSY
What?

MARIE
The sound of my mother going to the bathroom!

PATSY
I know!

MARIE
She even leaves the door open sometimes!

PATSY
Oh my stars not mine she is as private as a mole. She won't even cough in front of us.

MARIE
And you know what I hate even more? When she hugs me.

PATSY stops laughing.

PATSY
Marie.

MARIE
Last night? Calls me the Town Whore. Me! Who's never even been kissed. The Town Whore! I laughed so hard I almost puked.

PATSY
Didn't your father like, defend you?

MARIE
Edwin? *(laugh)* Edwin just sits in his chair, drinking his rye and lookin out the window for God knows what. That's why he's such a roaring success! *(pause)* Are you sure I should crash this party? What if, like, she asks me to leave?

PATSY
She won't.

MARIE
How do you know? I am, like, the only person in grade eleven who wasn't invited.

PATSY
Well. That's why I want you to come. To show her, if she has you at her party, that you won't ruin the party, that you can look pretty, and act cool and even get guys, just like everyone else. And anyways, there's gonna be lots of kids from St. Mike's and BCVI, they don't even know you.

MARIE
Are you… sure?

PATSY
Marie. Do you want to be the only one in the school sitting home tonight?

MARIE
No.

PATSY
Then you are crashing Cathy Corrigan's party and that's all there is to it.

Dog barking. PATSY runs to window.

MARIE
You won't desert me? Once we get there?

Pause.

PATSY
You know what I wish? I wish my dog would come back. She's been gone for so long.

Scene Four

Present.

The women are outside, looking out at the farm.

FRANCESCA
You must do very well with this farm, eh? Makin milk for alla our milkshakes, cheese for all our pizzas.

PATSY
Hey! I just heard Marie!

FRANCESCA
What?

PATSY
I said I just heard sweet Marie. Be careful, you might lose Francesca somewhere on the farm!!

FRANCESCA
Oh get off it. So do you ever think of takin it easy? Selling the property?

PATSY gets rubber boots.

PATSY
Oh I won't tell you how much Sealtest offered us for the place.

FRANCESCA
Really.

PATSY
Let's just say it was SEVEN figures.

FRANCESCA
Get outa town! 7! You could retire in Tahiti. Were you tempted?

PATSY
For about… a day. Oh we talked about it. We argued about it. But. Well, you know…

FRANCESCA
This is your life.

PATSY
Here. Put these on. Don't want to step on a snake.

They put on some boots.

Scene Five

Past.

MARIE and PATSY in school hallway. MARIE gives PATSY a note that the boys have passed to her.

MARIE
"When I was walking all alane
I heard twa corbies making a mane.
The tane unto the tither did say,
"Whar sall we gang and dine the day?"
–In behint yon auld fail dyke,
I wot there lies a new slain knight,
And naebody kens that he lies there
But his hawk, his hound, and his lady fair.

PATSY
And while you were saying this poem to the class they put this filth on your desk?

MARIE nods.

You saw them?

MARIE nods.

Why did you open it? *(pause)* What were you thinking?

MARIE burns the note and recites:

MARIE
'Mony a one for him maks mane,
But nane sall ken whar he is gane:
O'er his white banes, when they are
bare, The wind sall blaw for evermair.'

Patsy. You don't want to know what I was thinking. You do not want to know.

MARIE puts the burning note in the trash.

Scene Six

Present.

Ladies are walking on the property.

PATSY
So… you're not married right now are you?

FRANCESCA
No!

PATSY
So you're basically single.

FRANCESCA
Yup.

PATSY
And do you like that? Being on your own?

FRANCESCA
I love being on my own.

PATSY
Do you?

FRANCESCA
The peace. The FREEDOM.

PATSY
I would get lonely, I think. Don't you ever?

FRANCESCA
No. Never.

PATSY
I don't like to be alone.

FRANCESCA
Why not?

PATSY
I don't know. I just go really... hairy, you know? Don't you ever...

FRANCESCA
My dream, I mean a real dream I have? Is that I live by myself in the Arctic, near water, and giant shifting icebergs, surrounded by only violets and snowdrops and rough weeds, with the occasional hare racing by my little snow house, and I step out my door and see black seals in blue-green water, or walrus with their tusks, big white polar bears with Arctic Char in their mouths. And it is always just slightly above freezing? With a warm snowfall, and melting ice, and some days, when I'm very calm, I see one of those great grey sperm whales swimming by...

PATSY
Still as strange as ever!

FRANCESCA
Oh yeah? You think that's strange?

PATSY
Well, yes, actually, I have to say.

FRANCESCA
Hey. Remember how we used to arm wrestle?

PATSY
I always beat you because you had the brittle bones.

FRANCESCA
Peanut brittle bones.

PATSY
From malnutrition. That's what my mother always said.

Lights up on girls as they arm wrestle and roll around. MARIE loses to YOUNG PATSY. It is an uncomfortable moment for FRANCESCA.

Scene Seven

Present.

FRANCESCA
Oh. It's so unspeakably beautiful out here. I suppose you don't see it anymore.

PATSY
I see the roof needs fixing, the rusting trailer in the back, the new machinery we haven't paid for... the hand I know is stealing from us.... Just like you when you watch a movie, you likely see the cameraman, the lights, the ropes, the makeup.... Hey, watch the fence, it's electric now.

FRANCESCA
I always thought that would be a good way to go; electrocution... either by cow fence or lightning. I really like the idea of lightning.

PATSY
Sometimes I don't know if you're kidding or you're serious.

FRANCESCA
Oh I'm serious.

PATSY
You want to die by lightning?

FRANCESCA
Sometimes in a rainstorm I go for a walk. To the big park near me. No umbrella, just me, in a raincoat walking, up and down the muddy trails, over the fields.

PATSY
What are you trying to do?

FRANCESCA
I don't know. I think.... It's as if I need to feel that *power* again.

PATSY
You mean... like... the *power of the train*? *(pause)* You know what you need? You need a slap.

Scene Eight

Past.

Girls (15) are in the hay mow. MARIE, in a velvet cape with a hood, is performing a Mother Goose rhyme for PATSY.

MARIE
"Trip upon trenchers, and dance upon dishes, my mother sent me for some barm, some barm; she bid me go lightly, and come again quickly for fear the young men should do me some harm. Yet didn't you see, yet didn't you see what naughty tricks they put upon me? They broke my pitcher and spilt the water, and huffed my mother, and chid her daughter, and kissed my sister instead of me!"

PATSY
   Wow. That's really good. I think you're gonna get the part.

MARIE
   Thank you thank you. AND what do you have, Mademoiselle Patricia? *(She takes off her cape and wraps it around PATSY.)*

PATSY
   (pause) I don't have anything.

MARIE
   Patsy. You promised.

PATSY
   He didn't know I'd be walking out that way. I never walk out that way this time of year. But I was walkin out that way so I could practice my rhyme. It was the one about these girls? Skating in the summer? And falling through the ice and so I wanted to go way far out so Roger and Wayne wouldn't make fun of me–

MARIE
   Patsy?

PATSY
   And I'm walkin near the raspberry bush? You know where we get all the raspberries for Mum's pies? And this smell almost knocked me over and I hear the flies buzzin so loud and I look and I seen this… black and white thing, like, tied to the tree and the sound of the flies it's like they are inside my ear and I plug my nose and I go closer and when I seen her I threw up. I couldn't stay to bury her, because I kept gagging on the smell–

MARIE
   –It was Belle? It was Belle, and she was dead? Patsy?

PATSY
   See I figure he had to tie her to the tree, because otherwise she would run away when she heard the shot and he would have to shoot her again, and maybe he would just wound her, and then he would have to shoot her again, and she would have such terrible fear, and my Dad cares for dumb animals he does, so he had to tie her to the tree. And my Dad does not have the time to lift her and put her in the truck and take her down to the dump he is very busy he has to work the farm so he had to leave her there.

MARIE
   You found her? You found her tied to a tree? Shot dead?

   PATSY nods.

   But why did he shoot her, Patsy?

PATSY
She was nipping the cattle. And that spoils the milk. I remember him saying, "If she nips at them again..." but I didn't really.... Ya see when cattle get scared; it spoils their milk. My dad had no choice.

MARIE
But couldn't he... have... just...

PATSY
Don't you listen? Don't you know ANYTHING? *I said he didn't have any choice*! Now leave me alone!! Just LEAVE ME ALONE!!

Scene Nine

Present.

The women are by the pond.

PATSY
Remember this pond?

FRANCESCA
We used to skate on it.

PATSY
That's right.

FRANCESCA
And skinny dip. Summer nights.

PATSY
Ric and I, we still do. We love it.

FRANCESCA
I wonder if your mother and father did too?

PATSY
My mother? Oh no. She was as private as a mole. I couldn't imagine my mother ever taking her clothes off, even for a bath, let alone... you know it's funny, when my mother was dying her belly was all swollen, eh, from the fluid? And she's lying there, barely able to speak, eh, and she takes my hand and she says to me: "I'm feeling too sexy." I'm like, "What? Too salty? Want some water?" And she's like "No" she's gettin frustrated. It took me about ten minutes to understand what she was saying, eh. And I'm like, "You say you're feeling too sexy, Mum?" At first I thought she was just losin her mind, but then after about a day I got out of her that her insides were like pressin down on her vagina somehow, right? And causin her to feel, like aroused. Alla the time.

FRANCESCA just shakes her head.

I just felt so very bad when she told me that. It seemed like a very bad joke or something, right? Her being such a lady.

FRANCESCA
Yeah, but what's wrong with a lady feeling sexy?

PATSY
It's just not… dignified.

FRANCESCA
I would love to die feeling sexy.

PATSY
Without having any control, like a barn cat in heat?

FRANCESCA
Yes.

PATSY
I don't believe you.

FRANCESCA
That's the way I live. Why shouldn't it be the way I die?

PATSY
Highly sexed, are ya? Hah. I have a girlfriend like that. Lorraine. We tease her.

FRANCESCA
Many of us are like that, Patsy. Many women…

PATSY
I wouldn't care to be like that.

FRANCESCA
And why not?

PATSY
Because. I like to be in control of my feelings.

FRANCESCA
Are you, maybe, afraid?

PATSY
Afraid? Of what?

FRANCESCA
Of… your own… passion? I mean, isn't that, in a way, why you have never left… Marmora?

PATSY
No. I don't THINK so, but I could be wrong. I mean what would I know about myself? What are you talkin about "never left" Francesca? I went to Kingston, didn't I go to Queen's for two years in occupational therapy where I won a scholarship for further study, which I turned down? I have been on trips with Ric here and there to Toronto, to Montreal, to Vermont. One time we even went on a Caribbean cruise once. I leave SOMETIMES. It is you who never left, Marie. I mean look: just look at your face.

FRANCESCA touches her face/cheek, as MARIE mirrors the action in the next scene (acne cysts).

Scene Ten

Past.

GIRLS in kitchen. MARIE is burning her face with boiled water in a bowl, and washcloth. PATSY walks in with fresh eggs in a basket.

PATSY
What are you doing? Marie. What are you doing?

MARIE
Burning my face.

PATSY
BURNING your face? May I ask why?

MARIE
To kill the acne cysts.

PATSY
Marie. Did your doctor say that was okay?

MARIE
If I burn it, I kill the infection, see?

PATSY
But… *(MARIE shows her under the cloth.)* Oh my God. Oh my God Marie don't do that again. You hear me?

MARIE
Patsy, you don't understand. I would rather have this big burn on my face, which then scabs, and bleeds and everything, than have the acne. Because with

the acne, it's like alive, you can feel the bacteria crawling under your skin. And you know how that makes me feel?

PATSY tries to grab washcloth.

Patsy. I need to do this.

PATSY
No.

MARIE
Give it to me.

PATSY
No. Not in my house. You are not burning your face in my house. I like your face, Marie. And I don't want you to burn it.

Scene Eleven

Present.

On the property.

PATSY
I mean, let's be honest, there, Francesca. Aren't you the one who's afraid?

FRANCESCA
Of what?

PATSY
Well you haven't had any children, now have you?

FRANCESCA
That was a carefully considered choice, Patsy.

PATSY
Really?

FRANCESCA
Yes. There are many good reasons:

PATSY
Well. I suppose it is a lot of work.

FRANCESCA
It's not that.

PATSY
No?

FRANCESCA
I'm not afraid of work.

PATSY
Okay, then what is it?

FRANCESCA
Well for one thing I travel.

PATSY
You could bring a nanny along–

FRANCESCA
Patsy!

PATSY
I think you are scared. I think you are scared because children always see who you really are. And your child would see right through the fancy Francesca to my sad and lonely sweet Marie.

FRANCESCA
Oh come on I'm not so fancy now. And I wasn't just sad and lonely then.

PATSY
I just wouldn't want you to miss out, Marie.

FRANCESCA
I don't feel as though I've missed out.

PATSY
But you have. To be perfectly honest you have REALLY missed out. Big time.

FRANCESCA
YOU have missed out, Patsy. By staying here, in this closed and narrow little community, on this farm, hunkering down like a scared rabbit. Really. A couple of trips here and there is nothing. There's a whole world out there. An unimaginable world.

PATSY
Yeah? Like what? What is so unimaginable?

FRANCESCA
The underground cave cities in Turkey. The 13th century golden roof in Innsbruck, Austria, with the alps behind it…. The Tower of London, The Wailing Wall in Jerusalem, Stonehenge!

PATSY
Alright. I admit it. I have missed out. Somewhat.

FRANCESCA
You see?

PATSY
But *you* have missed out more.

Scene Twelve

Hay Maw. Girls, 15. Brushing the dog poop off MARIE's coat.

MARIE
If somebody would just tell me why they are doing this to me, I would be their slave for life if somebody would just tell me what is WRONG with me. I know I'm not UGLY, aside from my face, I do really well in school, I'm nice, I mean what the hell is wrong with me?

PATSY
Nothing.

MARIE
Nothing? You promise, nothing?

PATSY
Well, maybe, I don't know.

MARIE
What?

PATSY
Nothing.

MARIE
No, what?

PATSY
Well.

MARIE
Please. Please, Patsy.

PATSY
Well. Maybe… if you had… a…

MARIE
What? *(long pause)*

PATSY
Bath?

MARIE
What?

PATSY
I mean, no offense or anything, and it doesn't bother me at all, but I was just thinking that maybe if you like, took a bath or a shower more.

MARIE
Are you saying… I smell?

PATSY
No. Just a little. Sometimes.

MARIE
I smell? Really? But I wash under my arms with soap every day. I couldn't smell. You're crazy.

PATSY shrugs.

Patsy? *(pause)* Why didn't you tell me this before?

PATSY shrugs.

What… what does it smell like?

PATSY shrugs.

Like Linda Perchuk? Not like Linda Perchuk?

PATSY
My mom says that when a girl gets her period–

MARIE
What?

PATSY
That well, when you reach puberty all these strange smells start to happen and well that you need to take a bath once a week.

MARIE
Do you? Take one once a week?

PATSY
My Mom makes us.

MARIE
Once a week?

PATSY
Every Saturday night Mum fills up the bath That takes an hour or two and then all five of us take a bath so we'll be nice and clean for church on Sunday. I always go first cause I'm the cleanest.

MARIE slaps herself. PATSY tries to stop her, grabs MARIE in a hold/embrace.

Don't Marie. Stop that. Marie!! I'm sorry. I shouldn't have…

MARIE
See the thing is… I want to take a bath, right. I wanted to take a bath like every ten days. But the last time I filled the bath my Mum gave me a black eye cause we don't have any water see cause we don't hardly have any water in our well, we – is that Mud Lake? Near those trees?

PATSY
Yeah, that's Mud Lake.

MARIE
We should walk out there one day.

PATSY
No.

MARIE
How come?

PATSY
It's weedy. Brian Ring's cousin from Gan he died in it.

MARIE
Not to swim in it, just to see it.

PATSY
You can't even put a boat in it.

MARIE
Just to see it, Pats. Don't you want to see it?

PATSY
My mother, she grew up here and she's never seen it.

Scene Thirteen

Present.

Women are out by the lake.

FRANCESCA
My last long affair was with a family man. He had four children and he... turned away from them. The constant whining and sickness, the terrible nasty fighting, the unceasing sound of the television, the demands for money, and the latest toy, and fashion, he wanted away. And when he left them for me, he felt no remorse. We lived in a beautiful glass house, by a river; They would phone, crying, begging, and he would calmly tell them he had made up his mind. I found that very... discouraging, somehow.

PATSY
So what happened to him?

FRANCESCA
Oh. I got bored with him. After the thrill of breaking up a family wore off.

PATSY
The thrill...?

FRANCESCA
I'm not proud of it.

PATSY
Well. I'm sure you wouldn't do it again.

FRANCESCA
I probably would.

PATSY
If you did it to me I'd come after you with a baseball bat.

FRANCESCA
And I would deserve it.

Pause.

Patsy? I am afraid! I am afraid... that I would give birth to Marie Begg. You know? Do you know what I mean?

FRANCESCA screams, she sees a snake close by.

PATSY
What is it? Is it a snake? I know how you feel, I've been livin with them all these years and still whenever I see one I feel the way I did when Keith Knight punched me in the stomach.

FRANCESCA
I seem to be having trouble breathing. I don't know.

PATSY
It's just a garter. They are a nuisance but they're not at all poisonous honest, you don't need to worry–

FRANCESCA
Can you help me breathe?

PATSY
Breathe?

FRANCESCA
Would you please… help… me breathe?

PATSY
Are you… do you have asthma or…? Okay… okay… Marie… I want you to breathe in as I count to four, just deep and slow, got it? Okay 1-2-3-4 and out to the count of 4, here we go, 1-2-3 and 4. That's a girl…. Feelin better? Tell me, hon', you just tell me what you're feelin'.

FRANCESCA
I'm feelin'…

PATSY
Are you…?

FRANCESCA
I don't know, I'm falling apart here.

PATSY holds FRANCESCA in silence, Girls sing "Dark end of the Street."

Scene Fourteen

The two girls in PATSY's bed, sleeping over. They could be smoking. They sing in harmony.

PATSY & FRANCESCA
At the dark end of the street
That's where we… always meet.
Hiding in shadows
Where we don't belong

Living in darkness to hide our wrong.
You and me
At the Dark End of the Street
You and me…

PATSY
Peter Butler is the most beautiful kisser in this country. He's way better than Ric.

MARIE
What's it like? I can't even imagine.

PATSY
Kissing? it's like it's like… okay, you know last Sunday when we made strawberry ice cream by hand?

MARIE
Yeah.

PATSY
And the cream is in the cold salty steel and you're churning it round and round with that big steel spoon and then ya pour in the strawberries and the red juice runs through the cream and turns it deep pink and it's gettin colder and churning and if you put your face in right into the churning ice cream at that moment when it's goin pink with the red juice and turning from cream to ice cream… THAT… is the moment of a kiss.

MARIE
I want to kiss like that.

PATSY
You will.

MARIE
Not while I live in Marmora.

PATSY
That's ridiculous.

MARIE
I'm the town dog, Patsy. *(MARIE barks.)*

PATSY
Stop it. That is not true.

MARIE
My mouth aches, it aches, Patsy, from wanting to kiss.

PATSY
Who? Who do you want to kiss, Marie?

MARIE
Nobody.

PATSY
Come on, you can tell me.

MARIE
Nobody.

PATSY
Donny Neilson?

MARIE is quiet.

The shy one? Goes to St. Mike's?

MARIE
He talked to me today. At the free skate.

PATSY
No way. I've never seen him talk to a girl.

MARIE
He was talking about how he plays hockey. How he plays every day for hours and hours practicing his shot, just like Bobby Orr did when he was growing up; he says he's got the best shot in the province and he's gonna play for the Kingston Frontenacs, and then for the Montreal Canadiens. He said he dreams about hockey.

PATSY
He said all of that? To you?

MARIE nods.

Well, the Sadie Hawkins dance is comin up. Why don't you ask him?

MARIE
No way.

PATSY
Marie.

MARIE
No. Way.

PATSY
Marie! I'm gonna call him, and—

MARIE
Patsy. If you do that, I will never forgive you.

PATSY
Promise me you'll think about it.

MARIE
I am not promising anything. Now let me go to sleep.

PATSY
"Says the little girl to the little boy, What shall we do? Says the little boy to the little girl, I will kiss you!!!!!"

Present.

ADULT PATSY sings (refrain) 1ˢᵗ verse of "Dark End of the Street".

PATSY
At the dark end of the street
That's where we... always meet.
Hiding in shadows
Where we don't belong
Living in darkness to hide our wrong.
You and me
At the dark end of the street
You and me...

FRANCESCA
Patsy, let's go to the tracks. I want to go to the train tracks.

Scene Fifteen

Past.

Getting ready for the dance. PATSY hairsprays MARIE's hair, takes out hair rollers. AM radio music.

PATSY
Now, with the mascara, you brush over the eyelashes three times and then under 'em three times. And you have to wipe the wand off eh? So it doesn't get all goopy and make you look like white trash.

MARIE
Are you sure the blue mascara isn't too much?

PATSY
Oh everybody's wearin the blue. And with the baby blue eyeshadow, it's gorgeous. Oh my god your hair is perfect, you look like Miss America… it's shimmering.

MARIE
Like ice.

PATSY
Oh now make sure it falls over your shoulder, just so, it makes guys go insane with desire.

MARIE goes to touch it.

Now don't touch it.

MARIE goes to touch it.

DON'T TOUCH it.

MARIE
I wish you were coming.

PATSY
Oh this flu is so bad I can hardly see straight. Anyway, Ric's been weird lately, I'm playing hard to get.

MARIE
What do I do if he kisses me, Patsy?

PATSY
You just kiss back. But gently. Don't put your tongue in his mouth till he puts his in yours. And above all do not let him feel you up.

MARIE
How come?

PATSY
Marie. You know what they think of sluts around here. Look at Darlene Rowan.

MARIE
Yeah.

PATSY
You just slap his hand, hard. And make sure everybody sees ya.

MARIE has finished her makeup, shows her face.

MARIE
How's that? Is that okay?

PATSY
Beautiful.

MARIE
Are you sure?

PATSY
Yes I'm sure. You can hardly even notice your boils. Especially when your hair falls over them.

PATSY gets the dress.

And now… *(She makes a horn sound like a fanfare.)* Da Da Da Da!

She puts the dress on MARIE. It looks beautiful. We can see the beautiful woman she will become.

MARIE
Is it alright?

PATSY
(takes her to a mirror) You are gonna be the prettiest girl at the dance. And they're all gonna go like, "What happened to Marie Begg? I mean like where is Marie Begg?"

Scene Sixteen

Present.

The railroad tracks come into view.

PATSY
Recognize these?

FRANCESCA
Oh yes. Oh yes.

PATSY
Still comes by here, three times a day.

FRANCESCA
Smells. Oh my God. That smell.

PATSY
Yeah. Well. You know what that is. That's sewage, eh? They just dump it, right on the tracks.

FRANCESCA is going into pre-seizure mode. She is there, and not there.

FRANCESCA
(coughs) Ohhh. *(deep breath)* Ohhhh. Oh… oh… oh… that was me, that was how I smelled, after the dance; (*She starts wiping it off, trying to dry herself.*) I couldn't wash it off, you know? I tried, in the sink at the Tim Hortons, with lots and lots of that pink creamy soap but the smell it wouldn't come off, it just got stronger and stronger and I was so dizzy from the fumes I never told anyone I never told anyone about that, not even you but you could smell it. Couldn't you?

It was dark when it happened, wasn't it?

PATSY
Yes, I believe it was. It was dark.

FRANCESCA
But the air was fresh.

PATSY
That's right.

FRANCESCA
I had worn that green dress you made me–

PATSY
Yes you did.

FRANCESCA
And the white lace stockings…

PATSY
And I had brushed your hair until it shimmered–

FRANCESCA
–Like ice…

PATSY
You looked beautiful.

FRANCESCA
I looked beautiful. Except for the shoes with the broken heel – I was hoping no one would notice the shoes it was spring; white tulips tall, burgundy spray all over the sidewalks and the yellow forsythia everywhere and maples about to burst and the fragrance, the fragrance; I waited for him on the steps of the

Kentucky Fried Chicken and then there he was, his hair combed. His hands clean we didn't say a word, we walked and he actually held my hand, our hands were both sweating, I almost fainted with desire I had never been touched you see, by a boy I wanted to fall into the grass with him so we walked to the school, we went into the gym with the streamers and the punch bowl and the band was playing *(She sings.)* "smile a little smile for me, Rose Marie," he was still holding my hand, but the others, Pat Letour and Roly and them, they looked and they stared and after a while, they they started to cough they were laughing at him and there was that moment when he knew he was being laughed at… THE COUGHING… because of me. And the coughing. He suddenly knew I was the school dog he hadn't realized, you see, COUGHING… because he was from St. Mike's, so so he turned white white like the tulips… he shook off my hand and and and…

PATSY is wary, but with her.

PATSY
And then what, Marie? What happened then?

FRANCESCA
He never came back. I waited by the wall and I waited and they stared and they gathered and they threw spitballs and he never came back. I heard his car drive away I knew the sound of his car. I walked out my head down my legs shaking across the football field. In my mother's high heels and and– *(PATSY helps her.)*

PATSY
Do you want to go back, hon, we could go back.

FRANCESCA
And they were suddenly there, Pat, Roland, Mike and Jamie and they pushed me from behind, and then from the front and they were laughing. And saying my hair looked nice. And wouldn't it look nice with sperm all over it. I didn't understand that…. And I started to feel sick, sick to my stomach… and in my head like I was going to have a seizure. And all their hands, their fingers, touching me… I tried to walk past them. But someone grabbed my arms. So hard. They were all around me and there wasn't a space no space. They kept laughing. And coughing. And moving closer and closer. Their saliva spraying on my face and saying dirty words, filthy words I didn't understand. And then I fell backwards, on my back and them all unzipping their pants and then wham! I went into seizure in and out and when I would come out for a moment I would feel the spraying on my face, and see their faces, the sound, the spraying, the SMELL ohhhhhh Patsy the SMELL…

FRANCESCA collapses in PATSY's arms… she re-lives the memory.

Scene Seventeen

Past.

AM radio music. While listening to pop music on the radio, PATSY is making an apple pie, keeps her back to MARIE who enters the kitchen, her pretty dress a mess. The back is all muddy as if she lay on the dirt. The front is very wrinkled and ripped. There is blood, also on the back. She is shaking uncontrollably and her teeth are chattering.

MARIE
Patsy?

PATSY
How was it? Gimme all the dirt. I want every detail. Did ya dance a slow dance? Tammy phoned and said the band really sucked, and my Ric was there with *Gerette Blanchard*. I will never speak to her again I am so glad I have the flu. Temperature's 104 I'm not kiddin you. But I gotta do these pies for Mum, she's serving them to... Holy God. What happened to you?

MARIE cannot answer. She sits down, trembling, shaky. She has picked up a partially smoked wet butt off the road...

MARIE
Do you... have a light?

PATSY approaches her. MARIE smells terrible, of urine. She is having trouble breathing and therefore trouble speaking. When she speaks it is as if she is winded, without breath.

PATSY
Aww. *(She gags.)* Marie!?

MARIE
Will ya give me a light...?

PATSY
Marie, have you peed your pants Marie? Listen, do you... want to see a doctor?

MARIE
No.

PATSY
Well what's going on will you please tell me? You didn't take some of that acid they're passin around the school?

MARIE
No.

PATSY
Marie. What happened to you?

MARIE goes to the sink and pours water over her head and washes, washes.

PATSY
You are stoned. You are stoned and you're havin a bad trip. I'm takin you to hospital.

MARIE
No. No hospital. No.

PATSY
Marie. You're shaking. Did you get hit by a car or something? Where's Donny? Did he drop you off here?

MARIE
I walked from town.

PATSY
You walked! That's ten miles, Marie. Look at you, you're barefoot, where are your shoes, where are your shoes, Marie?

MARIE
Is it true about Holly French?

PATSY
What?

MARIE
That she does that…

PATSY
What?

MARIE
All the time. She does that all the time.

PATSY
WHAT?

MARIE
With all of them…. By the goalpost. That's what they said.

PATSY
I do not know what you are talkin about, Marie and I'm sure Holly French wouldn't neither. Now come on, I'm putting' you in the car and I am takin you to the doctor.

MARIE walks in circles round the room, speaking the following in a low continuous mutter.

MARIE
She she does it all the time she does that all the time all the cute girls do. All the cute girls do; the cheerleaders, gymnastic team, really really you gotta trust us: Okay, are you sure? Is that true? Really is that true that all the cute girls do this? Holly French, and Carol O'Roarke and Nancy Tanks they all do this? Really I don't believe you guys, you guys are teasing me. Oh yeah yeah, baby, promise promise on my mother's life that's what he said *On My Mother's Life*, right here by the goalpost every dance Holly and Carol and Nancy all the cute girls, we'll be gentle come on, you are so pretty we'll be gentle so pretty in that green dress. Me pretty? With my face? Then why did Donny take off like that? Oh he's an asshole we can see what a pretty face underneath, you're a good looking girl we have always liked your legs… such nice long legs let us see your legs pull up the dress. That's right nice knees pull it up way up oh yes oh yes and your hair such beautiful hair would look so nice with sperm in it.. EH? EH? EH? What's sperm? What's sperm? You can come to all our games now, Marie, and party after, go for pizza sit with us at lunch instead of all by yourself or with Patsy…. She's so straight, you're not straight like her… after the games we party hard we party hard over at Dave's…. Would you like to come with us and party… hard? "YOU DOG TURN OVER YOU DOG. I'LL SCREW YOU TO DEATH."

HAH HAH HAH and barking and coughing and barking… and Michael and Roland and Jamie and Frank and "TURN OVER BITCH."

BY THE THROAT, by the HAIR, by the GOALPOST!

And the moon was so low and so big and so yellow.

PATSY is silent, devastated.

Scene Eighteen

PATSY is holding FRANCESCA.

PATSY
Are you alright?

FRANCESCA
I don't know. I don't know.

PATSY
I think we should go back now it's getting dark.

FRANCESCA
Is the train coming, Patsy? Is the train coming soon?

Silence.

Scene Nineteen

Past.

PATSY is chasing MARIE, just outside of the house.

PATSY
Marie!! Wait up, wait up! MARIE. Where are you going? MARIEEEEE!! I'm freezing. My pie's in the oven. For God's sakes, wait up! Marie, where ya goin'?

MARIE climbs up the hill to the railroad tracks.

PATSY
Marie you are not thinkin of doin something stupid are ya?

MARIE
I'm waiting for the train, Patsy.

PATSY
Train doesn't stop here, Marie. Only stops in Belleville.

MARIE
It will stop for me.

PATSY
Marie, did you get hit on the head?

MARIE
I'll take the train to the ocean. As far from here as I can go.

PATSY
You are goin mental, Marie, I swear to God if you could hear yourself.

MARIE
Goin away now. Away from here.

PATSY
Marie, if you don't get down from there the train is going to hit you.

MARIE
The train will stop for me. It will stop for both of us, Patsy. Come on, come with me.

PATSY
Marie. I don't know exactly what you were talkin about back there, but it sounded to me like those boys… were botherin you. Were they botherin you? Cause I will call the cops on them, Marie.

MARIE
Their eyes their eyes like rats.

PATSY
Just come on down from here and we'll go to the police. It's the right thing to do, Marie.

PATSY reaches for MARIE arms outstretched. She is crying.

MARIE
Patsy?

PATSY goes to her and they embrace.

PATSY
Oh baby.

MARIE
I'm scared.

PATSY
Me too, Marie. You're acting so strange.

MARIE
Come with me. We have to get away from here, come with me.

PATSY
I can't. I can't, Marie. This is my home.

MARIE
I'm going to walk and walk along the tracks until I get somewhere else, that's what I'll do.

PATSY
Now now, ya can't do that, it's dangerous.

MARIE
Come with me, Patsy.

PATSY
Marie you come offa this track. I think I hear something.

Present.

ADULT PATSY
And I'm standing behind you and I'm sayin "You get right down offa here, Marie." I think I hear something.

MARIE
My best friend. Will you come with me? Please?

ADULT PATSY
And I know my damn pie is burning Marie, it's my mother's pie for her luncheon tomorrow you are not makin sense if you don't come offa that track you're not goin anywhere. Oh my God the PIE IS BURNING!

The sound of the train grows. A rumble.

MARIE stretches her hands towards the direction the train will be coming from. PATSY gets off tracks and tries to pull MARIE off.

And, and the train is coming, I can feel it in my feet and I pull… and I pull… wanna save my friend… wanna save my friend and then… and then….. and I can't explain it… I guess maybe it was my temperature of 104, and my thinking was muddled but suddenly I looked at that moon and I thought, "Yeah. Me and Marie, me and Marie.

YOUNG PATSY gets back on tracks behind MARIE, embraces her.

"We are gonna die beautiful, we are gonna get crashed by the train and then fly through the sky."

And I felt this deep yearning, Marie this yearning for for for nothing I could ever name, you know? Because there is just there is just no word for it and and I held your hand so cool and sweaty and we are holding hands together and we will become the TRAIN and the smell of the pie, and the pie is burning and oh orange light! And YOU are pullin on me *(MARIE's thinking clears, she gets off tracks and tries to pull PATSY off.)* pullin away but I am not gonna let you go I am stronger than you farm strong. I am going to stay on this track then I feel it I feel it in my feet and your fingernails diggin in I am the train I am big I am metal! I am moving so fast I am–

The crash.

Scene Twenty

In the kitchen area.

FRANCESCA
I wish I could stay forever.

PATSY
Me too. But you can't, I suppose. Hey. It must be at least five, sun's almost down.

FRANCESCA
Oh. I wish I could just stay – for a few days.

PATSY
Well go ahead. Stay. Phone and tell 'em you've got the stomach flu.

FRANCESCA
I'm tempted.

PATSY
You could meet Ric and the boys, ride the horses, sample all my different pies, we could look at old pictures, come on.

FRANCESCA
Well... no, I can't. I can't disappoint them.

PATSY
Marie. Is there... really... this gala happening?

FRANCESCA takes off boots and puts on her own shoes.

FRANCESCA
Of course there is, it's for a film I made a while ago, it's... there really really is, Patsy.

PATSY begins to make her ball of dough.

PATSY
That's okay. I do it sometimes, like we'll be visiting Elizabeth Ryan and I'll say I gotta get back and take my roast out, and I don't even have a roast.

FRANCESCA
Well I honestly do have an engagement. I could show you the invitation. But you are right, that even if I didn't... I don't know...

PATSY
You'd be afraid.

FRANCESCA
Yes.

PATSY
That if you stay too long.

FRANCESCA
I might never leave.

PATSY
And you would lose Francesca.

FRANCESCA
I have lost Francesca.

PATSY
Hooray. Are you gonna go back to Marie Begg?

FRANCESCA
I'm not Marie Begg either.

PATSY
Is this all good?

> *FRANCESCA embraces PATSY from behind; they hang onto each other with all their love and history, and even desperation. Slowly, FRANCESCA extricates herself and backs out of the set, looking at PATSY until she disappears.*

We aren't going to see each other again, are we, Marie…? We aren't going to see each other ever again. It's going to be like you were never here. Like you were a dream. I'll be sitting here six months from now and making my pastry and the snow will be falling and this afternoon will all seem… unreal.

FRANCESCA
I will think about you every day.

PATSY
And I'll be looking at that snow and I will feel the pastry dough in my hands and I will knead it and knead it until my hands they are aching and I think I'm like making you. I like… form you; right in front of my eyes, right here at my kitchen table into flesh. Lookin at me, talking soft.

> *FRANCESCA disappears. The girls are gone. Sound of a train. PATSY raises her hand.*

I will not forget you. "You are carved in the palm of my hand."

> *Slow fade to black.*

> *The end.*

AFTERWORD *by Helen Gilbert*

I first came across Judith Thompson's legendary work in the early 1990s when I attended a production of *Lion in the Streets* performed by actor-training students at the Queensland Academy of the Arts in Brisbane. Having recently finished a seven-year stint working and studying in Canada, I expected to find a familiar world on stage, to have insider knowledge about the characters and situations dramatised, to readily discern their Canadianness despite (or maybe because of) the play's relocation to Australia. The script, simply but energetically staged on this occasion, offered no such comfortable certainties. Thompson's themes, and even the rhythms of her dialogue, had travelled so well that they presented as uncannily local – and profoundly unsettling. Effectively, I saw a dense, poetic rendition of my own urban culture, our marginalisation of those who are different, our failure to fully acknowledge, much less atone for, the everyday violence that indelibly marks our lives. The burden of responsibility for this world could not be assigned so easily to another culture, another country, even if the narrative had been forged elsewhere.

To suggest that Judith Thompson's plays speak so poignantly across different times and spaces is not to invoke a false universalism in order to situate her now substantial oeuvre. Outside their own Canadian contexts, these plays mostly work through resonances not strict parallels; an image, a sound, a gesture, an emotion, a turn of phrase or even a tense silence strikes a chord, and we make the leap to imagine the larger symphony as it might look and feel in our own context. Thompson's enduring interest in the dark and turbulent inner world of her characters makes the outer world somewhat less specific in empirical terms, though it is never incidental to the action. Often, no distinctive setting is indicated at the outset; we are vaulted into a kitchen, a street, a children's playground, or even an indeterminate space which is later particularised, if at all, by the characters' relationships to it. Given this openness, it is not surprising to find that Thompson's texts have been staged in locations as diverse as South Africa, Israel, England and Scotland, as well as across the United States. Or that her work is studied across the English-speaking world and has become a perennial favourite among those actors anxious to extend their emotional range with a script that will tolerate adaptation and experimentation.

Of the plays collected in this book, *Sled* is arguably the one which most communicates a recognisable vision of Thompson's homeland, at least to the foreigner, yet its fascinating evocation of the Canadian North is more redolent with echoes of other spaces than might first appear. In so far as it treats the North as a geographical hinterland incorporated, in Rob Shields's terms, into the nation's "mythic heartland," the play's cartography allows us to imagine the North's possible connections with other much mythologised spaces, such as the Australian bush, the South African Weld or the American West. When I saw this text staged at the University of Washington in Seattle in 1999, the set featured ghostly white birches and a Great Snowy owl just as the playwright stipulates in her opening stage directions; yet, in this instance, the *mise en scène* easily morphed into a non-specific, epic space in which pressurised conflicts in contemporary American society might be played out and clarified.

One of Judith Thompson's greatest skills is her capacity to stage the inarticulate thoughts and half-recognised desires of society's less eloquent or less enfranchised subjects. She has admitted in interviews to being obsessed with the figure of the child and the nature of parenting, topics that also cross national and social boundaries, at least within Western culture. While *I Am Yours* and *Lion in the Streets* present children as idealised innocents through whom redemption may be offered to a spiritually sick society, other Thompson plays acknowledge the unspeakable cruelty that children unknowingly, or even wilfully, inflict. Her early monodrama, *Pink*, is exemplary in this respect, capturing in a few short pages the ways in which a child learns to endorse racial hatred and to participate readily in the seemingly minor but immensely significant acts of discrimination that ensue from it. This play can be read as a prologue to the more complex acts of violence committed by the schoolboys in *Perfect Pie* or the teenage outcasts of *Habitat*. The wider message that Thompson communicates through her focus on society's young is nevertheless a hopeful one, suggesting that children can and will learn to make moral choices if they are treated with tolerance and compassion.

For me, perhaps the most compelling quality of the plays in this book is their ability to shock even the seasoned critic. When confronted with the opening scene of *Habitat*, for instance, I find the rawness of Raine's language almost unbearable as she expresses open contempt for her dying mother; yet the scene registers instantly as a potent rendition of the most intimate pain we might witness. In *Crackwalker*, the image of Therese carrying her dead baby around in a bag would make my skin crawl were the act less mundane or less tender. And when Francesca reveals what the schoolboys did to her towards the end of *Perfect Pie*, I find myself wanting a sanitised version. Notwithstanding such graphic depictions, Thompson's work is anything but gratuitous; rather, the violence, be it verbal or physical, is designed to break down our defences, to elicit a politicised engagement with the issues at hand.

The great temptations when attempting to assess a playwright's significance are to look for influences on his or her writing and to read it in reference to familiar models or frameworks. While Judith Thompson's plays might momentarily evoke George Walker's disturbing black comedies, or Sarah Kane's chilling portraits of ordinary people in extreme situations, or perhaps even Harold Pinter's menacing family tapestries, they refuse to be pigeonholed generically or thematically. The label of poetic naturalism—the one most consistently applied to Thompson's work—doesn't quite capture the power of her dramaturgy or its unique, haunting qualities. In this respect, the plays anthologised here will retain their distinctiveness as they continue to travel to other theatrical spaces, even unexpected ones.

Work Cited
Shields, Rob. *Places on the Margin*. London and New York: Routledge, 1991.

Helen Gilbert teaches theatre and postcolonial literatures at the University of Queensland, Australia, where she also directs experimental performance work. She has published widely on Australian and postcolonial drama, indigenous theatre, performance theory and imperial travel.

ABOUT THE AUTHOR

Judith Thompson was born in 1954 in Montreal. She graduated from Queen's University in 1976 and graduated from the acting programme of The National Theatre School in 1979. Although she worked briefly as a professional actor, she became more interested in writing. At the age of 25, a workshop of her first script, *The Crackwalker*, was produced by Theatre Passe Muraille. Her work has enjoyed great success internationally. She is professor of Drama at the University of Guelph and currently lives with her husband and five children in the west Annex area of Toronto.